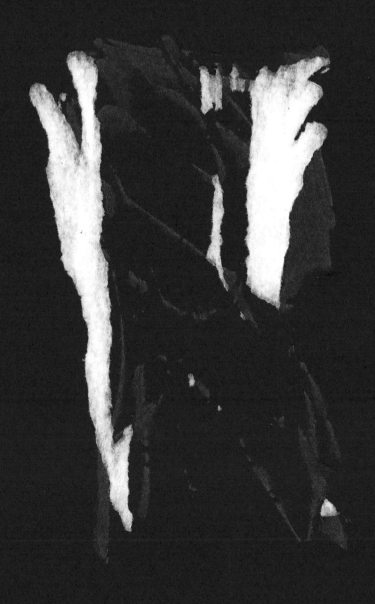

Praise for *The Greatest Game Ever Played*

'A thrilling, drawn-out contest . . . brilliantly told by Mark Frost. What makes this book special is the way it marries social history with sporting biography. So on top of his analysis of the technical evolution of golf, Frost produces vivid, often moving portraits of the two protagonists' *Sunday Telegraph*

'Frost's research into an event that took place almost ninety years ago is first-rate. He digresses expertly, capturing the atmosphere of a sport that was gradually finding its feet. A thoroughly enjoyable read' *Ireland on Sunday*

'Frost has researched his subject meticulously . . . his superbly detailed and paced 250-page account of the tournament begs to be read in one thrilling sitting, and more impressively requires no real love of golf to be enjoyed' *Sunday Times*

'Francis Ouimet's showdown with Harry Vardon was a watershed moment that changed the face of golf. At last this remarkable story has been given the epic treatment it so richly deserves' Butch Harmon, Tiger Woods' coach

'This is one of the best sports books I have ever read. If I had known there was this much excitement in golf I would have started playing earlier' Billy Crystal

'Anyone who loves golf, history, or just a great story will relish this wonderful book' Scott Turow

'A brilliant story, brilliantly told . . . a truly outstanding piece of sports writing' *Sunday Tribune*

THE GRAND SLAM

Bobby Jones, America and the
Story of Golf

Mark Frost

A *Time Warner* Book

First published in Great Britain in 2004
by Time Warner Books

Copyright © Mark Frost 2004

A CIP catalogue record for this book
is available from the British Library.

ISBN 0 316 72691 5

Typeset by Palimpsest Book Production Limited,
Polmont, Stirlingshire
Printed and bound in Great Britain by
Clays Ltd, St Ives plc

Time Warner Books
An imprint of
Time Warner Book Group UK
Brettenham House
Lancaster Place
London WC2E 7EN

www.twbg.co.uk

For my father, Warren,
and my son, Travis

CONTENTS

THE PLAYERS

British Professionals

JAMES BRAID, Earlsferry, Fife, 1870–1950
ARCHIE COMPSTON, Wolverhampton, West Midlands,
   1893–1962
GEORGE DUNCAN, Methlick, Aberdeenshire, 1883–1964
ABE MITCHELL, East Grinstead, Sussex, 1887–1947
TED RAY, Jersey, 1877–1943
JOHN HENRY TAYLOR, Northam, Devon, or Southampton,
   Hampshire, 1871–1963
HARRY VARDON, Jersey, 1870–1937
TOM VARDON, Jersey, 1872–1942

British Amateurs

JOHN BALL, Hoylake, Merseyside, 1861–1940
BERNARD DARWIN, Downes Kent, 1876–1961
HAROLD HILTON, West Kirby, Merseyside, 1869–1942
CYRIL JAMES HASTINGS TOLLEY, London, 1895–1978
JOYCE WETHERED, Maldon, Essex, 1901–1997
ROGER WETHERED, Maldon, Essex, 1899–1972

American Expatriate Professionals

THOMAS ARMOUR, Edinburgh, 1895–1968
ROBERT CRUICKSHANK, Grantown-on-Spey, Perth &
   Kinross, 1894–1975
JAMES BARNES, Lelant, Cornwall, 1887–1966
HARRY "LIGHTHORSE" COOPER, Leatherhead, Surrey,
   1904–2000
JOCK HUTCHISON, St. Andrews, Fife, 1884–1977

WILLIE MACFARLANE, Aberdeen, 1890–1961
STEWART MAIDEN, Carnoustie, Angus, 1886–1948
MACDONALD SMITH, Carnoustie, Angus, 1890–1949
CYRIL WALKER, Manchester, 1892–1948

American Professionals

MIKE BRADY, Brighton, Massachusetts, 1887–1972
LEO DIEGEL, Detroit, Michigan, 1899–1951
AL ESPINOSA, Monterey, California, 1894–1957
JOHN J. FARRELL, White Plains, New York, 1901–88
WALTER HAGEN, Rochester, New York, 1892–1969
WILLIAM MELHORN, Elgin, Illinois, 1898–1989
EUGENE SARAZEN, Harrison, New York, 1902–99
HORTON SMITH, Springfield, Missouri, 1908–63
JOE TURNESA, Elmsford, New York, 1901–91
ANDREW WATROUS, Yonkers, New York, 1899–1984

American Amateurs

PERRY ADAIR, Atlanta, Georgia, 1900–53
CHARLES "CHICK" EVANS, Jr., Indianapolis, Indiana,
  1890–1979
ALEXA STIRLING FRASER, Atlanta, Georgia, 1897–1977
ROBERT GARDNER, Hinsdale, Illinois, 1890–1956
JOHN GOODMAN, Omaha, Nebraska, 1910–70
S. DAVIDSON HERRON, Pittsburgh, Pennsylvania,
  1897–1956
WATTS GUNN, MACON, Georgia, b. 1905
HARRISON "JIMMY" JOHNSTON, St. Paul, Minnesota,
  1896–1969
ROBERT TYRE JONES, Atlanta, Georgia, 1902–71
WILLIAM LAWSON LITTLE, Newport, Rhode Island, 1910–68
CHARLES BLAIR MCDONALD, Niagara Falls, New York,
  1856–1939

FRANCIS OUIMET, Brookline, Massachusetts, 1893–1967
JESS SWEETSER, St. Louis, Missouri, 1902–89
WALTER TRAVIS, Maldon, Australia, 1867–1927
GEORGE VOIGT, Buffalo, New York, 1894–1985
GEORGE VON ELM, Salt Lake City, Utah, 1901–60

A NOTE ON THE TEXT

To avoid confusion I have used the modern terms for all the golf clubs in this story; irons and woods were not generally referred to by numbers until after Bob Jones produced matched sets with Spalding in the 1930s. All of the dialogue in this book is directly quoted from source material, chiefly the accounts left to us by Pop Keeler, Bob Jones, Grantland Rice, Walter Hagen, Chick Evans, Bernard Darwin, Al Laney, and Francis Ouimet.

PROLOGUE

In an average year lightning strikes the United States over twenty-two million times. Your chance of being hit by one of those strikes is 1 in 300,000: 7.7 casualties per million people per million lightning strikes. Lightning kills a hundred people a year in the United States alone, and critically injures over a thousand. An average bolt carries the power of thirty million volts, and somewhere between ten thousand and two hundred thousand amps, enough electricity to illuminate a hundred-watt bulb for six months.

He was America's most famous athlete, the crown jewel of a golden age; eight times a national champion, and on the verge of launching the most spectacular assault on the record books anyone in sport had ever seen. A dedicated amateur, he had within the last year launched his professional career as a lawyer: the world's greatest golfer only had time to play four to six tournaments a year. Preparing to play in that year's U.S. Open, on July 29, 1929, Bobby Jones and the three members of his regular Monday-afternoon game were making the turn onto the back nine at East Lake Country Club outside Atlanta when they noticed a bank of towering thunderclouds building to the southeast. Jones had grown up on the East Lake course, and dodged a hundred storms during his life there; he decided they would have time to finish their round before the body of the storm threatened. The first drops of rain fell as they putted out on the twelfth green, set near the right arm of the horseshoe-shaped lake that curves around the stately mock Tudor clubhouse and gives the course its name. As they made their way to the thirteenth tee, the sky above them still clear, a bolt of lighting struck the tenth fairway less than forty yards to their right. Jones felt an ominous tingle surge through his metal spikes. He stopped and yelled to his buddies to make a run for the clubhouse; they had no sooner changed direction than a second bolt hit a small tree at the back of the thirteenth tee, not twenty yards away, exactly where they would have been standing if they'd continued ahead. They sprinted across the small bridge that spans the northeast corner of the lake, leading back to the eighteenth green and clubhouse. Huddled under their umbrellas, Jones and his friends lost count of the lightning strikes hammering down on the course around them, a ferocious concentration of energy unlike any storm they'd ever seen.

As they hustled across the broad gravel drive, the last stretch of open ground before the safety of the portico sheltering the locker-room entrance, a monstrous bolt blasted the high double chimney on top of the clubhouse. The chimney exploded in a shower of bricks and mortar. Bobby felt his umbrella collapse around his head; he blindly staggered the last few steps to the protection of the door. Safely inside, the men shared a nervous, gasping laugh of relief. When Bobby discarded his umbrella and turned around, his friends gasped again: the back of his shirt had been ripped from collar to waist, and he was bleeding from a six-inch gash that ran from his right shoulder to the middle of his spine. A heavy fragment of the chimney had punched through his umbrella, struck him a glancing blow and torn the shirt from his back. He hadn't felt a thing. The men shared a moment of silent wonder at how close—inches—their great friend had come to certain death. Bobby was the first to break the tension with a joke—the golf gods were obviously displeased with him, but at least he knew where to send the bill for a new shirt. The luck of the Irish: what else would you expect from a man born on St. Paddy's day? Drinks flowed from the jug of bootleg corn liquor Bob stored in his locker, the worst-kept secret at the club, a survivors' warmth rekindled in them and the shadow passed.

When the storm moved through they walked outside and stared again in wonder: the driveway was littered, a debris field of bricks and mortar, some fragments scattered as far as the eighteenth-tee box, 300 yards away. Any one of which, thought Robert Tyre Jones, Jr., could have killed a man had it struck him on the head. Not that the gash on his back didn't sting like the deuce, but Bob was never one to complain. He never boasted either, nor made a show of his many great gifts; and he privately rated this innate sense of balance and moderation foremost among them. No matter what good fortune showered upon you, and by any reckoning he'd had far more than his fair share, he knew the gods would have the last laugh. They always did, with time on their side. Even if it took twenty years.

The myth that lightning never strikes twice in the same place is exactly that; the mast atop the Empire State Building, for example, attracts on average a hundred bolts a year. Lightning of an equally powerful but more metaphysical variety also centered Robert Tyre Jones, Jr., in its sights on the old twelfth hole at East Lake Country Club, and this time it had struck him square, sixteen years earlier. Its impact forever altered the course of his life, propelling him directly forward to the abundant promise of this moment in 1929, as surely as this second strike would lead to his ruin.

PART ONE

EVOLUTION OF
A GENIUS

"No matter what happens, keep on hitting the ball."

—Harry Vardon

CHAPTER ONE

EAST LAKE

O n September 22, 1913, America welcomed a new hero into
its sporting pantheon and for the first time the broad
middle of the country embraced with curiosity and enthusiasm
the exotic game he'd mastered. Playing alone on rain-soaked
fairways at the Country Club in Brookline, Massachusetts,
against the two greatest golfers in the world, Francis Ouimet
defeated Harry Vardon and Ted Ray in an eighteen-hole play-
off to win the United States Open Championship. The twenty
year-old former caddie personified a cherished American ideal:
that anyone with perseverance, modesty and backbone could
rise above the limits imposed by humble beginnings to achieve
greatness. Seldom discussed is how often a person's real problems

begin with the success. Lesser men might have failed a hundred ways under the pressures of Ouimet's sudden fame, but Francis stood up to that challenge and every other that life subsequently put in his path. You could find in him no trace of destructive pride, ego, false humility or spite. He never turned professional, choosing instead to focus on a business career and raising a family, in spite of which he remained a first-rate player for nearly twenty years and would go on to win two National Amateur Championships; but in the long run his sterling character contributed even more to the development of the game than his accomplishments as a player.

Vardon and Ray had toured America for months leading up to the 1913 Open, facing every one of the country's finest players without suffering a loss. Victory by one or the other of them had all but been conceded before the national championship; instead, Ouimet's shocking defeat of the two British immortals made banner headlines across America and around the world. Teenaged boys in particular embraced Ouimet as a role model and, for once, even their parents approved. Caddie shacks and clubhouses swarmed with new recruits, professionals and amateurs alike, eager to follow Ouimet into the game. Many would go on to memorable careers, a select few earning the credentials to land them in a Hall of Fame that hadn't yet been dreamed of. Only one of them would exceed the impact of Ouimet's historic break-through, relegate the memory of an entire generation of greats to also-ran status, and give rise to a legend that casts shadows over the American sporting landscape to this day.

While his improbable win spread the gospel of the game and heralded a bright future for native-born players, Francis Ouimet unknowingly served as a kind of secular stand-in for John the Baptist. The game's messiah was coming, and he was a lot closer at hand than anybody realized. He would emerge from the unlikeliest ground, and only after a cast of extraordinary char-acters necessary to shape his formative years had assembled around him. Call it destiny or coincidence; by October of 1913 all the elements necessary for the creation of a sporting miracle had aligned, but required one last spark to ignite the subsequent chain of events. As fate, or chance, would have it, the same two players who had precipitated Francis Ouimet's triumph were about to provide that spark.

Harry Vardon and Ted Ray sailed into New York and embarked on their barnstorming exhibition tour of America in early August, 1913. Designed to climax at Brookline in September with a Vardon or Ray victory at the Open, their grand scheme unraveled on that soggy Saturday when Ouimet seized the cup for the United States. The architect of that scheme, their patron, Fleet Street mogul Lord Northcliffe, sailed back to Britain bitter and empty-handed. The two defeated sportsmen, professionals to the end, declined Northcliffe's offer to join his early exit and vowed to complete an additional month of appearances, originally conceived as an extended victory march after their anticipated Open triumph.

A vibrant Indian summer had settled over Georgia when Vardon and Ray rolled into Atlanta during the second week of October, 1913. A two-day, seventy-two-hole match had been arranged with the best two local pros the New Center of the South had to offer: Willie Mann from Druid Hills, and Stewart Maiden of East Lake Country Club. On Saturday, October 11, the four men teed it up at East Lake, a sprawling entertainment complex built on the site of a turn-of-the-century amusement park.

East Lake's clubhouse and eighteen-hole golf course had officially opened for business on the Fourth of July, 1908, designed by the prolific Tom Bendelow. East Lake's list of playing members initially numbered less than twenty-five, ranging in age from six to forty. That original roster includes two names—one boy, one girl—who would not only reach golf's Hall of Fame, they are still considered by many as the finest players America has ever produced. Without knowing it, East Lake was already a nursery for genius.

Vardon and Ray arrived for their match at East Lake on Saturday morning, July 11, 1913, and enjoyed a hot breakfast from the club's kitchen, served on outdoor tables; despite their celebrity, as working-class pros they were not allowed—here or at any other private club in the world—to set foot in the clubhouse or members' locker room. First to welcome them was one of their opponents that day, East Lake's resident professional Stewart Maiden, a small, unassuming man from Carnoustie, Scotland. The members at East Lake called him "Kiltie," which today might be considered a demeaning cultural stereotype, but the intent was affectionate. A compact, flat-faced, perpetually sunburned man, Stewart Maiden embodied the stereotype of the dour, laconic Scot. He possessed an uncanny ability to pinpoint and correct swing faults with a minimum of words. Kiltie almost never addressed his student's problem verbally; for those who worked with him on a regular basis expressions or small gestures spoke volumes. By 1913 Stewart had also developed a serious dependence on strong drink, which did nothing to soften his sharp tongue, often to his detriment. But during his first ten years at East Lake, blessed with students of rare ability, he offered instruction of magnificent value, and inspired in them undying loyalty. A gifted player, he lacked the temperament for a sustained competitive career but his swing was a thing of beauty: balanced, rhythmic and deceptively powerful. That October he'd spent a week brushing up his game, and gone to bed without taking a single nip the night before his match against Vardon and Ray.

Knowing not only his employers but all his students would all be in the gallery, Kiltie was determined to give the big boys a tough fight. No players with their international pedigrees had ever ventured as far south as Atlanta before; this was golf's equivalent of Siberia, a million miles from the game's dominant Philadelphia–New York–Boston corridor, or its Midwestern stronghold in Chicago.

Among the reporters roaming East Lake's grounds to follow their match that day was Oscar Bane Keeler, O.B. to his colleagues, better known as "Pop" to his friends: thirty-one years old, and until this moment a man singularly devoted to making as little as possible out of a classical education. After flirting with a variety of careers, Pop was working as a reporter for the *Atlanta Georgian*. He had begun playing golf during a last romantic boyhood summer in Lake Geneva, Wisconsin, in 1897. He was not a gifted player, but fortunately Pop found substantially more skilled golfers to write about, beginning on that same October afternoon at East Lake Country Club.

Keeler could barely contain his excitement when he got off the streetcar at East Lake that morning. Pop connected with readers because he had such easy access to his own emotions; they showed up on his sleeves like chevrons. He picked up feelings in the air at a sporting event as if they were radio waves and boiled them down into strong, declarative sentences, letting you experience whatever he witnessed as clearly as if he'd let you borrow his nervous system.

Pop's struggles with his own game only increased his sense of wonder when he saw Ted Ray put the wood to a golf ball for the first time. While Ray wowed the crowd all morning, firing like a howitzer, making birdies and bogies with equal abandon, Vardon quietly went about hitting fairways and greens and recording pars with machine-like regularity. When his putter cooperated—the only weakness in his game; a nerve in his right hand had been damaged by a bout with tuberculosis—Vardon dropped his share of birds as well. Opponents often felt as if Vardon wasn't even aware of their presence, and they weren't far wrong: experience had taught him his real opponent was the golf course, not the other guy. He played against par, an elusive concept for the casual viewer. Not as spectacular a style in the heat of battle, Vardon's economical method was even deadlier than Ted's showy fireworks. This was the partnership they'd formed during their tour, reflecting their different temperaments, and it was the reason they were nearly impossible to beat in a best-ball match. In their morning round at East Lake Ray turned in a par 75, and Vardon shot 72.

Stewart Maiden and his partner Willie Mann looked intimidated by their famous competition and the size of the crowd that morning; both scored 78 and were three holes down at intermission with eighteen left to play. Although all was convivial on the surface between the four men, Stewart Maiden was determined to put up a stiffer fight that afternoon; he worshiped Harry Vardon like every other pro his age, but that didn't mean he couldn't beat him. Kiltie birdied three of the first eight holes to square the match. When he stuck his approach at the ninth within three feet of the pin and made his fourth birdie of the round, the home team went 1 up on Vardon and Ray and the crowd cheered the local boys like the Georgia Tech football team. They halved the first two holes after the turn, and came to the twelfth tee with the famous visitors still trailing.

Someone else was following the action at East Lake that day. A more plainly American name would be hard to conjure: Bobby Jones. Eleven years old, tow-headed, hair still worn in a nononsense bowl-cut, knock-kneed, a touch short for his age and a little chubby, baked dark brown with a spray of freckles sprinkled across his face. Knickerbockers, a white shirt, a jaunty little cap: from a distance he looked like a hundred other kids running around in that crowd. You had to get up close to spot the watchful intelligence in his slate-blue eyes, and the crooked right corner of his ready smile, shaded by a sense of irony. That face already owned a degree of self-possession that was almost

spooky; an old soul, you might have thought. He'd ridden out
from town that day on the streetcar with his best friend, Perry
Adair, son of East Lake's current president. A year older, taller
and leaner than his little sidekick, Perry enjoyed a growing reputation as the best junior player at East Lake, the city of Atlanta
and the state of Georgia.

Both families had taken summer homes in East Lake the year
the country club first opened. The Adairs—wealthier by far, on
their way to becoming one of the richest in the South; they also
owned the huge spread of land where Hartsfield Airport would
eventually rise—soon built a grand house with all the ameni-
ties. The Joneses lived a much more modest existence; they were
still apartment dwellers in Atlanta, albeit in the better part of
town. They spent their first two summers at East Lake in rented
rooms at a boarding house, before moving into a ramshackle
cottage on the edge of the second fairway called "the mule
house." Local lore on the origin of that name is muddled, but
it may at one point have been a stable for a Civil War-era farm
that once occupied the grounds.

The myth has persisted that Bobby's father, Robert Purdemus
Jones, was a wealthy man, but during Bobby's childhood he
worked as a corporate lawyer in Atlanta, under his own shingle,
and was bringing home a middle-class income at best. Robert
Purdemus was the son of an extremely driven and successful
man, Robert Tyre Jones. Folks called the Jones family patriarch
R.T., more out of respect than affection. At a ramrod six foot
five, two hundred and thirty-five pounds, R.T. commanded attention. A stern, fervently religious character without an ounce of
frivolity, he parlayed a small general store into a thriving cotton
mill—one of the first blue denim factories in the country.

The son of a struggling hardscrabble farmer, R.T. had lived
through the horrors of the Civil War and it informed every inch
of his character. Life on earth was not for the faint of heart;
you wrestled for every advantage, buried your dead, feared God,

and give Him all credit on those rare occasions when any was due. Fear and awe tended to be the reactions R.T. inspired in others. Finding even the harsh determinism of his parents' Presbyterian faith too liberal for his tastes, at twenty-one he had himself initiated as a strict Southern Baptist. He didn't drink, smoke, cuss, work on Sunday, or even break down and enjoy a refreshing Coca-Cola. He might indulge in a few hands of Rook every once in a while, but played no game that required the pagan idolatry of face cards. His instinctual search for a strong faith to sustain him proved sound, because that faith would be sorely tested; his father was later robbed and murdered on the family farm, and his first wife died suddenly at the age of forty-two. While raising seven children on his own, R.T. took the entire extended family under the shelter of his formidable arms. Building his legacy according to dynastic English traditions, R.T. selected a revealing motto for the rising Jones clan: *Coelitis mihi vires:* My strength is from heaven.

Born in 1879, R.T.'s oldest child, Robert Purdemus Jones—he always preferred Bob—grew up enjoying the advantages of his father's prodigious energies. Whether the result of genetic inclination or a rebellious reaction to his family, Bob's temperament could not have taken a more radically different turn from his father's. A gifted baseball player, Bob attracted the attention of some local scouts birddogging for big-league northern franchises, but when he was offered a minor-league deal by the National League's Brooklyn Superbas R.T. told him: sign that contract, and I'll disown you. His experience of the world out from under his father's shadow had taught Bob a few crucial facts about himself; he liked to drink, smoke, cuss, tell off-color jokes, hang out with the boys, and play poker, and do all of the above on Sunday if he felt like it. Father and son were destined to butt heads, but Bob might never have broken away without an ally to help him resist the pull of R.T.'s gravity. From another family whose Georgia roots ran six generations deep, Clara

Thomas stood barely five feet tall, weighed ninety pounds and was physically frail, but possessed the classic resolve of the Southern belle in the cast-iron petticoat. Bob and Clara met and married immediately in 1900. She insisted, and Bob agreed, that they would accept no money from his father in order to establish themselves in the big city. Strings came attached to such generosity; R.T. couldn't help but see it that way. When their first child William died after three agonizing months of illness, the tragedy devastated them.

Bob opened a small law office and within a few months picked up enough freelance contract work inside the burgeoning Coca-Cola empire to support his family; maintaining patents, drafting boilerplate bottling and distribution contracts. Networking with his fellow Georgia alumni, he joined the downtown Atlanta Athletic Club and befriended charter member George Adair. Clara took to her bed for the last few months of her second pregnancy, taking every precaution to avoid a repeat of their earlier heartbreak. When their son arrived on St. Patrick's Day, March 17, 1902, the young couple paid homage to R.T. by naming him Robert Tyre Jones. Bobby himself added the "Junior" years later, to complete the tribute. But at first, and for some time to come, the boy's prospects appeared every bit as bleak as those of his late lamented brother.

Weighing just over five pounds at birth, the baby struggled to maintain his weight, went through operatic fits of colic for weeks at a time, and couldn't keep solid food in his system long enough to do him much good until he was nearly five years old. Six doctors they consulted were baffled by the boy's infirmities, offering no treatment more useful than a strict diet of boiled egg whites. At the age of five Bobby still weighed less than forty pounds. Clara's heightened anxiety about her lost first child played a major part in shaping and disrupting the nervous system of her second. The experience of raising a second frail young boy convinced both parents that Bobby should grow up an only child. Terrified of infection from other children, in this era before routine vaccinations when childhood diseases were a potentially deadly threat, Clara kept the boy cloistered in their home, a virtual prisoner to her fears. Aside from the family's African-American live-in maid Camilla and her on-again/off-again boyfriend—who took glee in teaching him how to cuss—young Bobby could count his circle of friends on the knuckles of his thumb.

Hailing from a long line of strapping alpha males, Bob found the prospect of his sickly son wasting away like a hothouse flower distasteful in the extreme. Had Bobby inherited his wife's delicate constitution, or was Clara raising the child in her own neurasthenic image? It was time to find out. Big Bob, as friends and family had now begun to call him, decided to move the family out to East Lake for the summer to see if clean air and exercise would do for Little Bob what the advice of six doctors had failed to.

Big Bob's gamble paid off: given a chance to run around in the open air for the first time like a normal kid, Little Bob thrived. He spent a Huck Finn summer. The local boys played baseball, when they could find enough players, the first group activity Bobby had ever been allowed. He and Frank Meador, son of their boarding house's landlady, discovered a creek they could dam up for fishing, and didn't mind that they never caught anything. Bobby adopted an old broken-down pony at a nearby stable, naming it Clara, an honor his mother seemed reluctant to appreciate.

On one fateful afternoon, one of their fellow boarders, an earnest young man named Fulton Colville, noticed Bobby watching him practice chip shots on the front lawn. He asked the little boy if he wanted to try his hand at a few swings. The club was an old iron cleek, too big for Bobby to master. Fed up with how the damn thing was behaving, Colville sawed off the shaft below the grip and offered it as a gift to Bobby after dinner.

Bobby and Frank were too young to be allowed on the East Lake course, so they fashioned one of their own on a dirt lane beside the Meador house. Two fairways identical in length fashioned from the Georgia clay—one no more than an extended ditch—precious little grass, long stretches of wagon ruts as constant hazards.

It's an overstatement to say the game possessed Bobby from the start; he later had few specific memories of his first golf experiences, just another activity in a rich and varied repertoire of fun, but one stood out: Little Bob hated making a bad shot. When he knocked his ball into a briar patch under the bridge that crossed the ditch it made him mad enough to dance in the road. While such displays looked amusing in a five-year-old, a hunger for perfection and his furious inability to accept anything less from himself already loomed as the biggest mountain he'd have to climb in the first half of his life.

The family moved back to the city in the fall with a healthy son. Little Bob started school and Clara stopped fussing over him. Big Bob's practice advanced and, in deference to his warm and courtly Southern manners, friends and colleagues around town began affectionately referring to him as "the Colonel." The family headed out to East Lake again for the summer of 1908, and one evening on their way to the club for dinner they ran into their pro, Jimmy Maiden, about to move on to Long Island and in the process of saying his goodbyes to the members. He introduced them to his younger brother Stewart, not long off the boat from Carnoustie. In many ways a perfectly ordinary moment, but one that six-year-old Bobby would remember vividly.

There was nothing sensational about Stewart. He said very little and I couldn't understand a single word of what he did say. Jimmy and Dad and Mother did all the talking, and at first I wondered if Stewart could talk at all . . . There wasn't any sensation, any more than when I swung the first time at a golf ball. Stewart was just another little Scot, like Jimmy, only Scotcher. But it wasn't long before I was following him about the East Lake course and watching him.

Stewart never appeared to notice his little shadow, and if he did he never seemed to mind.

Upon arrival Kiltie instantly became the best player anyone at the club had ever seen. He had a classic swing built to the old Carnoustie form: flat, round, and fluid, guided by an even, leisurely tempo to keep the hickory shaft from torquing the head off target as it squared to the ball. Kiltie was all business on the course; hit the ball, find it, hit it again. Bobby couldn't then identify exactly what it was about the little Scot's game that so fascinated him, but it was no mystery: this was his first glimpse of perfection—consistent bio-mechanical precision, lit with a touch of poetry—and he drank it deep down into his unconscious. Bobby never carried a club when he tagged after the little pro; all his focus was on watching. After four or five holes, he would break off to return home, grab a hatful of balls and his three-club kit—his parents had also given him a cut-down two-wood and a short iron to go with his old cleek—head out to the thirteenth green and hit balls at the flag until the sun went down. Without any thought to technique, without a single formal lesson from Kiltie, he mimicked that perfect swing and absorbed it into muscle memory until he made it his own. He was old enough to be allowed out on the course with his parents now, never taking more than one club at a time. His interests continued to balance over the full range of an active boy's life, but slowly golf staked a greater claim in his sleeping and waking mind.

The game gradually became the center of the Jones family's social life. Regular Sunday dinners were followed by informal tournaments played by Big Bob, Clara, and their friends. Bobby's talent for mimicry became a favorite feature of cocktail-hour gatherings on the veranda, when his father would call on him to imitate the more hilarious swings of the regulars in attendance. The Adair family had moved into the Joneses' social orbit during this summer and their son Perry joined the kids' table. Two years older than Bobby, a tall and handsome blond, Perry had been taking regular lessons from Kiltie for over a year and was much further along in his game. The boys quickly became best friends. Bobby now enjoyed the benefit of regularly playing with, and competing against, a better player. A third player soon joined their regular outings, and she was better than both of them.

A red-headed tomboy, five years older than Bobby, Alexa Stirling was willowy, beautiful and spirited. She loved to hunt and fish as much as they did; and her father taught her how to repair automobiles, a skill Alexa retained her entire life. With the athletic, economical swing that Stewart Maiden had taught her, at 110 pounds she could drive the ball over 230 yards. Add to this a personality of charm and winsome modesty and you realize that Alexa Stirling was one of the remarkable young women of her day. (She was an early classmate of another such woman, Margaret Mitchell, who during her twenty years as an Atlanta housewife wrote a novel called *Gone With the Wind*.) Every boy she met fell under Alexa's spell and Bobby was no exception, even if he didn't yet know the word for it. Another extraordinary role model had found her way into Bobby's life, and the supporting cast around him was now complete; their impact began to affect his development like tumblers falling into place on a complicated lock.

Late that summer of 1908, someone suggested that a tournament for the kids might make an amusing addition to the grown-ups' regular games. A foursome of Bobby, Perry, Alexa, and Frank Meador was sent out to play a six-hole stroke-play match, a gallery of parents and friends in attendance. Bobby later admitted that Alexa won the contest, but her generosity of spirit changed the outcome. Sensing how much more it would mean to him, she suggested they award the three-inch-tall cup to six-year-old Bobby. Bobby liked winning, he found that out right from the start; he slept with his little silver prize that night and hung onto it for as long as he lived, always polished, in pride of place alongside some of the greatest trophies in the world.

This established the enduring rhythm of his boyhood. School years spent at home in Atlanta; he was always a good, if not exceptional, student. Idyllic summers at East Lake, where golf gradually overtook tennis, baseball, fishing, boating, and swimming. His temper continued to flare up hot and ready. During a round with Dr. Stirling and Alexa, Bobby hit a less than perfect shot, tossed his club, and let fly a shocking string of expletives.

In 1911 nine-year-old Bobby entered his first formal tournament, the junior championship of the Atlanta Athletic Club. His first experience with brackets and starting times, pairings and handicaps didn't daunt him for a second. Playing his way into the finals, Bobby faced a big sixteen-year-old named Howard Thorne, and beat him 5 & 4 over thirty-six holes. No one was prouder of Bobby's win than Big Bob; he carried Bobby and the trophy home on his broad shoulders, shouting out the news to Clara. Unlike so many kids of his generation, Bobby never had to walk the extra mile to earn his father's approval, and the big-hearted Colonel never gave him any reason to doubt how much he was loved. The harder-edged Clara played the bad cop when Bobby needed discipline. Scarred by R.T.'s scathing indifference to his once-promising baseball career, Big Bob never missed one of Bobby's important matches, and was always first to greet him with a hug when he came off the final green.

By 1913, the little golf academy that Kiltie Maiden had quietly gone about building at East Lake was about to yield a bountiful harvest. Forty-one-year-old club president George Adair won the first of two city amateur championships; his son Perry captured East Lake's junior crown for the second year in a row, and made some noise in local tourneys against grown-ups; Alexa Stirling played her first USGA event, and established herself as a presence to reckon with in the future. With the membership at East Lake expanding, George Adair contacted renowned Boston-based golf architect Donald Ross about adding a second course, and maybe redesigning their original layout.

Back in school that September, Bobby followed the exploits of Francis Ouimet at the 1913 Open, waiting eagerly on the front steps for his dad to return home with the afternoon papers. When Ouimet pulled off his improbable victory the story landed on the front pages and suddenly the quaint little game Bobby had grown up playing took on mythic dimensions. The news that the two British giants who had battled Ouimet were coming to the only course he'd ever known stirred up sensational excitement in Bobby, as if gods from another planet had announced a visitation. That he was far from alone in this feeling speaks to the subtle but profound sense of inferiority the South still suffered as a region, a culture, and a tribe of people. Their defeat at the hands of the Union had stripped them of their identity. Watching Vardon and Ray play the game in person, Bobby's young dreams for glory of his own took their first steps. But if he had caught a glimpse of his own future that day, would he even have believed it? That by mastering an ancient British game a young champion from a Southern state could help repair the damage done by a sixty-year-old war? That by becoming the country's first truly national sports hero, he would help knit back together the lingering wounds left by that terrible conflict?

When Vardon and Ray played exhibitions against local professionals, one of two things happened: the pros would either collapse under pressure or play the game of their lives. Stewart Maiden and Willie Man had mounted a comeback that put them in the second category; the two British greats knew they were now in a match. Kiltie had already played his second shot onto the twelfth green. Vardon followed, landing inside Kiltie's ball, even closer to the pin. Ray, as usual, had hit the longest drive, but pushed it right. He found his ball in the rough, 160 yards out and 20 yards behind a forty-foot-tall pine that stood directly between him and the green.

Bobby and Perry were in the gallery that scrambled around to watch Ray play his shot. So was Pop Keeler, although he didn't yet know either of the boys. As Ray walked to his ball, puffing on his pipe, wise veterans in his gallery—Keeler among them—speculated that he would have to punch back to the fairway around the tree and take his medicine.

"He'll lose a shot here for sure," Bobby remembered saying to Perry. "He's dead behind that tree."

Ray took one look at his ball, one at the tree, and a quick glance at the green. Without hesitation he pulled his favorite club—a one-of-a-kind hand-crafted thing he called a "Snieler"; the rough equivalent of a nine-iron—from his bag, planted his feet, and swung down at the ball as if he meant to kill it.

"He hit that ball harder than I ever have seen a ball hit since, as if he would drive it through to China," Bobby later wrote.

Up flew a divot the size of Ted's foot. Up also came the ball, buzzing like a partridge from the prodigious spin imparted by that tremendous wallop—almost straight up it got, cleared that tree by several yards, and sailed on at the height of an office building, to drop on the green not far from the hole. The gallery was in paroxysms. I remember how men pounded each other on the backs, and crowed and cackled and shouted and clapped their hands. As for me, I didn't really believe it. A sort of wonder persists in my memory to this day. It was the greatest shot I ever saw.

Keeler picks up the action from there: "And Ted Ray, his pipe in his mouth, the club tucked under his arm, was striding on toward the green long before the ball had come down, as if nothing at all had happened. He did not ever look after it."

Bobby watched the last six holes of the match in a state of wonder, as the drama shifted into high gear and held that crowd in thrall. Vardon made his birdie at twelve. Vardon and Ray went on to birdie the next three holes, but Kiltie birdied fifteen as well, and then got another at sixteen to cut the Britons' lead back down to one. After halving the seventeenth, Kiltie dropped a twelve-footer for his third birdie in the last four holes on the eighteenth. That left Ray with an eight-foot putt for birdie to secure the victory and avoid a sudden-death play-off. He studied the line from both sides for the first time that day, stepped up and slapped it into the back of the cup to win the match. All four men had played their second round in at least two strokes under par and received a sustained ovation. After witnessing such an amazing exhibition the home crowd didn't seem to mind that their favorites had been nosed out at the wire. O.B. Keeler waited his turn on the club's single telephone as reporters lined up to call in their headlines, while club members repaired to the bar and relived the great day long into the night.

Young Bobby could hardly sleep that night, lying in bed replaying every shot over and over. He had witnessed a display of astonishing skill, but beneath the placid surface of their polished play he had sensed a fierce struggle, capable of producing moments of rare wonder, delicacy, and power. Not so much man against man, but each man against himself, testing his limits and his capacity for rising to meet the test. The spent the following day at another Atlanta country club, Brookhaven, watching Vardon and Ray play two flawless rounds on yet another course they'd never seen before against another pair of local pros, the McKenzie brothers. Ray thrilled the crowd again by hitting his drive on the ninth across a swamp, a forced carry of over 280 yards, a shot no man had ever pulled off before. All Vardon did in Atlanta was play for par, and average 72 over his four rounds;

Ray's monstrous power shots had seized center stage in Bobby and O.B.'s memories, but in the days and weeks to come something about Vardon's quiet persistence loomed larger. Bobby later wrote: "Harry seemed to be playing something beside Stewart and Willie or the McKenzies; something I couldn't see, which kept him serious and sort of far away from the gallery and his opponents and even from his big partner; he seemed to be playing against something or someone not in the match at all."

A few weeks later that October Bobby experienced a milestone of his own, and he raced across four fairways to share it with his dad, near the end of his Saturday game at East Lake. As he walked off the eighteenth green, the Colonel was puzzled by the look on Bobby's face; the boy's hand trembled as he solemnly held out the scorecard. Big Bob read the card carefully.

"I made sure Perry attested to it," said Bobby. "He signed it, right there."

Bobby had shot his first 80 and made sure Perry signed the card so there'd be no question about its legitimacy. The Colonel smiled, held out his arms and wrapped his only son in a bear hug, blinking back some tears; only 3 percent of the people who take up the game ever break 80 in their lives. There would be a lot of whooping and hollering for the Jones boys on their walk home that evening.

The lessons Bobby had learned in golf were clear: the game was played for pleasure, but when you excelled in competition other people admired you, and your dad lavished you with praise, sometimes to an extravagant degree. By acquiring value in the eyes of others you could begin to believe you possessed it yourself, which in turn helped generate the self-confidence necessary to play this fiendishly difficult game at increasingly high levels.

Harry Vardon's method had quietly seeped into Bobby. He had been playing a match against Perry Adair in his record-breaking round, but for once never gave a thought to what his opponent was doing, or who was winning. It was the first round he had ever played against the only opponent that mattered, the invisible one he hadn't yet given a name to, the toughest of them all. Pop Keeler christened him Old Man Par.

The year 1914 is best remembered as a hinge on which the modern world swung into the open jaws of hell. Newsreel footage and photographs of Archduke Franz Ferdinand's assassination played in movie houses and newspapers across America. Everyone from Bobby Jones to President Woodrow Wilson saw these stark images of the crime. Wilson, the most dedicated golfer who'd ever lived in the White House, had given up the game that summer; his wife, Ellen, was slowly dying. During long nights keeping vigil over her decline, the President read the dispatches describing the string of firecrackers exploding across Europe with the horror of an educated humanist losing his faith in God and man. His ambassadors in France and Britain pleaded with him to intervene. When he learned of atrocities committed by the Germans as they marched through Belgium—thousands of civilians slaughtered, priests assassinated, cities burned to the ground—Wilson wept. But intervention did not reflect the national sentiment. Isolationist tendencies dominated every geographic, ethnic, and economic sector of the United States. Hundreds of thousands of recently immigrated Americans had fled Europe to escape this sort of senseless bloodbath; now that they were safely thousands of miles and an ocean away, most wanted no part of another. Wilson took the country's pulse and kept quiet, preoccupied with his own private tragedy.

Ellen Wilson died peacefully in her sleep on August 6. Ten days after he returned from burying his wife in her native Georgia, two weeks after Germany invaded Belgium, Woodrow Wilson formally articulated America's official response to the European conflict: neutrality in thought and action.

The opening moves of the war played in banner headlines, but the further one moved from the East Coast the more the conflict felt like distant thunder. Outside Atlanta, where the Jones family and their friends spent another untroubled summer at East Lake, the news barely registered on Bobby. East Lake's clubhouse had burned down in an electrical fire that spring and its replacement was under construction: the Joneses and new member O.B. Keeler, among many others, mourned the loss of their hand-crafted golf clubs for months. Stewart Maiden's shop ran over-time to address the crisis; Kiltie personally fashioned a first grown-up set of clubs for Bobby. Donald Ross's newly designed course opened for play that summer and was not an immediate success. Ross had reversed the routing to run counter-clockwise, one of his standard innovations. As old East Lake was the only course Bobby had ever played the new layout confounded him—it was over 300 yards longer—and his game went temporarily sideways. During their years together Kiltie gave him less than ten hours of formal instruction; Bobby learned primarily by watching and repeating. He responded to setbacks by concen-trating harder on the details; he noticed that a smaller, heavier ball called the Zome Zodiac flew a little farther and a lot straighter into the wind. A larger, lighter ball called a Black Domino went longer with the wind behind him. He began to study ways to attack a hole strategically, rather than just step up to the ball and swing: small but significant advancements to his game, and remarkable in a twelve-year old.

O.B. Keeler was typing up a story at the *Atlanta Georgian* one Friday morning when he overheard a fellow sports reporter named Milt Saul speaking with their chief editor. Like Pop, both men were avid golfers; Saul was a member at East Lake, and he was complaining about a tournament he'd entered there. "They really ought not to allow kids in these things. We've got three or four youngsters entered, and I've got to play one of 'em tomorrow—Little Bob Jones. He's a squirt, twelve years old. Of course I'll beat the wadding out of him, but what's the point of taking up time beating infants?"

The following week Pop overheard another conversation between the two men. The chatty Saul had been strangely quiet, and the boss stopped by to ask how the match had gone with Little Bob.

"He licked me eight and seven," said Saul, flustered. "I was right: they ought not to let kids play in these things!"

Little Bob Jones: Keeler filed the name away.

CHAPTER TWO

INTO THE FRAY

The origin of young Bobby Jones's hunger to succeed remains slightly mysterious; it appears to spring from the core of who he was. He owned an only child's conception of himself as the center of the universe, certainly a factor. His grandfather's Old Testament willpower at first glance seems to have bypassed the congenial Colonel, but Big Bob drove himself hard in business or any other competitive situation; he just did it in supremely affable style. Bobby inherited aspects of both men. Pleasing his father was important to him, but Bobby had ferocious expectations of his own, etched deep into his neurological and emotional codes. That's a quality which can drive a man to madness, and Bobby would come perilously close to the edge.

In May, 1915, Bobby set a new scoring record at East Lake, and club president George Adair decided he was ready for the next level of competition. George and Perry had planned a trip to Montgomery, Alabama, where both were entered in one of the South's biggest invitational tournaments, and they wanted Bobby to come along. First they had to convince his father; George offered to pick up all the expenses, but the Colonel hesitated over what would be Bobby's first tournament away from home. Not until Bobby made an impassioned plea did he give the okay.

Bobby distinguished himself in the tournament at Montgomery, but not by his own high standards. Although he missed qualifying for the first flight he made it all the way into the finals of the second before losing to a thirty-year-old left-hander; a man hitting from the "wrong side of the ball" made his defeat even more humiliating. Bobby pitched a fit afterwards and tossed some clubs around, feeling like an absolute failure. He was only thirteen, three months shy of high school, and already expected to beat experienced players more than twice his age.

Provided his game continued to advance, the Colonel had promised Bobby he could enter the prestigious Southern Amateur once he turned fifteen. Bobby returned from Montgomery convinced his career was ruined, only to discover his father had entered him in *that* year's Southern, two years ahead of schedule. What was more, since East Lake was hosting the event Bobby had been tapped for its four-man team in the inter-club competition. Kiltie Maiden had now taken the emerging prodigy firmly under his wing and Bobby had thoroughly assimilated his swing. When a friend of Kiltie's from Carnoustie arrived for a visit, he spied Bobby on the course from a distance, mistook him for the wee Scotsman and could not be persuaded otherwise until Kiltie appeared in person. Kiltie had a word with Big Bob about putting Bobby on the East Lake team—a word sounds about right; a full sentence was an oration for him—and that convinced the Colonel his son was ready.

Little Bob wasn't so sure. The night before the tournament he laid out his first pair of long pants to wear; self-conscious about his appearance, Bobby was afraid he still looked like a stumpy schoolboy in his usual knickerbockers.

Tuesday morning, June 15. A dangerous hailstorm held up play for over an hour. After waiting out the delay in the locker room, Bobby felt so nervous in front of the big crowd gathered at the first tee he had to "keep looking at the ground to keep from falling over." His little round face screwed in a mask of determination, he went out and shot the best round on his team—which won that part of the competition—and finished second for the qualifying medal, one stroke behind the leaders. In a field of 215 of the best players from every corner of the South. Out of that group the top sixty-four advanced to the matchplay brackets that would determine the championship. East Lake members crowded around to shower praise on their young hero, while the Colonel proudly held court in the bar; he'd qualified for matchplay as well. It should have been a red-letter day in the Jones household but all Bobby could think about as he lay in bed that night was how much better he could have played, reliving his mistakes over and over, establishing a pattern of perpetual dissatisfaction which would torment him for years.

The next day Pop Keeler traveled out to East Lake to cover the Southern Amateur, and watched this young Jones kid he'd heard so much about tee it up for the first time. Bobby handled his first-round opponent easily and advanced to the round of thirty-two. He drew a perpetual favorite in his second match, a stocky veteran in his fifties from Houston named Bryan Heard, nicknamed "the Commodore." It was a memorable duel, but the Commodore edged Bobby out with a snaking 30-footer at the seventeenth, 2 & 1.

Once Bobby was out of earshot, Pop asked the Commodore if the young lad had given him a fight. Heard removed his pith helmet and mopped his brow. "Did he? I would've shot 76 with a par at eighteen. That would have broken the best score ever by an amateur on this course. I only beat him by one." The Commodore watched Bobby mope toward the clubhouse. "That boy's going to be a great golfer. Maybe *the* greatest."

Young Perry Adair avenged his friend's loss that morning, eliminating the Commodore from the field of sixteen, which pleased Bobby no end. "Too many of these damned kids," muttered the Commodore as he walked off. Bobby, standing near the green, happened to overhear him, which put a smile a mile wide on his face.

The defeat dropped Bobby into the losers' bracket, where he ran off three wins against a trio of the best players in the region and advanced to the finals. Bobby was three down at the end of the morning, because this time his opponent—Frank Clarke of Nashville—did shoot 76 and set a new amateur record for East Lake. Clarke increased his lead to four up by the time they made the turn that afternoon; observers conceded the match was over. With his parents and friends watching, Bobby rallied to win the next four holes in a row and square the match. The cheers filled him with confidence; Bobby figured he had his man in the bag, and let up on the fury that had brought him back. He lost the next two holes, but still wasn't ready to quit, chipping in for birdie at the fifteenth, only to watch Clarke sink a 30-foot putt for a half. When Bobby put his second shot in a bunker on seventeen, Clarke closed him out, 2 & 1. His parents, Kiltie, and the crew at East Lake gushed over his resilient comeback. Atlanta's papers, with O.B. Keeler leading the chorus, raved about the youngster's performance: Bobby was the sensation of the Southern Amateur. In its write-up, *American Golfer* called his battle with Clarke the match of the tournament, and ran Bobby's photo with the story. An article in the sports section of the *New York Times* appeared shortly thereafter: GEORGIA'S GOLF MARVEL. Only the first of many headlines he would make that summer.

Bobby told no one his private feelings: "I felt I was a disgrace to my family, and to Stewart Maiden, and to the Atlanta Athletic Club, and to anybody or anything else convenient to be disgraced."

The lesson Bobby took away from that match was clear: never shake hands with yourself for your fine play before you shake hands for the last time with the man you beat. Bobby showed he'd taken that lesson to heart a few weeks later in Birmingham, at the Roebuck Country Club's invitational, another mainstay on the Southern circuit. Bobby squeaked by Perry Adair in the second round—the first time they'd faced each other outside of East Lake—and reached the finals against Bill Badham, a former collegiate star at Yale. Bobby played out of his skull against Badham, but got madder and madder than he couldn't shake this fancy-pants Ivy Leaguer, a man ten years his senior with a hundred tournaments under his belt.

The two were all square after eighteen but this time Bobby didn't pat himself on the back. He played Badham even to the twenty-first hole, looked him straight in the eye and struck a pitch dead at the flag to win his first big tournament. Any golfer who's ever won anything tells you the first win is the hardest. Bobby won twice more in Atlanta before the summer was over, breaking a course record at the Druid Hills invitational. Then he beat his own father, for the first time ever, in the finals of East Lake's club championship. Big Bob couldn't have been happier; he lifted him off the ground in triumph and they marched home arm in arm carrying the trophy and singing songs until Clara came out on the porch and yelled at them. Two weeks later, in the Atlanta City Championship, the climax of the local season, Bobby lost in the semi-finals to George Adair, who went on to defend his title. The next week Bobby set his

soaring aspirations aside and began classes, as a freshman at
Georgia Technological High school.

As Bobby's school year progressed, the specter of war drew
closer to American shores. President Wilson publicly reinforced
the country's neutrality, while privately encouraging increased
shipments of food and munitions to the Allies. The sport of golf
went into hibernation in Britain. Most courses were taken over
by the military, their clubhouses turned into convalescent hospi-
tals; fairways sprouted tents, training camps for new recruits.
Many were used as gunnery ranges. Seaside links were converted
to airfields for the British Army's air corps. Others were ploughed
over into farmland to support the war effort, sparing only the
greens.

   Harry Vardon had just turned forty-four, his condition fragile
at best; being accepted into any active branch of service was out
of the question. Realizing that to be seen practicing his profession might bring offense during a time when death lists filled
the newspapers, Vardon approached the Red Cross with the idea
of playing exhibition matches to raise money, and enlisted J. H.
Taylor and James Braid to join him. Their "Great Triumvirate"
events proved a solid success throughout the war, the birth of
a tradition in golf that has contributed millions to charities ever
since.

   Play went on in America. Four-time Amateur champion Jerry
Travers won the 1915 U.S. Open at Baltusrol Golf Club, joining
Ouimet as the only man to have won both national titles. The
gifted, pernickety Chicagoan Chick Evans fell one stroke short
when his putter failed him again.

   Ouimet, Travers and Evans were the overwhelming favorites
as the Amateur got under way in Detroit, but due to the unpredictable vagaries of matchplay all three were eliminated by the
second round. The trophy was claimed for a second time by
1909's Amateur champion Robert Gardner.

Ouimet returned home from Detroit and put golf aside for a while. After learning the trade as a sales clerk at Wright & Ditson, in the spring of 1916 he opened the doors of his own sporting-goods store in Boston. Raising capital from investors that included his father—who had come full circle on Francis's involvement with golf—he took as his partner a fellow member at Woodland, John Sullivan, his future brother-in-law. They offered a full range of equipment, including golf clubs and balls; what hacker wouldn't want to buy his gear from America's first champion?

On January 14 the United States Golf Association announced it had decided to redefine the rules of amateur status. Any player could, for example, still write articles about the sport for money, or accept a car as a "gift" for winning a big event, and retain his amateur standing. But this new interpretation declared that if you had anything to do with selling golf equipment—as an endorser, manufacturer, or retailer—the USGA now considered you a professional. Plans to open Ouimet & Sullivan had been in the works for months when Francis heard about the ruling. USGA president Frank Woodward was convinced that the line between pro and amateur had grown dangerously blurred, with nothing less than the integrity of the game at stake.

Ouimet had invested his life's savings in the store, and called upon the goodwill of friends and family to back him. He had been working full-time as a sporting-goods salesman at Wright & Ditson when he won the 1914 Amateur and no one had said boo about his status then. He had turned down dozens of offers to exploit his championships commercially—everything from appearing on the vaudeville stage to the growing movie industry—because of concerns over apparent exploitation. This decision threatened not only the modest dreams Ouimet had been nurturing, but his ability to make a living in the only business he'd ever aspired to. Although it wasn't in his agreeable nature to defy authority, make a public show of protest, or consider mounting a legal challenge—a restraint unimaginable today today—Ouimet felt the ruling was simply unfair. He made a conscious decision to contest the USGA's policy in the simplest possible way. He opened his store.

In late March, as applications were being accepted for that year's Amateur, Ouimet received a letter from Woodward, informing him the Executive Committee had revoked his status as an amateur in good standing. He would not be eligible to play in any USGA-sponsored amateur events until he severed connections with his sporting-goods business. John Sullivan received an identical letter. Knowing how much golf meant to his friend, Sullivan suggested Ouimet withdraw from the store temporarily and try to strike a compromise with the USGA. Francis refused. He had given his word to Sullivan that he was in to stay; loyalty came first. Woodward might have won the battle, but he lost the war of public opinion; a storm of controversy erupted, with a majority of people involved in the game leaping to Ouimet's defense. Kids like Bobby Jones refused to believe their hero would never play again. The greatest amateur of all, Old Man Walter Travis—publisher of *American Golfer* magazine—used his column to blast Woodward's decision.

As they had been in Britain for nearly a century, professionals in America were still looked down on as second-class citizens. In golf's privileged quarters, particularly the East Coast clubs where the American game took root, referring to someone as a "pro" was tantamount to calling him a hustler, a drunk, or a bum. Turning their line of work into a respectable profession remained an uphill climb, but in 1916 the activist vanguard of golf workers took their most important step in that direction.

Professional golfers in England organized their first representative body in 1901, the British Professional Golf Association. American pros followed suit in early 1916; the Professional Golfers of America came into existence when thirty-five members signed its charter in New York City. The PGA held its first pros-only tournament in October that year, a sparsely attended matchplay affair that over the course of the next decade would evolve into America's second major professional championship. Rodman Wannamaker, benefactor of the PGA, was in the gallery throughout the tournament and donated an ornate silver trophy of his own design, personally awarding it to winner Jim Barnes afterwards; the Wannamaker Trophy is still given to the winner of the PGA Championship today. Over the previous two decades the USGA had established itself as the guardian of the integrity of the game itself—in Woodward's persecution of Ouimet almost too zealously. With the emergence of the PGA, the often forgotten men who made their living inside the game, the caddies, pros, and greenkeepers who made the game possible at the ground level, at last had a protector of their own.

Minneapolis was the farthest point west to ever host a U.S. Open. With the spreading war overseas occupying public attention, only eighty-one entrants made the trek to the championship. Unwilling to incite a confrontation with the USGA, Francis Ouimet declined to even apply. Defending champion Jerry Travers also bowed out of the Open, announcing his retirement to concentrate on his work as a cotton broker on Wall Street. The absence of these key contenders opened up the field for perpetual bridesmaid, fellow amateur Chick Evans.

To help his putting, Evans brought his caddie with him from Chicago, along with half a dozen putters and his annually reconstructed putting stroke. He had done a lot of soul-searching about past failings in major tournaments over the winter, and placed the blame squarely between his own ears. In front of a sympathetic Midwestern gallery, Evans repeatedly whispered the word "relax" to himself before every shot—the first recorded use of a mantra by a golfer—and it worked wonders. Evans shot a blistering 32 on his first front nine, ending the day with a three-stroke lead over British expatriate Wilfred Reid. He went on to win the tournament with a new Open scoring total of 286, smashing the old record by four strokes. That record would stand for the next twenty years, surviving the transition to steel shafts, hotter golfballs and an upcoming rival named Bobby Jones. Small wonder Evans cried openly when they handed him the cup. After seven years of intense, public and often self-inflicted suffering in the fields of the golf gods, Chick Evans had broken through.

Pop Keeler had been through a season in hell. During the fall of 1915 he lugged his typewriter all over the South to cover Georgia Tech's football season, often in a cold, driving rain. On one raw, bone-numbing afternoon he watched Tech slaughter Cumberland State by a score of 222–0 (that is not a misprint). After that game Pop ended up in the hospital, his tonsils crawling with streptococci. He had barely survived his last bout with pneumonia and feared it was making a comeback, but this turned out to be even more serious. The Friday following his release, Pop was driving home, looked up at the evening sky, and saw two full moons. The following day his feet wouldn't work. Within a week he was back in the hospital, paralyzed from his toes to his throat, able to take water only by the spoonful, where it would likely as not come right back out through his nose. A neurologist recommended opening up his skull. He was outvoted. Pop wrote: "I suspect any effort to find something in my skull would have been futile anyway."

He had suffered a cerebral hemorrhage, the blood filtering down from his brain and creating nearly fatal pressure on his spinal cord. Nerve damage pinched his left hand into a claw with a dropped wrist; he was forced to wear a leather and steel brace full time to prevent further deformity. His tendon reflexes were virtually destroyed, and what muscle tone he'd had to begin with soon wasted away; he couldn't raise either arm above his shoulders. Months into his recovery Pop volunteered to appear before the Atlanta Neurological Society "as an illustration of what the human body would stand without a complete extinction of the life principle." Pop's struggle to live lasted six months, including two sanatorium stays where a variety of baths and electrical treatments did nothing but add variation to his misery. When one of his surgeons suggested Pop aid his recuperation by taking up golf again, he responded: "Haven't I been tortured enough?"

When he finally got home and tried to hold a club in his hands Pop didn't even have the strength to pick it up. For the time being he would only enjoy the game as a spectator. On his first day back at East Lake that summer he witnessed an epic encounter in the finals of the club championship between two best friends, seventeen-year-old Perry Adair and fourteen-year-old Bobby Jones.

Pop was amazed by the rapid maturation of Jones's game. Bobby had recently broken his own scoring record at East Lake with a 74 and won two local tournaments. He'd put on weight over the winter, and looked a little chunky now. Only five-foot-four, he weighed close to 160 pounds and could hold his own against any big hitters he went up against. It rained through most of his final match with Perry, but his golf was so compelling the fragile Pop risked his health to hobble around and watch Bobby win his second East Lake title. The kid had come into his own as a player, and Pop raved about what he'd seen: he could barely contain his excitement, which helped him forget his own troubles. Here was greatness, and he was the first reporter to grasp what that might mean to Bobby, to Atlanta and to the game itself.

Bobby's win earned him a berth in the first Georgia Amateur Championship, played in July, 1916, at Brookhaven Country Club in Atlanta. In a matchplay field of thirty-two, the draw pitted Bobby and Perry against each other in the finals. Playing as the favorite, Perry took a three-stroke lead into lunch; most agreed that as the older, more mature player he would win out. (This sentiment was so widespread that Pop overheard the chairman of the tournament, Ralph Reed, approach Bobby on the practice green between rounds to make an extraordinary request. So many spectators had traveled from all around the state to watch the afternoon's competition he wanted Bobby to agree to "play out the bye holes"—that is, the holes remaining in the round after he lost the match to Perry. Pop wrote that Bobby replied angrily: "Don't worry, Mr. Reed—there aren't going to be any bye holes!" Bobby later denied the conversation ever took place, but Pop stood by his story.

After losing the first hole that afternoon to go four down, Bobby's whole attitude about competitive golf changed completely and forever. He hit every shot harder than he'd ever swung in his life. His concentration took on a ferocity no one watching had ever seen before. He played the final seventeen holes in even par and beat Perry, two up, on the last green. Perry picked up Bob's ball, conceding defeat, and as he handed it to him stammered: "Bob, you are just the best."

Bobby had won Georgia's first amateur championship and crushed his best friend in the process. Although he would go on to win a handful of important titles in the South, Perry Adair retired from active competition while only in his mid-twenties to enter his father's real-estate business. He never made an impact in the game on the national stage and, after this loss in the inaugural Georgia State Amateur, he never beat Bobby Jones again.

George Adair took the Colonel aside after the tournament and told him that Bobby's victory earned him an automatic berth into the 1916 National Amateur Championship, to be held a few weeks later at the Merion Cricket Club in suburban Philadelphia. Bobby already satisfied the Amateur's other prerequisites: a verifiable handicap less than six, and $5 for the entry fee. Once again the Colonel hesitated—was his son really ready for the national stage?—and once again George Adair made a persuasive argument: winning the Massachusetts Amateur had been Francis Ouimet's only title before the Open in 1913, why shouldn't it be so for Bobby? George was planning to make the trip to Philadelphia—Perry had qualified as well—and insisted that Bobby come along, offering to pick up the tab.

The Colonel wrote a letter to Tech High School, requesting an excused absence for his son; the Amateur was being played right after Labor Day, and Bobby was going to miss the first week of his sophomore year.

Pop Keeler would not be making the trip north to Pennsylvania—budget constraints at the paper—but he made an important personal decision regarding his own future after watching Bobby win the State Amateur: writing about golf in general, and Bobby Jones in particular, was how he planned to spend the rest of his professional life.

Bobby's trip to Pennsylvania would be his first trip out of the Deep South, and his first stay in a grand hotel, where gourmet dining translated to three helpings of pie *à la mode*. The big city awed and fascinated the wide-eyed fourteen-year-old. At Merion, where they had gone to get in a practice round, Bobby fell in love with the pomp and hustle, the tents and colorful banners, the palpable electric atmosphere of a major championship; he had found a home. They played a practice round on the West Course, their first exposure to lightning-fast bent-grass greens; the severe heat of the South prohibited the use of anything but coarser-grained Bermuda. Bobby thought Merion's greens looked as smooth as pool-table felt, and couldn't wait to play on them. He had a steep learning curve: on the sixth hole, facing a 30-foot putt, he knocked the ball all the way off the green and out of bounds into a stream.

They arrived early the next day for the first of two qualifying rounds; the top thirty-two players in the field would advance to the matchplay tournament. Bobby was not only the youngest player in the field of 157, he was the youngest to ever compete in an Amateur. He stepped to the first tee of the West Course that morning wearing a crisp white shirt with a starched collar and a natty bow tie. Long light-brown wool pants, the only pair he'd brought with him on the trip. A jaunty cap, and a pair of high-topped army boots to which he'd nailed some spikes. Tanned and freckled as a farmer's kid, his sun-bleached hair still worn in a schoolboy bowl cut. Five foot four, 165 pounds; some accounts describe him as chubby, but he carried the weight well, most of it in his legs and rear end, the engine room of his deceptively powerful swing. He seemed a figure of curiosity, at best, even outright amusement for some; Bobby and the Adairs were authentic Southerners, an exotic breed here in the gentrified suburbs of the East. These jaded sophisticates were about to get a first-class lesson in talent.

Bobby shot 74, the lowest first-round score in the entire field. Word got out fast between rounds about what the Dixie Whiz Kid had done and when he made his way to the East Course for his afternoon round a thousand people waited at the first tee, the largest crowd Bobby had ever played in front of; what would become later in life an almost phobic aversion to big crowds had its start here. He played as poorly that afternoon as he had superbly that morning—although the much more difficult East Course had something to do with that—shooting 89 and landing in a tie for eighteenth place, four shots inside the cut line. Perry Adair came in after him, right on the cut line, and had to endure a play-off to secure the final slot in the matchplay field, but he survived. When Bob and Perry met up afterwards in front of the big scoreboard, the two hugged each other and jumped up and down in excitement; they were still kids first, golfers second.

They hurried to the bulletin board outside the clubhouse, where the USGA posted the next day's first-round match-ups. Bobby drew Eben Byers, a name that meant nothing to him, but one that drew groans from everyone around him. A thirty-six-year-old native of Pittsburgh, Byers was a former National

Amateur champion who had reached the finals two other times. Sick of receiving condolences from people he hardly knew before they'd even played the match, Bobby cockily fired back a line he'd heard from George Adair: "The bigger they are, the harder they fall."

Grantland Rice smelled a story brewing. A nationally syndicated columnist for the *New York Tribune*, the thirty-five-year-old Tennessean had found his voice in the last few years and was considered the country's most influential sportswriter. Concurrent with the popular culture being created by the movie industry, sports had in the last decade offered a unifying form of identity for twentieth-century America; teams became rallying points of pride for their cities, as all the age-old rivalries taken for granted today were just then being born.

And when Rice decided to write about you—as he would of Jack Dempsey, Babe Ruth, Walter Hagen, and Notre Dame football, all of whom enjoy their cultural immortality in large part because of his interest—it was a benediction from the Pope. You had arrived. Rice had served a four-year apprenticeship at Pop Keeler's future home, the *Atlanta Journal*, and during this time he struck up a casual acquaintance with a young lawyer named Robert Purdemus Jones; Rice and the Colonel had similar family backgrounds, and both had seen their pro baseball dreams crushed by patrician fathers demanding a more genteel career path for their sons. Because of his interest in golf as a player, he was also the first respected American sportswriter to treat the game as a major sport. When Rice realized that the Jones boy who'd created a sensation during qualifying at Merion was Big Bob's kid, he called Bobby at the Bellevue-Stratford Hotel, where he was staying, and arranged to take him out to breakfast early the next morning.

Bobby hardly touched his breakfast; he was about to go thirty-six holes with a former Amateur champion in his debut in a national tournament and couldn't wait to get started. Rice was struck by the fire and confidence in Bobby's manner, but also his gentlemanly manners; as a fellow son of the South, Rice appreciated the importance of good breeding. He wished Bobby well and said he'd be out to watch him that morning. He didn't voice his concerns about Bobby's displays of temper on the course, nor did he write about them; he thought they were an instinctive part of the boy's drive for perfection, but suspected that if Bobby failed to control them he'd never play the magnificent golf he was capable of shooting.

Most of the gallery attending Merion that day lined up to watch Bobby's match with Eben Byers, who kept his young opponent waiting on the tee in a classic bit of gamesmanship. As they walked off Bobby stuffed three sticks of gum in his mouth and offered one to Byers, who gruffly shook his head. Bobby shrugged: whatever. The crowd chuckled: with that casual act of innocence Bobby had already won them over. Byers consequently started the match angry—he was a proud man, humiliated that he had to play a little kid—and got steadily more steamed all day. Bobby already had a reputation for his temper, but it was never directed at an opponent, only at himself. Anger was the dark side of his startling, bulletproof confidence: he expected perfection on every shot and couldn't forgive himself for anything less. As someone to learn etiquette from in his first national match he couldn't have picked a worse opponent than Eben Byers. Early in their match, watching Byers violently reposition his tools after every lousy shot, Bobby decided it was perfectly acceptable for him to get in on the act. He'd been tossing clubs around in anger since he was six years old, when that sort of acting out tended to be viewed as "cute." Bobby also had a longshoreman's command of cursing, from years of trailing around East Lake after the Colonel and his salty pals, and he unveiled some shockers to the more delicate ears in the gallery.

Whilst Bobby was able to discharge his anger and get back

to business, Byers stayed in a permanent funk. At the lunch break Bobby had a three-hole lead, and moved around the grounds happy and carefree. Byers ate his lunch alone in the locker room, out of sight. Bobby's lead grew to five on the afternoon's front nine, but Byers crept back to within three as they made the final turn. The crowd sensed the kid might be ready to crack, that Byers would impose a stronger will, but they'd misread the situation: Bobby's pristine fourteen-year-old nerves were more than up to this task. Byers broke first. Bobby closed him out on the thirty-fifth hole, 3 & 1. The crowd cheered him all the way back to the clubhouse, and he blushed red, waving shyly to his new fans.

The next day Bobby went up against Pennsylvania's reigning Amateur champion, Frank Dyer. Untroubled by the attention Bobby brought along with him, Dyer jumped all over his young opponent, winning five of the first six holes. The "Whiz Kid's" club-throwing and cursing started immediately. The Byers match had played out as slapstick comedy, and its goofiness had helped defray Bobby's first-round jitters. Frank Dyer presented the kid with his first real test and journalists thought Bobby was close to losing control completely. George Adair recognized it, stepped in, and played surrogate father; he took Bobby aside between holes and told him he'd pull him right off the course and send him home if he didn't behave himself. Chastened, Bobby steadied his emotions and played even par golf the rest of the way. At the seventeenth hole he took the lead from Frank Dyer for the first time.

The eighteenth at Merion is a majestic par-four requiring a long drive over an open chasm, the last section of the scenic rock quarry. Dyer and Jones both carried their drives to the fairway, but caught bad bounces. The balls were lying by a tall mound, one at the base, one on top, both nestled in high rough. Their referee discovered his contestants were playing an identical brand of ball and neither had differentiated theirs with an identifying mark, as is now the universal custom. Both insisted theirs was the ball in the better lie—an examination once they got to the green revealed that Bobby was correct; his ball had a tar stain on it from an earlier bounce off a road—but to break the stalemate, Bobby volunteered to play the ball at the base of the hill. After hacking it back to the fairway he ended up taking six and losing the hole, which brought them to the lunch break all square, but the advantage was all Jones. When Bobby latched onto something external to draw anger away from his own performance he played his best golf, and this incident got him going. He won the opening hole of their afternoon round—after making a point of showing his opponent that he'd covered his ball with "J"s—and never gave back the lead, beating Frank Dyer 4 & 2. Bobby had passed the test.

Bobby's win over Dyer advanced him to the quarter-finals and confirmed his Cinderella status as the darling of the tournament. The evening papers covered his bed at the Bellevue-Stratford that night; Bobby read up about himself and found it a disorienting experience. Many of the stories focused on his temper; he had quickly been stamped as a "hot-blooded Southerner," reinforcing the cultural stereotype of a Dixie hayseed out of his element in sophisticated Yankee environs. Along that same patronizing line, reporters had the nerve to criticize his wardrobe, which hurt Bobby's feelings more than critiques of his temperament. He owned only the one pair of long pants he'd brought with him, and if his boots looked old and dusty compared to what the local swells were wearing, he'd never thought of golf as a "dress-up" game back home and for crying out loud he was only fourteen. But he took the criticism to heart; he swore that nobody would ever make fun of the way he dressed again. Within a few years Bobby would be considered a fashion plate and trendsetter well outside the confines of his sport.

There's a marvelous photograph from one of those sports pages, a posed shot of Bobby setting up for a swing, his gaze slanted down a fairway, with Merion's clubhouse in the background. His poised determination, tempered by a wicked Huck Finn smile, suggests a dangerous competitor at least a decade older than his actual age. This was only one of many photographs Bobby scrutinized that night, sizing up his image for the first time from the outside, as others saw him. He didn't have words to articulate the process at the time, but he had just taken the first step of his transformation from an ordinary kid into an object of fame, a face and persona and aura that the public would come to feel they owned more than he did. As Hollywood was discovering, film had revolutionized the creation of public icons; nothing would help Grantland Rice & Co. more in their creation of sporting and movie-star heroes than the mass reproduction of photographs and moving pictures confirming the romantic ideals of what star athletes were supposed to look like. The problems all that attention would create for their subjects hadn't even been considered yet; to suddenly see oneself as others do can rip the cover off a young psyche's protective innocence, and create chaos for the unprepared mind.

Finally Bobby put the newspapers aside and slept soundly. He needed every bit of his adolescent confidence the following day: as his next opponent he had drawn defending and two-time U.S. Amateur champion Robert Gardner.

Robert Gardner looked every inch the all-American Ivy League star athlete, from his styled, curly blond locks to the razor-sharp crease in his fashionable pants. At six-one, Gardner had to lean down to shake the schoolboy's hand. Despite the largest gallery he'd seen in his life, Bobby was over his stage fright; he played crisply all morning. Gardner appeared to be the more nervous of the two; he couldn't find a fairway and lost the first two holes. Despite his wildness off the tee, Gardner executed an impressive variety of recoveries to keep the match close. Convinced the man couldn't keep getting up and down forever, Bobby began to believe he had a chance to beat the defending champ, shot 76 and carried a one-up lead into intermission. The growing legend of the Whiz Kid dominated the grounds; almost every soul who'd made the trip out to Merion crowded around to watch their afternoon round.

They were all square coming to the sixth hole; Bobby stuck his approach close to the pin and Gardner missed the green, leaving himself a delicate downhill chip over a ridge onto a lightning-fast green. He whispered his shot up to within four inches of the cup and got down for a half, when Bobby missed his try at birdie. At the par-three seventh, Bobby left his tee shot in ideal position below the flag while Gardner pulled his well left of the green, staring down at another downhill tight pin; again he chipped to within a foot and knocked it in for the tie. On the eighth, Bobby's approach landed only ten feet from the pin, while Gardner pulled his long and left onto the ninth tee box. This time his pitch onto the green checked up short, outside of Bobby's ball.

"I felt the break had come," said Bobby. "He couldn't keep missing shots and getting away with it."

But Gardner sank his 15-footer for par. Although he'd just been shown the line, Bobby missed his third birdie in a row. Grantland Rice focused on this in his column the next day: "That would have broken the heart of any golfer alive."

"I felt I had been badly treated by luck," Bobby recalled a few years later. "I had been denied something that was rightly mine. I wanted to go off and pout and have someone sympathize with me, and I acted just like the kid I was. I didn't half try to hit the next tee shot, and I didn't half try on any shot thereafter. In short, I quit."

Looking back on it, Bobby was always grateful that he'd lost when he did. If Gardner had missed any of those chip shots during the heat of their match Bobby knew he would have beaten him. And if he'd gotten past Gardner he also knew there was a better than good chance he might have won the '16 Amateur.

"I had already become a bit cocky because of my success against grown men. I shudder to think what those years might have done to me," he wrote later. "Not so much to my golf, but in a vastly more important respect, to me as a human being."

Grantland Rice wrote this about Bobby's first Amateur: "At his age the game in this country has never developed anyone with such a combination of physical strength, bulldog determination, mechanical skill and coolness against the test. He is the most remarkable kid prodigy we have ever seen."

Although the papers reported that "the Georgia schoolboy" took the loss in his stride—whistling on his way back to the clubhouse, talking about the big bowl of ice cream he planned to dive into—something much darker and richer was going on inside Bobby. Underneath his smiling sportsmanship this loss hurt him to his core; he had outplayed Gardner almost throughout but it hadn't seemed to matter. He felt Gardner had only been a stand-in for something else, something implacable and strange, as if the match had been decided by some unseen hand. For the first time Bobby had bumped up against destiny. Bobby ate his ice cream, and accepted a hundred consolations as he sat in Merion's clubhouse, but the entire time couldn't stop wondering why fate, on this day, had chosen the other man. And if that was all that mattered, would it ever turn his way?

The next day Robert Gardner won his semi-final match against Jesse Guilford, and advanced to the championship against Chick Evans. Evans had played through his bracket without ever being tested, and their final match was watched by eight thousand spectators, including a mesmerized Bobby Jones. The USGA experimented with ropes to control the largest crowd that had ever shown up for an Amateur. Evans started the round with a birdie and built a three-hole advantage by intermission. Gardner came back in the afternoon to close within one on the tenth green, lying two and about to tie the match, when Evans sank a serpentine 40-footer to save par.

As soon as that ball dropped Bobby knew the match was over; he'd been right there in Gardner's shoes two days before. At this stage of a match played at such a high competitive level, Bobby now knew that winning had everything to do with state of mind; after a blow like that he sensed Gardner was psychologically finished. He was right. Evans won three of the next five holes and closed out the match.

Chick Evans had accomplished something no one else could boast about: not only had he captured the U.S. Open and Amateur—as only Francis Ouimet and Jerry Travers had before him—he'd done it in the same year. Boast about it he would, that was Evans's nature, just as it was for him to defensively explain to reporters how his was the more impressive achievement. Bobby learned a lot from watching him, both during and after the match, some of it negative, about how a champion behaves. He also identified Evans as the man he would someday have to beat, because he now owned something Bobby had during this last week realized he wanted more than anything. The title of best golfer in the world.

Fate played another hand that day. The game's Grand Old Man, forty-nine-year-old Walter Travis, had been in the galleries at Merion all week. He'd witnessed both of Bobby's matches, and been as impressed by the prodigy as everyone else. Grantland Rice bumped into him and asked him how he thought Bobby could improve. "He can never improve his shots, if that's what you mean," replied Travis. "But he will learn a great deal more about playing them. And his putting method is faulty."

Rice told George Adair about Travis's comment. Since Travis had a reputation as the greatest putter who ever lived, George sought him out and arranged a putting lesson for Bobby on the practice green the morning before the finals. The early trains coming out to Merion from Philadelphia were packed solid; Bobby and the Adairs were delayed by the crowd and arrived a minute too late to board the express. They caught the next one, but arrived twenty minutes late for his lesson with Travis, who had waited only five minutes for Bobby. The lesson didn't take place.

Back in Atlanta, Bobby's schoolmates seemed less impressed by what he'd done than a steady parade of admiring grown-ups, first among them Pop Keeler. The two would meet out at East Lake on Saturdays after Bobby's game and hoist a few Coca-Colas, which that summer introduced its iconic hourglass-shaped bottle. Bobby learned that Pop knew a lot more about golf than most people, and he liked talking strategy with him. Bobby also appreciated Pop's interest in him, and his lively sense of humor; he was the silliest grown-up Bobby had ever known, outgoing, socially fearless, and a shameless flirt with the ladies, an enlightening contrast to the shy young Bobby. Slowly, steadily, the unlikeliest of friendships was born.

CHAPTER THREE

FINDING A VOICE

E arly in 1917 President Woodrow Wilson made one last stab
at diplomacy in Europe, asking both sides to lay down their
arms and create what he called "peace without victory." His
plea fell on deaf ears. On January 31 Germany announced the
resumption of unrestricted submarine warfare. Three days later,
after another American ship went down, Wilson finally severed
diplomatic relations with Germany.

Major-league baseball continued play through the summer of
1917; boxing and horse-racing, the nation's two most popular
sports, carried on without missing a beat; the college football
season proceeded as planned; the U.S. Tennis Open was held as
scheduled, but billed itself as the "Patriotic Open." Only the

United States Golf Association canceled its scheduled championships in the year America joined the war. Perhaps the lingering public perception of golf as a wealthy man's game prompted the decision. The fledgling PGA soon followed suit and canceled its championship as well. The Western Golf Association in Chicago, four years the USGA's junior and often at odds with its Eastern cousins, went its own way and announced plans to conduct its tournaments as scheduled. It then went a step further in tweaking establishment noses by inviting Francis Ouimet, whose banishment by the USGA it had refused to recognize, to participate in the annual Western Amateur. Ouimet did not decide to accept until he had made one last appeal to the USGA's Executive Committee, but he was turned down again.

The following week Ouimet accepted the WGA's invitation to play in the Western Amateur at Midlothian. In front of a supportive Chicago crowd he won the only formal tournament in which he had competed for the last two years. Although he didn't make it past the first round at Midlothian, fifteen-year-old Bobby Jones told friends his trip to Chicago had been worth it because he got a chance to shake the hand of his idol, Francis Ouimet. They didn't have time for an extended conversation—Bobby was struck speechless when they met, making that difficult—but that would come later.

In the absence of the USGA's championships, the only high-profile golf played in America that summer was at charity tournaments modeled on Harry Vardon's benefits for the war effort. Top players from around the country lined up to participate. One name in particular now dominated golf in the South: Bobby Jones picked up right where he left off at Merion and opened his season in June with a victory at the Southern Amateur, the youngest player to ever win that title. As a result Bobby had been invited to play a series of Red Cross matches, a schedule that would dominate the next two years of his life.

An officer at Wright & Ditson Sporting Goods—Ouimet's old

employers—had the idea that a junior version of these charity matches might prove popular. He recruited his key participants straight from East Lake: Bobby, Perry Adair, and reigning U.S. women's champion Alexa Stirling. Elaine Rosenthal, a talented Chicago teen, completed the foursome. With Miss Rosenthal's mother serving as their chaperone, the kids set off on a whirlwind exhibition tour of resorts throughout New England. While on the road Bobby and Perry experimented with their first grown-up vice, sneaking cigarettes, a habit Bobby was never able to subsequently shake; he claimed they helped settle his nerves on the course. Treated as celebrities wherever they traveled—and acclaimed as fine young patriots for helping the war effort—these were heady days for Bobby, filled with golf, fawning interviews, and congratulatory dinners, an endless stream of unconditional admiration. Another swing followed through the Midwest and South, where Bobby broke scoring records by the handful. These tours proved such a success—the kids helped raise over $150,000—that invitations followed for them to participate in grown-up events.

Befitting his status as dual U.S. Champion, Chick Evans had taken the lead in the Red Cross effort and worked tirelessly on its behalf, traveling every weekend to participate in a match. He asked Bobby and Perry to travel to Chicago for a charity match against himself and Robert Gardner; another match followed a few weeks later in Kansas City. Before Bobby established himself as a serious rival, Evans couldn't have been nicer to the younger man; and Bobby was flattered by the champion's interest in him. When two players dropped out of a PGA tournament in New York to benefit the War Relief Fund, Evans called Bobby and Perry as last-minute replacements. This time the boys took the train alone, where they received a warm welcome as houseguests of Grantland Rice and his wife Kit. Rice introduced him to the chic, urbane world of big business and high society he would eventually inhabit. Both Rice and Jones later acknowledged that this week in New York formed the foundation of their close, lifelong friendship.

This was the first time anyone charged admission for an American golf tournament, the only obvious way to raise money for charity, but no one had believed people would pay to watch the sport under any circumstances. The War Relief matches proved them wrong. The rakish Walter Hagen agreed to captain the Home-bred Pro team, and put together a formidable squad. Bobby's amateur team was captained by four-time champion Jerry Travers, who came out of retirement to take part. Grantland Rice was also added to the team, more for press connections than golfing prowess.

The War Relief matches added a masterclass to Bobby's education: thirty-six holes a day at Baltusrol, Siwanoy, and Garden City against the best golfers in the world. The PGA had settled on an oddly weighted scoring system that substantially rewarded large margins of victory, a huge disadvantage for the amateurs, who were fielding the weakest team. Much of that blame fell on Granny Rice, a nice weekend golfer but miles out of his depth in this company; he got slaughtered in every match and failed to win a single point. Walter Hagen and the Home-bred Pros won bragging rights for the week by a wide margin; the Scots team finished second and the English Pros third, with the Amateurs in distant last place. The best performance on the Amateur team that week came from Little Bobby Jones, who won all three of his singles matches against seasoned older pros, and finished 5–1 overall. New York's press corps concluded that Bobby's spectacular debut at Merion the year before had not been a fluke after all. His fluid, natural swing was now hailed as the most elegant move at the ball anyone had ever seen.

There was simply no precedent for this in an American athlete's development. World events had conspired to provide an apprenticeship greater than any golfer in history could come close to matching. A fifteen-year-old launching drives of over

250 yards, showing unearthly composure under pressure, pulling off high-risk shots no one else dared to attempt, beating pros and amateurs twice his age in national tournaments. No one had ever seen a kid like this in the world of sports. Prodigies had appeared in chess, music, mathematics, but never before in this arena. His precocity could only be explained as a freak of nature, which was how the press began to slant portrayals of him. Stories and profiles appeared outside the sporting press in mainstream news magazines. Only a handful of articles mentioned, in passing, Bobby's increasingly out-of-control fits of temper directed at his failings on the course. He remained the perfect young gentlemen in every other circumstance, but these outbursts were becoming more volatile, and according to one observer were not confined to the golf course.

This was the secret cost of Bobby's sky-rocketing reputation: perfection became the only way he could hold up his end of the bargain. He expected nothing less of himself, which set him on a collision course with reality. The pressure was growing. The legend of Bobby Jones had begun to take on a life of its own.

In May of 1917, Pop Keeler was recovering from the previous winter's cerebral hemorrhage. But then he was struck by mon-articular arthritis, a devastating infection that took root in his left knee, the site of an old football injury, then rampaged through his system unchecked. Pop spent ten weeks in the hospital and, as he put it, "sixty hours on the rim of the Big Dark."

They saved his life again, and after months of tortuous treatment, breaking his knee on the operating table seven times in an attempt to restore mobility. For six weeks he was forced to lie in bed attached to an experimental device called "Buck's Extension," an elaborate weight-and-pulley system operated by electric motor that continually raised and dropped the lower part of his leg. He accepted all this punishment with stoic good cheer, and in the end they succeeded in straightening the leg so he could walk, though it remained as stiff as a plank for the rest of his life.

While Bobby was earning academic honors during his senior year of high school, American boys only two and three years older began dying overseas. Francis Ouimet didn't wait for the draft to call him. He became the country's first noted athlete to enlist after America entered the war, and by the fall of 1917 had been assigned to train at Camp Devens, north of Boston. Before he could ship overseas, a suggestion came down from command that Ouimet might do the army more good on a golf course than the battlefield. Ouimet spent the rest of the war playing fundraisers for the armed forces, often in uniform, and rose to the rank of first lieutenant. As civic-minded as his rival, Chick Evans volunteered for the Army Air Corps, which began life in 1917 with a total of fifty-five rickety training planes and a single combat squadron. Walter Hagen later claimed that he tried to enlist in the Air Corps but was turned down.

Ouimet appearances in uniform raising money for the war effort had scrubbed his slightly tarnished image, and a meeting of the USGA Executive Committee in January of 1918 finally gave him the news he'd been hoping for. With a divided heart he had decided to give up his sporting-goods business when he joined the army, but the USGA voted unanimously to restore his amateur status without his requesting it. Ouimet received the news with gratitude; always the good soldier, he never brought the matter up to anyone in the press and soon afterwards volunteered to work as an officer of the USGA. At that same meeting, the USGA also took one look at what was happening in Europe and canceled its championships for a second consecutive year.

After graduating with honors from Tech High School at sixteen, Bobby spent a second summer on the charity golf circuit, resuming his exhibition schedule with Perry, Elaine Rosenthal and Alexa. Early that summer he set another scoring record at East Lake with 70, but played his worst round of the season a few weeks later, at a charity match near Boston. He had come close to blowing up a few times during the match, then completely lost his cool; after a poor shot he scissored his club right over the heads of the crowd, then picked up his ball and chucked it deep into the woods. When the crowd recoiled and Alexa reprimanded him, Bobby shot back: "I don't give a damn what anybody thinks about me." He later apologized to Alexa, but seemed increasingly unable to control his emotions. A *Boston Globe* reporter agreed: "These pranks by Jones will have to be corrected if this player expects to rank with the best in the country. Although Jones is only a boy, his display of temper when things went wrong did not appeal to the gallery."

In September Bobby began his freshman year at Georgia's Institute of Technology, better known as Georgia Tech. Bobby's choice of school and mechanical engineering as his major surprised his family. An orderly approach to understanding the physical world was something Bobby wanted under his belt, and would lead to a more profound understanding of the physics of the golf swing than any player had ever possessed. During his first winter at Tech, consumed with a heavy class load, and raising a proper amount of hell as a popular young fraternity pledge, he played less golf than any other time in his life.

As the Great War ended, America turned away from the Old World, eager to immerse itself in forgetting and recreation. The booming war economy meant people had more means to indulge their appetites and more options than ever to feed them. Vaudeville had hit its peak in over four thousand theaters nationwide. Jazz broke out of its cult status into the mainstream, transforming the performing and recording industries with the first mass assimilation of an African-American idiom. Automobiles revolutionized urban lifestyles, encouraging mobility, giving rise to the suburbs and the beginning of a commuter culture. Movies experienced the greatest surge in popularity in history, and had developed the talent pool to produce a flood of full-length silent dramas and comedies. Married stars and business partners Douglas Fairbanks and Mary Pickford were sold as Hollywood's first royal couple; the mass-marketing of movie-star glamour was about to become a self-sustaining industry. (Both were avid golfers and commissioned Donald Ross to build a nine-hole course on their private estate in Beverly Hills.) Women's fashions loosened up, and hemlines began to rise. Up until now a relatively minor diversion, professional athletics were on the verge of becoming a national obsession. The stage was set for an explosion in the popularity of organized sports.

The war had done wonders for democratizing the sport of golf. The USGA's restraint in canceling its championships during combat had bought tremendous goodwill and elevated its reputation with the general public. Millions raised by the Red Cross and War Relief matches legitimized the game in the eyes of the common man as a sport for the masses. The box-office success of those events made it clear spectators no longer dismissed golf as an indulgent form of leisure but saw it as a thrilling competitive event. An explosion in golf-course construction took place across the country, as the newly wealthy hungered for more and better places to play. Club makers and ball manufacturers went back to their drawing boards to produce equipment that made the game progressively more accessible to the average duffer.

American championships resumed in 1919, and when the U.S. Open started at Brae Burn near Boston in June, the biggest cheers were reserved for local hero Francis Ouimet's official return to the game. Ouimet shot four under through his first ten holes and electrified the event, but, weakened by an attack of pneumonia that winter, faded quickly after his fast start. Bobby Jones declined to travel from Atlanta: the seventeen-year-old freshman had a full schedule of regional tournaments planned and wasn't ready to test the rougher waters of an Open. Walter Hagen stepped into the breach and the legend of "the Haig"—the fearless, devil-may-care, cocktail-swilling roué who created headlines and captivated the public's imagination—officially came to life at Brae Burn.

He dramatically won his second U.S. Open after spending the previous night whooping it up with Al Jolson and a bunch of showgirls. The press stories that poured out after this performance did more to create the aura of bulletproof showmanship which now surrounded Walter Hagen than a dozen championship trophies.

Not long after Walter returned to Oakland Hills, flushed with success, a pushy new member hurrying to make his tee time pulled up and whistled for Hagen to fetch his clubs from the trunk. Hagen shot one look at this moron, walked in to see the club's president and quit. He refused every offer that poured in from other top clubs. He had decided to become the first professional golfer in history to earn his keep without a job at a country club, a freelancer living off the fat of the land, which at this point looked plumper to him than a cattle car full of Angus beef. Almost to a man his fellow pros thought Walter was headed for disaster. Nobody could make a living just . . . playing golf. But the plain fact was that, until Walter took the leap, no one had ever tried.

Bobby put down his books at the end of his freshman year in spring of 1919 and picked up his sticks. He had grown to five foot eight, an inch shy of his full height, and lost fifteen pounds of baby fat; not a kid anymore, but a handsome, winning young gent. His cultivated fashion sense landed him in magazines; in classic Southern gentleman's style he wore cardigans, ties, knickerbockers, and two-toned shoes, accessorized with flair and impeccable taste. Only seventeen, Bobby was already the Big Man on Campus at Tech. He struck some people as cocky, but expectations had been rising around Bobby for years and so far he'd backed them up. Fans expected him to win every tournament he entered, and Bobby did too. He dominated his college matches as captain of the "Golden Tornadoes," Georgia Tech's varsity golf team but something went wrong when the summer circuit began. He chipped away at his East Lake scoring record, lowering it to 69 and then 68, but that wasn't tournament play. This time Bobby stumbled and took a backward step.

He lost the Southern Open at East Lake by a single stroke, furious at losing on his own turf. A few weeks later, playing as defending champ of the Southern Amateur in New Orleans, Bobby's tee shot at the first hole bounced into an old shoe on a workman's wheelbarrow. Uncertain of the rule governing this odd situation—as was the man refereeing his match—which allowed him a free drop, Bobby walloped the shoe with a niblick and knocked it out of the wheelbarrow onto the green, where the ball rolled free. But he missed the saving putt, took a bogey and, when told afterwards that he'd failed to use the rules to his advantage, blew up in a rage. Bobby lost in the semi-finals, disappointing an Atlanta contingent that had traveled south to see him play. This would have included his parents. Big Bob's law practice had flourished during the war. While Bobby roomed at his Georgia Tech frat house, the Joneses moved into a rambling clapboard house on Peach Tree Road, elevating their lifestyle into the upper middle class. For the first time the Colonel and Clara would have the means to travel to Bobby's tournaments and lead his cheering section. Pop Keeler also planned to spend his first full season tracking Jones, eager to cover every round he played. In addition to his gig with the *Georgian*, Pop would be writing pieces for *American Golfer*. Editor Walter Travis had realized there was value in having a correspondent dog Bobby's every step.

A trip to Ontario in July for the Canadian Open yielded another second-place finish, a distant sixteen strokes behind Douglas Edgar, pro from Atlanta's Druid Hills Country Club. For the first time the luck that had attended Bobby's every move seemed to have deserted him. He didn't understand; no wonder he was angry. During this summer, Bobby began to lean on Pop Keeler to help him sort it out.

They made an odd couple: the stiff-legged, lurching, extroverted Keeler, half a head taller and twenty years older than the modest, self-possessed young Jones. Bobby radiated a glow of robust good health; Keeler described himself at this point as "pretty comprehensively dilapidated." Bobby would soon be devoted to the one woman he loved during his lifetime, while Keeler was a compulsive ladies' man. Both had a love of learning, but Bobby remained a quiet intellectual; Pop never spent a day in college but broadcast his self-acquired mastery of the classics with a bullhorn, spouting verse or rhetoric suitable to different occasions like a jukebox. What bonded them was a shared passion for the game of golf. As inept a player as he was, made worse by his escalating infirmities, Pop understood better than all who'd ever written about it the inner turmoil of the sport, and the incredible strain winning at the highest levels demanded. They also shared a taste for hard liquor, and Pop helped initiate Bobby's early drinking habits.

Most importantly, they shared an unstated belief in the future greatness of Bobby Jones. A compelling conviction that he was supposed to conquer this game possessed the young man. He didn't talk about it much—and only with Pop—but this feeling seemed to derive from that mysterious influence he had begun to sense behind the curtain of human events. Pop called it destiny.

Although Bobby respected organized religions—and had been raised in and would preside over a traditionally religious home— his parents had never pushed it hard and he was too intellectually curious to swallow unexamined dogma whole. As a

Scots-American who'd been raised as a Scottish Presbyterian, Pop had absorbed that church's strict doctrine of predestination. It seemed logical to him that golf, the quintessentially Scottish game, sprang from the same philosophical fountainhead; destiny had been woven into the fabric of golf since conception. Bobby wasn't convinced; his studies in the physical sciences argued toward random chance as nature's governing idea.

The ongoing dialogue of their life together had found its principal theme and from this point forward the two became inseparable: bonny Prince Hal and his bawdy Falstaff. Both were convinced Bobby was headed for high achievement and, like a loyal squire, Pop pledged he would be there every step of the way to chronicle, aid and abet the quest.

Bobby's summer schedule had been designed for him to peak at the U.S. Amateur in late August at Oakmont Country Club, outside Pittsburgh. The course, designed by Henry Clay Fownes, was another of America's early jewels: long, muscular, and eccentric, layered with the deepest and most hazardous bunkers—over 350 of them in every shape and size—on any course in the country.

Every visiting player complained about Oakmont's lack of fairness after their first round, exactly the reaction Fownes wanted; he believed poor shots should be punished as if they were criminal acts. Fownes also was one of the first to double-cut his severely sloping greens—which he seldom watered—producing the fastest putting surfaces golfers had ever seen. Henry Fownes was a good player, but his son William became a great one, winning the 1910 U.S. Amateur, and assumed Oakmont's reins when his father retired. The younger Fownes made his father's course even more penal over time: if he saw members hitting consistently to some new spot on a fairway to avoid trouble, bam, in went another bunker. The 1919 Amateur would be the first of more than twenty national championships played at Oakmont, and attracted a great field from all over the country. They were about to experience the most terrifying golf course America had ever produced, one that separated the men from the boys.

Bobby Jones made a detour before his trip to Oakmont. That spring Kiltie Maiden had left East Lake—there is an unverifiable whiff of scandal about the circumstances, a run-in with a member in which alcohol seems to have played a part—to take a job at a country club in St. Louis. After watching Bobby struggle with his swing all summer, the Colonel felt a visit to St. Louis for a consultation with Kiltie was vital. The two worked steadily to straighten him out, but for the only time in their relationship not even Kiltie could fix the problem. Bobby's drives flew so persistently off line that Kiltie joined the entourage to Oakmont; the first recorded instance of a "swing coach" staying on call during a national championship.

As the tournament began the biggest story at Oakmont was the return to the Amateur of Francis Ouimet. The happy warrior had driven down from Boston with some friends in a convertible and caught a cold along the way, which quickly worsened. Not wanting to trouble anyone, or bow out when so many had come out to see him play, Ouimet sought no help and played the first two days with a raging fever. Chick Evans, technically the defending champ, made the trip from Chicago at the last minute. The USGA had tweaked the tournament's format: after a qualifying medal round they would trim the field of 136 starters down to sixty-four and ties. After a second medal round—this time over thirty-six holes—they would cut it further to thirty-two men, who would all advance to the matchplay action.

On its first day hosting a national competition, Oakmont attacked this distinguished field of players like a cornered wolverine. Francis shot an erratic 77, and considered it one of the finest rounds he ever played. Chick Evans carded an 80. Bobby came in at 82, and felt lucky at that considering what happened early that afternoon. After a clear, beautiful morning, a storm front rumbled in without warning and climaxed with a spectacular twenty-minute hailstorm that dropped golfball-sized chunks and sent the gallery running for shelter. Then, during the second round on Monday, the weather really turned nasty: three separate rainstorms brought howling winds that knocked down mighty oaks and blew the benches on the tee boxes around like matchsticks.

There were calls from stranded golfers for flat-bottomed boats to cross casual water, blimps to journey over occasional lakes, and submarines to locate balls that went into the drink. After shooting 79 in the morning, shaking with fever, Ouimet was so weak he topped three of his last six tee shots. Facing a ten-inch putt to finish his second round with an 87, a huge hailstone dropped in front of his ball just before it reached the cup and stopped it dead. He staggered off the course into the locker room, where a kind Oakmont member gave up his in-house lodgings so Ouimet could go to bed. The doctors called in to examine him couldn't decide if he had tonsillitis or pleurisy, but both agreed he was a very sick man. Certain he'd missed the cut, he was amazed to discover he was tied for sixteenth. Chick Evans came in tied for sixth. Bobby scratched out an 81–78 in those wretched conditions and finished one stroke behind the leaders; one of them was an Oakmont member, twenty-two-year-old S. Davidson Herron.

The weather improved and Tuesday's opening matches produced no upsets, but Ouimet—still weak and playing against his doctors' advice—had to win three of the last five holes to advance. Second-round brackets produced two irresistible match-ups. Bobby Jones faced Robert Gardner, the two-time amateur champ who had ousted him at Merion three years before. Even more anticipated, for the first time Chick Evans and Francis Ouimet would finally go head-to-head in a championship; if Evans was considered the front-runner, Ouimet was the overwhelming sentimental favorite. For the first half of their match Jones and Gardner replayed the script from Merion, with Gardner more nervous and Bobby carrying a three-hole lead into intermission, despite the fact that he couldn't find a fairway. Kiltie Maiden's final advice to him on Oakmont's range that morning was to stop trying to steer the ball and hit it as hard as he could. "So what if you end up on the next fairway?" said Kiltie. "On this damn course you're probably better off."

If Gardner entertained a thought that the kid would collapse again, Bobby quickly put it to rest: he finished Gardner off 5 & 4. Bobby, Pop, and Kiltie rushed over to watch Ouimet and Evans go at each other; their gallery grew to five thousand people. Still fragile and feverish, Ouimet steeled himself for the most important match of his comeback. Aware of Evans's resentment of him over the years, he felt Chick's behavior fell short of the game's standards of etiquette. Ouimet said nothing about him publicly, content to let his golf do the talking.

Evans set the tone by dropping a 45-foot eagle putt on the opening hole. Ouimet won the second and third to surge ahead. They traded superb shots all morning, passing the lead back and forth, never separated by more than a single hole, ending the morning round all square. Evans was so keyed up, and Ouimet so ill, neither man ate lunch; Ouimet could only down a glass of orange juice. The afternoon saw a thrillingly close battle; the match would be decided at the final hole.

Par-four, 456 yards. Elevated tee, uphill second shot. A solemn gallery lined the course all the way to the green. Adrenaline surged: both drives landed in the fairway, Ouimet slightly ahead. Evans pulled a fairway wood slightly into light rough, short and left of the pin. Ouimet pushed his long iron into a deep, dangerous bunker on the right. Advantage Evans. When they reached the green Ouimet realized his ball had somehow found a decent lie in the furrowed Oakmont sand, 60 feet from the pin. He climbed down into the pit, literally out of sight. He took an explosive swing through the sand and lofted his ball gently onto the green, where it rolled to a stop within the shadow of the flagstick. The crowd roared, then went stone quiet. Evans chopped his ball out of the tall grass and watched it skid fifteen feet past the cup on the glassy green. Advantage Ouimet. Evans stroked his uphill putt for par and came up a foot short. Ouimet had his left for the win; differences of opinion about the length of the putt reveal the way character affects memory. Ouimet remembered it as a 4-footer; most reporters placed it in the 6- to 8-foot range; Evans thought it was 10. In any event, "With no thought on anything but the hole, I stroked the ball accurately and it floated as nicely as you please into the cup for the win I wanted so badly." Which remains the strongest language Ouimet ever used in print to describe a competitive emotion. Walter Travis called it the most remarkable match in the history of American golf.

The crowd cheered Ouimet all the way back to the clubhouse—Bobby said he was "pop-eyed and gasping with excitement" after watching this "battle of giants"—but the grueling grudge match had left the winner terribly drained. After falling behind early the next day in his third-round match against Philadelphian Woody Platt, Ouimet once again rallied to even the match on the final hole. The cheers after he sank his tying putt at eighteen could be heard all over Oakmont. As they teed off for their first hole of sudden death the rains came again and they played in a steady torrent. Ouimet reached the green in two, while Platt was fifty yards short with his second, but he played an exquisite pitch that nearly rolled in to stay alive. Platt's gritty up and down sapped Ouimet of his last reserves; he lost the match with a bogey on his thirty-eighth hole of the day.

Ouimet's tournament was judged a huge success. His gutsy comeback thrilled the crowds, and he'd beaten his nemesis Chick Evans. The weather drew harsher reviews, one critic suggesting that Pittsburgh be referred to in any future golf guides as "a small, blunt town lying between two thunderstorms." Considering that the flu Ouimet battled all week had nearly developed into pneumonia and worn him down—although he never used it as an excuse—the press decided there was every reason to believe Ouimet would be a factor in championships for years to come. But golf's darling had other plans: he had married long-time sweetheart Stella Sullivan the previous fall, and after the failure of his sporting-goods store he was starting a new career as a banker in Boston.

Bobby won a sloppy, rain-soaked third-round match and advanced to the semi-finals against Oakmont's president Bill Fownes. Despite the former Amateur champ's supreme local knowledge he was no match for Bobby's all-around game. He had finally found his swing after losing his temper, played the second half of their match in a simmering fury, and dispatched the host club's president 5 & 3.

Bobby had reached the finals of only his second national championship, the youngest man to ever make it this deep in an Amateur. He was now matched against another Oakmont member, Davey Herron. Herron had grown up on the course and knew every warp and weave of Oakmont's treacherous greens. Pop described him as "a large, plump, curly-haired Pittsburgh golfer with an exquisite putting touch, and built like the proverbial brick barn."

Bobby spent the evening with his roommate Pop, trying to relax, but he was as keyed up as a racehorse kicking at his stall before Derby day. Pop tried talking about it, which did nothing to calm him, then tried not talking about it, which only made it worse. Finally he prescribed a single shot of whiskey—and three for himself—then turned out the lights. Both men stared at the ceiling until two in the morning.

"Hey, Pop."

"Yeah, Bobby?"

"This is what we're here for, right?

"That's right, Bobby."

The next day a boisterous hometown crowd of over six thousand showed up to cheer on Davey Herron. They weren't all country-club types; Herron spent summers earning money for college in a local steel mill and was currently working in a foundry, bending rails into horseshoe curves. Herron's cheering section had a raucous blue-collar make-up, and they failed to grant Bobby some of the game's basic courtesies, cheering when he found a bunker or the rough. The only people wishing Bobby well in that crowd were the Colonel, Kiltie, and, journalistic objectivity be damned, Pop Keeler. Even the marshals seemed partial. The *New York Times* reported one roaring through his megaphone at the crowd to "Get back, get back there; Davey's in the rough and we want to give him every chance!" Big Bob couldn't resist answering back: "And while you're at it, give Jones a chance, too!"

Bobby was the better player tee-to-green—Herron's swing was not a thing of beauty—which kept them even into the afternoon, but Herron's skill with a putter began to make the difference. Despite the fact Bobby shot even par on the front nine, after dropping three long-range bombs Herron opened up a three-hole lead by the time they reached the 600-yard par-five twelfth. Both hit decent drives, but Herron pulled his second into a bunker, the first opening to climb back into the match that Bobby had all afternoon. He took out a two-wood, intending to crank his second close to the green.

As he reached the peak of his backswing, a marshal standing nearby saw someone moving in the gallery and shouted, "Fore!" at the top of his lungs through his megaphone. Bobby flinched, fatally, and topped the ball, which hopped 20 yards into a bunker. Trembling with anger, Bobby failed to get out of the bunker in two tries, then picked up, conceding the hole to Herron. The damage was done; from a turning point that should have left him two holes in back of Herron, he was down four with only six to play. Pop said Bobby looked so mad that "he could've bitten his ball in half."

Bobby dropped another shot on the next hole and lost the 1919 Amateur Championship to Davey Herron, 5 & 4, who was picked up and carried away on the shoulders of his hometown crowd.

The press worked up a sweat trying to build the megaphone incident into a brouhaha. Even Walter Hagen chimed in; he was covering the Amateur for a newspaper syndicate to pick up a few bucks. The Colonel fed a couple of bitter quotes to reporters about the marshal's breach of etiquette and the ill-behaved partisan crowd, but when others tried to draw Bobby in that direction he declined. Davey Herron had beaten him fair and square, shooting four under par through the fourteen holes of their second round. "The better man won and he gave me a good drubbing," said Bobby. This was the only major title in Davey Herron's career, and his win established a strange pattern which dominates Bobby's career: his opponents in big matches often turned in the single best performance of their lives.

Bobby was shocked to realize he'd lost eighteen pounds during the week of the Amateur at Oakmont. This wasn't physical exertion: he could play two rounds a day for weeks and never lose an ounce. Nothing like this had ever happened before. Now Bobby began to realize that golf and championship golf were two different games, and the latter carried a much more exacting price. There have been many supremely gifted players who simply couldn't stand up to the competitive strain—what Bobby called "that stretching and stretching and stretching inside your head"—and turned away from the full expression of their talent. Grown men had cracked under that kind of pressure; during Bobby's early days the stark example of two-time U.S. Open champion John McDermott's nervous breakdown remained a vivid reminder. Today it's possible to make a living fit for a king from this sport without ever winning at the highest levels; early pros were playing for pocket change compared to modern purses. What would motivate a player today to push himself halfway to derangement when he's already set for life?

Yet Bobby never played the game for money; not one penny, during his entire career, at considerable financial hardship. At Oakmont he'd barely stuck his toe in the water, reaching his first final in his second major tournament, and the internal fire it ignited was already burning the flesh off him like wax from a candle. He was under no obligation to take this any further; he manifestly possessed the mind, character, and charm to follow any professional path he favored as far as he wished to go. This is where his drive to succeed takes on a mythic dimension; nothing was at stake other than his need to express the gift he felt was in him. Ouimet played the game for love and the joy of competition. Bobby played because he had to, and the price he would pay in physical and mental pain matched the epic scale of his achievements. As 1919 came to an end, that ordeal had already begun.

After returning from Oakmont, Pop Keeler lost an argument about his salary with the editor of the *Georgian* and ended up out on the street. He took a job as a publicist for a Hollywood studio, and hit the road organizing press tours for stars promoting their new motion pictures. The gig lasted only four months, but during Pop's absence Bobby made the acquaintance of another, younger, journalist who would bear witness to a crucial phase in his development.

Al Laney was a Pensacola native who'd just been discharged from the army and found himself at a loose end. Riding a train south from Washington he spotted a story in a discarded newspaper about the first Southern Open, then under way at East Lake, and on a whim decided to catch the last day of action. He'd worked for various newspapers before the war, mostly at the copy-boy level, and like so many others of his generation he'd been drawn to the sport of golf after Ouimet's victory in 1913. Laney switched trains and made it to East Lake in time to see Long Jim Barnes win the inaugural Southern Open, but he was more impressed by a post-game encounter with its seventeen-year-old runner-up. Bobby and the slightly older Laney, still in uniform, struck up a discussion about the war and golf and Georgia Tech that impressed Laney beyond words. He had sensed something special about Bobby, saw it on him as plain as a scarlet letter, but didn't know what it meant. He rode the train home to Pensacola that night and felt something like fate tugging on him. He had vague plans of heading for New York to look for work as a reporter, but this story in a newspaper someone had left on the floor of that southbound train changed everything. He acted on the impulse and secured a job with the Associated Press in Atlanta.

Over the course of the following fall and winter Laney got to know Bobby as well as anyone in Atlanta. He wrote a piece about Bobby's life at Georgia Tech, enjoyed frequent contact with him, saw him in many different social situations. Temperamentally drawn to writers like O.B. Keeler and Grantland Rice, Bobby was attracted to Laney for many of the same reasons: his outsider's perspective and a shared respect for the English language. But Laney was fifteen years younger than Rice or Keeler and more of a contemporary, so Bobby let down his behavioral guard more in his presence. Laney, in turn, was a psychologically astute observer, whose insights into Jones provide the clearest window into his state of mind during this period in his life. To most everyone who knew him, Bobby seemed happy and well adjusted, a carefree, immensely popular college kid enjoying the time of his life. According to Laney, who out of respect for their friendship did not write about this until many years afterwards, this was an illusion.

"I was fascinated with his personality," wrote Laney in his book. "So gentle, so intelligent and so pleasantly charming in an amazingly mature way on a surface that concealed a strong, almost uncontrolled temper. In young Bobby, passionate emotions were a chaotic mixture, with first one and then another in control. They were submerged most of the time, but at certain moments they threatened to dominate his personality, his view of himself and the outside world."

The prevailing belief, later shaped by Keeler, was that Bobby's anger was simply the product of a protracted adolescence. Laney maintains that the truth was much more alarming. Even though he'd only broken one club in anger at Oakmont—journalists kept track of these things—his loss in the finals wounded him much more deeply than his outward forbearance indicated. A few weeks later his pride took another blow when Alexa Stirling won her second consecutive U.S. Women's Championship. It was Laney's conclusion that his single-mindedness, this laser-like focus on perfection, was also his Achilles heel. In the spring of 1920, while traveling with Bobby and friends to a tournament in Tennessee, their car got stuck on a rain-slick, red-clay hill somewhere in north Georgia. Laney doesn't go into specifics, but he describes the incident this way:

> I twice had the frightening experience of seeing him come
> to the very edge of malice in fierce outbursts that neither he
> nor I understood. I was afraid for him, for I had seen him
> flushed and shaking in a rage of sudden anger, then drained
> white a moment later in sudden fear at the nearness of evil.
> In a sense I shared his deep inner struggle to overcome
> what, with his intellect, he knew to be ignoble. He knew
> well that he was poisoning himself with anger, that he must
> find the inner strength to rise above it.

It is telling that these confrontations occurred in the company of Laney and some college kids, and one infers from his account that they weren't isolated incidents. When he hurled a club in anger, those outbursts were easy to dismiss as part of the game; he was hardly the first person to lose his temper playing the world's hardest sport. What Laney describes is much more alarming: a young man fighting for his humanity, struggling with an impulse toward violence against other people that threatened to overwhelm all that was so obviously good about him. This was a face Bobby never showed Pop or Rice, his parents, or the other adults in his life. Everyone had expected so much of "Bobby Jones" for so long that he felt he wasn't allowed to fail at any level; he had no outlet for his doubts or fears. During a moment of sober reflection Bobby described this battle to Laney as "the critical match I thought I was losing."

Championship golf in Britain would have resumed in 1919, as it did in America, but a railroad strike crippled travel throughout the country and caused the last-minute cancellation of both the Amateur and the Open. The country's courses required months of rehabilitation to render them fit for play. British ranks had suffered heavy losses in the war: Jack Graham, a renowned amateur from Hoylake, died in battle, as did the British PGA's secretary, F.H. Brown. J.L.C Jenkins, the last British Amateur champion before the war, was severely wounded and never played to the same level.

Harry Vardon turned fifty in May of 1920. He knew that he had reached the end of his run, that a new generation stood in the wings ready to replace him, but, as all great athletes do at sunset, he longed for one last chance at glory. The first Open in six years would be played at Cinque Ports, in Deal, Kent, a seaside links that had hosted the championship once before in 1909. The best of both the old and new generations of British golfers joined the field. There was also one wild card in the deck, from across the pond.

Walter Hagen, reigning U.S. Open champ, had cleaned up during Florida's winter circuit and was flush with the cash to travel and take on the British Open. Hagen knew that turning himself into a household name was the key to making it as an unattached professional. Championships were the big game he hunted now—not for the paychecks, which remained pedestrian; most pros made more from side bets than they did from purses. Public recognition, enhancing name value; that's how Hagen planned to drive up his price for exhibitions and make a killing. And he knew that to maximize his reputation he needed to bag the Claret Jug, the game's oldest trophy. He persuaded Dickie Martin of the *New York Globe* to sail with him and ensure that American newspapers received a balanced account of his assault on the British citadel. Another first: a golfer with his own press agent.

During the month Hagen spent traveling around leading up to the Open he became a lightning rod for British disdain of American golf. The refrain was clear: if this loud-mouthed dandy was the best the U.S. had to offer then Britain had nothing to fear. When they got around to playing the Open at Deal, things really turned ugly. As poorly as professionals were treated in America, the British class system guaranteed theirs got it much worse. Upon arrival at Deal Hagen strolled into the clubhouse and asked to be shown his locker. The mortified club secretary whisked him out of the building to a row of rusty nails in the back of the pro shop, above a forlorn pile of shoes, their toes sticking up like skis. The man warned Hagen not to set foot anywhere near the members' private area again and told him that he'd be taking his meals in a shabby little caterer's tent out back.

Hagen plotted his attack carefully. Every morning he parked his rented limousine—complete with chauffeur and footman— right in front of the clubhouse, and made a show of changing his shoes on the running board in plain view of the dumb-founded members. He trained his footman to serve as his forecaddie, and instructed his chauffeur to meet him after his rounds on the eighteenth green holding a chilled martini and a tailored Savile Row polo coat. Most British pros still wore the frayed tweeds, knickerbockers and old boots common to the working class; Hagen had hauled over two steamer trunks filled with twelve color-coordinated outfits, complete with matching bow ties, monogrammed silk shirts and complimentary pairs of two-tone spiked saddle shoes.

Walter's wardrobe got better reviews than his golf. As every American in Britain had to learn, when the wind blew hard off the sea on a treeless links their high-flying iron shots lost their spin and couldn't find the greens. Hagen played the worst golf of his life, never broke 80 and finished fifty-third in a field of fifty-four. (George Duncan, a rising English player, won the Open Championship.) As his staff were loading his gear into the limo for the last time, the oily little secretary who'd snubbed him on arrival turned up to gloat at Hagen's departure.

"Sorry you didn't do better, 'Eye-gen, but golf over here is very difficult. I do hope you'll come back in some future year and try again."

"Don't worry about me, pal," said Walter. "I'll be back and you'll see my name on that cup."

During his freshman year Bobby had met a slim brunette beauty named Mary Rice Malone, the younger sister of two friends from Georgia Tech. The Malones were Atlanta natives, from the upper-class Druid Hills neighborhood, Irish Catholic country-club people like the Joneses. Mary's father John was a tax assessor for the city of Atlanta; her mother Mamie came from an old-established Georgia family. Catholics were relatively rare creatures in the high rungs of Southern society, and the Malones were wary of Bobby. He came from new money, ran a little wild and his fame made them suspicious of his intentions.

Their courtship proceeded quietly, traditionally. Bobby visited the Malones at home under the guise of seeing the brothers, taking meals with the family, exchanging shy smiles with Mary at the dinner table. Gradually he began to spend more time with Mary; he took her fishing, escorted her to dances at East Lake or Druid Hills in his sleek roadster. Neither felt any rush to marry because from early on it was clear they were absolutely right for each other. They would wait until Bobby was out of school and launched in his career, whatever it might be. Bobby also wanted to wait because there was the small matter of his future in the sport of golf to sort out.

Bobby turned eighteen, finished his sophomore year at Tech in May, 1920, and set out to assert himself in the national game. He broke his scoring record at East Lake again that spring with 66. Convinced no one could touch him when he was going right, he decided he would play fewer regional tournaments in order to focus on the big ones; he entered only forty tournaments for the rest of his career, and twenty-nine were majors. Pop Keeler encouraged him down that road; he had just returned to Atlanta after his Hollywood sojourn, and landed a job with the town's most respected paper, the *Journal*. But he had come home for a more important reason: Bobby was ready for the big time, and for the next ten years never went into battle without Keeler at his side.

Bobby set the U.S. Open in his sights for the first time in 1920, but needed a warm-up. In three successive weeks he played the Georgia State Amateur (semi-finalist), the Southern Amateur (champion, in a walk), and the Western Amateur. He broke the qualifying record in the Western, and in the matchplay semi-finals for the first time ran into Chick Evans. Chick was about to turn thirty, in his absolute prime, but Bobby was judged the favorite, which didn't sit well with the proud Evans. Bobby had played dozens of charity rounds with Evans during the war, preparing for this moment, studying his every move, but it turned out Evans had been holding something back.

After treating Bobby like his long-lost cousin, Evans came out of his corner trying to knock the kid's brains out. He watched Bobby and his caddie on every shot, guessing from their body language what sort of shot he was facing. When Bobby tried to do the same he realized with a shock that Evans used deliberate misdirection, giving the impression he enjoyed a good lie when his ball was deep in the woods. Bobby picked up the trick and returned the favor later in the match, decoying Evans into playing a risky shot over a tree. More a street fight than a golf match, the two played dead even through their first eighteen, but in the second round Evans's experience showed: he exploited every mistake Bobby made, played flawless golf, and was up three with seven holes to play. Furious at himself for letting Evans sucker him, Bobby canned three birdies in a row to square the match. He looked poised to take the lead when Evans's approach at the next hole found a grass bunker and Bobby landed on the green, but Evans got up and down, sinking a 12-footer. Bobby's putt ran off line, leaving him a 6-footer to halve the hole. His next hit the cup, spun all the way around, and spit back out toward him. "It looked me in the eyes and said you're licked," wrote Bobby. "I was licked, sure enough. Chick out-finished me, and I thought I had him."

Evans won the match, one up. Bobby claimed he learned whatever he knew about the game from losing, not winning, and this was one of his hardest lessons ever.

Bobby went back to Atlanta, and Evans went on to win the Western Amateur for the fifth time, his crown as the game's top amateur secure for another day.

When Bobby and Pop returned home, Big Bob met them at the station, took Pop aside and grilled him about the match with Evans. Pop told him about Evans's gamesmanship, Bobby's comeback, and how Chick had beaten him at the last. The Colonel's face turned red; he almost snorted in anger. "Well he'll sure as hell never beat him again," he said, and stormed off.

The Colonel wasn't just blowing smoke. Bobby never lost to Chick Evans again. Even more startling: during sixteen years on the national stage, Bobby never lost another match to the same man twice.

CHAPTER FOUR

FATE AND NOTHING ELSE

Harry Vardon had been invited to tour South Africa and Australia soon after the war, but the trip he and Ted Ray had made to America in 1913 remained the most successful of their careers. They had discussed a return trip after the last one ended, but the war had made overseas travel impossible. They weren't getting any younger—although still holding his own with the young bucks, Ray had just turned forty-three—so why not give it a go? They might even take another shot at winning a U.S. Open.

"Crazier things have happened," said Harry.

"And we've both seen 'em," said Ted. "Count me in."

Vardon and Ray arrived in New York on the liner *Olympia*

during the first week of July, 1920. The American press welcomed the old-timers with affection, warming their hands over shared memories of a more innocent age. Their American tour of 1913 had earned the two men legions of friends—as had Vardon's first solo visit in 1900—and they rekindled many of those relationships as they criss-crossed the country. Their tour manager, an aspiring golf-course architect named Arthur Peterson, had scheduled wall-to-wall exhibitions throughout the East and Midwest for six straight weeks, with the men sleeping on overnight trains as they hurtled on to the next stop.

Both men were impressed with the improved courses they saw in America, and felt that the level of play had risen dramatically: Ouimet's victory had transformed the state of the American game. "Unless Great Britain is able to produce some fresh blood to take our places," Vardon told a reporter, "our supremacy in the Royal and Ancient game is about to be seriously challenged."

As it had in 1913, their tour was designed to climax at the U.S. Open in the second week of August, being held in Toledo, Ohio, at Inverness Country Club. One of the last stops they made beforehand was in St. Paul, Minnesota, where Harry's brother Tom had long since settled in as resident professional at the White Bear Lake Yacht and Country Club. Harry and Ted played their last exhibition at Inverness the day before qualifying began, and beat two local pros 2 & 1.

The Western Open had been played in nearby Chicago only a week before, so the 286-man field at Inverness included every top dog in the game. Defending champ Walter Hagen slipped into town the day before qualifying. Playing as many exhibitions as he now did, Hagen didn't need practice to stay sharp, and liked the challenge of walking onto a course cold. His defiance of the English at Cinque Ports had generated great press in America. When players gathered at Inverness they were greeted with the welcome news that the members had voted to open their clubhouse for use by the visiting professionals. This breakthrough—and the august presence of Vardon and Ray—created the most festive mood of any Open in memory. The USGA, mindful of putting on a good show, created a marquee pairing for the qualifying rounds: Harry Vardon and Bobby Jones, playing in their last and first Opens respectively.

After Vardon and Bobby had posed for photographers, Pop took Bobby aside and urged him to control his temper while playing with the legend. Bobby had a harder time controlling his excitement; he chatted and bubbled away at Vardon throughout their first round. Vardon saved his compliments for reporters until after the round, when he pronounced Bobby's methods as sound and predicted a bright future for him. He also wrote, months later, that despite Pop's admonition to him, Bobby "apparently needed a little more time to get his temper under control."

During their second round on Wednesday, Bobby made an effort to adopt Harry's more serious demeanor, and they played the first six holes in silence. At the seventh, after watching Harry nestle a classic bump-and-run shot next to the pin, Bobby skulled a wedge over the green into deep rough, costing him a stroke. As they walked to the next tee, Bobby tried to break the ice with some bashful self-deprecation.

"Mr. Vardon, did you ever see a worse shot than that?"

"No," said Vardon, ending the conversation.

When their round was over—both qualified without difficulty—Vardon spent an hour in the locker room with Bobby, discussing and answering questions about his iron play. Bobby's engineer's mind had been astonished by the faultless mechanics of Vardon's swing and was eager to absorb as much as he could from the master. Although he lacked formal education, Vardon had applied more thought and theory to the golf swing than any man alive and he could discuss or write about his conclusions in dizzying detail. Bobby was equally impressed by his dignity, and vowed to renew his efforts to behave himself on the course. Vardon's message to the youngster was as simple as his professional code: learn the trade, not the tricks of the trade. Bobby told Pop that after this encounter with Vardon his Open was a success no matter what happened. Pop reminded him that the tournament hadn't actually started yet; beginning tomorrow, sixty-four men would play for the American championship in earnest.

Bobby felt it the moment he walked out to the first tee. This was the same course he'd played the day before, the pleasant weather almost identical, but the air felt electric, knotted with tension, harder to breathe. Bobby's first taste of Open pressure rocked him. His knees shook as he took his stance in front of the massive gallery. He couldn't find his swing, and there was no one to help him. By the time he steadied late in the round he had shot 78, nine strokes behind the leader. Bobby skipped lunch between rounds and loaded up on pie *à la mode*, a boyish habit Pop had been trying to break that often led to second-round let-downs. In this instance the comfort food helped settle his nerves; he shot a 74 in the afternoon and came off the course seven strokes in back of the leader at the halfway mark. Veteran professional Jock "Hutch" Hutchison, a thirty-six-year-old expatriate Scotsman from St. Andrews, was in front. An eccentric, high-strung twenty-one-year-old American pro from Detroit named Leo Diegel, also making his Open debut, stood second, one stroke back. Tied for third a shot behind Diegel was a trio for the ages: Walter Hagen, Harry Vardon, and Ted Ray.

Seeing all those worthy names in front of him freed Bobby from his pressure to succeed. Sure he was already out of the running, the next day he went out and played what he called "typical kid golf," unconcerned with winning or what anyone else was doing, and shot a third-round 70. When he saw the scoreboard Bobby realized he had turned in the morning's best round: he was only four shots in back of Vardon, who had leapfrogged the other challengers to grab the lead. Hutchison and Diegel were in joint second, a stroke back, with Ted Ray a shot behind them. Of the players clustered at the top only Hagen had fallen out of contention. Chick Evans had crept up from the pack to trail Bobby as low amateur by a stroke. Bobby decided all he needed was another 70 and the Open was his, then helped himself to some more apple pie and ice cream. Harry Vardon marched out to play his final round in a U.S. Open that afternoon convinced he had the title in his grasp. A rowdy crowd of over ten thousand flocked around him, hoping to see history in the making.

Vardon played a flawless front nine, and increased his lead to four by the time he had reached the twelfth hole. Bad weather hadn't been a factor all week, but at the precise moment Vardon teed up his ball a storm of Biblical proportions bolted down across Lake Erie out of a clear blue sky. Hitting dead into the teeth of a sudden gale, Vardon needed four full shots to reach the par-five green, and two-putted for bogey. Then the rain came, sideways, lashing, a torrent running off the rim of Vardon's hat. Just walking into the wind became an effort. Stretched to the limit of endurance, Vardon weakened, and when that happened his vulnerable right hand—nerves ravaged years earlier by tuberculosis—lost its grip on his putter. He missed a 2-foot putt for par at the thirteenth when his right hand jumped, banging the ball off the back of the hole; it jumped up and stayed out. Another shot lost. The storm raged around him like King Lear on the heath; it almost appeared, one writer observed, to be directing its wrath at him alone.

Vardon three-putted each of the next three holes. Not knowing how the storm had affected those playing behind him, he knew he needed to par the last two holes to keep his fading hopes alive. The seventeenth faced straight into the storm; 430 yards, the green protected by a brook that now threatened to break its banks. His drive traveled less than halfway, but he had to gamble now and go for that green; he hammered a brassie right on the screws but it ballooned up into the wind. The ball just cleared the brook, then caromed off the far bank and rolled back into the water. Harry's shoulders slumped as he walked forward; he dropped a ball behind the stream, got up and down for six, and collected a par at the last, but the damage had been done. One stroke under par through eleven, then seven strokes lost in eight holes. As he stumbled to the clubhouse, the mysterious storm that had destroyed Vardon's chances now vanished as quickly as it had come.

Bobby was already off the course by the time the storm hit. The pressure had gone to work on the young man from the start of his final round: he finished with a slack 78, tied for eighth. The 70 he'd thought he needed that afternoon wasn't necessary; even par 72 would've won Bobby his first U.S. Open championship. He finished only four strokes in back of the winner, but with this added indignity: Chick Evans posted a 75 and slipped in to best Bobby as low amateur. Evans had then gone back out on the course and thrust himself into the action, taking Leo Diegel's bag away from his caddie and slinging it himself in an attempt to steady the jumpy Diegel to victory. But Evans's presence on the bag wasn't enough and, although Diegel was too polite to say so, may have been a distraction. With the crowd, Bobby among them, cheering on the only American-born player left with a chance to win, Diegel lost four strokes over the final four holes, ending in a tie with Vardon.

Playing just ahead of him, the amiable giant Ted Ray had survived the punishing squall, the only man in the field sturdy enough to stand up to it. In fact, Ray turned in the round of his life. He drove the 320-yard par-four seventh green and cashed in a birdie. During the height of the storm he collected three crucial pars on the same holes Vardon had bogeyed. He caught Vardon at the sixteenth, and then moved a stroke ahead of his old friend at seventeen. Facing a 5-footer for par on eighteen,

Ray learned at this exact moment that sinking the putt would give him the lead. He screwed on his hat, handed his putter to his caddie, refilled his pipe, lit it, took the club back, and calmly dropped the putt to finish a stroke ahead of Vardon and Diegel. A pro from Philadelphia named Jack Burke reached eighteen with a chance to tie Ray, but missed his putt. That left only Jock Hutchison on the course with a chance to catch him, but he missed a birdie chip at seventeen and was down to his last chance at eighteen. Hutch was paired with Hagen, already well out of the running. Playing first, taking a casual swipe at his ball, Walter drained a 60-footer for birdie, then threw back his head and laughed as the gallery of ten thousand roared. "I wish that had been yours, Jock," said Hagen.

Facing a putt half as long as Hagen's, his face twisted with strain, Hutchison came up short and missed his chance. Great Britain had carried the day; as often before, when Vardon faltered, Ray stepped up in his place. An immensely popular champion with press and public alike, Ray's gallant charge to victory took the sting out of Vardon's collapse. The trip had been delayed for seven years by Francis Ouimet, but the U.S. Open's silver cup was going back to Britain for the first time since Vardon had won it in 1900. But Vardon's pre-tournament prediction that American golf was on the verge of dominance over Great Britain in the royal and ancient game was prescient: a British golfer would not win another U.S. Open for the next fifty years. Harry also predicted that it wouldn't be long before an American player achieved the unthinkable, and won Great Britain's Open.

The members of Inverness invited professionals into their clubhouse at the Open and changed the social order in America; Ted Ray's win provoked a watershed event in the British game as well: members of the club that employed him as its professional—Oxhey, in Hertfordshire—voted to celebrate his victory by awarding him an honorary membership. Their gesture rocked the foundation of the English sporting establishment; hysterical class-system hard-liners interpreted it as a sign the apocalypse was near. Vardon's employer, South Herts, soon followed suit, as did the home clubs of J.H. Taylor and James Braid. After five decades, their struggle for acceptance had finally broken down the door to the private English clubhouse.

Later in the year, in response to Inverness's generosity, Walter Hagen and a group of pros presented the club with a towering grandfather clock, inscribed with these words:

God measures men by what they are, not what in wealth possess
    This vibrant message chimes afar, the voice of Inverness.

The author remains unknown, but one suspects Walter had a hand in it. The clock remains in the club's entryway to this day.

When Pop Keeler sat down to write about everything he and Bobby had witnessed on that last remarkable day at Inverness—how that tempest had howled down out of the sky to write a heartbreaking end to the final chapter of Harry Vardon's competitive career—the committed fatalist phrased it this way: "Fate and nothing else beat Harry Vardon that day."

Bobby didn't feel the same sting of disappointment he had after losing at Oakmont. The compelling finish at Inverness had mesmerized him: five players with a chance to win on the final green! "I concluded right there that the Open championship was the thing; it is my idea of a tournament."

He also had no regrets about his finish. "Of all the luck I've had, and I've had a lot, the best luck is that I didn't win at Merion as a kid of 14 at my first Amateur, or at Inverness, in my first Open. I might have got the idea that it was an easy thing to do."

Pop tried to gently steer Bobby away from his unreasonable expectations for perfection. Bobby had watched Leo Diegel closely as he fumbled away his chance to win at Inverness down the stretch, "wondering why his face was so gray and sort of fallen in." The lesson, as Pop summarized it, was that when you find yourself blowing up in a championship—and you will— just remember that "the other fellows are blowing up, too, so keep your own lid on as tight as you can." But Bobby was stubborn and prideful, and still felt he had the game figured out. Keeler saw how much Bobby didn't know and didn't have the heart to tell him. He'd have to learn it the hard way.

The 1920 National Amateur was held in September at Engineer's Club, on Long Island. Having reached the finals the year before—and tasted success in his first Open—everyone from his legion of fans to his own father thought it was time for Bobby to collect a title. The Colonel traveled with Bobby and Pop, convinced that the breakthrough they'd been waiting for was at hand. They were reunited with Grantland Rice, who had just taken over the reins of *American Golfer*.

Bobby won the qualifying medal at Engineer's, then played his way into the semi-finals without breaking a sweat. He appeared confident, boyish and grinning, then found out his next opponent was Francis Ouimet. The two had never met in competition, but a friendship had formed during the previous year. Bobby looked up to Ouimet more than any man alive with the exception of his father, and he served as a role model for Bobby not just on the course but in life. According to Al Laney, Bobby's struggles with his temper were at their most dangerous at this time, but Ouimet's approval meant the world to him, and Bobby was always on his best behavior in the older man's presence.

A resolutely private and modest man, Francis respected those qualities in others above all else. It wasn't until spending time together during this tournament at Engineer's that the two began to realize how much they had in common: a love of classic literature and thought, a deep respect for the history and conventions of the game, and an ingrained aversion to what Ouimet called "people making a fuss over me." Although ten years older, Ouimet granted Bobby the deference of a contemporary, recognizing the brains and sensitivity that made him more than a youthful marvel.

It wasn't so much what Ouimet said to Bobby that made such an impact, but who was saying it. Which is not to say that Ouimet took it easy on him once they stepped onto the course; that was a crucial part of his character as well.

Bobby later called this match with Ouimet the end of his boyhood, an assessment that proved optimistic. As mature as he seemed for his age, Bobby was only eighteen, and the easy path he'd had in the draw left him unprepared, while Ouimet knew exactly what to expect and had readied himself "for the stiffest sort of a contest." To his discerning eye, Bobby had two weaknesses: an uncertain grip on his emotions under pressure, and a shaky putter under any circumstances. Both would come into play.

Ouimet came out strong and won the first two holes. Bobby appeared flustered and unsteady on the greens, canceling out solid drives and approaches with a cluster of three-putts throughout the morning, which, as he later wrote, "didn't help my youthful conceit of myself." Ouimet capitalized on every one of those mistakes to either win or halve a hole, and increased his lead to three during the back nine. At seventeen, Bobby's temper flashed for the first time after a poor bunker shot. On the eighteenth green, after Ouimet made bogey, Bobby missed a 2-foot gimme for the win, picked up his ball and kicked it into the weeds; Ouimet's lead was three at the halfway mark. Bobby loaded up on pie and ice cream again at lunch and won the first hole that afternoon. Both men played steadily and halved the next five holes. The match turned on the seventh green.

They were both putting for birdie from the front of the green, Bobby slightly away. As he took his stance a flying insect, a bee or yellowjacket, landed on his ball. He shooed it away and prepared to putt again. The bee circled and set down on his ball a second time. When he waved it away this time, the bee flew back and settled on the grass right on his line to the hole. A marshal, trying to be helpful, stepped forward and set his megaphone down over the bee. By now the gallery was beginning to giggle, and when the bee emerged from the open mouthpiece of the megaphone they roared with laughter. When the bee zeroed in on Bobby's ball yet again, the laughter doubled. Laughing himself now, Bobby pulled off his cap and, wildly waving both it and his putter, theatrically chased the bee off the green and out of sight. Bobby got a round of applause for his antics, but his concentration was fatally blown. Getting back to his ball, he left his putt 6 feet short and missed the next one. Ouimet won the hole. As they walked off together, Francis turned to him and said, not unkindly: "Let's just play golf, Bobby."

Bobby burned with shame at the stark realization of what he'd done to himself. "That bee flew away with a good bit of my juvenile fancy for the game of golf," he said later. He couldn't shake the anger out of his system and lost the next two holes as well. Ouimet's lead was five holes with nine to play, not because of that bee, Bobby knew, but because of how he'd reacted to it: like a child, playful and scatterbrained. Their match ended on the thirteenth green, 5 & 4. When the gallery greeted Bobby with gracious applause as he walked off it brought tears to his eyes; for the first time in his life he felt as if he'd let them down.

Ouimet absorbed a similar beating the next day from Chick Evans before the finals began. Suffering from a sudden bout of amnesia, Evans declared, "Although we have never played together under circumstances that afford a fair chance to judge our games, it seems the unanimous belief of all the golf writers that Francis will win." On this issue he was mistaken; the two men's talents being more or less equal, it's safe to say most of them simply would have *preferred* Ouimet to win.

The USGA let Bobby work as a marshal so he could watch their showdown. He saw Evans win the 1920 National Amateur from Francis 7 & 6, his third major win, putting him ahead of Ouimet and Hagen. After reaching the finals of the championship for the first time in six years, Ouimet said afterwards: "His play was magnificent and his putting left nothing to be desired. I had no regrets because I was simply outclassed by a great player." Evans's comments were typically mealy-mouthed.

Bobby won a small invitational tournament and played a couple of exhibitions in New York, even beating Vardon and Ray in one of them before returning home to Georgia. But those lesser victories felt hollow to him; the Open and the Amateur were the only titles that mattered now. Soon afterwards, Alexa Stirling had won her third straight Women's Championship. Having failed to win any of the four majors he'd entered, and realizing his mental and emotional approach needed an overhaul to succeed at that level, Bobby felt lower about his game than he could ever remember. But when he got together again with Al Laney in Atlanta, his friend noticed a crucial difference in Bobby's temperament.

I could see at once that he had changed. I tried to question him about this and about the Ouimet match. For a while Bobby would say little more than "Francis helped me. You know what I mean." I began to have a certain faint understanding. I began to see that the young Bobby had for Francis what amounted, if not to actual reverence, then to the greatest possible admiration for him as a human being. I was a long time in getting it out of him, and I had to wait much longer to understand that this relationship with an older person of Ouimet's character was the most important thing in the young life of Bobby Jones. Understanding began with his remark, "Francis helped me" and with the feeling of vast relief with which it was said.

Bobby's outbursts would continue, although in the opinion of Laney the time spent with Ouimet was the turning point. But there were still dark days ahead, and Bobby was about to endure the worst of them.

In 1920, the USGA and the Royal & Ancient Golf Club tried to reconcile their differing rulebooks during a summit at St. Andrews. One of the few issues agreed on during the meeting involved the ball. With no established standards, manufacturers had been winding the ball smaller and denser to increase distance. Big hitters like Ted Ray could now pound it so far they threatened to render older, shorter courses defenseless, an argument eerily reminiscent of today's debate about the game's evolving technology. For the first time since golf began, limits for the ball's weight and measurement were established with pleasing symmetry: 1.62 inches in diameter and 1.62 ounces in weight. The only other idea approved during the summit: an annual international competition.

In the spring of 1921, Oakmont's Bill Fownes assembled a team of American amateurs and set off for Britain to play their counterparts. USGA president George Walker, maternal grandfather of future President George Bush, announced he would donate a trophy for the event, which appeared the following year and has since borne his name: the Walker Cup. Bobby made arrangements to finish his junior year at Georgia Tech a month early so he could sail from New York on the last day of April with a team that included Fownes, Francis Ouimet, and Chick Evans. This was the last major golf trip on which Pop Keeler did not accompany him: the cost of the trip came to nearly $10,000, well beyond the budgets of the *Journal*, *American Golfer* and Pop himself.

Arriving in Liverpool on May 9, two weeks before the event, Bobby got his first look at Britain, and the English press got their first glimpse of the man Harry Vardon had praised as the rising star of American golf. They liked the look of him and called him "Bonnie Bobby"; his natural reticence played a lot closer to the British house style than Walter Hagen's brassy horn-tooting.

Hoylake provided the perfect setting for the first American–British competition. Built in 1864, it was the second oldest English links, but first to host some of the game's most historic traditions. The British Amateur had begun here in 1885, defining the line between amateur and professional. In John Ball and Harold Hilton, both of whom grew up there, Hoylake gave the game its first great amateur champions. In 1911, the Royal Liverpool Club bought Hoylake for its members, since when Hoylake has also been known as Royal Liverpool. With its tight fairways, tiny greens and the wind blowing stiff off the Irish Sea, Hoylake provides as harrowing a test as any course in the world.

The Americans needed those two weeks to acclimatize to the links style of play. Liverpool had suffered through an eight-month drought and the fairways were as hard as a parking lot. Bobby made the adjustment to bump-and-run shots quickly. Team events were a new phenomenon in golf, but the American squad embraced this locker-room camaraderie and spent their evenings formulating strategy on how best to attack Hoylake. Two days prior to the start of the championship, the eight-man teams faced off for their friendly competition. They played alternate-shot foursomes in the morning—a format unfamiliar in America—followed by singles in the afternoon. To everyone's shock the Americans swept the foursomes, took five of the eight singles matches and won the event decisively, 9 points to 3. The sound of stiff upper lips falling slack with amazement could be heard all over Britain. Predictions that the invaders would march through the Amateur with equal ease filled the newspapers.

The British Amateur's format departed from the American in two significant ways: with an invitation-only field no qualifying rounds were required, and every match in its eight matchplay rounds—with the exception of a thirty-six-hole final—was played over eighteen holes. Although this ensured a strong field it often led to early departures by better golfers when lesser talents got hot, a flaw longer matches tended to equalize.

Bobby's gallant, go-for-broke style struck a deep chord with knowledgeable fans. Ladbrokes established him as an early favorite at 5–1, with Ouimet and Evans close behind him. All eight Americans won their first-round matches, but in the second Ouimet lost decisively, and Bill Fownes ousted Chick Evans. A battle of two giants, Boston's Jesse "Siege Gun" Guilford and Oxford's Cyril Tolley, turned on a bizarre twist when Guilford's prodigious drive at the twelfth scampered 300 yards down the fairway and dove into a rabbit hole. Forced to accept a penalty for an unplayable lie, Guilford lost the hole, his composure, and the match.

Bobby went up against an unknown florist from Wrexham named E.A. Hamlet. Employing a quaint, old-fashioned swing, Hamlet displayed the quivering indecisiveness of his namesake and shot a dismal 87. Bobby should have slaughtered him, but after losing his temper at an early mistake he couldn't find a green, couldn't buy a putt, and found himself down two with three to play. Bobby rallied to even the match going into eighteen. Hamlet left his par putt hanging on the lip of the cup. Bobby's putt for par, off line, hit Hamlet's and dropped in. Hamlet's ball stayed out. Match over.

Bobby coasted to an easy third-round win and reached the final sixteen against another obscure Englishman named Allan Graham. Ouimet watched the match and had to close his eyes on the greens: Bobby couldn't sink a putt over 2 feet. It ended at thirteen, 6 and 5, one of the worst trouncings Bobby ever absorbed. His anger at his performance carried over into post-match comments, when he said he wouldn't enter the British Amateur again unless they changed the matches to thirty-six holes. This outburst earned Bobby his first negative reviews from the English papers. He was about to give them a much stronger reason to reconsider their enthusiasm for him.

The last American in the field, Freddie Wright, lost in the fifth round to celebrated British golf journalist Bernard Darwin. A failed career in law had propelled Darwin sideways into journalism, where he fell by chance into writing a golf column in 1907. Darwin had single-handedly elevated golf writing in England into a respected profession, but few realized what a fine player he was in his own right. His career reached its apex with this win, sending him into the semi-finals of the Amateur for the second time. The kindliest man imaginable off the course, Darwin often fell victim to fierce, self-critical temper on it, one of the reasons he responded so instantly and fully to Bobby Jones. With the entire field rooting for him, Darwin lost his last chance to win an Amateur. It was a rousing all-English finals in any case, won by twenty-eight-year-old Willie Hunter.

Despite his disappointment at Hoylake, Bobby's British adventure was far from over. He and four other team members decided to stay on and play in the Open at St. Andrews ten days later. A group of American professionals, led by Walter Hagen, had also journeyed to Scotland ahead of the Open to participate in an international team competition against British pros. They met at Gleneagles, an inland American-style parkland course that suited their style of play more than the traditional links. Six years and a few gatherings later this low-key affair would evolve into the Ryder Cup, the most consistently dramatic team competition in the game. At Gleneagles, the British pros defended home turf stoutly, winning 9–3, avenging the British Amateur defeat.

This brought together the largest contingent of Americans ever to enter a British Open: fourteen professionals and five amateurs. In 1920, Bill Tilden had become the first American to win the tennis crown at Wimbledon, and golf remained the last unsullied bastion of British sporting might. No foreigner had won the Open since Frenchman Arnaud Massey in 1907, and no other had done it before or since. There was much more English concern about an immigrant Scotsman from the States capturing their title than about some home-grown American.

For Bobby and most of the Yanks this was their first visit to the sacred ground of St. Andrews. They found the old college town charming, but Bobby couldn't make head or tail of the golf course. The flat terrain, lack of guiding visual features, blind pot bunkers and double greens confused him; the layout seemed haphazard to his eye and he decided a good score owed far too much to chance. He kept these reservations to himself, not wanting to offend his hosts, but more practice rounds did nothing to change his opinion. Hagen took a more positive approach; in the year since his dismal showing at Deal he'd played all the best seaside American courses, trying to master the links style. He'd squeezed in as many practice rounds and exhibitions in England as he could with Vardon, Ray, and other British greats, developing what he called a "quail-high stinger", a ball hit hard and low below the wind. But Hagen quickly learned that St. Andrews rewarded precise placement of every shot over raw distance, and that could only be mastered by diligent study of the course and frequent play.

Fourteen Americans survived the Open qualifier, with Bobby low amateur. Expatriate pro Jock Hutchison captured the qualifying medal on the strength of a unique advantage: he had grown up in St. Andrews. One of the game's most meticulous professionals—winner of last year's PGA Championship, his most important victory to date—Hutch had traveled to St. Andrews four months earlier and played every day, sometimes twice, to prepare for this Open.

Bobby paired up with Jock on the first day of the Open, and saw an astonishing performance. Jock aced the par-three eighth, teed up his ball on the 306-yard par-four ninth and clobbered a drive that ran all the way to the hole, lipped out and stopped three inches away. The men on the green when his drive arrived told Hutch that only bad luck kept his ball from dropping for a double-eagle one. Those miraculous back-to-back shots have never been equaled in championship golf, and Jock rode them to a two-shot halfway lead. Bobby described Hutch as "set like a piece of flint to win." Playing better than he'd expected after his practice rounds, Bobby came in six strokes behind him, tied for ninth. Hagen was a stroke in back of Bobby, completing a solid American showing. Tied with Hagen was a tall, elegant young English amateur named Roger Wethered.

Bobby woke the next morning with every expectation of having something to say about the Open. Instead, in ways and for reasons he couldn't decipher, the bottom fell out of his game. He topped his first drive and couldn't keep his others on line. The precision of his irons vanished, a death sentence at St. Andrews. His putting woes worsened, and for the first time in his life neither Kiltie or Pop was around to set him right. By the time he'd reached the turn—the term originated at St. Andrews; an outward nine holes, then a literal turn back toward the clubhouse for the inward nine—he'd carded a 46 and shot himself far out of contention. The crowd that had gathered to follow the glamorous young challenger slowly drifted away. He took another double bogey at the tenth. Bobby's temper, which had been running hot all day, finally boiled over, and led him into disaster.

The eleventh at St. Andrews is a long par-three called High, for it stands on the course's tallest ground, although virtually at sea level it barely qualifies as a hillock. The hole features a large figure-eight green set on its side as it faces the tee. The left front is protected by a difficult bunker called the Hill Bunker. That's where Bobby planted his tee shot. After digging in to play a recovery, Bobby failed on his first attempt, and then on his second. At which point he said to himself: What's the use? What followed next was a matter of controversy only recently resolved; he took either one or two more swings at the ball, which remained in the sand. Some contemporary newspaper accounts claimed he then picked up the ball and tore up his scorecard. Others reported he had done one or the other, but not both. In his column for *The Times*, although he'd been elsewhere when it happened, Bernard Darwin wrote that Bobby teed up his ball and whacked it into the River Eden. Blind with rage, Bobby admitted he picked up his ball, but insisted he only tore up his card in a figurative sense, and denied ever hitting his ball anywhere but onto the twelfth fairway from the next tee. Jones expert and scholar Sidney Matthews recently found an eyewitness whose account appears to settle the dispute: the man claimed to have seen Bobby pick his ball out of the bunker after a third failed attempt, then tear up his card and scatter its pieces in the Eden.

Bobby then played out the round, completing every hole, and never turned in a card, an automatic disqualification. But no account of the incident, including Bobby's, disputes the fact that he had committed the one unpardonable sin in the game of honor: he quit in the middle of a round. During his first visit to St. Andrews. In the heat of battle. On the last day of an Open.

Bobby was nowhere near the player or public figure he would become, and with most attention that day focused on prodigal son Jock Hutchison's pursuit of the Claret Jug his actions didn't generate a fraction of the scandal they would have a few years later, or anything approaching the media firestorm that would have resulted today. A few British reporters took Bobby to the woodshed for it, but most treated the incident as a minor failing, allowing readers to draw their own conclusions about his character. If any other players on the course or in the locker room afterwards spoke to him about it none of those comments have survived. None were needed to reinforce the shame Bobby felt as soon as he walked off the eleventh green. Although players retire from medal competition for a variety of reasons during every tournament, this was the only time in his life Bobby quit in the middle of a round and it scarred him deeply. "I have some sterling regrets in golf," he wrote later. "This is the principal regret—that ever I quit in competition. I've often wished I could offer a general apology for picking up my ball. It means nothing to the world of golf. But it means something to me."

How he reacted in the immediate aftermath said even more about him. Having committed the crime, he could have compounded it by leaving town; it would have spared him the whisperings and scrutiny when word spread of his misdeed. Instead he got right with himself and marched out that afternoon to play his final round. Bobby shot a 72 in the fourth round, one under par, but the simple act of showing up did more to address the damage he'd done to himself than a hundred excuses.

Roger Wethered's third-round 72 vaulted him into the lead and the hearts of his countrymen, one stroke ahead of Hutchison, who recorded a third-round 77. Wethered then went out early in the afternoon with the entire gallery behind him and broke his own record with a 71. Bobby played directly behind Wethered, and watched him put together that remarkable score as he took his humbling medicine. On the sixteenth fairway he also saw him come to grief. Wethered landed his tee shot at the base of a small mound and to get a clear line to the flag he climbed the mound, then backed down toward his ball to keep the line in sight. He stepped backwards onto his ball and was compelled to call a one-stroke penalty on himself for violating Rule 18: thou shalt not move a ball at rest. Without complaint Wethered finished the hole and his round, and the score that should have been his winning 70 turned into a 71. He refused to voice any complaint afterwards about the rules or his misfortune, saying only, with a smile, "My feet are just too big."

Bobby hooked up with Ouimet and Hagen after his round and went back out to root Jock on, taking turns as they nipped from Hagen's silver monogrammed flask. Hagen finished a respectable sixth, a huge improvement over his embarrassing debut at Deal. Bobby was amazed to hear him dismiss it as just another disappointment; first place was all that counted, anything less made you an also-ran. Hagen's steel-eyed focus on winning made a big impression on Bobby, but so did his casual attitude. Despite the fact that as the world's only unattached pro he was living from one tournament paycheck to the next, Hagen appeared to be the most supremely at ease man in the world.

"What's the point of losing your temper, kid? It's only a game," he said. "Isn't that right, Francis?"

"That's right, Walter."

Bobby stared at the two men in disbelief. No one in his deadly earnest pursuit of perfection had ever even posed the question to him in that way before. Crowds love a winner, they were saying, but they'll damn well worship somebody who can show them grace under pressure.

Jock Hutchison helped reinforce both lessons that afternoon. Starting his final round as Wethered had finished his, he found out he needed a mistake-free 70 to force a play-off for the Open Championship. In front of three generations of his own family— his father was caddying in the tournament, his own son was in the gallery—and a rowdy hometown crowd, while carrying the standard of the United States as the first American with a legitimate chance to win an Open, knowing he needed a nearly impossible three-under-par 70, Jock Hutchison went out and shot his number. His final round remains one of the great performances ever turned in during any major championship. Hutchison carried that same determination into the next day's thirty-six-hole play-off, where he easily bettered a visibly weary Wethered by nine strokes. Although it was a stretch to say he'd won the title for America—he was a St. Andrews man, born and bred in the grand traditions of the game, and the town took great joy in his victory—Hutchison had broken the British stranglehold on the game's oldest trophy. The press consoled itself by focusing on Jock's divided heritage; it wasn't as if a *real* American had captured the Jug.

The members of the Royal & Ancient Golf Club, the Open's administrator and the British game's governing body, took more drastic action, voting to outlaw the square-grooved irons Hutchison had used at St. Andrews, which allowed him to put backspin on the ball and grip the hardened, windswept greens. (The USGA refused to follow suit.) But even this questionable defense could not stave off the inevitable: Hutch's win turned out to be lightning on the horizon signaling the approach of a deluge; only one British player would win their Open during the following thirteen years.

Bobby had tasted the air now at all four of golf's biggest tests. He had experienced the best and worst of international competition, but the poise and maturity he'd seen in Ouimet, Hutchison, and Hagen renewed his determination to wrestle against the darker angels of his nature. After his dishonor at the Open, Bobby had not succumbed to self-pity or despair; he had faced the music. The ordeal left him sadder, wiser, more knowing of himself. Pop Keeler recognized the change as soon as he laid eyes on him: Bobby had turned a corner. For the first time he admitted to Pop that his sense of infallibility might be based on a false assumption; the shot that required perfection to succeed was not always the one to play. Maybe he wasn't as smart as he thought he was. The road to the top of this game ran longer and a lot rougher than early success had led him to believe.

Bobby arrived home in early July with little over a week to prepare for the 1921 U.S. Open. Pop Keeler took the train up to meet him at Columbia Country Club just outside Washington, D.C., hosting the event for the only time. America's President took in the championship for the first time in its history. Warren Harding, in office since November, 1920, had taken up golf four years ago while still a senator, and gone golf-mad. He played three rounds a week, usually at Chevy Chase Country Club, and resented any responsibilities of office that got in the way of his game. He enjoyed imbibing adult refreshments during and after; less than a year into Prohibition, this presented something of a public-relations challenge for the chief upholder of the Constitution. Harding was also the first president to welcome star athletes in for photo opportunities at the White House. He used these occasions as an excuse to meet his favorite golfers—chiefly Walter Hagen and Chick Evans—whom he often tapped to play as his partners in Washington area pro-ams.

The players put on a rousing show for their president at Columbia. It was announced that the field of 274—another record number—would be trimmed for the first and only time in Open history by a single qualifying round.

Approaching the first tee in his second U.S. Open, Bobby told Pop he felt as nervous as he could remember. Expectations had reared up in the press again; each time he played a major now he carried more weight. Bobby hooked his opening drive into the woods, which Pop described as "the type written in the story books as impenetrable." But Bobby found his ball, and a narrow opening toward the green. He also had a safer, more conservative option sideways to the fairway, but chose the riskier path. His slashing recovery attempt smacked dead into a tree and bounced deeper into the forest. Pop heard a man next to him mutter: "There goes Bobby." Pop felt a sinking sensation in back of his belt buckle and his hair turning gray. Disaster. Bobby smashed his third shot as hard as he could toward a thin section of foliage; the ball blasted through the branches and barely trickled onto the fairway. He got down in three from there for double bogey six. Other flirtations with doom followed—including a 30-foot putt for par that dropped at seventeen—but he squeaked by them and barely qualified with a 77, one under the cut line.

Bobby was partnered with Gene Sarazen, a brash young former caddie from Apawamis Country Club, New York, who was making his Open debut. A stocky five foot five, Sarazen made up for his lack of stature with confidence, powerful hands and a king-size personality. Both players knew the other had a reputation for losing his cool on the course and they made a friendly wager that the first man who threw a club owed the other $10. In the first round Bobby played wildly and posted a 78, but the bet helped both men maintain their cool; neither tossed a club all round. In the afternoon their fortunes reversed: Bobby channeled his anger into a superlative front-nine 32, and finished with 71, picking up four strokes on leader Jim Barnes.

Bobby appeared poised for a serious run at the lead, but in the third round his putter turned skittish; he needed only thirty-seven strokes getting onto the greens, with a birdie putt on all but two of them. He took forty putts getting the ball into the hole. Bobby was right back where he'd ended the first round: nine strokes behind Jim Barnes.

Bobby decided to "shoot the works" in his final round and birdied three of the first four holes. After a towering 280-yard drive at the fifth, a long par-five, he pulled his two-wood to go for the green, and yanked the shot out of bounds. Instead of cooling off he dropped another ball and hooked that one out of bounds. He scored a nine on the hole, and his Open was over. Pop watched him closely and never saw Bobby betray a flicker of emotion when those shots sailed left and killed his chances. He didn't quit; no ball was picked up in anger, no scorecard got shredded. Bobby appeared so unconcerned by his demise he might have been mistaken for Hagen. He finished his round without further incident, in fifth place, three slots better than his Open debut the year before. Sometimes progress, decided Pop, can mean more than victory.

Jim Barnes won the '21 Open nine strokes ahead of Hagen—who treated second place with his customary disdain—and 1908 Open champion Freddie McLeod. Chick Evans snuck in ahead of Bobby by a stroke as the low amateur in sole fourth place, the only thing Bobby was mad about afterwards.

In his second Open, Bobby had been bested by only four men, all former Open champions. More importantly, he had embraced Pop's advice about the two things a man had to overcome to win a championship, neither of which had anything to do with his opponents. They were Old Man Par, and his own damn human limitations.

Pop Keeler ended up in a car with Hagen, driving back to Washington for dinner after the awards ceremony. Knowing that he'd spent a lot of time with Bobby during their trip to Britain Pop asked Hagen for a candid assessment of his friend's progress.

"Bobby's playing some great golf, in spots," said Walter. "He's got everything he needs to win any championship, except experience; and maybe, philosophy. He's still a bit impetuous."

"I'll drink to that," said Pop, and they did.

"But I'll tip you to something, Pop: Bobby's got more game than anybody out there. He's going to win an Open before he wins an Amateur."

The last chance for Bobby to redeem himself in 1921 came in late September at the National Amateur, held at St. Louis Country Club in Missouri. Kiltie Maiden was still the current professional; their reunion with Kiltie was a warm one that made Bobby long for simpler times. Wherever he traveled now Bobby carried the trappings of a star, the worshipful press clippings, a growing entourage, an adoring fan base, the dashing good looks and signature style of a fashionable trendsetter. The only thing missing was a trophy to justify all of the above. The title of "best player to have never won a major," worn until recently by Phil Mickelson, hung on his neck like a millstone, and the more everyone whispered that a breakthrough must be at hand the heavier it got. The one Amateur final he'd reached ended early, he had never led an Open after three rounds and had yet to seriously challenge down the stretch in the fourth.

Thanks to Grantland Rice and the omnipresent newsreel cameras, the idol worship of athletes in the early 1920s was well under way. Bobby did so little to seek it out that all the attention he attracted remained a mystery to him. His magnetism didn't derive from the narcissism of a needy movie star (although he was every bit as handsome), or the boastful crowing of a childish athletic demi-god. People were drawn to him by a radiant quality he barely seemed aware of, one that invited the fantasy projections of strangers. He evoked a complex excitement in his fans; the way he held himself hinted at secrets only he seemed to know, a coiled power, withheld, and an emanating decency. He seemed deeply and knowingly amused, without arrogance, rich in human understanding and sympathy. It raises a question of enduring human mystery: what exactly is charisma? In Bobby's case, beyond obvious talents and physical attractiveness, it had something to do with his taut stillness. Beneath that placid exterior simmered a volcano barely held in check. People knew that Bobby could erupt, which lent him an element of danger.

Bobby was still a troubled young man. As he and Pop rode the train out to St. Louis, they sat on Bobby's berth and quietly talked it over.

"I wonder if I'm ever going to win one of these things," said Bobby.

Pop had never heard him question his chances before. He recognized that Bobby's confidence was dangling over a ledge. Pop took a chance, and got tough with him.

"If you ever get it through your head that when you step out on the first tee of any competition you are the best golfer in it, then you'll win this championship and a lot of others. Because it is my honest conviction that you are the best golfer in the world."

Bobby laughed, ruefully. "Please, don't be an idiot. I've seen these fellas play. They're good. They're awful good. And I know it."

"I've seen 'em play, too. And I've seen you play, which you have never done. And I tell you you're better."

Bobby shook his head in disbelief. His mind still ran along the empirical lines he'd learned at Georgia Tech: where was the evidence?

"Men succeed in spite of their flaws," said Pop. "The sooner you realize what they are the faster you'll overcome them. That's when you'll win, and not before."

Bobby went off to mull it over; Pop had gotten through. Without ever calling it by name, Keeler had added another shingle to his crazy-quilt résumé: sports psychologist.

This was Bobby's fourth Amateur. A strong field had gathered in St. Louis: Ouimet and Evans and the others who'd traveled to Britain on the international team. A rising young player from Los Angeles named George Von Elm made his first appearance, and one Tommy Armour sailed over from Scotland. But there was a new name in the field that caught Bobby's eye and riled his competitive fire. The man who had won that year's British Amateur at Hoylake, Willie Hunter, had also made the trip across the briny to compete, amid statements to the press that winning both countries' titles in the same season would make up for Jock Hutchison's win at the Open.

Just let me at him, thought Bobby.

Ouimet shot 69–75 to take the qualifying medal, and with typical modesty said "it was my good fortune to win." Willie Hunter had no trouble on an American course and finished a stroke behind him; Tommy Armour trailed by another. Defending champ Chick Evans appeared poised to rush past them all, until the twelfth hole of his second round. He struck his tee shot 15 feet from the cup. His birdie try drifted 4 feet past. He missed the come-backer by inches. Then, annoyed, he tried to swipe the ball in one-handed, missed again, and while the ball was still moving struck it a second time, a penalty. Lying one on the green, Evans had to put a seven on his card. Six putts from 15 feet. From there he was lucky to qualify, and the damage to his brittle confidence would linger. Bobby played cautiously in the qualifier, finishing seven strokes in back of Ouimet. They posted brackets that evening and Bobby saw that, if both men survived into the third round, it set him up for a shot at Willie Hunter.

Bobby couldn't wait: he slaughtered his first man 12 & 11. He abused his second 9 & 8. Pop's pre-tournament pep-talk had gotten through. Based on those beatings everyone, including Bobby, expected him to stomp wee Willie Hunter. Partisan feelings in the crowd ran high and Bobby absorbed the benefit. He shot an even-par morning round and stood two up at the lunch break, but found himself saying, "Only two up." That worried him; it worried him even more that it worried him. He changed his pants for luck, donning a pair of pinstriped flannels he'd worn in his previous matches. Despite Pop's rants about nutrition Bobby still indulged his sweet tooth between rounds, and this time he went back out after twin helpings of pie *à la mode* to resume the fight.

In the afternoon Hunter picked up a hole at the third, then gave it back at the seventh. Bobby was still only two holes up with eleven holes left to play. "He's sticking to me like a bulldog," Bobby told Pop as they walked the fairway.

Bobby was playing American-style, high-spinning irons to the greens, where they were landing hard and picking up mud from wet pitch marks. The rule allowing players to remove mud from their ball on the green was years away and the mud on Bobby's ball was sending every birdie putt off line, forcing him to settle for pars. Hunter was playing British bump-and-run shots to the green, not to avoid the wind—there wasn't any—but to keep his ball clean by the time it got there. He was sinking clutch putts to save par and stay close. This bulldog had lockjaw.

When they reached the eighth Bobby decided to try something drastic to shake Hunter loose. A short, sharp dogleg right carved through the woods; Bobby had driven straight over the dogleg to the green in practice rounds—about 280 yards as the crow flies—and pulled it off every time, resulting in easy birdies. The risks were obvious: fail to clear the trees and you brought double bogey into play. A rocky ditch below a steep bank protected the green on that side if the shot came up short. He knew Hunter didn't have enough *gluteus maximus* to duplicate this shot, and picking up a birdie here might just break his obstinate will. When Pop saw his friend teeing up toward the shortcut he had to bite his lip to keep from shouting a warning; Bobby had been lured into playing his opponent, not the scorecard.

Bobby launched a rocket over the tallest tree in the woods; dead on line to the green. At the top of its arc the ball caught the uppermost branch—Keeler called it "a twig no bigger than a pencil"—and fell like a bird shot from the sky into the rocky ditch. Hunter played a safe tee shot down the fairway to the corner of the dogleg then landed his approach on the green. Bobby found his ball in a patch of dense weeds and tried to blast it out; out came a shower of stones, followed by a startled rabbit, but the ball stayed put. The crowd laughed at the rabbit, and Bobby joined them. Bobby's next shot reached the green, but he missed his putt; Hunter collected an easy par and won the hole. Instead of driving a stake into Hunter, Bobby's lead had been cut in half, and the failed gamble cut out the heart of his confidence. Hunter won the next hole to square the match; nine holes left to play.

The flow leaked out of Bobby's game and with it all his

advantages; he was grinding for pars now, as Hunter continued to do. They were still all square with four to play. At fifteen, a long par-five, Hunter outdrove Bobby for the first time all day. Bobby pulled his two-wood to go for the green but pushed the shot to the right, pin high, where it only stayed in bounds by bouncing off a man in the gallery. Hunter's second shot came up well short of the green, but safely in the fairway. Bobby played a superb pitch to the green that rolled to within eighteen inches of the cup, lying three. Hunter pitched up to 10 feet, also lying three, and then sank the putt.

Bobby missed his eighteen-inch tap-in for birdie.

Hunter had his first lead of the day, one up with three to play. At the par-three sixteenth, both men landed tee shots 10 feet away on opposite sides of the cup. Bobby missed his putt, Hunter dropped his and went up dormie two. At the seventeenth, Bobby ran out of chances when he missed a 15-foot birdie. Willie Hunter had beaten him and Bobby graciously conceded. To demonstrate that good manners ran in the family, the Colonel was the second man to step up and shake Hunter's hand.

But just prior to that, dissatisfied with his approach shot, Bobby had thrown his club back toward his bag, lying on the ground near the gallery. The club glanced off the bag, bounced up and hit a female spectator in the lower leg. Bobby apologized profusely and appeared more shaken by it than she was; he then missed the short putt that ended the match. Most hardly noticed the incident—some newspapers failed to even report it— but others leaped on it to run out another round of stories about Bobby's lack of self-control.

When Pop heard reporters bitching about Bobby's lack of character in the press tent afterwards he stood up and delivered a spirited defense. "You'll all be writing headlines about him some day," he challenged them. "You'll all be saying it, mark my words; he's the greatest golfer in the world."

Pop went out to drown his sorrows with a few cocktails that night. When he got back to the hotel room he found Bobby waiting up for him, still agonizing over the loss.

"Why did I lose?' Bobby asked. "How's it possible for a guy like him to beat me? It was that putt, wasn't it? That God damn little putt on fifteen—"

"Don't chase rabbits. It was the drive, at eight over those trees. You had the lead, you should have sat on it, forced him to catch you. Instead you tried to gamble and let him right back into the match: you handed it to him, Bobby."

"Maybe so, but I don't know how to play any other way. I have to play every shot for all there is in it—"

"That's a laudable frame of mind. And it'll provide you with plenty of chances to get used to losing championships. The best shot's not always the one to play."

Bobby heard him but wasn't ready to absorb the lesson. It would have to come in its own time, the same way he was learning to control his emotions.

The pressure was mounting, eating at him, and starting to affect him physically. Although he never mentioned it in St. Louis so as not to appear to be making excuses, he suffered from an almost crippling case of varicose veins in his left leg (brought on, Pop felt sure, from internalized stress). Bobby had realized Hagen was right: nobody gave a damn who finished second. With so little money at stake beyond first place, winning was all that mattered to professionals anyway; but as a committed amateur Bobby had no financial incentive no matter where he finished. Maybe it made sense if you needed the game to put food on your table, but Bobby still had a year of college to go before he even started worrying about making a living.

"I was still just a boy playing golf," Bobby wrote. "And now in a gradual but apparently universal sort of way, I was expected to win a national championship, not just shoot a fancy round here and there, or beat some classic opponent. Not drubbing the boys back home in a state or sectional tournament. Championship. Championship. So that's it. No matter how prettily you play your shots. No matter how well you swing or how sweetly the ball behaves."

Pop insisted that another element was needed to win one of the Big Shows, in addition to talent and persistence and willpower. Fortune had to smile. Call it luck, call it fate or chance or whatever you like, but you couldn't win without it, that fateful bounce of the ball or turn in the wind that delivered you to victory. The Scots had grasped this mysterious part of their native game long ago, knew how central it was to every outcome. They called it "the rub of the green."

"Chance is bred in the bone," said Pop. "You've no control over it, in life or in golf, and in the end what's the difference between 'em anyway?"

"So what do I do?"

"You wait and prepare, and when you're meant to win it'll happen, not because of your willing or wanting to, but because when it's your turn the outcome's inevitable."

Boston's big-hitting Jesse Guilford went on to win the 1921 Amateur, defeating two-time former champ Robert Gardner 7 & 6. Pop Keeler reported that lightning snaked down out of a moody sky and struck a policeman watching the finals that morning. He was badly shaken, but otherwise uninjured. Bobby knew exactly how he felt.

The cold comfort of philosophical perspective aside, another season was over with nothing to show for it. Bobby returned home to begin his senior year at Georgia Tech. A few weeks later he received a letter from USGA President George Walker, taking the young star to task for his behavior and warning: "You will never play in a USGA event again unless you can learn to control your temper." As a result of his childish display the incident at St. Louis, coming so close on the heels of his surrender at St. Andrews, had brought Bobby to the verge of exile from the game.

Contrite and humiliated, Bobby focused on completing his degree. In need of emotional security as never before, his relationship with Mary Malone quietly deepened; they spent long hours discussing their future together. Marriage seemed almost a certainty, but Bobby was determined to finish his education and be able to support a family before they took that step. He had realized a career in mechanical engineering was not going to provide the satisfaction he'd imagined as a freshman. Bobby had traveled a long way up in the world since then, and his ambitions had wider horizons. His father's law practice had continued to thrive, and the Colonel lobbied hard for his son to join. He had always preached the exalted English ideal of a man embracing a profession; engineering or, worse, professional sports were little better than blue-collar trades. On a simpler, personal level the Colonel was also Bobby's closest friend.

It's uncertain whether Bobby had made up his mind about his future when he applied to Harvard. His stated intention was to round out his college career with a bachelor's degree from their English Department. Perhaps he was already looking for a foundation in reading law, while acquiring an institutional pedigree that would improve his prospects. The literary influence of Keeler can also be detected: if technical science hadn't given him the answers Bobby was looking for, maybe he could find them through immersion in two thousand years of literature. Bobby was only twenty, and despite his athletic achievements still struggling with fundamental questions of personal identity. Two years at Harvard might provide the perfect harbor, just far enough away from Atlanta, and buy him time to chart a surer course.

That spring Bobby wrote a sincere response to USGA President Walker, apologizing for his temperamental outbursts and resolving to eliminate them, but in private conversations with

Pop he seriously contemplated giving up competitive tournament golf. Walker's letter had forced Bobby to confront the question: was the ongoing strain to his health and mental wellbeing
worth the, at best, elusive rewards? The alarming weight losses
he experienced during majors had continued. If he didn't break
into the winner's circle soon, what possible reason could he have
for stepping back into that fire? Scholarship has gone back and
forth on the subject of how close Bobby came to abandoning
his quest. Bobby later denied it, and Pop appears to be the only
person he discussed it with directly; years later he had too much
stake in maintaining Bobby's legend to confirm it. The approach
of the 1922 golf season forced the issue. That spring Bobby
underwent four medical procedures to repair the varicose veins
in his leg. During his stay in hospital, Perry Adair came to see
him with a request.

Perry's father George, Bobby's first patron in the game, had
died suddenly in November of 1921, at the age of forty-eight. His
friends in golf had decided to dedicate a new trophy for the
Southern Amateur in his name; that year's tournament, where the
Adair Trophy would debut, was scheduled to take place at East
Lake. Knowing he had sworn off regional tournaments, Perry had
come to ask whether Bobby would agree to play in this one as a
tribute to his father. The Southern was scheduled less than two
weeks after his release from the hospital and his doctors warned
against putting any strain on his leg. But Bobby couldn't say no
to Perry; he got in four hours of practice—his only golf in three
months—and snuck out to play nine holes the day before the
tournament began. With his leg heavily bandaged, Bobby finished
in a tie with Perry for the qualifying medal, then breezed through
five matchplay rounds to win the championship easily.

Bobby's name became the first to grace the George Adair
Trophy, and in a satisfying coda Perry would follow him in
victory the next year.

His effortless victory had convinced Bobby he shouldn't turn his back on golf, but from this point on he would concentrate exclusively on the Big Shows. He had just turned twenty-one and graduated from Georgia Tech near the top of his class. The chase was on. He had one week to get ready for the 1922 U.S. Open.

The 1922 Open was being played at a new venue, Skokie Country Club just north of Chicago. Bobby and Pop boarded another train; in the usual cramped sleeping berths, not a roomy Pullman compartment, a hard and wearying way to travel. First class was well out of reach of Bobby's budget and would remain so for the next five years. Now reinstalled at East Lake as resident professional, and back on the team as Bobby's swing coach, Kiltie Maiden made the trip with them. The Colonel had decided to remove himself from his son's entourage, feeling his presence added too much pressure. Pop took on the added responsibility of sheltering Bobby from increasingly aggressive reporters who chased him for quotes; he let it be known among his brethren in no uncertain terms that if they wanted any words from Bobby to spice up their stories, from now on they were going to have to go through him. If Pop hadn't been so likeable they might have hated him for it.

The voluble Pop and the taciturn Kiltie added comic contrast to Bobby's inner circle. Although they eventually grew fond of each other, Pop's non-stop chatter and good cheer rubbed Kiltie the wrong way, particularly in the mornings before the first drink had wiped away the cobwebs. Forever trying to improve his own desperately impoverished game, Pop constantly badgered Kiltie about his theory of the golf swing. Although few men alive knew more on the subject, Kiltie just plain hated to talk; the more questions Pop fired at him, the more reticent the little Scotsman became, and the more he clammed up the harder Pop pressed him for answers.

This was Skokie Country Club's debut as a national

championship venue. The course was scorched bone-dry after a spring drought, and in practice rounds players torched the course with record low scores. Bobby found the layout surprisingly easy, giving rise to optimism in the Jones camp that this might be his week. With over 320 entries, qualifying rounds took three days, with thirty-six holes restored as the standard. Bobby cruised in with a 72–76, and on the first day of the Open proper found himself paired with Walter Hagen.

Hagen had just made history as the first native-born American to win the British Open. When he returned in triumph from England with the Claret Jug, hundreds of fans and a military marching band greeted his boat as it docked in New York. In the first parade ever given by the city to a sports personality, Hagen claimed he rode in a fleet of limos down Broadway escorted by a squad of motorcycle policemen as crowds lined the streets. With most of Hagen's accounts, dividing his estimates by half is a safe way to arrive at reliable numbers; it was more likely one limo, escorted by two motorcycle cops. A raucous dinner followed that night in the ballroom of the Biltmore. After a few days of round-the-clock celebration, a bleary-eyed Hagen caught a train to Chicago and showed up at Skokie on the eve of the tournament. He wasn't about to miss a chance to become the first man to win both Opens in the same year.

Based in large part on the box-office success of Hagen's exhibitions, the USGA had decided for the first time to charge admission. After a heated debate over whether selling tickets would drive people away, over ten thousand showed up willing to plunk down $1.10 at the gate. With paying customers walking the grounds the USGA decided to pair the two biggest names in the field: the marquee match-up of Bobby and Hagen drew thousands to the first tee. Rising to meet expectations under pressure, Hagen threw down a flawless 68 in the first round to take the lead, besting Bobby by six strokes. But his frenetic travel schedule caught up with him in the afternoon; he found bunkers on five of the front-nine holes and fell back to a 77, tied with Gene Sarazen in third place. Bobby shot a steady 72 to settle in one stroke behind them in fifth.

The next morning found Bobby paired for the final rounds with a dashing Scotsman, George Duncan. Now the harsh lessons of his last few years, and the steadying influences of Pop and Kiltie, began to pay dividends. With every club in the bag working, Bobby shot his best round in an Open, 70, landing him in a first-place tie with a young Chicago pro named "Wild" Bill Melhorn. Bobby had climbed another step up the mountain: he held a share of the lead at a major going into the final round. Hagen was three strokes back. One shot behind him, almost unnoticed, stood Gene Sarazen.

The path to Bobby's first big win looked wide open. His game felt sure and steady and, keeping faith with the promise he'd made to George Walker and the USGA, he had kept his emotions in check throughout the week. He'd improved by two shots during every round and told Pop he thought he could shoot 68 in the final and win going away. Bobby played well but 68 proved optimistic: two missed putts gave him 36 for his outbound nine. As he reached the tenth, word drifted back to him that Sarazen, playing ninety minutes ahead, had just finished with the 68 Bobby had hoped for. The math was simple: Bobby needed a 71 to beat Sarazen and win the championship. That meant he'd have to play the long back nine in 35, one under par.

Bobby crushed his drive at ten, but his approach ran through and over the green. He pitched back to the flag and rolled ten feet past it. Pop and Kiltie stood next to each other in the gallery watching Bobby line up the putt. He struck it firmly, on line, but it caught the lip and spun out. A stroke lost to par. "Kiltie and I looked at each other under the long, moaning sigh the gallery exudes on such an occasion," wrote Pop. "The little Scot was ghastly under his tan. He shook his head slightly. Bad business."

Bobby described the pressure bearing down on him now as "the iron certitude of medal competition. You *know* what you have to do in that last round. It is not one man whom you can see, and who may make a mistake at any moment, with whom you are battling. It is an iron score. Something already in the book."

He needed to par in now just to tie Sarazen, but lost another stroke at the twelfth, flying the green, pitching back long and missing a 30-footer for par. After missing the green again on thirteen he chipped up and sank what Pop called "an ugly little four-footer" to save par. That seemed to revive him. Bobby pounded his drive at fourteen straight down the middle, nearly reaching the green. Bobby, Pop and Kiltie put their heads down and started walking; Bobby was working harder than he ever had in his life, and looked ready to stay in the fight to the end. As a grim Pop trudged down the fairway he felt someone come up from behind and clap him on the back.

"Don't let your chin drag," said Bobby. "It's not as bad as all that."

His tone sounded chipper, but despite the attempt at bravado Pop said Bobby's "face was gray and sunken and his eyes looked an inch deep in his head." Bobby thought Pop looked even worse than he did.

Bobby misplayed his easy pitch at fourteen, leaving himself a tough 35-foot putt for the birdie he desperately needed. As he made the stroke Bobby put so much unconscious body language to it that by the time the ball dropped in the hole he was lying flat on the green. The crowd, now containing every one of the day's paying customers, roared in approval. One of those lost strokes had come back, but he still needed a second birdie to catch Sarazen. The eighteenth was his best chance, a reachable par-five, but he had three tough holes ahead to get there. At fifteen he just missed a 15-footer for birdie. Kiltie and Pop could barely breathe when that one stayed out, but Bobby calmly accepted the result and marched on. He collected another work-manlike par at sixteen. Make par at seventeen, then that birdie at the last would deliver him into a play-off.

Bobby cut off the dogleg with a booming drive on seventeen, carrying a strategic bunker at the elbow to discourage that approach. That should have left him with an easy second shot, but when Bobby and the crowd reached the fairway they discov-ered the ball had taken a dreadful kick, dead left, out of the fairway and onto a dirt service road where it came to rest under a low-hanging tree. How such a bold, well-executed drive could end up in such a rotten lie seemed cruel, inexplicable.

Bobby betrayed no emotion. He worked himself into position over the ball, visualizing a low runner under the tree to the green over 150 yards away. The shot came off perfectly but ran out of gas just before it crested a small slope to the green, and rolled all the way back down to the fairway. But Bobby left his crucial chip to the hole short, and his putt for par came up short as well. Bogey five.

Standing on the tee at eighteen, Bobby needed a miracle eagle three for the tie. He walloped another drive, then pulled his three-wood to try for the green and set up an eagle putt. The ball was struck so purely it ran through the green into the gallery standing off the left side. The chip he needed to drop into the hole rolled right over the cup. Bobby made the 6-foot putt for the birdie he'd been banking on, but the bogey at seventeen had killed his chances.

Gene Sarazen had won the 1922 Open, with Bobby in second by a stroke.

He'd made progress, that much was undeniable. In three Opens he'd gone from eighth to fifth place and now to second by a single shot. He'd never been low amateur in the championship before; at Skokie he finished thirteen ahead of Chick Evans, who was playing in his own hometown. Last year's Amateur champion Jesse Guilford was sixteen strokes behind him and Bobby beat the reigning British champ Willie Hunter, his nemesis at St. Louis, by seventeen.

No amateur ever finished ahead of Bobby in an American or British Open again.

Most importantly of all to Pop, Bobby never once lost control of his emotions. In years past that horrendous bounce at seventeen, which cost him the tournament, might have sent him into a blind rage. The next morning, Bobby and Pop ran into Sarazen on the train headed east. At twenty years and four months, Sarazen and Bobby were almost exactly the same age, but their lives could not have followed more divergent paths. Sarazen had worked as a caddie since the age of eight, and dropped out of school in his early teens. Coming up the hard way had given him a helping of Hagen's bluster and braggadocio—his best friend during childhood, an Irish kid named Ed Sullivan, didn't do too badly in life either—and as the shortest pro in the game Gene felt the constant need to make a big impression. A few weeks later he would follow up his breakthrough at Skokie with a victory over Hagen in the PGA Championship. After these early back-to-back major victories in his career Sarazen cashed in aggressively on all the deals that came his way; his future seemed assured. At that moment Bobby, the modest, educated young man from a loving and supportive family, could not say the same.

Bobby didn't let anyone see how low his spirits had sunk until he was on the train home with Pop and Kiltie; all three felt tired and discouraged. As Bobby put it, "this championship quest was getting a bit thick." For all the great golf he was capable of playing, Bobby had clocked forty rounds in ten national championships and never once broken 70. Other players, lesser talents by any measure, managed to do so repeatedly, often winning because of it. The game seemed to select its winners by nothing more sensible than the random conferring of lucky breaks. Neither Kiltie nor Pop could argue with that point; they'd seen it happen too often, and that was a bitter pill to swallow. Trying to offer consolation, Pop asked Bobby what he'd do if he played the game as poorly as he, Pop, did.

"I'd probably get a lot more fun out of it," said Bobby.

Bobby was brushing up his Latin and studying Einstein—whose startling theories of relativity were in the popular news—a month later when the three men took another train north, this time to Long Island and the National Golf Links. Bobby was scheduled to play in the first official Walker Cup competition with Great Britain. The event would serve as a final tune-up for the National Amateur, played a week later at the Country Club in Brookline. Bobby won his alternate-shot match and in singles against Englishman Roger Wethered, as the American team prevailed 8–4. The evidence was mounting that American players had caught, if not surpassed, their British counterparts on both the amateur and professional levels, but one unlikely old soldier put up quite a fight.

When British team captain Robert Harris came down with tonsillitis on the eve of the tournament, forty-six-year-old Bernard Darwin stepped in as an emergency replacement. Making his first trip to America since 1913, Darwin had come to cover the even for *The Times* but instead found himself losing a first-day match against his old friend Francis Ouimet. The next day Darwin rallied to beat American captain Bill Fownes in singles.

A raucous dinner marked the end of the festivities—fueled by their host C.B. McDonald's extensive wine cellar—and the next morning both teams ferried across Long Island Sound to Connecticut, where they jumped on a train bound for Boston. The Colonel traveled up from Atlanta and rejoined Team Jones, ready to put his fear of being a jinx to the test. The American favorites qualified easily, with defending champion Jesse Guilford capturing the coveted gold medal. Playing on the hallowed ground of the Country Club meant a lot to Bobby; he got in a practice round with Ouimet before the start of competition and heard first-hand the story of his friend's great victory in 1913.

Bobby won his first three matches in the Amateur, none by wide margins, but his game felt solid. In the semi-finals he came up against Jess Sweetser. Bobby joked afterwards that on the first tee he shouldn't have reminded Sweetser, 1920's collegiate champion from Yale, that he was about to enter Harvard. They halved the first hole and then Sweetser, played a blind shot from 90 yards to the second's elevated green. The roar of the crowd told them what had happened: Sweetser had holed out for an eagle. Bobby then played his second shot to the green, and heard another roar, followed by a groan; his ball landed six inches from the cup but stayed out. Watching from the gallery, Bernard Darwin called them "the greatest little shots" that he'd ever seen. A kick-in birdie, and Bobby was already one down. It was like a punch in the face, and five years later Bobby wrote that "it still makes me groggy when I recall it."

His eagle sent Sweetser on a rampage while Bobby was still reeling. Seven holes later Bobby found himself six down. A tall, handsome, and, some said, excessively cocky player, Sweetser went on to break Ted Ray's nine-year-old course record with 69. Bobby steadied to shoot two under par on the back, but could only pick up a single hole on his streaking opponent. Five down at intermission, Bobby tried to continue the fight but this was Sweetser's day; after lunch Sweetser parred the first eleven holes and the match was over, 8 & 7, the most lopsided, decisive defeat of Bobby's entire life.

"Jess Sweetser chopped my head off," said Bobby. "I remember thinking it was adding insult to injury, beating me at the most distant point from the club house, so I would have to haul my bedraggled self nearly a mile before I could sit down and rest."

The next day Sweetser won the 1922 Amateur by beating Chick Evans, 3 & 2. When Bobby congratulated him after he collected his trophy, Sweetser said: "Thank you, Bobby. I beat the best man in the field yesterday." Not much consolation; Bobby had failed even to reach the finals and, after Skokie, felt he'd taken a step backwards. He felt even worse that his father had come all that way to Boston only to see him get trounced; the Colonel left Brookline convinced he was jinxing Bobby. Pop tried to defuse their frustration by suggesting Bobby always brought out the best in his opponents, that an inspired performance like Sweetser's only confirmed his greatness.

Bobby took no comfort from it. Sweetser was a month younger than he was; for the first time he had lost to a player catching up with him from behind. As they summed up the Amateur at Brookline golf writers echoed that sentiment; there hovered around Bobby now an air of disappointment, as if people had begun to tire of his perpetual promise, receiving no pay-off for the long-term investment of their affections.

Bobby began to believe he lacked what it took to win championships. He could hit great shots with the best who ever played, and the mechanical perfection of his form took your breath away, but he seemed to be missing a key ingredient to put him over the top. What was it? Luck? Mental toughness under pressure? The will to win? More than one observer of the sport had concluded that a big brain wasn't an asset in golf. Could intelligence and emotional sensitivity, among his most valuable human qualities, actually be holding him back? The questions haunted them all on the trip back to Atlanta; if he had greatness in him, would it ever show itself when it mattered most? Only Pop Keeler's faith was unshaken, convinced that the toughness Bobby needed could only be acquired through defeat in the heat of championship competition. Pop noted that Brookline erased all talk of Bobby quitting the game; it only increased his resolve.

On Saturday, September 16, a week after returning from Brookline, Bobby went out with his dad and regular weekend foursome to play a round at East Lake. He had broken the scoring record six times since he was thirteen; it stood at 66, a number he'd subsequently matched three times. That day Bobby shot his seventh record score at East Lake, a 63. This was 1922, the era of hickory shafts and irons with sweet spots the size of a pea, on one of the toughest courses in America. Bobby never shot a better round in his life and that record would stand at East Lake for seventy years. It became the talk of the town when Keeler wrote it up in the papers. Pop raved to Bobby about what he'd done when he saw him the next day, but he was in no mood to hear it.

"The place for that round was at Brookline—or Skokie," said Bobby. He took no pleasure in his achievement, and even less pride. Although he empathized with his young charge's anguish, secretly Pop couldn't have been more pleased. He could see the striations forming in Bobby's steel-blue eyes. Still only twenty, he'd been cured by the fire and shaped by the lathe, battle-tested. Strong enough, at last, to carry his burdens. It won't be much longer now, thought Pop.

Four days later Bobby left for Harvard.

PART TWO

THE CHAMPIONSHIP
YEARS

"No virtue in this world is so oft rewarded as perseverance."

—Bobby Jones

"Golf is a humbling game."

—Francis Ouimet

CHAPTER FIVE

BREAKTHROUGH

President Warren G. Harding played his final round of golf during the last week of July, 1923. He was so weak from congestive heart failure that he only had the energy to play the first six holes of that last round, in Vancouver.

Harding did a lot to popularize golf during his term. Unlike one of his predecessors, William Taft—whom Harding appointed as Chief Justice of the Supreme Court, a rare sound decision—who concealed his obsession with the game for fear of appearing élitist, Harding never missed an opportunity to have his picture taken on the course with his famous partners. In the years after the war golf had entered the mainstream of American life; thanks to Ouimet and Hagen and attractive young players like Bobby it was now viewed as a wholesome, healthy pastime to be enjoyed by the middle class.

The Roaring Twenties in America are often depicted as a non-stop cocktail party; a far cry from the truth. The early part of the decade brought tumultuous upheaval, when the furious rate of societal and technological change we take for granted today thrust the country into a future it was not prepared to embrace. The rapid transition from nineteenth-century stability to churning postwar turmoil threw two generations into disarray and created a combustible mix of anxiety amid a world of new-found freedoms. Small wonder that sports and sporting heroes offered a comforting refuge.

Along with Jack Dempsey, Walter Hagen and Babe Ruth, the public embraced running back Red Grange and Knute Rockne's championship Notre Dame teams in football, Big Bill Tilden in tennis, and racehorse Man o'War, who won twenty of his twenty-one career starts at the track. New York sportswriters, with Rice in the lead, continued to feed the country's appetite for heroes, but these figures bore no resemblance to the air-brushed celebrity pitchmen manufactured by today's sports-entertainment complex. They were all colorful, quixotic individuals who'd risen to the top through hard times. The public responded as strongly to their personalities as to their achievements in the arena, which made the sports writers' jobs that much easier; who needed to pump up the details when Ruth or Hagen were so much larger than life? Olympus was quickly becoming a crowded pantheon, but Granny Rice knew there was always room for one more.

Bobby Jones turned twenty-one on March 17, 1923. He'd spent the fall and winter immersed in Harvard's rigorous academic program. Having exhausted his collegiate eligibility at Georgia Tech he'd been turned down by the Harvard golf team, but worked and traveled informally with them as assistant manager. They needed him: Bobby once played a best-ball match against the entire six-man squad, and beat them soundly. The school awarded him an honorary letter, and later voted him into their Varsity Hall of Fame. He resisted joining the Harvard chapter of his old Tech fraternity, evidence of his focus on education, but still had time to daydream; Bob drew up designs for an ideal driver he hoped to build some day that he called the Dreadnought. The girl he'd left behind was also much on his mind; after almost four years together, Mary and Bobby had decided they would marry the following spring, but held off making a formal announcement until he returned home. He played a few rounds of casual golf with Francis Ouimet around Boston, on one occasion setting a course record at the Charles River Country Club, but when he asked the school for permission to leave early in order to participate in the British Amateur and the second Walker Cup they said no; a unique experience for Bobby, but this was Harvard, where final exams trumped championships.

This brought Bobby to the eve of the year's U.S. Open without a single warm-up, and scarcely any practice. He despaired that his game had never been in worse shape, to such an extent that Kiltie Maiden decided to accompany him to Long Island, where the Open was being played at Inwood Country Club. A long, harrowing, penal course carved out of an old potato farm on the marshy shores of Jamaica Bay, Inwood offered one of the toughest layouts in championship history. Half links style where it fronted the water and half parkland, the course anticipated the USGA's future template for Open set-ups: narrow fairways, impenetrable rough, and glassy greens. The trip also allowed a sentimental reunion for Kiltie with his older brother Jimmy, resident pro at nearby Nassau Country Club since leaving East Lake in 1907. As every aspect of Bobby's game continued to languish during his practice rounds—he couldn't even break 80—the Maidens consulted with each other on how to turn him around. The greens, they decided. Build up his confidence there and the full swing must follow.

Jimmy pulled a battered old putter out of a barrel in the back of his pro shop and handed it to Bobby. It was an unlovely instrument which had come over from Carnoustie with him nearly twenty years before. Its goose-necked blade bore a number of nicks and rust spots. The hickory shaft had partially splintered at some point in its life; three bands of black whipping just above the neck held it together. With a face bearing two degrees of loft more than standard, Jimmy thought it might help Bobby get the ball rolling better on Inwood's undulating greens. (When he held it in his hands years later, Jack Nicklaus said it felt more like a three- or four-iron than a putter.) Before the mass manufacture of clubs these hand-crafted tools often acquired affectionate nicknames. Jimmy Maiden called this one "Calamity Jane."

Bobby liked her the moment he took Jane in his hands. One account claims he went out to the practice green and sank twenty-four of his first twenty-five putts. That may not be true, but there's no question she boosted his confidence over the ball at a crucial moment. After putting all his life on the South's grainy Bermuda grasses, his season in Boston had helped him acclimatize to the northeast's bent-grass greens. Pop observed that Bobby was sagging under the weight of expectation at Inwood more than ever before, so worried about disappointing expectations that he'd forgotten he'd come to play golf. Although he'd mastered his temper, Bobby still lacked Hagen's ability to laugh off a loss or forget a bad shot; he felt every ounce of pressure acutely, and knew he'd reached a turning point in his ability to stomach it. Although he never came out and said so, Bobby dropped enough hints for Pop to conclude that if this Open ended badly for him—in second place or anywhere south—they might have reached the end of the road. Winning a major, as the two now agreed, wasn't up to the players anyway. Fortune cast the final vote.

"I was fearfully depressed," wrote Bobby the following year.

Over 360 golfers from around the world showed up when qualifying began on Monday, July 9. Rounds were split over the next four days, and only seventy-seven would advance to the Open proper. When they published the draw on Sunday night, Bobby found out he would have to wait until Thursday to play his way in.

The smartest decision Bobby made before the tournament was to break his customary routine of bunking in a hotel with Pop; several weeks before, Bobby and Francis Ouimet had agreed to share a room in the attic of the Inwood clubhouse. Ouimet had played well that spring, leading the US team to victory in the Walker Cup at St. Andrews, then reaching the semi-finals of the British Amateur. They spent their spare time watching early qualifying, getting in practice rounds, and discussing the tough Inwood layout. Both agreed there were no breather holes; every shot demanded discipline and a sound game plan. Patience would be rewarded, but not panache. More than any other Open in memory, this tournament would be won by the man most willing to measure himself against Old Man Par.

Bobby broke 80 for the first time at Inwood twice on the day he qualified, 77 and 79, six strokes in back of the lead in the middle of the pack. The perfect pace and positioning, Pop decided: no point in shooting your best rounds now. Qualifying medal winners almost never won an Open or any other tournament, so the prevailing superstition said. Bobby had a chance to confront another superstition the next day, Friday the 13th, when he was paired with Walter Hagen for the Open's first two rounds.

Hagen had only three weeks ago returned from defending his British Open crown. He had interrupted the most lucrative exhibition tour of his life, a year-long schedule with a unique performer named Joe Kirkwood, an Australian-born pro and the game's first trick-shot artist. Kirkwood's repertoire astonished galleries; he could launch booming drives with the ball balanced on the crystal of a volunteer's watch without leaving a scratch, or a woman's open-toed shoe without removing a digit. Left-handed, right-handed, wearing a hood, standing on his knees, Joe wove a brand of effortless magic that no golfball could resist. He attributed his unique ability to steady nerves, regular exercise and strict clean living. How he managed the latter during years on the road with Hagen is a Mystery.

During their tour Hagen and Kirkwood contributed a significant technological advance to the game. Three years before, a New Jersey dentist and frustrated hacker named Dr. William Lowell had whittled a small wooden peg on which to place his ball on the tee box, forgoing the traditional pile of wet sand. Lowell patented the gadget and took it to market, painted fire-engine red and sold in paper packets as the Reddy Tee. Despite advertising in every golf publication the doctor's novelty hadn't caught on until the desperate Lowell offered Hagen and Kirkwood $1,500 to use his tee on tour. They handed them out as they walked the fairways, and left samples behind on every tee box, where kids scrambled after them as souvenirs. Both men began using Reddy Tees in regular tournaments as well and before long so many people were clamoring after them, according to Hagen, that the USGA had to start roping off tee boxes and fairways. Within a few months the Reddy Tee started showing up in pro shops around the country; even touring pros grudgingly admitted they were useful. A wealth of imitations flooded the market and the little wooden tee became a universal accessory; Hagen took the Reddy Tee to England and it caught on there as well. The reason tees aren't all still red today is that their paint ran off in high heat and humidity. The first time Hagen went out with a pocket full of them in those conditions he saw a stream of crimson running down his tailored plus fours and thought he'd been shot. Not about to turn his back on Dr. Lowell's endorsement money, Walter took to carrying a spare Reddy behind his ear.

During the first round of the Open, Inwood stood up to the most accomplished field ever assembled, yielding only two scores under par. Front runner Jock Hutchison fashioned a flawless 70. Clicking with Calamity Jane on the greens, and chipping brilliantly, Bobby needed only fourteen putts on the back nine to finish with 71. No other player managed even par; Hagen came in with a loose 77, in twentieth place. Francis Ouimet, who had barely qualified, shot himself out of contention with an 82. The afternoon rounds saw Hutchison follow his fast start with a solid 72. Bobby stayed on his tail with 73, two strokes back at the halfway mark. Hagen improved to ninth with a 75, nine strokes back but teetering on the cusp of irrelevancy. Alone in third place, one stroke behind Bobby, stood Robert Allan Cruickshank.

Standing five foot four, an inch short of Sarazen and fifty pounds lighter, Cruickshank had built a solid reputation as an amateur in his native Scotland before the war. Enlisting early as an infantryman, he'd been thrust into the thick of the fighting. In the trenches at the Somme, from only a few feet away he saw his younger brother torn apart by an artillery shell. Eventually taken prisoner, he organized an escape from the camp, led three other men to freedom, rejoined his unit and refused reassignment back to Britain, seeing out the war on the front lines. When the war ended Cruickshank returned to university, finished his degree and emigrated to the States in 1921, intent on starting a law career. When he realized it was possible to not only make a living at golf in America but be considered a first-class citizen, he detoured back into his sport and turned professional. He reached the semi-finals of the PGA Championship during his first two tries, losing to eventual champion Gene Sarazen. After all he'd been through, if any man in the game could stand up to the pressures of a U.S. Open, Bobby Cruickshank ended the search.

Two rounds in and the Open was already down to a three-man race: Jock Hutchison and the two Bobbys. At the end of the first day a press-tent straw poll gave Hutchison the edge. This surprised and alarmed Pop: faith among the press corps that Bobby could close the deal had begun to fade.

Bobby went out ahead of his closest competitors that morning paired for the final rounds with Sarazen. Cruickshank followed ninety minutes later, playing with Hagen. Jock Hutchison went out last in a pairing with Joe Kirkwood. Bobby had momentum and his regular caddie Luke Ross at his side, Kiltie and Pop in the gallery, and a hot putter in his bag. He then shot a five over 41 on the front, including two penalty strokes, but never lost his composure and didn't relinquish hope as he had in the past; everyone blows up during at least one rough patch during an Open, he'd banked that knowledge now and relied on it. This was his bad round, and that was all, not fate turning its back on him. "Stick to your business and save all the strokes you can," he kept saying to himself.

Despair beckoned and for the first time in such critical circumstances he resisted: Bobby carded a superlative 35 on the back nine to finish with 76. He was shocked to discover that both Hutchison and Cruickshank had blown up worse than he had, with 78 and 82 respectively. Hutchison stood four strokes back and was running on fumes, his rabbity energy spent. Bobby led Cruickshank by three. Expecting to find himself mired in third place, Bobby held the lead going into the Open's final round for the second year in a row, this time all by his lonesome.

He took his lunch break with Ouimet and Pop—tea and toast, no more indulgences at the dessert tray—all three keeping a healthy silence about his situation. Privately Bobby calculated 73 would be enough to hold off Cruickshank and Hutchison; that was the number in his head as he set out for his final round. Somewhere between the lunch room and the first tee he fudged that number upward, figuring 75 marked the edge of his margin for error. His eternal battle with Old Man Par had been momentarily forgotten; sometimes the last lesson you learn is the first one to slip your mind.

Was his name already written in the Book? Did the gods want him to win a championship? How much control did he have over what was about to happen? A skittish Pop put it this way: "He was playing against something besides famous professionals and amateurs, and narrow fairways and terrible traps. He was playing against a grim fate that in every start had ridden him and crushed him to the turf in tournament after tournament when it seemed his time had come."

Bobby bogeyed the first hole, chalked it up to nerves and moved on. He reclaimed that lost stroke with a bold birdie on the par-five fifth, when two tremendous woods put him on the green and Calamity Jane did the rest. So far so good. Then trouble at the seventh, a challenging 223-yard par-three; he smacked a three-wood down the right side of the fairway, it took a wicked bad hop off a spectator's foot, and jumped out of bounds. Two strokes lost to par—what might once have been a crushing blow to his confidence—but again he stood firm and didn't let it rattle him. Three strokes to finish the hole, then two straight pars to reach the turn with 39. The course's toughest stretch was behind him; he'd never shot higher than an even par 35 on the back all week, which would put him at 74, smack in the middle of his safety zone.

A short par-four began the inward nine. Reaching the green easily in two, he dropped a 20-foot putt for birdie and the crowd roared. Word spread over the course that Bobby was finally on his way; his gallery swelled and snaked around the fairways. They saw him knock off three more pars in a row, confident and strong. Playing with the house's money now, he gambled at the long par-five fourteenth and came up aces: a birdie four and he was back to even par for his round with only four holes to play. Pop limped along after the exultant gallery, not allowing himself to believe the moment could be at hand, gasping for air.

Bobby dropped his tee shot in a bunker at fifteen, a par-three, then lofted a soft recovery to within 4 feet and dropped the putt dead center for his save. Luck appeared to have thrown in with him at last. Three holes to go; three par-fours. Twelve strokes to a 72; Cruickshank would have to card a tournament-best 69 just to tie him, and news had already filtered back that the Scotsman was stumbling on his first couple of holes. The worst Bobby had played these finishing holes during the Open was even par; twice he'd birdied the eighteenth. Numbers and calculations cascaded through Bobby's head, colliding with the clear cold intentions he needed to finish the job.

Pressure is a hazard in the game, as plain as sand or wind or water and all the more insidious for being out of sight. Bobby landed his drive at sixteen in the middle of the fairway. A simple mid-iron would put him on the green with a chance at birdie and almost certain victory. Bobby rushed his swing, came over the top, pulled the shot left and watched it sail out of bounds. The crowd froze in their tracks. Dead silence. He never changed expression, dropped another ball, went through his routine and rifled it right of the green toward a bunker. The ball kicked left off a mound on its first bounce, rolled onto the green and stopped 6 feet away from the cup. Calamity Jane came through for him again; he made the putt for bogey, a sensational up and down from 150 yards out. The crowd reacted as if he'd bagged another birdie. Only one stroke lost after a potential disaster; Pop listened to the buzz as the gallery tallied up the cost of Bobby's stumble, deciding it was an extravagance he could easily afford. Pop wasn't so sure; he saw a shade of gray come over Bobby's face and felt his own stomach flop over like a trout in a net.

Again Bobby's drive at seventeen found the short grass, long and on line, leaving an even simpler iron shot to the green. The crowd gasped when he overcooked the easy approach, watching his ball bounce and over the green into a patch of deep rough.

After a ticklish pitch back toward the flag he was left with a 10-foot putt for par.

He missed it.

The buzz turned to solemn stillness, broken by whispers of concern: *He couldn't. Not again. He mustn't, he can't.*

His gallery didn't want to see this; not another soul on that course did. If Bobby shot himself out of this lead with so much riding on it he might never recover; no one knew or felt that more acutely than Keeler. Pop found his mind involuntarily wandering back to a tournament Cruickshank had played in two years earlier; Cruickshank had trailed Jock Hutchison and Jim Barnes by nine strokes with eight holes to play, and he'd caught them both and forced a play-off, and then beaten them decisively the next day.

But he hadn't been playing for the National Championship, Pop reminded himself. Bobby could still make par at eighteen for 74, the edge of his safety zone. Cruickshank would then still need to break par in the last round of an Open to tie.

The eighteenth at Inwood stretched 425 yards, the fairway a narrow chute closely lined with trees. A shallow lagoon protected the front of the green, forcing a key decision on the second shot; go for it or lay up. Bobby steered his drive onto the fairway. He was nearly 200 yards out with a strong breeze in his face, but he had no choice: he had to shoot the works. He pulled his three-wood out of the bag. Pop went pale: the shot screamed for an iron, a hard crisp iron over the pond, straight at the flag. Bobby tried to finesse the wood, and pulled it left, over the green and just beyond a nasty pot bunker. They found the ball nestled down in short rough beneath a decorative chain that marked the boundaries of the twelfth tee box.

Now fate truly did seem to conspire against him; the position of the ball prompted a paralyzing five-minute discussion among a covey of rules officials about what to do with the chain. Bobby sat on a mound behind them and brooded while they deliberated; his eyes smoldered, his mental gears seized up. Pop watched from a distance, helpless, and sensed Bobby's collapse would now become complete. Ouimet joined him, speechless and equally stricken. When the officials finally decided the rules allowed them to remove the chain—a clear-cut option Bobby had pointed out at the start of their filibuster—Bobby had already talked himself into the cellar. He half-heartedly chopped the ball out of the rough and dumped it in the pot bunker. Another swipe at the ball in the bunker put him on the green, and he used two putts to get down for a double bogey six.

Disaster. Four shots squandered in three holes. He'd finished with 76, one stroke outside the margin he'd set himself at the start of the day.

The crowd looked away, reluctant witnesses to a one-car accident. Pop painted on a brave face and hauled himself forward to meet Bobby coming off the green. "His face gave me such a shock that for a moment I forgot what I meant to say. His age seemed to have doubled in the last half hour."

"I think you're champion, Bobby," he said, after swallowing hard. "Cruickshank will never catch you."

Bobby wasn't buying that line for a second: Pop later catalogued two different quotes as his response. In the more sanitized version available in the "authorized biography" Bobby said, "I'm afraid I finished too badly. I had a great chance to shut the door, and I left it open."

Bobby remembered looking up and seeing Pop standing before him as he left the green, blinking at him repeatedly, unable to swallow, before he could speak. His own unvarnished version of how he responded, sharp and bitter, also shows up in Pop's earlier drafts of the story: "Then I said what was in my heart and had been there longer than I like to admit: 'Well, I didn't finish like a champion. I finished like a God damn yellow dog.'"

Alone in every way, Bobby walked inside to his room in the clubhouse to wait for the jury to come in. Ouimet decided to follow him after a respectful interval. What he found there was an image that recurs frequently during the next seven years: a haunted young man, pacing the floor of some small, spare club-house room, spent and shaken after running the gauntlet, a strong drink in hand to blunt his jangled nerves, waiting for word about some other poor bastard's battle with fate.

Pop found Grantland Rice and the two struck out across the course with the rest of the gallery to watch Bobby Cruickshank. They caught up with the little Scotsman on the sixth green, just in time to watch him sink a birdie putt; at roughly the same moment, the news about Bobby's dreadful finish reached Cruickshank. It energized him; he made the turn in 36, a stroke under par, began the back stretch with two no-nonsense pars and then picked up another birdie at the twelfth.

Cruickshank was three shots ahead of Bobby with six holes to play.

"I was good and sick and utterly empty," wrote Pop. "I had passed up breakfast and lunch and was rattling like a gourd. Also my feet hurt. If there was any less happy person in the world than I, he inevitably was looking for a red barn with a rope over his arm."

But Cruickshank still had to finish those last six holes. This was the Open and he was human. He bogeyed the thirteenth and then dropped another stroke at the fifteenth; his lead had been reduced to a single shot. He reached the sixteenth tee confronting the same test Bobby had encountered two hours earlier: par the last three holes and the championship was his. Cruickshank double-bogeyed the sixteenth.

"I felt as if the burden of the world had rolled off my shoulders," said Pop. He slipped away from the gallery and franti-cally wheeled his bad leg back to the clubhouse and up the stairs to Bobby's room. News of Cruickshank's breakdown had preceded him; Ouimet and several others were already there congratulating Bobby. Pop took Ouimet aside to ask him in confidence if he thought Bobby's win had been salted away. "Absolutely," said Ouimet. "No man on earth could play those two holes in seven shots under these circumstances." But Bobby knew at least one man who had; Ouimet had done exactly that himself ten years earlier to win his Open.

A USGA official entered the room and asked Bobby to come downstairs and prepare himself for the trophy ceremony. Bobby said he'd rather wait until Cruickshank had finished and the last putt was in the hole.

Pop decided to go back down and watch the finish. As he walked back onto the course word filtered in that Cruickshank had secured his par at seventeen, at 405 yards the easier of the last two holes. He still needed to birdie the treacherous Lagoon Hole to tie Bobby and force a play-off. Pop reached the gallery in time to see Cruickshank land the long, accurate drive he needed. From 175 yards out the Scotsman pulled the iron Pop had been praying Bobby would use earlier. The ball left the club straight, low, and perfect, touched down on a dead line to the flag 20 feet away and rolled to a stop within six.

"The cheer of the gallery crashed out like artillery," wrote Pop. Bobby and Ouimet could hear it in the clubhouse: Cruickshank had given himself a chance. He wasn't going to miss that putt; Pop knew the ball would drop before he hit it. So did Bobby, watching from his high window.

Cruickshank's stroke was sure and solid and the putt fell for a birdie three. Brave Bobby Cruickshank had caught him, and deserved to. Bobby called it "one of the greatest holes ever played in golf." Their eighteen-hole play-off was scheduled for 2:00 P.M. the following day, Sunday afternoon.

Ouimet stepped in. With the help of two friends he cleared some space around Bobby, cordoning off their section of the clubhouse, leaving Pop the job of feeding quotes to the clamorous press. At first Bobby seemed inconsolable, and couldn't shake his finish at eighteen out of his mind; unless that pattern was broken, this was a fatal psychology. Ouimet suggested a change of scene, away from the bustle at Inwood; they went downstairs, avoided the crowds and climbed into a friend's borrowed car. Ouimet drove them a good twenty miles through the open countryside, all the way to the northern side of the island and Roslyn, New York, where they shared a quiet dinner at the Engineer's Club, the course where Ouimet had beaten Bobby after his encounter with the bee in the semi-finals of the 1919 National Amateur. His selection of Engineer's was deliberate: this was the scene of one of Bobby's last self-destructive juvenile meltdowns. He was a man now, with an opportunity to demonstrate a wholly different reaction to adversity. Over the course of their dinner, in thoughtful and spare discussion about the game and his situation, Bobby worked his way around to a crucial mental adjustment that allowed him, as he put it, "to get square with myself."

"If Cruickshank had bogged down at the finish, and I'd been left in front, I'd never have felt I won the championship," he told Ouimet.

"How so, Bobby?"

"I'd have felt that Cruickshank lost it. This wasn't between Cruickshank and me, though I made the mistake of thinking so. It's between me and Old Man Par. Like it will be tomorrow."

By the time they drove back to Inwood through the gathering dusk, Bobby seemed at peace. There wasn't a better man on the planet for Bobby to share these hours with, or one who better understood what he was going through. This was the tenth anniversary of Ouimet's win at Brookline, the last time an amateur had faced a professional in a play-off for the U.S. Open title.

Neither man was given to effusive or emotional statement of the obvious; both appreciated a silent, deeply felt sympathy that only established friends could share. On this occasion that understated, slightly distant ease did Bobby a world of good, more so than the complex emotional bonds his connection with Pop would have required of him. Ouimet was also a fellow competitor, another shared experience that needed no underlining; he'd walked this lonely path and come out the other side a champion.

It's tempting to imagine Ouimet dispensing detailed advice to Bobby about how to handle himself in an Open play-off, but that doesn't fit either man's character. Bobby was facing a trial by fire that would decide his entire future, and precisely because Ouimet was the only other man alive who had lived through that same ordeal he didn't presume to know he had the answers. When the stakes were this high a man's response could only emerge out of the deepest part of who he was.

According to Ouimet, the evening ended this way: "Bobby picked up a book, read a few chapters, and turned in for a fine night of rest."

An afternoon start presented its own set of challenges. The next morning Ouimet assumed a practical role and appointed himself a policeman "to keep well-wishing friends away from Bobby, because one of the most tiring things in the world is to talk golf just before a big match." He ordered breakfast brought up to the room, and then barred the door to anyone but Bobby's closest friends. When Pop came in, Ouimet reported that Bobby had slept well, and Bobby insisted he felt fine and ready, but the sight of his young friend gave Pop a jolt: "The boy's face was drawn and pinched and his eyes were far back in his head, and introspective, with the look of a chess player exerting all the powers of his mind."

Shortly after noon Luke Ross came to collect Bobby and take him down for his warm-up. He seemed calm and centered, and only reported later that he felt "kind of numb." Pop appeared to be in much worse shape; he felt like hell hit with a ripe tomato. Ouimet grabbed him and a couple of his newspaper friends and they took a walk out onto the course. Pop suggested they try to alleviate their anxiety by singing, so the four men sat alone on a bank behind the third green and self-consciously sang a couple of little songs. "It was silly, of course," he wrote, "but there was an utterly indescribable tension in the close air. The sky was overcast. I could not get it out of my mind that fate was closing in." Pop's mind kept wandering and then got stuck like a phonograph needle on a line from Kipling's poem "Danny Deever": "'I'm dreadin' what I've got to watch,' the Colour-Sergeant said."

For a few moments on the Saturday, the USGA had considered delaying the play-off until Monday; there was still a lingering puritanical bias against playing golf on Sundays, particularly the closer one got to New England. A forecast of foul weather tracking toward Long Island helped decide the issue: it might arrive as early as that afternoon, and Monday looked to be a wash-out. The play-off's late starting time was a compromise to allow people to first attend church. Neither the threat of a storm nor religious feeling seemed to stop anyone from attending: the gallery started assembling shortly after noon, and as the hour approached there were close to ten thousand people around the clubhouse. Distant lightning flashed occasionally through a forbidding blanket of cloud; rumbles of thunder and high humidity added to the oppressive, brooding atmosphere. This was before the USGA provided organized security, so as the players moved toward the first tee Ouimet recruited a couple of large acquaintances to help him surround Bobby and prevent spectators from accosting him during the match. Jones and Cruickshank walked out to the tee right on schedule, at 2:00 P.M. Both men wore knickerbockers, white shirts and bow ties. They posed for pictures together on either side of USGA president Wynant Vanderpool.

Then, a brisk handshake with words of mutual good luck exchanged, and off they went with two perfectly played tee shots.

Unless someone blew up under pressure this would be match-play disguised as medal. The front nine featured more back-and-forth action than singles at Wimbledon; they wouldn't halve a hole until the eighth. The start went like this: Advantage Jones, even, Cruickshank one up, even, Cruickshank up one—his third birdie in the first five holes; he hadn't yet carded a par—then Cruickshank went two up at the sixth despite Jones playing at even par. Cruickshank's lead fell back to one when Bobby attacked the seventh with a tremendous three-wood to the long par-three green; protecting his lead, Cruickshank played safe and short off the tee, chipped up, and then missed his putt for par. Bobby later felt that unerring tee shot at seven, down a tight tree-lined chute to the tiny green, was his most important shot on the front nine. Their first half came at the eighth, and then Bobby won the ninth with a solid par when Cruickshank missed a 5-foot putt. That squared the match at the halfway mark. Both had shot 37, Bobby matching par for the first time on the front nine all week. Dead even.

Pop saw a contained ferocity in their focus; the strain felt palpable, crushing, but neither man gave in to it. They played swiftly, with purpose, in silence, the gallery staying as quiet when they were over the ball as if they'd never left church. Thunder rolled closer. The wind picked up, announcing a genuine threat of rain. Ouimet had to take his role as bodyguard seriously: in the middle of play, as Bobby walked down a fairway, a man approached and invited him to spend a week at the fellow's summer home. Bobby had never seen the man before and politely told him to come around after the match was over. The man wasn't satisfied and insisted on an answer; Ouimet and his friends stepped in to distract him and Bobby slipped away. Another stranger greeted him like a long-lost brother as they walked between holes; this time Ouimet and company inter-vened at once.

Now the tension began to creep into their heads and hands

and arms: Bobby seized the lead again with a bogey at ten when Cruickshank doubled badly. Both bogeyed the eleventh with sloppy approach shots, the worst hole of the day for each man. Bobby recovered quickly; at the par-three twelfth he landed his towering approach 2 feet from the flag and watched it roll right by the cup; he made his birdie, Cruickshank settled for par, and the younger Bobby's lead was stretched to two. For the first time Cruickshank looked as if he might be on the verge of breaking.

They halved the thirteenth with pars, only the third and last time that happened all day. Then, coming off the ropes, at the par-five fourteenth Cruickshank nearly holed a brilliant approach shot for an eagle, settled for birdie and halved Bobby's lead. Almost like a boxing match now, thought Pop; that shot seemed to stun Bobby momentarily. Bobby double-bogeyed the par-three fifteenth with two loose shots—Cruickshank took a bogey—and just like that they were back to square with three holes left to play.

The sixteenth had given Cruickshank trouble the day before and it did again on Sunday; he recorded a bogey to Bobby's par. Advantage Jones. Both missed the fairway at seventeen and pitched up short of the green; Bobby appeared to gain a formidable edge when Cruickshank's recovery crawled into a greenside bunker. Bobby chipped up toward the flag but left it 10 feet short; Cruickshank came out of the bunker, landing just outside Bobby's ball, and then sank his par-saving putt; Bobby missed his and lost the hole and his lead. Three hours and seventeen holes into the match and they were back to a flat-footed tie. Both men appeared completely out of bullets; the gallery looked nearly as spent as they did. Friends like Pop, Ouimet, Kiltie, and Rice didn't know what to do with themselves. No one had ever seen a play-off like this one.

They staggered to the eighteenth. Either the fearful Lagoon Hole would decide the match, or they'd have to play another eighteen—on another day, by the look of the dark clouds rolling overhead as Cruickshank stepped to the tee. The wind picked up severely, dead into them; the storm appeared to be no more than half an hour off. Cruickshank intended to hit a low draw to stay below the breeze and catch as much roll as he could toward the green. Instead he misplayed a tee shot for the first time since the tournament began, a half-topped hook that sizzled through the rough, traveled less than 150 yards and skidded to a halt behind a tree near a service road. The green was completely out of reach from there; he'd have to lay up sky of the lagoon and hope his short game could salvage another par. A perhaps fatal unforced error. But could Bobby capitalize?

Bobby stepped to the tee and cracked a long high fade down the right side, setting up the preferred approach to the green. Losing its energy, the ball just dribbled off the fairway to the right and looked as if it would settle in the rough, but an extra roll carried it onto a patch of dry, hard ground, surrounded by loose dirt. When Bobby and his gallery reached the spot, Ouimet felt a chill run up his back at the choice Bobby faced. Two hundred yards from the green, over water, a clean lie but one that demanded perfect contact to pull off. He could lay up short and try to outpitch or outputt Cruickshank to the flag, but he wasn't playing Bobby Cruickshank now, in fact hadn't given him a moment's thought all afternoon; he was in the ring with Old Man Par, and that meant he needed to be on that green in two.

The work of seven long years all narrowed down to this one swing, one that Ouimet and Pop already knew Bobby was about to try, and dreaded having to watch.

The crowd, stacked ten deep behind them and stretching in a long curve across the fairway, paused long enough for Cruickshank to punch his second shot, as expected, out of trouble and short of the lagoon.

Jones later claimed he remembered nothing about the decision or the shot itself. By everyone's account he didn't waste a second, as if not wanting to give himself time to consider how many ways this could go wrong. He glanced over and made eye contact with Kiltie for the briefest moment then pulled a driving iron—the equivalent of today's two-iron—stood up to the ball, and swung the club back. Ouimet shuddered when he saw the club selection and closed his eyes; Pop couldn't take his eyes off it. All three men later said they'd never seen Bobby hit a ball with less deliberation or more decisively. Ouimet heard the crisp *click* of the club as it made contact, opened his eyes, looked up, and found the ball soaring like an arrow straight for the flag. Pop said it "went away on a ruled line." While it was still in the air, Kiltie took off his new straw hat, raised it up and smacked it down on caddie Luke Ross's head. Ross claimed he never felt a thing.

The ball cleared the water, bounced twice on the green, checked up, nearly hit the flag, and stopped just 6 feet past the hole. Now the thunder came; it came from the assembled congregation, and they wouldn't let up.

Bobby saw the ball lying near the hole and for the briefest moment wondered how it got there. The next thing he remembered was Ouimet grabbing him by the arm and propping him up as the gallery stampeded around and past them to surround the green. Grantland Rice shook his hand as they moved forward; Bobby didn't even see him.

"Finest shot I've ever seen, Bobby," said Ouimet. "Finest shot I've ever seen."

Luke Ross took the club back from his boss before someone tried to steal it. Bobby and Ouimet shuffled ahead, jostled by the crowd, in a daze. Pop, tears in his eyes, took his other arm. Kiltie was grinning from ear to ear—there's a first time for everything—and holding his ruined hat.

I don't care what happens now, Bobby thought.

Cruickshank had to hole his pitch or land stone dead and hope that Bobby missed the putt, but the bell had already tolled;

he hit the ball thin, ran it into a bunker, saw it roll 20 feet past the hole coming out, and missed the putt. Double bogey six.

Bobby putted twice to collect his par. Cruickshank walked straight over and held out his hand, and the world followed hard on his heels.

Bobby Jones. U.S. Open Champion.

"And now that he had won I could say things that had been locked up in my heart for four long years," wrote Pop Keeler.

> I could not say them before. They would have been misunderstood as alibis by those who did not know Bobby as I knew the boy. And one of the things I had wanted to say was this: All those years he had been the victim of too keen a mind and too fine an imagination. It was never his heart that was at fault. In his breast beat the heart of a lion. And the world knew it now. But to me, Bobby Jones was no greater on that day than he was the day before, or than he was last year. He had showed the world—that was all.

"Man, it was a bonnie shot," Cruickshank said to Pop as they waited for the trophy presentation. "There never was such a golfer, and I'm proud to have stepped so close to him. He is now what Harry Vardon was at his best: the greatest golfer in the world. To be defeated by him is glory enough."

In 1986, the members at Inwood planted a plaque in the ground to commemorate the spot where Bobby hit his fateful approach to eighteen.

Pop asked Kiltie Maiden what he was thinking while Bobby was standing over the ball at eighteen. Kiltie said he wasn't thinking at all. "Well," said Pop, keeping after him as usual, "then why did you bust your new straw hat over Luke's head when the ball hit the green?"

"How the hell should I know?"

Bobby and Pop sat on the clubhouse steps a short time after the play-off, waiting for the ceremony to award the trophy—a day later than planned, but infinitely better now, on his own terms. "How do you feel?" Pop asked him.

Bobby looked at him for a moment, as if puzzled by the question, and took his time answering. "Why, I don't care what happens now."

When they handed him the cup, when he saw Ouimet's name engraved there, and Walter Hagen's and Chick Evans's and old Harry Vardon's and Ted Ray's, when he felt the great shining weight of the silver in his hands, he couldn't speak. He managed to croak out a couple of modest thank-yous before his voice broke. A bagpipe was playing somewhere as the crowd swept forward to lift him on their shoulders.

CHAPTER SIX

HALFWAY THERE

P op and Kiltie decided to splurge on the way home and
reserved a first-class drawing room on the train south. Pop
bought all the New York morning papers—there were seven
then—splashed with stories about Bobby's win, and spread them
out around the compartment so they could look at the photographs as they rolled out of town. Pop kept catching Kiltie
staring at the cup in the corner, wearing "an expression similar
to that of a cat who has recently come across a pan of cream
uncovered." None of them remembered talking a great deal—
a novelty for Pop, a welcome relief for Kiltie—but for once few
words were necessary. Every once in a while Bobby took out
the gold medal he'd won in addition to the silver cup and said

in his dry, understated way: "You know, it's remarkably hard to get one of these things."

When they stepped off the train in Atlanta the town had turned out to greet him with flags and a brass band. When they cheered and Bobby saw them all filling the station he had to turn away to compose himself. His mother Clara rushed to him, the Colonel crushed him in a hug, and then Bobby shyly kissed Mary in front of all those people, and they all piled into an open-topped car and his city paraded him home. Pop Keeler couldn't remember the last time Atlanta had given anyone such a welcome.

A grand dinner at East Lake a week after his return honored his accomplishment, followed by a program of speeches and salutations: the Mayor of Atlanta expressed the city's gratitude and pride in Bobby, and the Colonel contributed an emotional salute to his son's tenacity. Bobby had always dreaded public speaking, but he capped the evening with a brief, eloquent speech summing up his deep feelings for the place that had nurtured his dreams:

"You gentlemen have said some beautiful things about me and what I've been fortunate enough to do. But one thing they all have absolutely wrong. They spoke of my honoring the Atlanta Athletic Club. No man can honor a club like this. The honor lies in belonging to it. I am prouder of being a member of this club than I could be of winning all the championships there are."

Bobby spent two months catching his breath, enjoying unhurried days out at East Lake. He played only ceremonial golf the rest of that summer, with family and friends and various dignitaries; nothing close to the pressurized ordeal of a championship and a welcome respite from it. There was a full life to be lived outside of the game, time to spend with the Colonel and his cronies at the club, plans to make with Mary. Bobby wouldn't put himself back into the heat of competition until it was nearly time to return to Harvard that fall and finish his degree.

The 1923 U.S. Amateur was played in September at Flossmoor Country Club, a tough new 7,000-yard layout just south of Chicago. Bobby arrived as the favorite, and he tied Chick Evans for the qualifying medal. Pop couldn't remember seeing him more relaxed before a championship and he knew exactly why: the monkey was off his back. Bobby spent his evenings reading the English translation of Giovanni Papini's controversial best-seller *The Life of Christ*; not exactly light bedtime fare, although at that moment he had a specific, personal interest in this partic-ular title. In anticipation of his marriage Bobby was considering a conversion to Catholicism, and reading Papini served as part of his decision-making process.

The American Amateur title would continue to elude him. In the second round Bobby ran into a red-hot golfer named Max Marston, a thirty-one-year-old veteran from Pine Valley—amateur champion of both New Jersey and Pennsylvania—who would go on to beat Ouimet and then win the title against defending champion Jess Sweetser. After Bobby built an early lead, Marston played the final nineteen holes of their thirty-six-hole match in five under par, the hottest streak of his entire career. Bobby lost the match, 2 & 1, his earliest exit from the Amateur in six appearances.

Bobby sank into melancholy that night as he reviewed his performance, convinced that matchplay would always bring him up against a golfer who played above his abilities and knocked him out of the Amateur. By now the only round in which he'd never been eliminated was the first, and in the years ahead the fear of losing that early in the championship would become something close to a phobia.

Pop countered by pointing out that Bobby had also *won* a match in every round of the Amateur except the last one. Maybe his luck would change next year. Bobby remained convinced that his game just wasn't suited to the matchplay format.

Local favorite Chick Evans had suffered an even more shocking defeat, losing to Willie Hunter in the first round. When they ran into each other the night after Bobby lost to Marston, neither man with any official golf left to play, they agreed to square off informally the next day, with the gold qualifying medal for which they'd finished in a tie at stake. There was sportsmanship in the gesture, but also a trace of spite. Bobby's loss meant Evan's 1916 record of winning the Open and Amateur in the same year still stood. As Ouimet had been before him, Bobby couldn't help but be aware of the envy Evans radiated toward any amateur who threatened to equal or surpass his accomplishments. What rankled with both Ouimet and Bobby was Evans's inability (or unwillingness) to acknowledge those natural, aggressive feelings face to face or make a joke of them in a playful way as Hagen or Sarazen would have done.

"Why of course I'll play you for the medal, Chick," said Bobby. "Looking forward to it." The next day, with the USGA squeezing their match into the Amateur schedule at Flossmoor, Bobby broke the medal-play course record with a 72 and spanked Evans by four strokes. Pop watched the contest closely and realized that Bobby paid no attention to what Evans was doing all day long; he was playing the course, not the man. "That's the way to win at matchplay," he told Bobby afterwards. "You're out there against Old Man Par and no one else."

For Bobby the insight was a revelation. He had always followed the conventional wisdom of treating each hole in a matchplay event as a separate entity, like the rounds of a prize fight. It didn't matter what score you had by the end of the match as long as you won more holes than your opponent. As a result his concentration wavered whenever holes got away from him, which in the long run negated his greatest strength: the power of his mind. Bobby worked through every stroke of a medal-play tournament the trained engineer-artist he had become—with a structure, a design, a plan of attack—and that discipline focused and freed him to work wonders when called upon to improvise. In matchplay a *savant* like Walter Hagen, who excelled at it like no one else in history, could switch his game off and on at will as fortune dictated with no emotional erosion, but Bobby needed his engine room stoked from start to finish. Playing against Old Man Par, the one opponent who never faltered, kept him on that edge.

During his round with Evans, Bobby found his mind circling back to the first time he'd ever seen Harry Vardon play at East Lake in 1913. Ted Ray's showy drives were the shots people tended to take away, but the memory of Vardon quietly collecting par after par was what won the match for the Englishman that day, conclusive evidence that his was the ideal approach for the format. What if he could sustain the mental effort demanded by championship medal golf throughout an entire match? He left Chicago determined to give it a try next year at Merion. He had his recollections of Vardon, and his growing friction with Chick Evans, to thank for that idea. And his first gold medal from a National Amateur to remember them by.

Eager to get back to Atlanta and Mary and launch the career he'd decided on, Bobby increased his class load and finished his degree in Literature at Harvard by the start of the new year, a semester ahead of schedule. He limited his golf that fall to a few charity exhibitions, including a match against Ouimet to benefit the Caddie Welfare Fund. A few weeks later Bobby and Sweetser bettered Hagen and Sarazen in a best-ball match at Winged Foot in suburban New York, raising $7,000 for the Rotary Club's crippled children fund.

After disappointing finishes at the British and U.S. Opens, Hagen had lost the 1923 PGA Championship for the second straight year to Sarazen. In addition to a dizzying tournament schedule Hagen's on-going tour with Joe Kirkwood had kept him on the road for the last two years; he now decided that for the first time in his life he was golfed out. He climbed into his chauffeured Cadillac with his socialite wife and drove down the Atlantic coastline to winter in Florida. Combined with the new mobility made possible by the automobile, Florida emerged as the perfect destination for the new phenomenon of resort living and second homes.

Here land was abundant, credit was cheap; waves of speculators moved in to corner the middle of those transactions and walked away with millions. The Florida legislature did its part, voting to outlaw state income and inheritance taxes, and legalized horse and dog racing to attract high rollers. All of it worked: the state's population doubled in less than five years. Resorts lined the pristine beaches on both coasts and golf courses figured prominently in the lifestyle; they sprang up on every corner of the state.

Like Walter Hagen, Bobby Jones had also chosen real estate as his game off the course. When he returned from Harvard in the spring of 1924 he accepted an offer from Perry Adair to join his thriving family business. Perry had given up competitive golf in 1921, and along with his older brother Forest assumed the reins of Adair Realty and Trust. They quickly became major players in the Florida frenzy, buying up huge tracts of coastal property near Sarasota. Bobby set golf aside, rolled up his sleeves and went to work on the company's lowest rung, looking after a portfolio of minor rental properties. This was a far cry from the glamorous professional beginning he'd envisioned; he was beating the pavement collecting rent checks while living at home with his parents.

Although he had collected a postgraduate degree, Bobby's education in golf was far from over. Over the winter, while visiting the nearby resort area of Augusta, Georgia, Bobby ran into the game's Grand Old Man, Walter Travis. One afternoon, in the basement of the old Augusta Country Club, Bobby cashed in an eight-year-old rain check and collected the putting lesson Travis had planned to give him on the practice green at Merion back in 1916.

In his brisk, no-nonsense manner, Travis diagnosed that Bobby's stroke had been tooled for the South's grainy Bermuda grasses; it functioned as a hit at the ball, rather than a smooth stroke through it. Travis told him that style would never hold up on bent-grass greens. He changed Bobby's set-up drastically, placing his feet closer together, heels nearly touching, with the weight shifted toward the left, which stabilized him and prevented any swaying that could throw the club off line. He adjusted his grip to the standard reverse overlapping, creating more of a hinged stroke and encouraged him to feel the sensation of tapping a tack into the back of the ball. He also suggested Bobby practice a form of breath control to neutralize the nervousness that sometimes afflicted him while standing over a putt. The importance of this encounter to his future success can hardly be calculated. Although he needed most of the year to assimilate the Old Man's instruction, from this moment forward putting would never again be the weak link in Bobby's game. By the end of his career some mentioned him in the same breath as the game's greatest clutch putter, with Travis himself.

Bobby took away something else from his day with Walter Travis. The Old Man was often described as possessing the perfect temperament for golf: he was such a congenital pessimist that whenever anything went wrong during a round it only met his underlying expectations. Bobby never tasted the full, saturnine richness of Travis's perpetually half-empty glass, but he took a sip which helped his ongoing effort to accept the vagaries of the game without heaping all the blame on himself.

The 1924 United States Open was played at Oakland Hills outside Detroit. (Only two months before, the USGA announced their decision to allow clubs with steel shafts into competition.

No pro or amateur of any note played with steel shafts yet; Bobby wouldn't even experiment with them until after his retirement.) After working all spring for the Adairs with little room for golf, Bobby arrived a week ahead of the tournament to sharpen his game and defend his championship. Walter Hagen showed up at the same time, and the two played some competitive practice rounds together. Although always professing great respect for Bobby as a person and a player, being beaten by any amateur was a blow to Hagen's professional pride, a wound Bobby would aggravate repeatedly in years to come. At Oakland Hills, coming off the course after losing a practice round to Jones, that pride prompted Hagen to make a side bet with a local big shot that he would come to regret.

The tournament began on June 5, and for the first time in USGA history qualifying rounds had taken place at various regional locations prior to the Open. The eighty men who began play at Oakland Hills had already earned their way into the field. Bobby sent a clear signal he was ready to become the first man since Johnny McDermott in 1911 to repeat as Open champion; shooting 74–73 on the first day, he held a share of the lead with Wild Bill Melhorn. Hagen played well on his old turf and landed three strokes back, in fourth. Between them, alone in third and only a stroke out of the lead, stood this year's designated unknown, prototype for the obscure, intriguing figures that the Open's format annually thrust into the spotlight.

His name was Cyril Walker, a thirty-year-old native of Manchester in England, working as a professional out of a country club in Englewood, New Jersey. Only five foot six and unhealthily wizened at 118 pounds, Walker had done nothing during a decade in the States and dozens of tournaments to suggest he belonged on the leader board with Jones, Melhorn, and Hagen. He didn't look like championship timber; he had a crooked smile, squinty eyes, snaggle teeth and big ears that struck straight out from the sides of his head. He suffered from severe nerves during competition, which deprived him of sleep, disrupted his digestion, and decelerated his pace of play to an aggravating crawl; Walker was the slowest pro in the game by a long way. But the wind was blowing hard off Lake Michigan that week at Oakland Hills, and Walker had served his apprenticeship on the links of Royal Liverpool near the Irish Sea. In spite of his size he had large hands and powerful wrists and had mastered the British art of punching the ball below the wind. He had also undertaken a rigorous exercise program prior to the Open, and felt his game had reached rare form.

Cyril Walker caught Bobby by the end of the third round with his third 74 in a row. Hagen, Melhorn, Macdonald Smith and Bobby Cruickshank all lurked within three strokes. The wind kicked up fiercely that afternoon, and picked off the contenders one by one. Hagen stayed in contention until the sixteenth, when he dumped his drive in a water hazard. Melhorn finished with the early lead, and after an erratic round Bobby came to the final hole needing a birdie to get past him. Unlike his "yellow dog" finish during the last round at Inwood, Bobby bagged his birdie and grabbed the lead from Melhorn. But this time the tenacious little Brit playing an hour behind him didn't falter down the stretch.

Pop watched from Walker's gallery, and was "hypnotized by his methodical determination. I have never seen anything like it, in sport or out. His work in that last round displayed the peculiar inevitableness of a natural phenomenon, and it impressed less by mechanics than by the invincible spirit, the grim determination, which sent that seemingly frail human machine along hole after hole." Throwing down the round of his life, Walker had two strokes in hand over Bobby by the time he reached the last three holes, and confronted the dire challenge of knowing exactly the score he had to beat. Pop became obsessed with the idea that as Walker stood on each successive tee he seemed to be saying to himself: "This one golf hole is the single problem of my career. It is the problem of my existence. There never has been any other problem. There never will be any other problem. I was created, developed, trained, drilled, to play this one hole in par. It shall be done."

Cyril Walker played those last three holes in one under par and won the Open like a man whose hour had come. "Any man who can shoot that last nine in par today deserves to be champion," Bobby told Pop. "My hat's off to Cyril Walker."

Offering Walker nothing but compliments, Bobby demonstrated that a sportsman treats defeat and victory with the same good grace. After ending up in fourth place, Walter Hagen's mood was nowhere near as sanguine; he forked over a much larger amount than Walker had won, in cash, to that unidentified bookie from Oakland Hills. Their bet: that Hagen would finish ahead of Bobby Jones.

Bobby rushed home from Detroit and on June 17 he married Mary Rice Malone. At some point the Jones family patriarch, Bobby's formidable old grandfather R.T., had caught wind of Bobby's flirtation with Catholicism, and put his foot down. Under no circumstances would a Jones from Canton hold truck with the Church of Rome. There's no record of exactly how this went down inside the family circle, but in the end Bobby declined to convert to Mary's faith.

The wedding took place in the evening under a full moon on the lawn of the Malones' family home, and not at Atlanta's Catholic Church of the Sacred Heart, although one of their senior priests conducted the ceremony. Bobby's celebrity attracted the interest of all the local and regional society pages, every one of whom remarked on the warm, romantic mood and the couple's obvious devotion to each other. Hundreds attended, spread out across the broad moonlit lawn, the trees aglow from a thousand glittering lights, some in the shape of shamrocks symbolizing the Malones' heritage and Bobby's St. Patrick's Day birthday. A full orchestra played throughout the preamble to the ceremony, then began the traditional Wedding March as Mary walked down the flower-strewn aisle.

A nervous Pop Keeler stood in the audience, his attention wandering fearfully: "Queer what vagrant thoughts get in your mind at times. I catch myself thinking it is a well-behaved gallery, but packed awfully close. Will the players have room to swing!" He spots his little mock antagonist Kiltie Maiden standing on tiptoe near the back of the audience, struggling to see the couple as Mary reaches Bobby at the altar; he swears the stoic little Scot looks closer to tears than most of the dowagers around them. Then Pop finds his own glasses fogging up.

After five years of courtship, Bobby and Mary were at last husband and wife. As Pop makes his way toward them in an endless reception line he has never sounded more like Falstaff, ill at ease with his princely companion's new worldly status, agonizing over what he's going to say to him. "Old friends always say something supremely foolish at important junctures." When Pop finally got to them all that came out is: "Hello, Bobby."

"Say, O.B.," said Bobby, "I found your belt in my trunk when I was unpacking."

Pop beamed at them both: "And looking from Bobby to Mary standing there together—really together, under the flowers—I wished I knew words delicate and happy and graceful enough to say something fitting of the culmination of this charming romance. There is something beautifully old-fashioned and tender about it. It is not a matter for words, perhaps, but rather for the thoughts and hopes and emotions that are never spoken but lie deep in the heart. God bless them both!"

The once sickly infant born into a middle-class Atlanta home, deep inside the borders of a dispirited, reconstructing culture, had grown up to become the South's first twentieth-century hero. A modest young champion whose feats were about to transcend any claims of regionalism and astonish and inspire the world, who by virtue of his gifts would become a friend to princes, presidents, and kings. And, every bit as remarkable, his destiny had been foretold by one lonely, limping prophet: Oscar Bane Keeler had prophesied all this years before when Bobby was just a boy. There's a minor note of melancholy to Pop's soaring spirits as he hovered on the edge of the crowd that night on the Malones' broad green lawn. Now Pop would have to share him with Mary and the multitudes.

Bobby was invited to meet his first president, Calvin Coolidge, at the star-studded opening of the Congressional Country Club in Bethesda, Maryland, one of his few other golf excursions that summer.

When Warren Harding had died unexpectedly in 1923, Vice-President Calvin Coolidge was sworn in at 2:47 A.M. in his sitting room at home in Plymouth Notch, Vermont.

Although golf had become an established ritual among politicians and captains of industry, Cal couldn't bring himself to embrace it. He played left-handed, poorly and reluctantly. To dedicate the number of daylight hours required for a full round ran contrary to his plain Yankee nature; that was time for making hay, exactly what he was doing on his father's farm the day of his inauguration.

As the season wound down the third annual Walker Cup matches were played once again on Long Island, this time at Walter Travis's masterpiece, the Garden City Golf Club. The United States won the cup for the third time in a row, 9–3, and this served as a final tune-up for the National Amateur Championship, where thoughts of camaraderie would be quickly set aside. With travel costs proving too onerous for amateurs on both sides of the Atlantic, it was agreed that from this point forward they would play for the Walker Cup on a biannual basis, instead of every year.

From Garden City Bobby, Pop and caddie Luke Ross traveled

to Philadelphia and suburban Merion. Instead of the downtown Bellevue-Stratford they checked into the Greenhill Farms Hotel in Overbrook, much closer and more convenient to the course. When it rained heavily during practice rounds, Bobby told Ross to stop polishing his irons, a tactic he would employ in rough weather for years to come; his engineer's training told him that letting a light coat of rust form on the forged steel encouraged friction, increased spin, and prevented the ball from slipping off the club's wet faces.

Dozens of articles and magazine profiles couldn't resist contrasting the brash boy from Dixie who'd charmed them all so thoroughly in 1916 with the sleek, confident young conqueror he'd become. The course at Merion had matured over those years as well, a fitting test for the game's improving amateur field: longer, tougher and featuring over a hundred new bunkers. Chick Evans, the returning champion from 1916, would lose in this year's first round and in a classic soundbite afterwards said: "The course isn't so tough, unless those 'white faces' get you." As if they weren't part of the course. They *had* gotten Evans, and the name he applied has stuck to those bunkers ever since. This was Bobby's seventh Amateur, and armed with his recently completed education in classic literature he recognized a perfect opportunity to dramatically complete his journey. Pop agreed: winning the Amateur at Merion, where Bobby's career had begun, would bring a satisfying wholeness to Pop's favorite story.

Bobby had also taken to heart the lessons he'd absorbed the year before in Chicago about Old Man Par; he vowed to stay focused on playing the scorecard, not his human opponent. Analyzing his own record, Bobby had determined that if he'd followed this disciplined strategy he would have already won at least one Amateur and a second Open. If anybody he went up against could match or beat par in a game with more success than Bobby did they deserved to win. But theory wasn't practice, and this new philosophy would be quickly put to the test.

Bobby finished second in qualifying, two strokes behind Clarke "Ducky" Corcoran, a streaky veteran who broke the course record his first time around Merion with a 67. Knowing that in every Amateur he'd lost to some beneficiary of random chance who'd played brilliantly, Bobby was not surprised to look up after an easy first-round victory and find Ducky Corcoran waiting for him. This made him more determined to stick to his new strategy, and no one could argue it wasn't working when Bobby went four up on the twelfth hole of their afternoon round. At the thirteenth, a short par-three, Bobby airmailed a dart at the flag and stopped four feet shy; the match poised to end right there, Corcoran answered with a pitch only six feet away. Both made their birdies and the match moved to the fourteenth, with Bobby up dormie five.

Pop Keeler felt so confident of the outcome at that point he wandered off to watch some other matches—and half an hour later was shocked to hear that Bobby and Corcoran were still playing. Corcoran had won both the fourteenth and the fifteenth; they now stood dormie three. The sixteenth is an extraordinary hole, a long, serpentine par-four, its fairway navigating a sinuous curve around the course's old marble quarry. Beating Old Man Par on sixteen demands a long accurate drive just short of the quarry, and then asks for a nerve-racking iron that must carry the yawning rock pit to an elevated green or find disaster. Pop scuttled back to the quarry just in time to see the two men hit their approaches; Corcoran went first and found the front of the green. The pressure shifted to Bobby. He rifled a four-iron that bracketed the other side of the flagstick; both men lagged close, made their pars, and Bobby finally bade Corcoran adieu.

The next day it looked like Bobby might fall victim to another golfer gone wild. After playing each other dead even through the morning, Bobby's third-round opponent Rudy Knepper began the afternoon with three straight birdies. Bobby never faltered, kept his powder dry and fired away at the scorecard.

Under mounting pressure Knepper collapsed and Bobby won out handily, 6 & 4. So Pop was shocked when he returned to their hotel room that night to find Bobby sitting on his bed, distraught and near tears. The draw had conspired to send Bobby into the next day's semi-finals against his greatest friend in the game, Francis Ouimet.

"I don't want to play Francis," said Bobby. "I'm going well and his game's all shot to pieces—"

"Then you should be able to beat him—"

"Damn it, I don't want to beat him."

Pop realized he was serious and chose his words carefully. "Well, do you want to win an Amateur championship?"

He did. He just couldn't think of climbing over Ouimet to get there.

"And how's your plan coming along, shooting at par and letting the other fellas take care of themselves—"

"It's working just fine," said Bobby impatiently. "Keep shooting pars at them and they'll all crack, sooner or later."

"All right," said Pop. "When you go out there on the first tee tomorrow, you're not playing Francis Ouimet. You're playing the card of the Merion Cricket Club's East Course. And so is Francis. And whoever plays it closest goes into the finals on Saturday."

Less than twenty hours later, the two men walked off the eighth green—their twenty-sixth hole of a thirty-six-hole match—with their arms around each other's shoulders. Ouimet was smiling happily and Pop thought Bobby "looked like a man who had just been notified his bank balance was overdrawn." Bobby had played the scorecard and showed it no mercy. Ouimet had been systematically destroyed, 11 & 10. So completely did Bobby dominate the match that when he looked upset after losing the eighteenth with a double bogey, the last of only two holes Ouimet won all day, Francis smiled gently at his young friend and said, "Bobby, you could afford to lose that one."

"What Bobby did to me was criminal," said Ouimet to Keeler afterwards, good-natured as ever. He also endorsed Bobby's disciplined new approach to matchplay—which Bobby had shared before they started, to show there were no hard feelings—and predicted there would be no stopping him in medal or matchplay from then on.

One last man had something to say about the 1924 National Amateur. Making his second appearance, George Von Elm meant as much to the game of golf on the West Coast as Bobby did in the South. Born and raised in Salt Lake City, he'd been a star high-school athlete in three different sports, and won Utah's Amateur Championship at fifteen. After wearing out local competition, George had recently relocated to the sun-drenched playgrounds of Hollywood. The twenty-three-year-old Von Elm had dispatched defending champ Max Marston in the semifinals, becoming the first golfer representing California, or anywhere west of the Rockies, to make it this deep into the Big Show.

It was as if Central Casting had supplied the perfect man for the role of the Formidable Opponent; sun-bleached blond, tanned Teutonically fit, impeccably dressed, formal to the point of *hauteur* in manner and bearing. Pop Keeler later said of Von Elm that as he swaggered down a fairway you could practically hear his saber rattling. Von Elm and Bobby, diametric opposites in style and temperament, would over the next few years become bitter rivals, equaling Bobby's simmering differences with Chick Evans. But when they met in the finals of the '24 Amateur it was the first time they'd ever played each other. Von Elm had a bone-crushing handshake and a habit of staring down opponents on the first tee, like a boxer's pre-fight psych-out. Neither cut any mustard with Jones. Pop observed that he had never seen Bobby look more cool, confident or businesslike at the start of a match; the Californian's bristling arrogance brought that out in him. Once they teed off he paid no attention to Von Elm, which seemed to bother him more than anything else Bobby did that day.

Von Elm won the first hole, the only time Bobby had trailed in a match since the first round. It would also be the last. By the turn Bobby was two up, and he stretched it to four by inter-mission. After a light lunch Bobby hammered Old Man Par, and Von Elm absorbed a beating by proxy; Jones won five of the next nine holes. On the tenth green Bobby was about to putt out after George had finished when Von Elm stopped him.

"Don't putt that one, Bobby. I've had enough."

They shook hands. The final score was 9 & 8, and seemed even worse. Bobby had collected the second half of the American double championship that only Ouimet, Evans, and Travers had won before him. The circle had been rounded, back at Merion where he'd rocketed into the country's consciousness as an unknown boy wonder. This fairy-tale quality of Bobby's career was something Pop didn't even have to underline, and it contributed to his conviction that Bobby's future was all in the hands of destiny. Hard to argue with, given what would follow, but from a practical standpoint Bobby had won at Merion by sticking to his strategy of playing against par and ignoring his opponent. Not only had it reduced his stress, it didn't even require him to play his best golf; focusing on the scorecard kept him from feeling obliged to produce something heroic on every shot.

As they handed him the Havermeyer Trophy he'd sought so fervently for the last eight years, Bobby experienced a curious pang of guilt. "I don't really feel like I did anything," he told Pop.

"No fireworks, no blood and guts, no abject suffering?"

"That's right."

"Bobby, you might want to keep that to yourself," said Pop.

People would still play over their heads against him on a regular basis, no matter the format. He tended to bring out the best in opponents and always would. But it had come to him at last that all he had to do to win the damned thing, any tournament against any man in the world, was go out there and play like Bobby Jones.

CHAPTER SEVEN

THE BATTLE OF
THE CENTURY

Atlanta turned out at the Brookwood train station, and the
crowd that welcomed Bobby home from Philadelphia was
even larger than after his Open victory. Pop reported that he
was "blushing, speechless and inexpressibly happy." They threw
another big party at East Lake, giving speeches and reading
telegrams which poured in from all over the world. When dinner
was done they dimmed the lights, lowered a screen, and showed
a movie someone had found: rare footage of Bobby and Alexa
Stirling playing at East Lake as youngsters, followed by footage
of Bobby winning at Merion. All wide shots and silent, not
tight enough to convey the action or excitement, but a thrilling
novelty. Just as the Open cup had the previous year, the

Havermeyer Trophy went on display in East Lake's lobby, with Bobby's name newly engraved at the top, the last of twenty-eight carved on the cup itself before they added a ring around the base to accommodate the future. Neither of American golf's two greatest prizes had ever traveled south of the Mason-Dixon Line before.

Bobby spent the first few months of 1925 in Sarasota, Florida, where Adair Realty and Trust had opened an office to handle its real-estate holdings—over two thousand acres of land. The Adair development was called Whitfield Estates, one of the first in the state to anchor around a golf course: Whitfield Estates Country Club. Perry hired Donald Ross to design the course, construction began in 1925, and he named Bobby as sales manager for the adjoining lots. So Bobby went to work selling lots and homes to customers, but Perry soon realized that his friend's greatest value was out on the golf course, so that's where he spent his afternoons, wooing potential buyers.

The Florida land boom had reached its peak; the state had experienced a frigid winter, which kept vacationers away. So many new houses had gone up so fast that demand for building materials overwhelmed the railways, which slammed the brakes on construction at new developments. When prices stopped ramping up, the speculators who'd piled onto the pyramid late in the game found themselves stranded and strapped for cash. The result was rampaging inflation, which sent the cost of living through the roof; many of the middle class who had migrated to Florida in pursuit of affordable housing suddenly discovered they couldn't afford to stay. Newspapers picked up the theme and ran with it, warning buyers to keep their distance. The bad winter of '25 was followed by a blistering hot summer and then disaster: an early-fall hurricane that killed four hundred, left nearly twenty thousand families homeless and caused $80 million worth of damage. This kicked the crashing land market and the state itself into severe depression. Florida's collapse served up a chilling foreshadow of what was in store for the rest of America just four years down the road.

Bobby spent two winters as sales manager of Whitfield Estates. Although his own writing about the experience remains circumspect, it was clear to him from the beginning that he was desperately ill-suited to the life of a salesman. While Hagen was happily bamboozling buyers at nearby Pasadena—where he worked as resident pro for four months a year, selling county-club memberships and receiving land in exchange for playing exhibitions that attracted potential buyers—and chuckling all the way to the bank, Bobby couldn't summon up the forced gaiety and hand-holding that comprise so large a part of every real estate transaction. He didn't find fault with the industry, or pass judgment on it; Bobby wasn't a prig, he just didn't have the sales gene in him. "I had to sell a little piece of myself with every sale," he wrote later.

There were other privations. He was newly married and away from his bride, who provided the emotional bedrock on which his increasingly demanding life would center. Mary was in the late stages of expecting their first child in April, and stayed home in Atlanta while Bobby went south. He returned briefly when she gave birth to Clara Malone Jones. Beginning a family raised new anxieties about making a living; the fact he felt miscast in real estate did nothing to allay them.

The best thing that happened to Bobby during his seasons in Sarasota was his decision to room with Tommy Armour. The suave young Scotsman and war hero had immigrated to the States in 1921, hoping to start a career in business. Walter Hagen introduced Armour into the upscale golfing universe of Westchester County where, short on cash but with faultless British manners more useful than a résumé, he landed a job as the social secretary at the Westchester-Biltmore Club in suburban

Rye. The Westchester-Biltmore was America's first gargantuan golf complex, built in 1922 with two golf courses, a polo field, a race track, and twenty tennis courts at a cost of $5 million. As the cash-rich early twenties picked up momentum, many resorts built to this epic scale would follow. While working at Westchester, Tommy was introduced by Bobby Jones to Perry Adair; Adair soon afterwards offered Armour the job as resident professional at Whitfield Estates. Tommy jumped at the chance and announced he was turning pro. The loss of his eye during the war had remarkably little effect on his golf game; he often wore a black patch instead of his glass replacement, which contributed to his piratical look. He'd gone into the army a private and come out a major, with a reputation as the fastest gunner in the entire Tank Corps. Rangy and outsized, he was a larger-than-life figure in the carousing Hagen mold; his capacity for liquor was even more legendary and factually based. Whereas the Haig often watered down drinks to polish his reputation as a boozer, Armour was hardcore; his glass was never half empty. It also, according to eyewitnesses, never diminished him mentally or physically. Armour's strength was legendary, leaving alone the fact that he'd killed a German officer with his bare hands after both their tanks had been reduced to scrap metal. Those hands were so powerful he could grip a billiard cue by the tip with his arm extended by only his thumb and forefinger and hold it straight up in the air. Try that after a half dozen cocktails sometime.

Armour's move to Florida gave him a chance to play its informal pro winter circuit, where he fell in with Hagen and the other free-spirited scoundrels who gravitated around him off the course. Armour not only matched or beat Hagen drink for drink, he could also hold his own with him in a lying contest; the antithesis of the stoic Scot, Armour loved to gab and was a dazzling raconteur. At first glance Hagen didn't seem the type of alpha male to tolerate the presence of another equally

outlandish character, but the two developed a mutual appreciation without either feeling threatened. The fact they were
starting to make a decent living on the golf course had a lot to
do with their tolerance. Realizing they needed each other to
draw spectators to their exhibitions went a long way toward
keeping the peace in the professional ranks; these low-key tournaments in Florida were the seeds of what would eventually
become the PGA tour.

That largesse didn't always extend so generously to Bobby
Jones, although the pros all professed to like him personally,
and he never had any trouble fitting into their towel-snapping
locker-room culture as one of the boys. Even though Bobby
never cashed a check from a victory, and his winning never
reduced the amount anyone received—first-place money simply
went to whichever pro finished second—whenever an amateur
won a tournament the pros viewed it as a blow to their pride.
Winning the biggest championships had huge economic reper-
cussions; a victory in either Open boosted a pro's exhibition fee
by hundreds of percent, and no one profited more from that
than Hagen. As the decade progressed, and Bobby's reputation
continued to grow, Hagen increasingly became the spokesman
for the anti-Jones point of view.

The next chance the pros had to beat their amateur came in the
1925 Open at the Worcester Country Club outside Boston. Nearly
450 players from around the country attempted to qualify; Bobby
traveled to Long Island and worked his rounds in during a business trip with Perry Adair. He played his way into the Open on
one of the country's most unusual new courses, the Lido, recently
built as part of a real-estate development on the island's marshy
south shore by the Methuselah of American golf, Charles Blair
McDonald, at an unheard-of cost of $800,000.

Bobby shot two brilliant rounds at the Lido, the second a 70
in a blinding rainstorm; he considered it one of the best rounds

of his life. Ouimet qualified here as well, as did Hagen; Bobby finished four strokes ahead of him, adding fuel to their pro–am rivalry. Mindful of box office appeal, the USGA paired the two titans together at Worcester during a practice round—where they charged admission for the first time, and lucky patrons who paid a buck witnessed a new course-record 66 by Bobby and the first hole-in-one of Hagen's career—and again on the first day of the Open.

The USGA had set up the course for maximum difficulty, par had been lowered two strokes to 70, and at 7,100 yards it was the longest parkland layout most had ever faced. Ouimet knew the course well, but business and family obligations had recently limited his competitive golf, so he astonished everyone when he seized the lead with a first-round 70; Boston papers had a field day. Bobby got his bad round out of the way early, a 77 that he attributed to the desertion of his irons. It was his action between shots on the eleventh hole that morning that would come back to haunt him.

Bobby's approach to the elevated green fell short, settling in deep grass on a steep embankment. As he took his stance to play a short pitch up to the flag, his clubhead grazed the grass and to his eye caused his ball to move a fraction of an inch. No one else saw it happen, but after playing the shot he informed his partner Hagen and the USGA official covering their match that he was calling a penalty stroke on himself. Hagen was dumbfounded and tried to talk Bobby out of it before he spoke to the official, but Bobby insisted he had broken Rule 18—moving a ball at rest after address—and had to pay the price. He finished his round, and then argued again with USGA officials afterwards who tried to dissuade him from assessing himself the penalty, which wouldn't be written in stone until he signed and turned in his scorecard. Bobby remained convinced he had caused the ball to move, end of story. His 76 turned into a 77. Hagen walked away shaking his head; although he played by

the rules and was never accused of bending them, given an identical dilemma, it's safe to say he wouldn't have felt the same
ethical compulsion to confess to an unwitnessed crime.

Many writers later trumpeted this act of contrition as a wonder
of sportsmanship, praise which made Bobby furious. Rules were
rules and he was astonished that anyone who knew the first
thing about the game would expect him to do anything less. His
widely reported quote to Pop afterwards: "You'd as well praise
me for not breaking into banks." Pop felt even more strongly
about it, and told him so. "If it turned out that one stroke stood
between Bobby and the championship, I would be prouder of
him than if he had won." Given the game's Presbyterian predilec-
tion for punishing anyone who flirted with fate, Pop would soon
be given a chance to test the limits of his pride.

Bobby's first round left him in thirty-sixth place, dead and
buried according to one Boston front page, which led its early
edition with this banner: JONES OUT OF NATIONAL OPEN. Whoever
slugged that headline underestimated the effects of self-disgust
on Bobby's game; he shot his way back into contention during
the afternoon with a 70, climbing all the way back into a tie
for tenth, six strokes behind this year's surprise leader, a thirty-
five-year-old transplanted Scotsman named Willie MacFarlane.

MacFarlane was an even more unlikely figure than Bobby
Cruickshank or Cyril Walker, a thoughtful, slender, bookish
professional from Oak Ridge Country Club in Tuckahoe, New
York. He had a reputation for shooting unbelievable rounds
among the Westchester County cognoscenti, setting scoring
records at many tough courses in the area, including an eye-
popping 61 on his home track. Content to quietly ply his trade
from behind the counter of his pro shop, Willie had never won
a tournament in the United States and had played in only one
other Open, Inverness in 1920, where he finished in an eighth-
place tie with another debutant, Bobby Jones. Reporters turned
up the fact that McFarlane had recorded only thirteen scores in

the nine months prior to qualifying. Despite the lay-off—or maybe because of it—Willie MacFarlane turned in one of his genius rounds that afternoon at Worcester, a 67, sparked by an astonishing 31 on the back nine. He had just shot the lowest single round ever recorded in U.S. Open history. (The average score that day was 78.) He ended up tied with Leo Diegel for the lead, and found himself exposed to the hot glare of the public spotlight. Ouimet was tied with two others in second.

More sweltering heat and high humidity greeted the sixty-six golfers who made the cut for Saturday's final two rounds; these were the hottest June days on record in Boston. Before the advent of air-conditioning, heatwaves presented the gravest health hazards; hundreds had already died throughout New England. Growing up in the South's semi-tropical summers gave Bobby a big advantage in these conditions; while others wilted, the heat never seemed to bother him. Although Bobby had never broken 70 in an Open, he matched that number, his personal best, for the second straight time in the morning's third round and moved into a tie for fourth. Willie MacFarlane appeared to be on his way back down to earth after carding a 40 on the front, but he hit his stride on the way in again with a 32 and maintained his lead by a single stroke over a handsome young club pro from White Plains, New York, named Johnny Farrell. Ouimet held his ground in third place with a 73, a stroke ahead of Bobby.

This set up the most wide-open finish in tournament history. Eight men had a chance to win the Open that afternoon. Leo Diegel went out in 34, found himself in the driver's seat, began twitching again and shot himself out of contention with a dreadful 8 at eighteen. He looked so debilitated over the ball that Bernard Darwin began using his name as a verb: to natter nervously over any task became "to diegel." Hagen and Sarazen both made late runs; Sarazen fell short with a par at eighteen when he needed birdie. A par would have secured the lead for Hagen, but his lust for birdie led to a bogey five, and he finished tied for fifth with Sarazen, just ahead of old Boston warhorse Mike "the King" Brady. Farrell blew up with a 78, but his par at eighteen gave him the clubhouse lead. Ouimet reached sixteen a short while later needing only three pars to jump ahead of Farrell; his bid for a second Open win in his home state fell one stroke short, but he tied Farrell for the lead.

Bobby played solidly down the stretch against Old Man Par; his pairing with Tommy Armour seemed to steady him. He matched the best final-round score turned in by any of the contenders, 74, and with a par at eighteen he came in a stroke ahead of Ouimet and Farrell. Only one man who could catch him was still on the course. Playing half an hour behind Bobby, MacFarlane succumbed to final-round nerves; as he made the turn he was barely hanging onto his lead. He then played his worst back nine of the week and needed a par at eighteen to catch Bobby.

MacFarlane reached it in two, 40 feet from the cup. His long lag stopped 5 feet short and settled in a divot mark; this was before players could lift and replace balls on the green. He was forced to putt with a mid-iron to get the ball rolling, but it dropped. The next day Bobby and MacFarlane would play off for the U.S. Open title. One can always look back on a dozen misbegotten shots over the course of four rounds that could have changed the outcome of a championship, but that playing field tends to level off over time. An act of character, not fate, had made the difference here. Just as Pop had predicted, the penalty stroke Bobby had called on himself during his first round had cost him sole possession of first place in the 1925 Open.

Sunday's play-off appeared to be a complete mismatch: Bobby was not only over a decade younger but infinitely more seasoned in high-stakes tournaments. He looked strong and solid next to the bespectacled Scotsman. Bobby had drawn his usual adoring galleries and had his team at his side: Pop, Kiltie, Ross. MacFarlane's wife and ten-year-old daughter were his only support in the crowd when the play-off began, although a number of pros reminded him of his sacred duty to hold off the amateur. MacFarlane's caddie was a man he'd only just met, a friend of a friend from the area named Bill Savage. Turning down MacFarlane's original offer of $10 a round, Savage had taken pity on the unimposing Scot, suggesting light-heartedly that he only get paid if Willie won the Open, in which case they would split the purse down the middle. At least he had a highly motivated caddie.

By now experts should have realized that MacFarlane had a previously undetected gift for upsetting expectations. Sunday morning's eighteen-hole play-off ended in another tie. Both men shot 75, and Bobby felt fortunate to still be in it. The heat intensified through the day, and it was ninety degrees when they teed off at 11:00 that morning. Already down a stroke, after duffing his approach on fourteen, Bobby slam-dunked a miraculous 30-yard pitch from the rough for a birdie to even the score. MacFarlane took another lead at sixteen; Bobby birdied seventeen to get back to even. Then a gift: MacFarlane missed an easy 5-footer for birdie at eighteen that would have won it outright. Bobby had to sink a side-winding 5-footer for par to send them into a second overtime.

For the first time an Open play-off had been extended to thirty-six holes. As they broke for lunch the mercury crawled to over 100 degrees in the shade. When Bobby mentioned this to MacFarlane on the first tee that afternoon he said cheerfully, "Thank goodness we don't have to play in the shade." The odds all favored Bobby now. The sauna-like heat and accumulated strain would wear the older MacFarlane out. That missed putt for the win at eighteen was bound to rattle around in his head and knock something loose. On the front nine that afternoon those predictions looked accurate: Bobby ignored MacFarlane and matched Old Man Par with a 35. MacFarlane slowly faded to 39; Bobby had a four-stroke lead with nine to play. Watching from the gallery, Ouimet told Pop as they made the turn that he "would not give MacFarlane a nickel for his chances." They should have checked the scorecards and remembered how MacFarlane had been torching the back nine at Worcester all week. He birdied the par-three tenth. After two halved pars, at thirteen Willie sank a 20-footer for another birdie, while Bobby, pressing now, three-putted for bogey. His lead had shrunk to a single stroke. At the par-five fifteenth, Bobby tried to push his advantage in length off the tee and break MacFarlane's back with a birdie; he went for the green in two and got buried in a greenside bunker. Playing conservatively, MacFarlane reached the green in regulation and collected an easy par. Bobby's bid for par came up short and they were dead even with three to play. Now Bobby appeared drained; Pop thought MacFarlane looked fresh as a daisy.

Both men parred sixteen. After their drives, as Bobby waited for MacFarlane to play his approach from the other side of the fairway on seventeen, he walked over to Pop. "This thing's getting funny," he said, lighting up a smoke. "Still tied after a hundred and six holes."

"Looks like a third play-off," said Pop.

Bobby's face turned grim. "There won't be another play-off. I'll settle it now one way or another."

They halved seventeen and came to the home hole tied. Three hundred and thirty-five yards, uphill, to a small green cut into the ascending slope like a shelf. The hole was set four steps from the front edge, fiercely protected by a long, deep bunker that ran across the front. Bobby outdrove MacFarlane by 20 yards. MacFarlane played his approach long and safe to avoid the bunker, leaving himself a 40-foot downhill putt to the flag. Good as his word, Bobby tried to end the ordeal by sticking his short pitch a foot beyond the front edge and letting it trickle close to the hole.

The ball landed four inches short of his target, but instead of rolling forward sucked slowly, painfully, back off the green, down the slope and into the bunker. His blast out of the sand left him a 10-foot putt for par. Completing his role as tortoise to Bobby's hare, MacFarlane coaxed a perfect lag to within inches and collected his four. Bobby needed to sink his putt to force a third play-off. To nearly everyone's relief, he missed.

MacFarlane had defended his profession's honor and beaten Bobby to win history's longest Open. He was also the first Scotsman to win a U.S. Open since Alec Smith in 1910. Willie cashed his winner's check, and as promised paid half of it to Bill Savage, in crisp fifty-dollar bills. Only one more of his countrymen would win a U.S. Open in the next eighty years; American domination of the old Scottish game was now nearly complete.

Walter Hagen declined to defend his British Open title in 1925, but fellow American pro Jim Barnes went over alone and won his fourth major. Aside from two brief stretches during the next forty years, before and just after World War II when American pros gave up traveling overseas, from this point forward they would dominate the British Open.

Bobby hadn't captured either of the game's oldest championships, but they were coming back into his thoughts. The day after his disappointment at Worcester, he and Pop stopped off for a day in New York. Over dinner they discussed a return to Britain. Bobby's inglorious withdrawal from the Open at St. Andrews in 1921 remained the sole blemish on his sporting escutcheon. With time and maturity under his belt, Bobby was determined to erase that first impression from the British public's mind. The Walker Cup would be played at St. Andrews in the summer of 1926, and the USGA paid travel expenses, still a vital consideration for Bobby. The British Open and Amateur were both scheduled within weeks of the Walker, so being named to the team would allow him to play in all three. Although there was little doubt Bobby would be invited onto the Walker Cup team, a good showing at the 1925 U.S. Amateur would guarantee it.

The Amateur returned that September to Oakmont. A change in format had been announced: only sixteen men would make it through qualifying, and all ensuing matches would be played over thirty-six holes. Before Bobby made the trip to Pittsburgh, he made a decision closer to home that affected that year's championship even more directly: he brought along Watts Gunn.

Since Bobby's arrival at the top of the game, the golf hothouse of East Lake Country Club had produced another young wonder. Twenty-year-old Gunn—one of the greatest names in sport's history—was a student at Georgia Tech, a Georgia Amateur champion in 1923, and an unabashed admirer of Bobby Jones, the local legend who had first inspired him to play. Although only three years his junior, when in Bobby's company Gunn looked and acted like a high-school kid. Without condescension, Bobby referred to him as his protégé and Watts felt flattered by it.

When he found out they'd been awarded the Amateur, Oakmont's patriarch Bill Fownes decided that his pet project, already the hardest course in the country, needed toughening up. He sprinkled in bunkers like birdseed, shipping in train cars full of sand. The obstacle-course layout, combined with the new format, eliminated a boatload of strong players from the field who contended for the final sixteen: five former Amateur champs, including Ouimet, failed to qualify. Bobby made the cut, and to everyone's surprise, none greater than his own, so did Watts Gunn, with the fifth best score in the field. From that point forward the Amateur title required only four wins, each played over the thirty-six-hole length that Bobby favored. The penal ordeal of Oakmont actually increased his advantage: nobody else seemed up to it. Bobby walked through his first three matches without being tested; in the semi-finals he beat George Von Elm for the second year in a row. Imagine his surprise when he looked up and realized that in the finals he'd be going up against none other than little Watts Gunn.

Something wild had gotten into Gunn. Too unworldly to fully comprehend what he was up against, there was something kind of mechanical and uncomplicated about his approach that just clicked at Oakmont. Pop watched him at work and said "there didn't appear to be anything on his mind but his hair."

Gunn had been three down after eleven holes in his first-round match against Pennsylvania's champion Vincent Bradford; he had no idea how he'd done it afterwards, but he won the next fifteen holes in a row and beat Bradford 12 & 10. A streak like that had never been produced in an Amateur before or since. He faced former champ Jess Sweetser in the second round during a savage rainstorm and gave him the worst beating of his life; Gunn won seventeen holes, lost only two, and halved twelve. Sweetser was gone before he knew what hit him, 11 & 10. Afterwards Bobby asked Gunn about the match with Sweetser and he couldn't remember any of it in the proper order, holes all jumbled together. When Pop Keeler asked him how he felt after the match, Gunn looked at him with a dreamy faraway cast in his eye and said: "Gee, I'm awful hungry. I'm so hungry my pants are about to fall off."

In his semi-final match against Dick Jones from New York, Gunn found himself up by only a hole at the lunch break. Based on his experience to date this wasn't how big-time matches were supposed to go. He pulled himself together that afternoon and dispatched Jones of New York, 5 & 4. First to greet him coming off the green was Jones of Atlanta, whom he now had to face in the finals of the 1925 Amateur.

Bobby made it clear that his protégé would get no special favors. Much as it upset him personally to beat a friend, he had found a way to do it against Ouimet at Merion and would follow the same prescription here; his game was played against numbers on the scorecard, not his endearingly goofy sidekick.

About an hour after their match was set, Watts ran up to Bobby and Pop, suddenly remembering that he should cable Judge Gunn in Macon that he'd made the finals.

"Don't worry," said Bobby. "He knew it long before you did."

After dinner that night, Bobby ran into Gunn in the hotel, trying to sneak out for a date he'd made with a girl who'd flirted with him that day in his gallery. "I'm just going out for a bite," he said. "I'll be right back."

"Oh no you won't," said Bobby. "I'm going to lick hell out of you tomorrow and I don't want any excuses when I do."

By setting up an all-East Lake final, Gunn made possible another record for the Amateur that has never been equaled: two members from the same club facing each other for the Havermeyer Trophy. Till that point in its history, no two contestants from the same *city* had ever reached the finals. Atlanta newspapers fell into a lather at the prospect; the story was splashed across their front pages, sports pages and human-interest pages. Church bells rang. Civic pride hit a high-water mark; if any athlete could resuscitate the self-respect of an entire city, Bobby was the man. He especially looked the part standing next to his youthful opponent. Gunn's childlike nature made it easy to forget that Bobby was only twenty-three; in comparison he seemed like the Ancient Mariner.

It would be dramatically pleasing to report that Gunn continued his inspirational run and gave his mentor the match of his life, and for the first eleven holes he did exactly that; Bobby was one under par, and one down to Gunn. Maybe Watts didn't know what he was doing, but there's no space on the scorecard for state of mind; Pop described his play as "strangely able" and worried that he might never wake up. The match turned on the same hole at Oakmont where the megaphone incident had derailed Bobby's first trip to the finals in 1919; the long par-five "Ghost Hole." Gunn had reached the green in regulation and looked certain to collect a par. Bobby was lying three in a calamitous Oakmont bunker to the right of the green. Bobby had an intuitive suspicion that, if he couldn't match Gunn for par here, the kid might sprint away on a hot streak and disappear in a cloud of dust. He splashed his shot to within 10 feet and drained the par-saving putt. Gunn's putt for birdie hung on the lip and they halved the hole. Gunn looked perplexed. Momentum swung hard in Bobby's direction; he evened the match on the next hole and played the next six in two under par to carry a four-hole lead into the lunch break. From there the outcome was not in doubt; Gunn never gave up, but the meter on his beginner's luck had run out. He lasted until the eleventh hole that afternoon, where Bobby collected his second consecutive Amateur championship 8 & 7, then put his arm around his young friend and consoled him all the way back to the clubhouse. But Gunn didn't need much consoling; he was happy as a clam in mud just to be there.

An Atlanta crowd lifted both favorite sons onto their shoulders when they returned home the next day, and East Lake threw another celebratory dinner. Bobby generously included Gunn in every speech and interview he gave, allowing the younger man to feel as if he'd won a share of the championship. Bobby had successfully defended an Amateur title for the first time since Jerry Travers in 1913 and had now won an Open or Amateur for three straight years. After they got back to Atlanta, Bobby shared a confidence with Pop: if he could win either cup for six years running—only three more—he'd be satisfied enough to walk away from the game.

They didn't speak of it again for a while, and Pop never pressed him on the point, but for the first time the subject of the end was in the air, and Pop knew why. Although his sport had given him a huge head start in life, like most young men his age Bobby was wrestling with fundamental issues of adult identity and responsibility. He and Mary were still living with his parents, in their big white house on Lullwater Road. With the birth of their first child he felt the daily pull and obligation of providing for his family. As hard as it might be to accept, Bobby knew that unless he turned pro a day would come when golf would only be an obstacle to that end. Although he had already realized that selling real estate made him miserable he still had to put bread on the table; Bobby agreed to spend another winter in Florida working for Adair Realty at Whitman Estates. This year he went down in late October and took Mary and baby Clara with him.

There he bumped into Walter Hagen, who had won his second consecutive PGA Championship in the summer of 1925 and was setting up shop in Florida for the winter. Bobby spent a lot of his time on the links with Hagen, Tommy Armour and the other hearty brutes who comprised the emerging pro tour. There's no question that Bobby privately considered joining their ranks during that season. Less than a decade removed from under-class status, professional athletes in every sport had garnered unprecedented legitimacy. Their income had been headed due north for years. Bobby's fame had never been higher and continued to rise; he was nuts not to cash in on it, in the opinion of his freebooting friends.

The temptation was almost irresistible: chained to a demeaning salesman job he despised, mouths at home to feed, with the minions of corporate America eager to open their check-books to the commercial exploitation of the decade's Golden Boy. While Bobby mulled this over, an electrical fire destroyed East Lake's clubhouse for the second time; among the losses were all of Bobby's favorite clubs—except Calamity Jane, who always traveled with him; he'd become so devoted to her that he slept with her under his bed—and the original Havermeyer Trophy, which Bobby had let the club keep in the lobby.

Bobby weighed the idea. He listened to Hagen and Armour check off a pro's bountiful advantages. He even made plans to play in the Florida Winter Golf League. He certainly discussed the idea with Mary at home, but he never brought it up to Pop Keeler or his own father, a telling indication that his traditional upbringing as a Southern gentleman—in a line of men born to follow careers, not practice common trades—still occupied the high ground of his conscience. The Colonel had made it clear once again there was a place for Bob in his law practice, should he see fit to follow that path. The events of 1926 would finally make up his mind for him.

The Winter League was canceled abruptly in January for lack of interest: the number of people wintering in Florida had dropped precipitously. Perry Adair had a hand in developing the idea that followed, but Hagen came up with it first. He was the sport's reigning professional champ, Bobby was on top of the amateur game—why not arrange a grand exhibition match to settle the issue of who was the game's best player? The press and public had already been clamoring for such a match, like a heavyweight title fight. The idea took shape: thirty-six holes on Bob's home course at Whitfield Estates followed by thirty-six the following week at Hagen's home, Pasadena, drawing well-heeled crowds to help both struggling developments move some inventory.

His own promoter advised Hagen not to go up against Bobby. Hagen's stock was sky-high on the exhibition circuit; losing to Bobby would bring more risk than winning would bring benefits. Nonsense, argued Hagen: everybody wins here, particularly me. He was assured of a $5,000 guarantee as an amateur wasn't playing but his Adair Realty salary. He couldn't share in the gate with Hagen either, and they were planning to charge an unheard-of $3.30 for tickets. For his part Bobby agreed to the match largely out of a sense of obligation to Perry; he saw it as part of his job. Hagen loved reading that the press predicted victory for Bobby, the Polly Purebred amateur, while the scallywag pro was inevitably cast as the black-hatted villain.

When they tossed a coin and Bobby won the right to play the first thirty-six at Whitfield Estates, Hagen realized he'd be playing the first half of the match in front of a hostile gallery cheering against him on every shot. He had Bobby right where he wanted him.

They had never played a head-to-head match, but Hagen knew enough about Bobby's emphasis on perfection to believe he carried a huge advantage: Hagen could forget a bad shot the moment he hit one, but Bobby couldn't shake off a mistake with anywhere near the same facility. Hagen also felt that in this version of a street fight, away from the niceties and rituals of a USGA event, he could get into Bobby's head. He knew that in matchplay nothing mattered but who won the hole, and it didn't matter how. Bobby had come up against an opponent who didn't give Old Man Par the time of day, a clash of philosophies as much as of style and credentials. Pop Keeler traveled down to watch; so did Grantland Rice and a squadron of important writers from New York. They billed it as the Battle of the Century.

Promoters limited ticket sales to 750, but hundreds more crashed the gate on the last day of February to watch the Battle's first round at Whitfield Estates. Hagen hit one fairway out of the first nine and built a two-hole lead. His recovery shots were even more supernatural than usual and his putter was hot as a pistol: twenty-seven putts in the first round. Bobby appeared off-key from the start. Although he drove beautifully, his irons were loose and uncertain. He compensated by pressing around the greens, as Hagen predicted he might. Bobby worked the lead back to one with a birdie on twelve, but Hagen pushed his lead to three as the morning round concluded. While Bobby sweated and strained to place every shot perfectly, Hagen continued to hook, slice, push, and pull everything off the tee, and still Bobby could gain no ground until canning a birdie on the afternoon's fifth hole.

At the sixth Hagen hit another terrible drive to the edge of the rough, dead behind a towering pine. Bobby played a flaw-less tee shot and a solid iron to the elevated green, leaving himself a good chance for birdie and a possible turning point. Hagen stood up to his stymied ball, half-topped a wicked slice that ran a hundred yards at an altitude of three inches, hopped through a greenside bunker, climbed a steep embankment, and came to rest on the green 12 feet from the pin. When you learn that Bobby missed his birdie putt and Hagen made his you start to appreciate why Hagen was getting under Bobby's skin. A disheartened Pop believed the match turned on this hole. Hagen held onto his three-hole advantage through the final turn and then decided, what the hell, as long as he had him down he might as well try to put his foot on Bobby's neck. He shot 32 on the back nine, and when the smoke cleared he had shot a two-under-par 70 and built an eight-hole lead. Asked to analyze the reason for his success that day, Hagen pointed to his putter; both men played well but he had taken exactly eight fewer putts than Bobby.

The match resumed the following Sunday, on Walter's course at Pasadena. His commanding lead put a dent in attendance, but for once Hagen was more interested in pride than his pocket-book. Bobby only played golf against the problems of the course in front of him, trying to match the blueprint of perfection he carried in his head; he was his own worst critic and the pres-ence, absence, or behavior of galleries made no difference to him. Hagen was a born performer. In front of his hometown crowd he fed off their energy like a Broadway ham milking curtain calls on opening night. He confessed later that he used to set up shots like a movie director, trying to extract every last ounce of drama and suspense. After putting so beautifully at Whitfield Estates, Walter went crazy on the familiar greens at Pasadena. He sank a 50-footer to go up nine on the second hole. Twice on the first fourteen holes that day his drive hit a tree and bounced into the fairway and he got up and down for birdie.

Somewhere during that morning round Bobby abandoned his strategy of playing the scorecard and tried to match Hagen shot for shot. His game actually improved but nothing seemed to matter: he played the last twenty-five holes at Pasadena in even par and steadily lost ground. By then it was clear that, for this match anyway, Hagen's name had been written in Keeler's Book of Predestination, although it was only natural to suspect Walter had snuck in the night before under cover of darkness and jotted it down himself.

By the time they reached their twenty-fourth hole of the day, Hagen was up twelve with twelve to play. Both men were just off the green, lying two. Bobby chipped in from 45 feet for birdie. Hagen stepped up to his ball, pulled a three-iron, and chipped it toward the flag.

"My little sweet potato went for that hole as if it had eyes," he said. His ball hit the stick and dropped for a birdie to halve the hole. The Battle of the Century was over. Technical knockout.

"Walter chopped my head off," wrote Bobby soon afterwards. "He played the most invincible match golf in those two days I had ever seen, let alone confronted. And I may add that I can get along very comfortably if I never confront any more like it."

Hagen had won the match decisively 12 & 11 and along the way established new scoring records at both Whitfield and Pasadena. He needed only 69 strokes that last day; Bobby joked that he needed sixty-nine cigarettes, but he'd shot a respectable 73. For his troubles Hagen collected the largest single check ever paid to any golfer for an exhibition match, $7,600. As a show of gratitude he went out and bought Bobby a set of diamond and platinum monogrammed cufflinks, so his net was reduced to $6,800.

"Sure I grandstanded," he admitted later. "But don't get the idea I was merely being amusing and brassy. To me that stuff was all part of my game. It helped fluster my opponent as much as it delighted the gallery, and was equally important in releasing the tension from my game."

The disappointment of his loss to Hagen had several positive effects on Bobby. First, any thoughts of turning professional were shelved. He realized that stepping down off the altar of amateurism would drop him into an arena where no holds were barred in the scramble for a buck, and this clashed with his evolving self-image. The modern perception of "amateur" is of someone who does something poorly or with a lack of professionalism, but the Latin root of the word is *amator*, someone who pursues a pastime out of love. Bobby embraced his amateurism as more than a label; it defined him as thoroughly as "professional" described Hagen. Fate had not tapped Jones only to send him out on the road nine months a year with a bunch of scruffy nomads chasing penny-ante purses in half-assed tournaments. He wanted a life centered in Atlanta, to be part of a community, a solid wage-earner for his wife and children and family.

Second, Hagen's masterful performance increased Bobby's desire to keep climbing the mountain; there were still many goals ahead of him chief among them winning a British Open. The match with Hagen had also exposed a weakness in his game that could prove fatal overseas: faulty iron play. Bobby went to his former roommate Tommy Armour and asked for help. Armour pointed out that Bobby was trying to steer the shots with his right hand, instead of pulling down and through impact with his left. Bobby made the correction and noticed a startling improvement: his iron shots flew on line again. In fact Bobby found it was almost impossible to hit them *off* line. Armour also gave him a refresher course on the punch shot, a vital part of any player's arsenal in Britain. Perhaps most importantly of all, Tommy talked him through a shot-by-shot tutorial on how to play St. Andrews, the course that had baffled Bobby in 1921, where the coming year's Walker Cup would be played. By the time they were done Bobby felt he had begun to understand the singular strategic genius of the Old Course, and went to work developing a detailed plan of attack.

The friendly sparring with Hagen wasn't quite finished, though. A couple of weeks after their epic match they met again in the Florida West Coast Open, played at Pasadena, a medal-play tournament that was part of the winter tour. Hagen won, but only by a single stroke, with Bobby second. He was already gaining ground.

As expected Bobby was named to the Walker Cup team and began planning his return to Great Britain. He and Hagen made one last sociable wager: whoever scored the lowest in both that year's Opens and their qualifiers would buy the other a hat. The joke was that Bobby seldom wore a hat when he played, and Hagen never did; he was being paid a fat endorsement fee by Brylcreme to keep his lustrous, groomed black mane out in the open air whenever he stepped on a course. A serious-money rematch between the game's two heavyweights seemed certain to follow, but the USGA, sensitive to any perceived breach of the amateur/professional barrier, put an end to the speculation. They issued a ruling that if Hagen were to cash another check from a match with Jones it compromised Bobby's amateur status. There would be no rematch.

Who was the better golfer? Despite Hagen's convincing win the question still hung in the air. Walter had this to say about it: "The closest I can come to an answer is that any champion golfer—with his nerves steady, his game at its peak, the weather and course conditions equalized by his skill and luck—can beat any other champion golfer on any given day. I happened to play Bobby on my particular days." Bobby was too modest to compare his game to Hagen's or any other player's; that was someone else's job. Because he always insisted he learned more from the matches he lost than those he won—and it's clear he learned a great deal from losing to Hagen—the memory of this loss remained a far from unpleasant one.

"When you play a lot of intense and interesting competitive golf with and against a man," he wrote, "you develop a real affection for him. The respect and admiration you have for him as an immediate adversary ripens through the years because of the memory of the tense and thrilling experiences you have shared."

Bobby and Walter both left Florida in the spring of 1926. The real-estate bubble had burst and the remainder of the decade would pass before it turned around. For once in his life Hagen got out of a failing investment with his nest egg intact—he'd received a dozen prime lots as payment but never put any of his own money into them—while Bobby went back to work as a low-level wage earner in the Atlanta office of Adair Realty. He had privately made up his mind he was going to leave the real-estate business soon, and told Mary so. According to sports-writer Paul Gallico, who spoke about the matter with him later, Bobby "became convinced he and his golfing titles and prowess were being employed merely as a front to dispense wastelands." A professional transformation was in the offing, but first there was the matter of an extended trip overseas to attend to.

What he was about to do that summer changed everything.

CHAPTER EIGHT

THE YANKS
ARE COMING

The Walker Cup team sailed out of New York for England on May 5, 1926, on the *Aquatania*. Francis Ouimet was on board, along with Jess Sweetser and Jesse Guilford, team captain Bob Gardner, and the imperious George Von Elm. Thanks to his showing at Oakmont so was twenty-one-year-old Watts Gunn, a true innocent abroad. And along to record all their adventures on his first trip away from American shores was Oscar Bane Keeler. The USGA threw them a grand dinner in the ballroom of the Waldorf-Astoria the night before they departed and the city arranged a big send-off at the harbor, with flags flying and trumpets blaring. Irving Berlin contributed a special version of his hit "Always," with lyrics rewritten to predict the team's success. Bobby's parting from Mary had been more difficult than usual; she was four months pregnant with their second child.

As they steamed through the harbor past the Statue of Liberty and into the open sea, Pop looked back until the light of her lamp disappeared from sight before turning in. He wrote his first column that night; he would wire back to Atlanta a series of colorful dispatches chronicling their travels throughout their trip, less than half of them about golf, many about the comic challenges of chaperoning the unpredictable Watts Gunn. As he lay down in his bunk that night Pop's mind was filled with musings on man's mastery of the oceans and the march of human progress. His transcendent mood was short-lived when he woke up with a start at 3:00 that morning. The ship had slipped into the rough open Atlantic and he was suddenly, catastrophically seasick.

While Pop seldom ventured out of his cabin in the early days small intrigues broke out on board through the crossing. Gunn read *The Great Gatsby* and wondered aloud what all the fuss was about. Bobby caught a cold, and gave it to Sweetser. Ouimet battled a bout of seasickness to rival Pop's. Together they haunted the infirmary, experimented with a variety of remedies but found no relief until somebody slipped them a white powder remedy in a blue bottle called Carlsbad #2. In a calm sea with the ship as steady as a church, Pop felt revived enough afterwards to take his first walk around deck in the bracing fresh air, and even downed a cautious lunch. Then the powder wore off and "I went back down to my room to die." But when he woke from his next nap the seasickness had mysteriously vanished, and didn't return. The boys got a kick out of investigating a rumor that Marion Davies, William Randolph Hearst's notorious movie-star mistress, was on board; it remained unconfirmed.

On the third night out Ouimet organized a singing squad,

and regaled the dinner guests with a barber-shop-quartet version of "Moonlight Bay." At dinner that night the discussion revolved around the general strike that had paralyzed much of Britain, affecting everything from food delivery to medical care and basic transportation. There was suddenly real uncertainty that the tournaments they were traveling to take part in would even be allowed to take place; shipboard editions of the *Daily Mail* appeared every evening, keeping them apprised of the degenerating situation. It wasn't until the *Aquatania*'s last night out at sea that they received a cable from the Royal & Ancient confirming that the British Amateur, the first of their events, would proceed as scheduled.

On the morning of May 11 Pop Keeler went topside at 3:45 A.M. to steal a look at the town of Cherbourg off the starboard bow, his first glimpse of a foreign country; he'd never even seen Canada before, and the romance of those distant lights affected him deeply. They docked a few hours later that morning in Portsmouth and discovered the general strike had canceled their boat train, so they made their way into London by motor coach. As they drove out of the harbor onto the motorway Gunn was terrified by his introduction to British traffic: "Good Lord, Pop, they're driving on the wrong side of the road!" The team checked into the posh Savoy Hotel on the Strand, spent a whirlwind day and a half sightseeing, and then news broke that the strike had been settled. Britain went back to work and so did the Americans; they climbed into their motor coach and drove southeast to Sussex, where the team played a one-day exhibition at Rye and decisively defeated a composite Oxford–Cambridge team.

Making their way north, the team spent one day back in London, where Pop and Bobby visited the Cheshire Cheese, Samuel Johnson's famed eighteenth-century hangout on Fleet Street. The organizational genius behind the first English dictionary, and subject of James Boswell's legendary biography,

Johnson had long been a literary hero of the language-loving Pop; within a few years he himself was routinely being referred to as "Bobby Jones's Boswell." Bobby got a big kick out of the pub's atmosphere, but when they got back to the hotel that night he confessed to Pop he was terribly homesick for Mary and their baby. He had decided to drop out of the British Open, the last event on their agenda, and return to Atlanta two weeks earlier than originally planned. Pop was disappointed but understood the decision; he was already yearning for home and hearth himself.

The next evening the team boarded the *Flying Scotsman* and rolled north out of Kings Cross Station toward Edinburgh. Occupying an entire car and a half, they covered four hundred miles in nine hours and arrived at Muirfield the next morning. After checking into the Marine Hotel in nearby Gullane they got in a single day of practice rounds, attended a dinner in the team's honor that night, rested on the Sabbath—still the custom in Scotland—and on Monday, May 24, play began in the British Amateur.

Lying inland near the Firth of Forth, the venerable Muirfield layout felt more hospitable to the American player than the links courses that run along the shore. Although Walter Travis had won the 1904 event as an American, he was originally from Australia; no home-grown American had ever captured the British Amateur. The British bookmakers nevertheless established Bobby, George Von Elm, and a late-arriving Chick Evans—not part of the Walker Cup team, he had sailed over on his own—as the early favorites. Bobby was less sanguine about his chances; with the eighteen-hole limit on every match in the first six rounds of the event, the format posed what he felt was the toughest challenge of all the major titles. He was also shaking off the effects of the persistent cold that had bothered him since the crossing; Sweetser was in an even worse way. The sturdy Ivy Leaguer nearly collapsed during the practice round, but the last-minute withdrawal of his first-round opponent allowed him to spend a day in bed and regain his strength.

Ouimet edged Von Elm in a close second-round match, then came up against Sweetser in the third. Growing weaker due to his advancing illness, Sweetser rallied to take their match to the eighteenth hole for the third day in a row, where he won it once again. In spite of reservations about his ability to win the event, Bobby drew an easy path through the first few rounds, his game gaining an edge as keen as Pop had ever seen. In the fourth round he drew the reigning British Amateur champion, Robert Harris, the first time in the event's history—in either country—that a current American champ met his British counterpart head to head. In one of the commanding performances of his life, Bobby dispatched Harris in twelve holes, 8 & 6. Little doubt remained in experts' minds that Bobby would march through the rest of the field to win the title. He and Sweetser were the only Americans left as the tournament reached the semi-finals.

Bobby felt unaccountably restless after winning his match with Harris. The weather had been unusually warm and this far north so close to the summer solstice the sky remained light until eleven at night. Bobby left the window open, and slept with only a sheet covering him; a chill wind crept in off the sea and he woke with muscle spasms and a severely stiff neck. He thought he heard the left side of his neck "give a loud, rasping creak like a rusty hinge." He could barely lift his arms to his shoulders and seriously considered withdrawing from the tournament. The hotel summoned a local physical therapist who worked on Bobby for over an hour. Accounts about the results differ; Bobby claimed he felt loose enough afterwards to at least go over to the course, hit a few shots and make up his mind about playing; Pop privately worried that the therapist had done more harm than good. Muirfield had no practice range, so Bobby hit a few balls on the eighteenth fairway and was soon called to the first tee; during that 100-yard walk he made up his mind to play the match.

"It is the player's business to come to the tournament not only in proper practice insofar as his golf is concerned, but also in proper physical condition. If I had failed in either respect, it was the fault of no one but myself. I would go out and do the best I could, so long as I could lift the club at all."

Bobby's opponent in the fifth round was a twenty-year-old from Glasgow named Andrew Jamieson, making his debut in the Amateur. He was a nervous, fragile lad, who rode his bicycle to the tournament every day from the nearby village where he was staying. Jamieson had spent three hours the night before working on the putting green with a brother who was caddying for him. Without question he was the lowest-regarded golfer still in the tournament, the unlikeliest figure to knock Bobby out of the Amateur. Bobby never mentioned his physical problem as an excuse—he didn't even write a word about this difficulty in his first autobiography, and wouldn't bring it up at all until his final book, written half a lifetime later in 1958—but it was clear from the start that his injury made it impossible to swing freely or avoid flinching at impact. Still, Bobby at 60 percent was good enough to beat 95 percent of the men in any field; his reputation alone by this point was worth two strokes. Jamieson showed up wearing a novice's blinkers and cobbled together a cautious, risk-free round of thirteen pars and one birdie. Bobby didn't win a single hole from him. He felt his neck begin to loosen as the match advanced, and if they'd been playing thirty-six holes he probably would have felt enough improvement to mount a comeback. This was exactly the worst-case scenario he had dreaded going in: Andrew Jamieson, complete unknown, had ousted him, 4 & 3. Jamieson didn't stick around long; after losing in the semi-finals that same afternoon the mild-mannered giant-killer climbed back on his bicycle and rode quietly out of town.

Bobby's devoted Scottish caddie, twenty-nine-year-old Jack McIntyre, cried his eyes out after the match, and pledged that his new boss would find him waiting on the tee a few weeks later at Royal Lytham & St. Anne's for the British Open. "I know he's the greatest of them all," he said. Bobby didn't have the heart to tell him when they parted that he was going home before the Open.

Alone in his room, Bobby got to thinking about his last early exit from a British tournament, five years earlier. He felt depressed and disappointed, but not angry.

> And I didn't want people to think so. If I went home now it would look somewhat as if I were sulking. I had little hope of winning the British Open. No amateur had won it since 1897, five years before I was born. But I thought maybe I could make a decent showing. I was determined, no matter where I finished, that I'd not pick up this time. The British are a wonderful sporting people, and I wanted them to think kindly of me and to believe I could shoot a little golf.

He told Pop of his change of heart when the latter returned from a rueful evening stroll, and Pop's spirits revived instantly. They spent the next twenty-four hours supporting Jess Sweetser, the last American in the Amateur draw; Pop practically func-tioned as his nurse. Sweetser had been carried to twenty-one holes before winning the semi-finals, and sprained his wrist during the match. Pop wrapped his wrist, and tried to treat his fever, but Sweetser rejected any suggestion that he withdraw so close to the summit. Despite being able to down only a few sips of orange juice, he marched out the next day to play the thirty-six-hole final match and defeated Scotsman Alexander Simpson 6 & 5 to win the British Amateur Championship. The gallery was gracious in defeat, and applauded him as his teammates carried him, elated but on the brink of exhaustion, all the way back to the clubhouse. Walter Travis had found a worthy successor.

A remarkable scene followed in the hallowed chambers of Muirfield's clubhouse. This was the sacred home of the Honourable Company of Edinburgh Gentlemen, founded in 1740, the oldest organization in golf—founded a full decade before the Royal & Ancient of St. Andrews—whose walls are covered with portraits of red-coated captains that predate the American Revolution. The club's members, some of them prominent British golf writers, stood by in wide-eyed amazement that night as the victorious Americans, filled with high spirits of both the emotional and distilled variety, broke into song. Ouimet led them through the repertoire they'd been working on since the crossing, tight harmonies echoing through halls that had never heard a single note sung in their history. (Pop called Ouimet and Sweetser "occasional singers: they sing at every occasion." Their formal hosts gradually decided that their distinguished forebears looking down from on high might not be spinning in their graves. By the end of the evening Ouimet and the boys were taking requests from some of the honorable gentlemen.

On the last day of May the team traveled eighty miles north by coach, around the Firth of Forth to St. Andrews, and checked into the Grand Hotel to prepare for the Walker Cup competition, which followed three days later. Sufficiently recovered from his neck problem, Bobby reacquainted himself with the Old Course. Looking at it with fresh eyes, acquired during his winter's work with Tommy Armour, he began to grasp the genius of the place, and each successive round he played reinforced his conviction that here was the world's greatest test of golf.

One idle afternoon Pop took Bobby and some of the other Americans on a visit to the factory of legendary club maker Tom Stewart. In the aftermath of the East Lake fire, Bobby had cobbled together a set of mismatched clubs to replace those he'd lost; a handful turned out to be the products of Tom Stewart's forge. The son of a blacksmith, Stewart had been crafting irons for over thirty years, the last of the old school club makers.

Entering the anonymous shop on Argyle Street Bobby and Pop witnessed "twenty hardy Scots toiling like a platoon of Vulcans in the forge room, sixteen more at the finishing wheels next door." Out of these grubby, cramped rooms emerged what those in the know considered to be the game's finest instruments. Old Tom Stewart seemed equally impressed with Bobby's knowledge of club design and mechanics; their meeting signaled the start of a significant relationship. Stewart provided Bobby with a duplicate set of clubheads before he left Britain—they wouldn't be fitted with shafts until he returned to East Lake—and continued to supply him for the next few years.

The Walker Cup began on June 2. The entire town of St. Andrews—with the exception of Tom Stewart's forge—shut down for the duration and over five thousand turned up to watch; Pop thought it had the feel of a national holiday, which was close to the truth. In alternate-shot, two-ball foursomes in the morning Watts Gunn paired with Bobby and helped him gain revenge against Andrew Jamieson and his partner Cyril Tolley. Gunn struck the decisive blow, an improbable 120-foot putt for birdie to win the thirteenth. The American team took three of the four foursome matches—the British specialty—and a 3–1 lead. That afternoon the British struck back in singles, winning four of the first six matches and halving another. Only Bobby had an easy time of it, clobbering Cyril Tolley 12 & 11, with his finest burst of golf since arriving in Britain. It was left to George Von Elm to eke out a heroic half in the final match against a gigantic military man named Major Hezlett, allowing America to retain the Walker Cup for the fourth straight time, $6^1/_2$–$5^1/_2$, the narrowest victory in the event's history.

The teams marked the end of the event with a formal dinner that night; Jess Sweetser excused himself early, appearing spent. At midnight he knocked on Pop's door, eerily composed but white as a sheet and holding a blood-stained handkerchief to his mouth; he had suffered a severe lung hemorrhage. Doctors were summoned. They debated at length about whether Jess was fit to travel; he was gravely ill with tuberculosis. He took the news calmly but insisted on being allowed to return home; if he was going to die he didn't want to go on foreign soil. The team helped him onto the train the next day; the doctors had given him heroin, and instructions to Pop and Ouimet on how to inject him with it. He suffered another hemorrhage during the crossing, and the British Amateur champion returned home with his trophy as an invalid, heavily sedated, and was carried off the *Aquatania* in New York on a stretcher.

Bobby and Von Elm left for the Lytham and St. Anne's Club to begin their practice rounds for the Open, while Pop made a side trip to visit Paris. Meanwhile a second group of American golfers made the passage over on the *Aquatania*. Walter Hagen was captaining a team of top professionals coming to compete in the biannual international matches, the event's last edition before these matches officially became known as the Ryder Cup in 1927. Whether they were still groggy from the crossing or looking ahead to the Open, the American pros struck out against the British, who were captained by Ted Ray. The U.S. team lost $13^{1}/_{2}$–$1^{1}/_{2}$—only Wild Bill Melhorn won a singles match—their most lopsided defeat in international competition. The victory helped soften the blow struck by Sweetser at the Amateur; press and public alike now reckoned the issue of which country held supremacy in the sport would be settled at the Open.

Bobby told Pop he had played "moderately well" at Lytham and St. Anne's before traveling to Sunningdale, Surrey, where his thirty-six-hole Open qualifier was scheduled. There were three regional qualifiers that year—in north, south and central England—an R&A experiment, the first time qualifying rounds had been played away from the site of the Open.

Considered Britain's finest heathland course, Sunningdale was set on gently rolling, sandy terrain southwest of London. Sunningdale's beauty belies its demanding combination of

precision and menace. Bobby befriended the resident professional, 1904's British Open winner Jack White, who presented
him with a superbly crafted driver that he had named Jeanie
Deans, after the heroine of a Walter Scott romance, *The Heart
of Midlothian*. Bobby appreciated the literary reference and fell
in love with the club; he hadn't yet found a driver he liked to
replace the one he'd lost in the East Lake fire. (This was actually Calamity Jane II; Bobby had retired the first Jane a few
months earlier. Jane had been warped by caddies over-enthusi-
astically applying an emery cloth while cleaning the blade after
a round.)

It was June 18, a sunny, breezy, beautiful day. Par was 72;
the course record for competitive play was 70. That morning,
a powerful Welsh pro named Archie Compston lowered it a
notch with a 69. Bobby began his round at noon and proceeded
to play the single perfect ball-striking round of his entire life.
He hit every fairway and green in regulation, save one—his only
mistake of the day—a 175-yard par-three where he got up and
down from a bunker. He hit all four par-five greens in two. This
was no driver-wedge course; he was usually hitting four-irons
or more to the greens. He shot 33 on the front and 33 on the
back, six birdies, no bogies, for a record-shattering 66. He took
33 shots from the field, and 33 putts on the greens; Pop fanta-
sized afterwards about what damage he might have done if
Calamity Jane had been equal to Jeanie Deans and his irons.
He missed two birdie putts of 5 feet or less, and holed only one
over 10 feet. The cheers went on long and loud after Bobby
holed his last putt beneath the magnificent oak that frames the
eighteenth green. Bernard Darwin wrote that the crowd looked
awestruck, "realizing they had witnessed something they had
never seen before and would never see again."

That night Bobby still felt keyed up after his round so he,
Pop, Von Elm and the gigantic Archie Compston took a long
walk after dinner. They went out of a rear gate of the Wheatsheaf

Hotel, where they were staying in the town of Virginia Water, and walked toward a lake in nearby Windsor Great Park. After passing a lovely little waterfall, they followed a winding path down near the shore and as they neared the site of an ancient wharf came upon an astonishing sight: four large carved marble faces, beautiful, feminine, and severe, with serpentine hair like the locks of Medusa. The statues appeared to be an entreaty to the goddess of love from an adoring wife longing to have her husband returned to her. Bobby had gone out that evening worrying that his record-breaking performance might be peaking too soon. The realization of what they had found moved the four men deeply and they walked back in silence, reaching the hotel just after midnight. His cares had dissipated: Bobby shot a 68 during his second time around Sunningdale the next day, ahead of every other qualifier for the 1926 British Open by seven shots.

After passing a rigorous inspection process that had begun in 1923, the Lytham and St. Anne's Club was hosting its first Open. (The "Royal" prefix, which Lytham and St. Anne's now carries, is attached to a club which at any point in its existence has counted a principal from Great Britain's royal family among its membership.) Named after two nearby villages, it first opened for play in 1897 and was at inception a true links course from which you caught an occasional glimpse of the Irish Sea. Situated a few miles south of Blackpool and a mile inland, civilization had steadily encroached on it until by 1926 the course ran along a railway line in the middle of red-brick suburbia. Among its eccentricities were an opening par-three, and back-to-back par-fives on the front. Bernard Darwin called it "a beast, but a just beast."

This was also the first time the R&A charged admission for its Open championship—as they did weeks before at the Amateur—a change spurred by an unruly mob that had run amok at Prestwick the previous year. Although the plan was put into play to limit attendance and keep out the hooligans, with Bobby Jones in the field they sold over eleven thousand tickets each day. The championship began on Wednesday, June 23. Good as his word, caddie Jack McIntyre had paid his own way to St. Anne's to carry Bobby's bag; both Bobby and Pop felt Jack's stalwart, Sancho Pansa-like presence was like a four-leaf clover. Just as they had at the Amateur, touts established Bobby as the early favorite at 6–1. By the time they teed it up, and word of Bobby's qualifying performance had sunk in and the line on him had fallen to 3–1, the shortest odds on record for an Open. The weather held through all three days of play, just as it had at Sunningdale; but the wind stayed up and steady, prevailing off the ocean from the northwest, which rendered the shorter back nine the tougher passage. Thirteen Americans had qualified: the four amateurs who had remained—Watts Gunn, Roland McKenzie, George Von Elm, and Bobby—and the entire professional team who had made the trip over.

Just as Bobby had done at Sunningdale, Hagen led all qualifiers who played their way in at St. Anne's, completing his first round with a dazzling course-record 68. Bobby finished four strokes behind, alone in fifth place. Like many players he was never above superstition: he wore the same sweater, shoes and socks he'd had on his first day at Sunningdale; "This is my 66 outfit," he told Pop. Bobby would wear a completely different outfit the next day, but for the rest of the tournament he carried around a smooth old English penny he'd won from J.H. Taylor when he'd bet that Hagen would make his last putt to break the record.

The wind swirled unpredictably on the second day. Hagen fell off during his second round with a 77. Bobby snuck past him with a steady 72, landing in a tie for the lead with fellow American Bill Melhorn, with Hagen only a stroke behind. This looked like America's week as Yanks crowded the top of the leader board; the nearest British player, Archie Compston, sat all the way back in a tie for seventh. With few home-grown heroes to root for, the crowds lined up behind Bobby; if an American had to win their Open, the galleries made no secret that they preferred the modest, sportsmanlike amateur over the mercenary Hagen. They had already begun to perceive Bobby as more British than the British—well-mannered, reserved, self-contained—while Hagen was easy to cast as the soon-to-be clichéd Ugly American.

The final two rounds would be played on Friday. Bobby teed off at 9:00 A.M. with a brawny twenty-six-year-old pro from Yonkers, New York, named Andrew Albert Watrous. Considered a rising player at home, Watrous stunned the galleries that morning with a 69 to take the lead from his famous partner, who stood alone in second two strokes behind him. Fifty-six-year-old legend John Henry Taylor, the last of the Great Triumvirate still playing competitive golf, had announced this would be his last Open. Playing inspired golf, he stirred the hearts of his countrymen that morning by shooting 71 and inserting himself into the hunt. Hagen finished two strokes in back of Bobby and four off the lead, a dangerous position from which to close if he put together one of his finishing kicks. After a magnificent run in the third round, George Von Elm sat a stroke in back of Hagen. These were the only men left with a chance at the '26 Open.

When they finished their third rounds, Bobby saw Watrous staring in shock at the scoreboard, took him by the arm, and led the young pro back to the room he was sharing with Pop at the Majestic Hotel. Pop pulled their shoes off, yanked the shades, and ordered tea and cold ham sandwiches from room service while the two men lay down on the twin beds and tried to rest; Bobby warned Watrous that, whatever he did, "For God's sake, don't take a nap." According to tradition, a nap between rounds was fatal. They chatted fitfully. All Watrous could manage to eat was a single slice of ham. As they walked back to begin their final round an hour later, Pop overheard Bobby encourage Watrous: "Remember, Al, the winner and the runner-up are in this pair."

Reaching the players' entrance on his way out in the afternoon, Bobby realized he had left his identification badge on the dresser in his room. The guard minding the gate, apparently fresh off the boat from another galaxy, didn't recognize him. Bobby refused to make a fuss, hurried around to the public entrance and bought his way in with a ticket.

The wind was whipping. Bobby had every part of his game working at peak efficiency, except Calamity Jane II. Jeanie Deans was finding the fairways, and his irons threatened every flag, but he didn't one-putt a single green all day. This was before sprinkler systems; with the greens dried and hardened by constant wind and sun, Bobby said it was like putting on ice. Watrous put his head down and played sturdy, determined golf, twice yielding half his lead to Bobby, but Jones gave it right back with three-putt greens. Both men played the front in even par. Starting an hour after them, Hagen made a move on the front nine and closed into a tie with Bobby. Watrous took back his two-stroke lead at thirteen with a solid par. The players and gallery walked to the next tee in heavy silence. Pop was so distraught he wandered off for a while.

The rest of the round would be played dead into the wind. Although Pop missed most of it, other writers on hand felt that Bobby now put on the finest demonstration of skill from tee to green in his career. He parred the 455-yard fourteenth; showing the strain, Watrous took three putts and bogeyed, cutting his lead back to one. With the wind whipping their pants legs both men reached the 463-yard fifteenth in two, but again Watrous three-putted; the two Americans were tied for the lead with three holes to play.

After matching pars at sixteen, they stepped to the seventeenth: 462 yards, a slight dogleg left, the left side protected by a run of pot bunkers. Watrous hit a perfect drive down the right side, leaving an ideal angle to the green. After outdriving him all day, Bobby came over the top and hooked it into the waste area down the left side. When they found his ball he'd salvaged a small piece of luck: it had avoided the deadly bunkers and come to rest cleanly on a firm patch of sand. Watrous was judged away and played a safe long iron to the front of the green. Meanwhile, Pop was back in the clubhouse bar, as he put it "taking in a liberal dose of antifreeze."

Bobby's ball was 175 yards out, all of it hazardous, not a foot of fairway between this spot and the hole. His view of the green was almost completely obscured by sand dunes, gorse, and heather. He had heard the crowd's reaction, knew that Watrous was on the green and what he had to do in response. He walked to the fairway to get a look at the flag, then marched back and didn't hesitate. In moments like this, Bobby consciously slowed his languid backswing even more than usual, taking it back a notch further to avoid the tendency to rush. Bobby's old friend Al Laney, who had landed a job on the staff of the *New York Herald Tribune* and spent most of the last two years covering the paper's European beat from Paris, was standing close enough to see the look on Bobby's face and said that "what I remember more acutely than the shot itself was how drawn and almost ill Bob's face appeared as he stepped into the sand and settled his feet." Bobby asked Jack McIntyre for his four-iron; Laney noted that the similarity in lie and distance to the shot that had won him his first Open at Inwood in '23 was uncanny.

This time he hit an even better shot. The ball nipped cleanly off the sand, barely cleared the dunes, then made straight for the flag like a sniper's bullet. Benefiting from the resistance of a stiff headwind, the ball landed on the front edge, bounced twice and snaked to a stop 10 feet inside of Watrous's ball. The crowd went mad.

The blood drained from Watrous's face as they walked to the green. News spread to the clubhouse, and Pop rushed out from the bar. When he got his first look at Watrous he thought the tournament might already be over; he was just about right. Watrous misread the green and three-putted for the third time in the last four holes. Bobby got down in two for his par and took a one-stroke lead, his first of the tournament. He never glanced at Watrous, so fierce was his concentration on the next tee. He closed his final round with another par; Watrous gave away another stroke.

Bobby left the course in first place with a final score for the championship of 291, matching the Open's all-time low set by James Braid in 1908. But Hagen was still out on the course, with six holes left and a chance to catch him. Bobby locked arms with Watrous and walked him into the clubhouse, where they poured stiff drinks and waited for word. Rumors flew around them: Hagen had finished his front nine two under par; he was mounting a charge on the back. Pop grew worried enough to start for the press room; on the way there a reporter informed him that Hagen had bogeyed twice down the stretch. Pop went right back into the clubhouse to shake Bobby's hand. Still, Hagen came to the final hole needing a par to tie Watrous for second place. Hagen, it was widely known, had no interest in second.

While Bobby, Pop, and a hundred others watched from the clubhouse balcony, and thousands waited in the gallery, Hagen paced off his second shot from the middle of the fairway to the edge of the green and back again, over 150 yards; he made it melodramatically clear he was going to try to drop his second shot in the hole for an eagle from the fairway, a last-ditch attempt to tie Bobby for the lead and force a play-off.

Hagen let the tension build, then took out his five-iron and swung—time stood still while that ball was in the air—and almost pulled off a miracle; the ball landed less than a foot from the hole, jumped over it and skipped into a flowerbed behind the green. Bobby later told Walter he had to turn his back, unable to watch because he knew Hagen was just lucky enough to make a shot like that. With his chance gone, Hagen took three more strokes for a diffident bogey, dropping into a tie for third with George Von Elm, his worst finish in a British Open in the last four he had played.

It should be noted there's an urban-legend quality to this account. Although it became a treasured anecdote in the lore of the game, Al Laney said he remembered Hagen's final shot landing nowhere near that close to the hole. When decades later Laney finally got around to asking him about it, Hagen laughed and said: "Don't you remember, son? I never deny any story about myself. I don't go around breaking down my image this late in life." Whatever the truth might be, the crowd around the eighteenth green that day cheered mightily when Hagen's shot went astray: the man they loved to hate had fallen from contention.

Bobby had won the British Open. He was the first Open champion who ever had to buy a ticket in order to play his final round.

Bobby stepped in off the balcony and the clubhouse around him filled with living history. The Great Triumvirate were there to shake his hand: Vardon, Braid, and Taylor, along with former champions Ted Ray and Sandy Herd and George Duncan and fifty-seven-year-old Harold Hilton, the last amateur to win the Open in 1897. Pop did a quick calculation and figured at least forty national championships were represented by this crowd around his young friend, and they weren't acting all that British either, slapping him on the back, even hugging him. This was Bobby's official welcome into the great fraternity of his sport. The balance of power, still a subject worthy of debate over the previous few years, forever shifted during that summer. An American had won their Amateur for the first time and their Open for the fifth time in the last six years, but all these glorious champions of a passing age recognized that Bobby was a player who transcended nationality.

In his speech awarding the Claret Jug to Bobby shortly afterwards, with tears running freely down his face, J.H. Taylor gave perfect voice to the sentiment that crowd was feeling. "We have just watched the greatest golfer in the game win the game's greatest prize."

Bobby never lost his dread of public speaking, but in these moments he was often at his best, shy, sincere, and emotionally vulnerable. He told the crowd, and all those assembled British champions, that his greatest honor was simply adding his name to a trophy that already held so many who had done so much. Turning to Taylor, he paid tribute to the old warrior's third-round 71 and said it was "better than I could do."

When Bobby and Pop left their hotel in the early evening to begin the trip back to London they stepped off the elevator and there was his faithful caddie Jack McIntyre, come to say goodbye, but as he held out his hand and tried to speak he couldn't get the words out. Bobby put an arm around his shoulders, and with his own voice faltering told him: "Jack, old man, I'd never have done it without you." Jack sat right down on the floor of the hotel lobby and sobbed like a baby.

Bobby and Pop made the fifty-mile drive to Liverpool through the "soft English twilight" to catch a night train back to London, the two of them alone with the Claret Jug in the back of a cab. Both men later described this drive as the happiest hour of their lives.

"I think Bobby and I were not especially coherent on that ride," wrote Pop. "We sat up and grinned idiotically at each other frequently; and at times pounded one another on the back. And we talked a lot about what the folks at home were doing at that moment. That really was the best of all, thinking of the folks at home." "When I see that old *Aquatania*," said Bobby, "I'm going to pick it right up in my arms and hug it."

During their final day in London, Bobby gave a series of interviews to the English papers that underscored his humility and
sportsmanship. Walter Hagen, on the other hand, shot off some
parting remarks about the sorry state of British golf—the word
"lazy" was mentioned—and then spent the better part of the
next month trying to extract a size-12, two-tone saddle shoe
from his mouth. British professionals didn't have the luxury of
abandoning their club positions to pursue freelance careers, as
Hagen had done and other Americans were starting to do; no
organized system of tournaments that would have allowed them
to support themselves yet existed in Great Britain or Europe,
and wouldn't for decades. Hagen's unflattering implication was
that they lacked the initiative to create such a system themselves.
The truth was that their fixed, inferior position in the British
class system still made such a step impossible.

If Hagen thought the English lacked enterprise, he trailed them
by a greater distance in graciousness. Bobby received a telegram
at his hotel that day from Andrew Jamieson, the young amateur
who had defeated him in the Amateur at Muirfield. It was in
Latin, but Bobby and Pop deciphered it this way: "Congratulations
from a small nobody who was impudent enough to beat you."

Bobby, Pop, Hagen, and the rest of the American invaders
boarded the *Aquatania* and set forth for home on Sunday, June
27. A hundred cabled messages of congratulations were waiting
for the champion on board. It was a joyous voyage, and the
relentless schedule of celebrations and dinners gave Bobby plenty
of chances to regain the pounds he'd dropped at St. Anne's, but
precious little time to get the rest he needed.

There would be even less after they arrived. The U.S. Open
was scheduled to begin in two weeks.

CHAPTER NINE

THE DOUBLE

As the *Aquatania* passed through the Verrazano Narrows into New York Harbor, the city's municipal steamer, a small packet ship called the *Mecom*, sailed toward them. Pop called Bobby up on deck for a wonderful surprise. Close to a hundred friends and family had made the trip to New York and sailed out on the *Mecom* to welcome him home: Mary, both his parents, even his crusty old grandfather, R.T. (who claimed to already be in town on business; God forbid he make a special trip for such frivolity). Also among the welcoming committee was a senator or two, over forty reporters and photographers, and a band playing "Dixie" as they pulled alongside. The *Aquatania* came to a stop while Bobby and company went on board the

Mecom and were taken to Pier A on the Battery. It seemed everyone in the city knew he was coming: ships saluted him with their whistles and horns, a fireboat trailed them spraying water like the Tivoli Fountain.

A wall of newsreel cameras greeted Bobby as he stepped off the gangway. The party was waived through customs, a privilege reserved for visiting royalty, and thousands cheered as they climbed into open cars and began a three-mile trip toward the heart of the city. With their sea-legs still wobbly beneath them, they got out to walk behind a succession of marching bands when they reached Broadway, as a phalanx of motorcycle cops cleared the way, sirens blaring. "Ticker tape flying in white spirals from the skyscrapers, and a continuous roar echoing like thunder through the canyon of downtown New York," wrote Pop. He estimated a million people lined the parade route to City Hall, and that as they walked along Bobby looked like "an embarrassed, happy little boy." Although Hagen could claim the city had thrown something similar for him after his first British Open win, it didn't begin to approach the scale of this reception. No single individual, certainly not a sports figure, had ever received anything like this procession through what would become known as the Canyon of Heroes.

New York's flamboyant playboy mayor, Jimmy Walker, gave a speech on the steps of City Hall that was broadcast live on radio throughout the northeast. Visibly overwhelmed, Bobby added a few simple words before cheers began anew. Bobby and Mary couldn't steal a moment alone together until they checked into the Vanderbilt in mid-afternoon, where a gala dinner was held for him that night. Attendees remarked that their guest of honor had a solemn look on his face throughout the evening. Keeler chalked it up to exhaustion, but Bobby felt dazed and disoriented.

He couldn't put a name to it yet, but Bobby was experiencing the strange transformation from a local hero into an utterly famous household name. He didn't belong to just Atlanta or Georgia or even the game of golf anymore; now the whole country laid claim to him. The elegant way in which this young man played an incredibly difficult sport without expectation or reward of a single red cent in return appealed to people in a way no athlete had ever done before. Ouimet had put golf on the map and Hagen had created the game's first larger-than-life personality; Bobby was the first American to transcend his sport in a way we would recognize today as a superstar. Bobby was hot; he was cool. He was like us, only better. The air around him felt charged with the dreams of millions of strangers, but his modesty made him still seem as approachable as the kid next door; after being humbled by his struggles with the game, none of his success seemed to have affected his hat size. This was a dynamite combination and the hysteria in New York was only a taste of what life had in store.

The glare of the spotlight spilled over onto everyone close to Bobby, particularly Mary. Romance magazines wrote about their marriage; fashion magazines wanted to photograph her clothes and their home. Mary knew she had married a man on a mission, but until their tumultuous welcome had never realized that from this moment forward she would have to share her husband with the multitudes in ways no bride in her right mind would have imagined.

Huge life decisions hung in the balance. The next day Bobby and Mary boarded a westbound sleeper train together along with his parents and left for Scioto Country Club, in Columbus, Ohio. During the trip Bobby sat down with the Colonel and discussed his leaving the Adairs' real estate business and entering the law.

Six hundred and ninety-four players attempted to qualify for the 1926 U.S. Open, requiring seventeen sectional events; both record numbers. One hundred and forty-five survived the cut

and would tee it up at Scioto; the more than one hundred creden-
tialed reporters who flocked to the Midwest to cover the event
were interested in exactly one of them. No golfer, of any nationality, amateur or professional, had ever won both the British
and United States Opens in the same year. He was about to try
to turn the trick within three weeks.

Scioto was a Donald Ross design, just over a decade old and
already considered one of his better efforts. The club's head pro,
forty-six-year-old George Sargent, was a great friend to the sport,
a founding father of the PGA who had been Ouimet's playing
partner during his final rounds in the 1913 Open. As players
arrived in town so did a heatwave and a rigid band of high
humidity. When practice began on Monday, Sargent told the
press to expect high scores: a month-long drought had left both
fairways and greens hard and unforgiving, but the rough he'd
cultivated had somehow flourished. The city of Columbus sent
over emergency water wagons to spray down scorched areas of
the fairways. During the middle of Bobby's practice round on
Tuesday a thunderstorm blew in off the Great Lakes and chased
everyone off the course, canceling the scheduled pro–am event.
Bobby didn't mind: he needed rest more than practice.

He might have appeared sharp to the undiscerning eye, but
to Pop he looked "stale, jaded and dull." After two months of
steady pressure and constant travel he was used up and longed
to be home. When he met Keeler just before his tee time on
Thursday morning he said something Pop had never heard from
him before: "I wish this was over."

Then Bobby went out to play his first round, breathed in the
electricity and adrenaline crackling in the championship atmosphere, and shot 70. The assembled reporters, many of them
newcomers to golf who had been sent to cover Bobby as a
general news story, fell all over themselves. "The perfect golfing
machine at work" summed up the sentiment in dozens of stories.
Bobby and Pop knew differently: this had been a sweating,

grinding piece of work, eking out pars while skating on the rim of disaster. Bobby was out of gas; his 70 was the work of nothing but will and strained mentality, and it further exhausted him. Pop watched him slump to the showers, his shoulders broken out in heat rash; Bobby came back afterwards, leaned his wet head on Pop's shoulder and asked with only half a laugh: "Why can't I play this damn game?"

But that 70 left him in second place two strokes off the lead behind Wild Bill Melhorn. Bobby spent a restless night; Grantland Rice encountered him before the second round and was shocked at how exhausted he looked. That morning Bobby couldn't sustain his high-wire act. Where he had caught good breaks and bounces the day before, this time they went against him. He was forced to take a penalty stroke at ten to gain relief from a stone wall next to a water hazard. He rallied, briefly, until he reached fifteen. Playing in a steady wind, after grounding his putter in front of his ball to square his line, when he moved it behind the ball to begin his takeaway the exposed ball wobbled and turned over. Once again, no one else saw it move. Once again, Bobby called a penalty stroke on himself. Once again, he expressed dismay that people should compliment him for simply following the rules.

He was barely hanging on by the time he reached eighteen, a reachable par-five birdie opportunity; he needed one to finish with 76. After pushing his drive into the right-hand rough Bobby tried to make up for the day's sins with an overly-aggressive swing that came in too steeply; the hosel of his two-iron snagged in the grass and the ball advanced 20 feet. Annoyed at himself, he swung again without changing clubs and hooked the ball into light rough on the opposite side of the fairway. His pitch to the green came up short. A chip from there left him a 5-foot putt. He rushed it, and missed it, and took double bogey seven for 79, his highest single-round score ever in a U.S. Open. At the halfway point Bobby trailed Melhorn by six strokes, and stood four shots behind a twenty-five-year-old pro from Elmsford, New York, named Joe Turnesa.

The USGA had changed the format that year, extending play to three days—as the R&A had done earlier, although the USGA's intent was to increase revenue, not limit attendance—with the final two rounds still played on the last day of competition. The field was trimmed after the second round to the top fifty players and ties. The added box office helped increase the prize money: the purse had grown to $2,145, with the top twenty players finishing in the money. First place earned you a check for $500—unless you were Bobby Jones.

Bobby felt disgusted by Friday's performance, particularly the final hole, where he had lapsed into poor judgment and the kind of juvenile mistakes he thought he'd put behind him. Mary and his parents worried that he was driving himself close to collapse. When he woke Saturday morning, Bobby was violently ill, vomiting repeatedly. Pop and a friend from Atlanta rushed him to a local doctor's house at 7:00 A.M. Dr. Ryan couldn't diagnose the problem precisely—it was symptomatic of exhaustion, but Ryan wasn't about to tell Bobby Jones not to play the last rounds of the Open—and gave him something to settle his stomach. Refusing payment or free tickets, Dr. Ryan said he was coming out to watch the last two rounds and asked Bobby only for a ball he used that day. They returned to Scioto where, digging into his dangerously depleted reserves, Bobby summoned his best golf of the week, an error-free third round of 71. He picked up a stroke on Joe Turnesa, trailing him by three in third place, behind Wild Bill Melhorn by one shot. Bobby rested in the clubhouse between rounds; he tried to eat a light lunch of tea and toast but couldn't keep anything down despite Dr. Ryan's medication. He would have to play the Open's final round on borrowed energy, a bad stomach, and wobbly legs.

The wind picked up throughout the day, heralding the approach of another Great Lakes blow. Rain fell in spurts.

Melhorn fell out of contention quickly, creating a two-man race. Turnesa teed off two groups ahead of Bobby, but two-thirds of the crowd was in Jones's gallery.

(Following him all week at Scioto was a teenage drugstore clerk named Charlie Nicklaus. Two decades later, raising his son Jack on the fairways of Scioto where he was now a member, Charlie held up Bobby as the game's ideal both on and off the course. Jack never had a bigger hero in the sport.)

Joe Turnesa was an unflappable character and didn't seem to mind playing with the lead. They played the first eight holes dead even with each other and the scorecard. On the short par-three ninth, protected by a large tree overhanging the right side of the green, Bobby made his first mistake for bogey while Turnesa got his par. Joe's lead increased to four, with nine holes left to play.

Bobby could keep track of Turnesa just by listening to the reactions of his gallery. Joe parred the tenth and the eleventh. Bobby matched him. But as Bobby teed off on twelve, Turnesa tried to gamble at the par-five thirteenth; he went for the green in two but playing into the wind came up a bounce short and got caught in the high grass. An aggressive gamble at this stage of the tournament, it ended up costing him a six. By the time Bobby reached twelve he knew Joe had given back a stroke; now he went all out to grab another one from him. His drive was long and low, shearing like a clipper into the wind. His second cleared the patch of rough that had trapped Turnesa, and kicked onto the front fringe of the green. A simple chip and putt and he had his birdie.

Turnesa's lead had been trimmed to two. A sudden absence of wind cost him another stroke at the 445-yard thirteenth, when it failed to move his approach off line as he'd intended and found a greenside bunker. Another bogey.

Bobby's second shot ran into a bunker on the other side, pin high. But the bunker had a low lip, and Bobby elected to putt the ball out. That got him to within 4 feet, and Calamity Jane saved his par. The roar that went up reached Turnesa on the fifteenth tee. He realized his lead over Bobby was down to a single stroke.

They matched pars on the next two holes. At sixteen, Turnesa bounced his approach through the green and left his chip short coming back. He missed a 9-foot putt for par. Bobby capitalized, recording a routine four: they were tied. On the par-three seventeenth Turnesa betrayed his only sign of tension all day: short with his tee shot, short with his chip, and just like that another bogey. When Bobby came through and collected his three he had his first lead of the tournament.

It lasted all of thirty seconds. Just ahead, playing the par-five eighteenth, aware he needed a birdie to stay even with Bobby, Turnesa went for the green in two and pushed into the rough. But his pitch from there was nearly perfect, leaving him an 8-footer for birdie. He sank the putt for four. The roar reached all the way back to the eighteenth tee.

Tied for the lead.

He looked focused and strong to the seasoned observers crowding around him, but only Bobby knew how deeply the exhaustion had wormed in his bones. He felt nauseated and weak and hadn't eaten a bite of food all day. He'd burned off the twelve pounds he'd regained on *Aquatania* and then some. Another eighteen-hole play-off the next day might just finish him; he knew he didn't have the strength to win one in his weakened state. He'd lost two Open play-offs in the last three years when he was on top of his game. Today, sick as he was, offered his best and only chance.

Winning the Double Open, history, was in his grasp. All he had to do was match Turnesa's birdie at eighteen and he could close his hand around it.

Into that whistling crosswind, Bobby smashed a 310-yard drive that split the seam of the narrow winding fairway. Some estimates claim it was even longer; Pop paced it off to be certain. Pop said the only sound you could hear among the crowd of ten thousand as Bobby reached his ball was the racket of typewriters from the clubhouse roof; reporters had been stationed up there all week to watch the action. Even the typewriters stopped as Bobby ripped another fateful mid-iron on the Open's final hole. His knees were shaking as he swung; they nearly buckled as he walked after it.

The crowd began cheering before the ball reached the green, then exploded as it touched down on the front edge and rolled 20 feet right past the flag. Bobby lagged his eagle putt to within four inches. Four inches left to win the Open. His mind played tricks on him over the ball, the imp of the perverse taunting him to stub his putter on the ground and whiff. Bobby clamped down those thoughts, held the putter a half-inch off the grass, and tapped the ball home for the win.

Double Open Champion. Pandemonium broke out around him.

But the celebration was slightly premature; there were still two players on the course with theoretical chances of catching him. Bobby dragged himself out of range of all the well-wishers and back-slappers—not before remembering to slip the last ball he'd used to Dr. Earl Ryan along the way—and staggered back to his hotel room. His father found him outside, clamped both hands on his shoulders, and told him: "It doesn't matter if you win now; what matters is that you finished at all, and finished the way you did."

"Thank you, Dad," he said.

When Bobby reached his room his mother was already there, packing his suitcases. He filled her in on the round as he poured himself a highball with hands shaking so hard he could barely hold the glass. Then it all crashed in on him. He slumped into a chair and burst into shuddering, convulsive sobs.

Empty. All the strain and tension of the last three months

lived in the glare of that spotlight. Bewildered. All the uncertainty of his real life in such stark contrast to the "conquering hero" of the newsreels. Lost. He was twenty-four, soon to be a father of two, between careers and short of cash. An idol to the nation in a sport from which, as a matter of principle, he had firmly decided he would derive no financial reward. Adored by uncomprehending thousands still celebrating less than a hundred yards away, and millions around the world. As far as Bobby could remember it was the only time in his life he'd ever broken down like this, at the exact moment of his greatest triumph and the most remarkable achievement in the history of golf. In front of his own mother, no less. If he could only stop bawling his eyes out for a second he'd burst out laughing.

Clara took a long, puzzled look at him. Not the warm, cuddly type, she had always been the backbone and disciplinarian in the family, keeping Bobby on the straight and narrow while the Colonel stayed his pal. The sight of her only son falling apart threw her for a loop. This was supposed to be his idea of fun, wasn't it? That's why he did this. Honestly, Bobby?

He couldn't even answer her.

"Well," said Clara finally, "I think that's about enough championship golf for you."

The larger question he was confronting, when Bobby could get his mind around it, was simple, and every person comes to it at some time or another in their life. He nearly killed himself to win these damn things and now that he'd finally done it all he could ask himself was: *Is that all there is?*

The phone rang, Pop calling from the clubhouse with confirmation: By the way, you've won the Open. Come and get it.

An equally dramatic scene was unfolding in Scioto's locker room. Walter Hagen had played poorly in the Open; he finished a distant sixth and had never been a factor. That didn't stop him from marching in after it was over and lashing out at his fellow pros as they were packing up to leave.

"Whenever I fail to stop Jones the rest of you curl up and die, too. All that goddamn amateur has to do is show on the first tee and the best pros in the world throw in the towel. If we don't stop him he's going to walk all over us." Dead silence. "Well I'm going to ask you all this: What are we going to do about it? It's about time we stand our ground!" Then he stamped back outside to pose for pictures and sign autographs.

Bobby pulled himself together and walked back down to the eighteenth green. He put on a weary smile but told USGA officials he preferred to just collect the trophy and not give a speech; he was afraid he might break down all over again. When the officials saw his ashen face no one put up any objection.

The champ held the cup for photographers while the cheers began again. He'd never been part of a more incongruous moment: torn to shreds inside, a champion, standing alone on a mountaintop no one had ever reached before.

BOBBY'S BRINGING HOME THE BACON. That was the banner headline waiting for him in Atlanta. His two Open trophies, Claret Jug and silver cup, rode on the back of a flatbed truck, together for the first time, as the parade wound through downtown and ended at the Atlanta Athletic Club's posh new headquarters. Pop's eyes filled with tears at the sight of that crowd; he described in his column how hard it was to get tired of these affairs. But Bobby was tired, period. Tired of golf, tired of traveling, tired of being on constant display, knowing the demands on his time and attention would only get worse.

For the first time in his career, Bobby felt compelled to give Pop an "official interview" for national syndication, to satisfy the public's hunger for insights into "Bobby Jones." Just as he and Pop had always been able to discuss his swing and golf game as if it belonged to some neutral third party, they now begin to think of his public image as a creation distinct and separate from himself. The interview reads as exactly what it was: a friendly chat between two old pals over a couple of cocktails.

Bobby attributes his success to luck. Principally, the luck of growing up next to East Lake and the presence of Kiltie Maiden. (The word "fate" is never mentioned; Pop felt it might come across as too deep-dish for broad consumption.) When prompted, Bobby talked about technique, reluctantly, but it's clear how deep and precise his thinking about the golf swing had become. The self-deprecation he displays in describing his game never reads as false modesty; his faults still pained him and he despaired of ridding himself of them. He uses the words "wretched" or "terrible" more often than any superlatives. When Pop brings up the great shots that had won championships and were starting to crowd his résumé, Bobby doesn't remember much about them. He can recall thinking about what he wanted to do as he assessed a situation—on the four-iron at Inwood, for example, but all he could remember was looking up and seeing the ball outlined in the sky against a black cloud.

His most revealing comments come on the subject of nerves. "I do not think nervousness hurts my game. The more nervous I am, the better I play, usually. I suppose it means being keyed up. Some of the sloppiest rounds I have played, I wasn't nervous at all. As to the strain, I don't seem to be conscious of it during a round. Afterward—well, I know something has been done to me." He insisted you had to be nervous to play golf well. The man who could keep himself on edge was a hard man to beat. "Nerves are what differentiate a thoroughbred from a plough horse," he said.

Despite which, Bobby also mentions that he's trying lately to learn how to relax between shots, chatting with his partner or some friend in the gallery—usually Pop—to relieve the tension. "Then when I get to the ball I can snap on the concentration as hard as I need to."

When Pop tries to bring up the subject of the penalty shots,

Bobby feels an invitation to moral flattery approaching and holds up a warning hand. "There is absolutely nothing to talk about," he says, "and you are not to write about it. There is only one way to play this game."

Pop decided to risk violating Bobby's confidence, and used that line to close the interview.

His ethical rigor on the course would continue, but there would be no more uphill fighting on the private side. The decision had been made between Scioto and home that in the fall Bobby would attend Emory University's law school in Atlanta, the finest program of its kind in the South. The choice of Emory seems dictated by an overwhelming desire to spend time close to home, but the Colonel grilled him about the bigger decision: was Bobby sure about the law? He said he was. The mental challenge, the precision of the language, the clean crease between right and wrong all felt like a tonic to the life he'd been living. And after Emory's three-year program, once Bobby passed the Bar he knew a desk would be waiting for him at the firm which would be known as Jones, Evins, Moore & Jones. The Colonel's fondest lifelong wish had come to pass.

Bobby picked up his sticks again in August and began preparing for the season's final test. The 1926 Amateur Championship was held at Baltusrol Golf Club in Springfield, New Jersey. For the first time the USGA introduced the concept of seeding the top amateurs, and to no one's surprise Bobby claimed the first spot. Behind him came Jess Sweetser, still recuperating from tuberculosis and unable to play, then George Von Elm, Francis Ouimet, and Chick Evans. Bobby arrived with a chance to become the first man to ever win three Amateur championships in a row, and match Evans's 1916 Open–Amateur double into the bargain. Both press and public had every confidence he would pull it off. Qualifying began on September 13, and Bobby won the medal at one over par, a shot off the Amateur record. The USGA had tinkered with the format yet again: after qualifying on Monday and Tuesday, seeding determined brackets for the top thirty-two survivors who would play two eighteen-hole matches on Wednesday. The final three matches leading to the championship, all thirty-six-hole affairs, would follow on Thursday, Friday, and Saturday.

Bobby breezed through both of Wednesday's matches without incident. On Thursday, in his first thirty-six-hole match, he met Chick Evans. The two hadn't played each other in competition for six years, when Evans psyched him out at the Western Amateur in Memphis. Evans did an unseemly amount of crowing at the time; then only eighteen, Bobby had vowed to one day even the score. Their paths had diverged; Evans had gone six years without a national title, while Bobby had become the king of the game. Although as friendly as ever to Bobby's face, the envy rose off Evans like a vapor and Bobby saw no reason to let his advancing dislike of Evans stand in the way of beating his brains out. Revenge is a dish best served cold. Bobby opened a two-hole lead after the first eighteen, but Evans stuck close and Bobby was tempted to give up playing against par in order to fight him head to head. But he kept to his disciplined approach, Evans cracked on the final nine and Bobby finished him off at their thirty-fourth hole, 3 & 2.

Friday morning's semi-final brought Bobby together again with Francis Ouimet. Ouimet had barely qualified, squeaking in through a play-off, but his game had come back to life since his poor showing against Bobby at Merion two years before. Both played a superb first round, Ouimet coming in at even par, no easy achievement at Baltusrol, one of his best performances of the year. Bobby shot three under, which on this course seemed superhuman. After lunching together the two friends went back to battle in the afternoon; Ouimet opened with an eagle to get within two, and he closed out the front nine with a phenomenal 34. Bobby shot 33 and stretched his lead to four. Ouimet parred the next four holes, and lost the match 5 & 4. Just for fun, because they so enjoyed playing with each other, they finished the round together and hardly a soul in the gallery deserted them. Ouimet shot 69, a stroke off the new club record of 68, which had just been turned in by his opponent Mr. Jones. Francis could only shake his head and laugh.

Saturday's final brought Bobby up against that haughty Californian fashion plate, George Von Elm. After spending the summer in Britain together the two men were getting on each other's nerves. Von Elm felt he had established himself as the country's second best amateur—he was right; even Hagen had said he was the only other non-pro who ever worried him—but the gulf between Bobby Jones and second place was so vast that Von Elm felt permanently slighted. As a regional champion George ruled California, but without any major titles that hadn't translated to national respect; the same provincialism colored Midwesterner Chick Evans's attitude toward the Eastern establishment even after he'd won his majors. Both men always forgot that, as an outsider coming from the South, Bobby had faced far more innate prejudice at the start of his career than either one of them. He was simply a better player, something neither was ever willing to concede. Bobby and Von Elm had a personal stake in beating each other. Von Elm stood between Bobby and a trophy case of previously unapproachable records: three Amateurs in a row, the Open-Amateur Double, and three major victories in the same calendar year, which sportswriters had started to call "the Triple Crown." Bobby stood between Von Elm and the legitimacy he craved.

Everyone expected Bobby to trounce Von Elm again; everyone except Bobby. He'd seen too much of this tough-minded son of a bitch's game. On their way to the course that morning, Bobby told Pop: "Nobody's going to keep beating a golfer as good as George Von Elm."

They were dead even through sixteen, both playing even par

golf. On the seventeenth green, after Bobby missed a long birdie attempt, and sank a tough come-backer for par, the huge gallery rushed ahead to the next tee. But Von Elm still faced a tough 6-footer for par to halve the hole, and he stepped away from his ball when the gallery made its move, visibly upset. As Bobby described it later, "I don't know exactly what prompted me to do it, but I felt that there was no way to stop the crowd and that it was definitely unfair for George to have to putt with all the commotion going on." Bobby walked over and knocked Von Elm's ball toward him, saying: "I'll give you that one, George." Von Elm put an arm around Bobby's shoulder and thanked him as they walked on to the next hole. On the next green, Von Elm returned the favor; while Bobby was studying a 4-footer, he picked the ball up and stuffed it in Bobby's pocket, halving that hole as well. Their referee, Bill Fownes, called them together as they left the green and said: "Now listen, boys, this Alphonse and Gaston stuff has gone on long enough. Let's play golf." In the best amateur tradition, despite their private feelings about each other, rivalry was not allowed to get in the way of sportsmanship.

Von Elm played relentless golf over the second eighteen that afternoon; he never faltered. Bobby appeared to have slipped past his peak, but he never gave up. Von Elm opened up a two-hole lead—the only one either had been able to build all day— as they reached their thirty-fifth hole. A par-five, over 600 yards in length, the longest hole in the history of USGA competition; Von Elm reached it easily in regulation. Bobby hit his drive in the rough. After advancing it back to the fairway he tried to land a knockout punch while practically lying on his back, and nearly holed his third shot from 170 yards, but the ball rolled 20 feet past the flag. When he missed his birdie putt and both men settled for par, the match was over, 2 & 1. Bobby had shot one over par for thirty-five holes but his reach for history had been turned away by Von Elm's steady brilliance, and for the first time an American golf title belonged to a man from west of the Mississippi. Pop later wrote: "Of all his championships, I loved him best in that long and losing battle."

Bobby offered no excuses, and gave Von Elm credit for the win he deserved. "It was George's turn," he said. Visibly relieved, Von Elm collected the new Havermeyer Trophy and appeared to have gained the respect he needed, but the feeling was short-lived; most of the next day's newspapers blamed the result on sub-par golf by Bobby, rather than Von Elm's masterful one-under-par performance. He realized it would take more than one win over Bobby Jones to earn him a place beside him up on the pedestal.

Two weeks later Bobby traded his clubs for law books and began his first term at Emory University. That same week he learned that the Royal & Ancient Golf Club of St. Andrews had named him an honorary member for his win in their Open. Bobby accepted proudly, but announced with regret that because of his studies he would be unable to travel overseas the following summer to defend his British Open title. There would soon be more distractions: Bobby and Mary's second child, Robert Tyre Jones III, was born less than two months later.

The greatest year anyone had ever played in golf was over. It was impossible to imagine a player could ever match it, let alone surpass it. And for the first time in history, all four of the game's major titles belonged to American-born players: Sweetser, Jones, Von Elm.

As Bobby turned his hand to the building blocks of a future career that winter, in the back of his mind an impossible thought began to take shape. Something had been missing in his matches at Baltusrol, particularly in the finals against Von Elm; for the first time in any national championship he hadn't felt nervous. He told Pop about this alarming loss of competitive edge, but privately interpreted it as a sign that the time was coming, sooner rather than later, for him to move on in life. He began to look for a way out of golf, one that would both satisfy his ambition and allow him an exit with his dignity intact that no one would argue with.

And then it came to him: what if all four major titles could be won in the same year . . . by the *same* American-born player?

CHAPTER TEN

CONSOLIDATION

B obby set the game aside that fall and well into the winter of 1926–7; his course load was simply too demanding for any other kind of course work he was more accustomed to. According to Pop Bobby played exactly two and a half rounds of golf between November and late February. The lay-off didn't seem to hurt his game; during one of his earliest spring rounds, playing with Kiltie at East Lake, Bobby scored the first hole in one of his life. Pure luck, he called it. A month later he won the Southern Open, played at East Lake against a field of the game's best professionals and amateurs, by eight strokes. The longer he played, the luckier he got.

During a decade of exclusivity, Bobby had used Pop as a shield from the inquiring national press, and in return Pop received unfettered access to the private thoughts of his friend, and became a respected national sportswriter. Along the way a lot of journalistic feathers got ruffled. A false perception had started to form that Bobby considered himself to be bigger than the game. The resentment directed toward him from professionals like Hagen was well documented, although under-publicized by reporters maintaining the day's more forgiving journalistic standards. In 1927 some of Bobby's fellow amateurs—principally Chick Evans and George Von Elm—started to get in on the act.

Evans and Von Elm believed that the USGA danced to Bobby's tune, organizing tournaments to suit his schedule and handing him preferential starting times. They also complained they let him hand-pick his playing partners. Some of those grievances had a foundation in fact, but not because Bobby was asking for them. The USGA needed to sell tickets to its championships to survive, and Bobby had become the sporting world's biggest attraction. They needed him on the golf course when the most people had a chance to see him. If that meant pairing him with someone he knew or had developed a rivalry with, so much the better. One of the eternal axioms of showbusiness is the star gets his name in lights and the biggest dressing room. That never stops the grumbling from the second rank, but if anyone felt slighted all they had to do to change it was beat him a few times. Most never beat him once. It's interesting to note that these same complaints would surface later, during their primes, regarding Ben Hogan, Arnold Palmer, Jack Nicklaus, and Tiger Woods.

Bobby heard the gripes and decided that there was no percentage in addressing them publicly. But he did tell Pop he felt ready to accept the responsibilities of stardom and was prepared to deal with other reporters on a one-to-one basis. He also let everyone around him know that from now on he preferred to be called Bob, a name more suited to the grown-up he had become. (Pop took to calling him "Rubber Tyre," but he was the only one who could get away with that.) Seizing additional control of his image while struggling to subsidize his education, Bob accepted an offer from Jack Wheeler's Bell Newspaper Syndicate to write a series of first-person columns about the game of golf. Bob discovered he enjoyed the work, and the columns would continue until 1935. He also began contributing to Grantland Rice's *American Golfer* on a semi-regular basis. Something of a loophole in the USGA's definition of amateurism, sportswriting for a paycheck without turning pro had well-established precedents; both Ouimet and Evans had taken similar jobs after winning their national championships. No one complained when their articles first appeared, but some sticklers did about Bob's; for the rest of his playing days he would remain under greater scrutiny, and be held to a higher standard, than any other amateur in history.

The general interest in Bob had grown so great that he signed a contract with a New York publishing firm to co-write his autobiography with Pop Keeler. In his introduction to *Down the Fairway*, published later that summer, Grantland Rice pointed out that "one person in ten million might have an interesting autobiography to put out at the age of twenty-five." The book is still a wonderful read and although Pop had a major hand in shaping it, Bob's voice comes through clearly. This was the first of four books Bob would publish during his lifetime, and he already possessed a distinctive literary style, in some ways typical of the better writers from the South: lyrical, ironic, understated, with a keen eye for the unexpected detail. His writing in this way resembled his golf swing: powerful and precise, with a touch of poetry. It's no exaggeration to say that by the end of his life he had become the most insightful writer on the subject of golf who had first been an outstanding player. For what was originally intended as a quick catch-the-money sports biography, the point of view he offers of himself in *Down the Fairway* remains grounded, self-deprecating and refreshingly clear-eyed. One detail on which he agreed with his less modest profilers: Bob expressed shock at realizing he'd already been competing at the national level for thirteen years, more than half his lifetime. He'd won five major championships and astonished the world.

They hadn't seen anything yet.

After the beatings it handed the Amateurs in 1919 and 1925, Oakmont Country Club learned the USGA wanted it to host the 1927 Open. Bill Fownes once again went to work, adding more hazards and obstacles to his ongoing experiment in testing the limits of the human spirit; in many spots he let the rough grow up over a man's knees. Of the heavy rakes he'd invented to carve two-inch furrows into the sand—perpendicular to the line of the hole—and turn his 220 bunkers into death traps, Jimmy Demaret would later say: "You could have combed North Africa with 'em and Rommel wouldn't have got past Casablanca."

Among the men in the field that year were members of Great Britain's first Ryder Cup team. After the 1926 matches at Wentworth, the international competition between American and British pros found a sponsor in a former nursery owner from Hertfordshire named Samuel Ryder. After watching the British team trounce the Americans at Wentworth, Ryder invited members from both sides to tea, and offered to provide a trophy if the teams would agree to formalize the event as a biannual affair, played on alternate years with the Walker Cup. Shortly thereafter Ryder commissioned the delicate gold chalice that bears his name and has since become one of the world's most fiercely contested trophies. In June of 1927 the first official Ryder Cup competition was played at Worcester Country Club outside Boston. Ted Ray captained the British side, with Hagen his American counterpart; the Americans prevailed 9½–2½, gaining revenge for the bloodbath at Wentworth.

Press and public expected a great deal of Bob at Oakmont. Although he was speaking to reporters, he refused to offer any forecasts, despite having won the Amateur on this course two years earlier. He knew going in that his game was a long way from what this monster layout demanded. Bob had recently won the Southern Amateur in a walk against nearly the same field, it was true, but that was at East Lake, the track he knew so well he could kick a ball around it in par. Oakmont punished anything less than perfection without mercy.

He must have sensed something. Bob's tournament ended, in effect, on the fourth hole of the first round when he hooked his drive into one of those furrowed bunkers. Not just any hazard, but Oakmont's most feared one: the 60-yard-long Church Pews. Bob needed four shots to get out of church. He shot 76 that day, and 77 the next. That should have been the end of the Open for him, except that Oakmont was kicking every other behind in the field. Bob was only six shots out of first, but told anyone who would listen he had no chance to win. He supported this prediction with the 79 he shot in the third round, eight strokes out of the lead, but still it wasn't over. When he finally put together a decent stretch during the final round, the field drifted back toward him, and as he reached the thirteenth tee he learned he was only a single stroke behind the leader, "Lighthorse" Harry Cooper. Bob looked to be on track to shoot 70 or 71, and word spread that he was making a run at his third Open. The nerves of every other player in the hunt rattled and pinged, while Bob's gallery inflated back to its normal size.

The thirteenth at Oakmont is a par-three, the shortest on the course. Bob yanked a five-iron into a narrow ditch way left of the green. From a lousy lie in the ditch he hacked it into a massive bunker. He needed two to get out of the sand and onto the green, leaving himself an 8-footer for five. "Then," said Bobby, "I carefully missed the putt."

Triple bogey six. Pop watched the air go right out of him.

Two holes later he double-bogeyed the fifteenth. Bob finished with 79, tying his personal worst for an Open round. He ended tied for eleventh, his lowest finish ever in a U.S. Open. His exit cleared the stage for one of the most exciting back nines in the history of the championship.

Harry Cooper was a twenty-three-year-old transplanted Englishman, the son of a golf professional who'd taken a club job in Texas when Harry was a boy. He appeared to have this Open all wrapped up, until he faltered down Oakmont's brutal home stretch. Gene Sarazen nearly caught him, but failed to sink a 50-foot birdie at eighteen and fell a stroke short. Wild Bill Melhorn and Emmett French both had shorter putts to tie at eighteen but failed to capitalize. Only Tommy Armour—the Black Scot, as they'd taken to calling him—was left with any hope of catching Cooper. With six holes left to play he trailed Lighthorse Harry by three. By the time Armour reached eighteen, Cooper's lead was down to one.

Pop and Bob stationed themselves on the edge of the green and watched Tommy drill a four-iron to within 10 feet; he needed that putt to force a play-off. The tension was so thick Pop could feel it in his ears. They heard two men arguing behind them that under these circumstances no one could make that putt. Bob reminded them that a man who had snapped the neck of a German tank officer with his bare hands to save the lives of his crew knew a little something about pressure. Armour made the putt.

Pop couldn't stick around to watch the play-off. He had a train to catch to New York, where he was scheduled to be married (to sportswriter and golf lover Eleanor McIntosh McAuliffe) the next day. Bob left the same day for Atlanta, upset but philosophical about his poor performance; without his ever offering it as an excuse, law school had demanded too much of his time. But his four-year streak of consecutive championships was in jeopardy. He vowed to return home and prepare for the Amateur later that summer.

Both missed a great play-off the following day, won by Tommy Armour for his first major victory. For once the professional ranks had held serve against Bobby Jones. The Black Scot proved an enormously popular champion with press, public, and fellow players. Instead of cashing in on his victory with a grueling exhibition tour, Armour took a different approach. He would spend the remainder of his life working as the resident pro at a succession of upscale private clubs in and around Palm Beach, whose members lined up to be charged outrageous sums of money for lessons. After the win at Oakmont Tommy's fee went up to $100 an hour. Twenty years later, from his rich, eager clients, he would be able to ask, and be eagerly paid, $1,000 a lesson.

After their civil marriage at City Hall in New York, Pop and Mommer, as he called her, had two days to kill before boarding the *Aquatania* to begin their honeymoon in Paris. Pop wandered into the midtown headquarters of the USGA to give his regards to the organization's secretary, Tommy McMahon. McMahon said: "You might be interested in this," and handed him a telegram.

The telegram was from Mr. Robert Tyre Jones, of Atlanta, asking Mr. McMahon if to his knowledge the entries to this year's British Open at St. Andrews—scheduled to begin in just over two weeks on July 11—were officially closed. And if they weren't, would Mr. McMahon mind cabling Mr. Jones's entry to the R&A. "It's cabled," said McMahon.

Pop broke into an ear-to-ear grin. Bob later explained that he hadn't wanted to bother Pop about the decision on his wedding day. Pop walked back to his hotel where, at length and with the same poetic finesse with which he'd wooed her, he explained to Eleanor that there was going to be slight change in their honeymoon. It was a good thing she loved golf; an Open at St. Andrews sounded like more fun than Paris to her anyway.

Bob had gone home before announcing his plans about

Scotland to a single soul because he needed to talk it over with
Mary. After three years of marriage Mary had begun to assert
herself in Bob's life. She had lobbied hard for his staying close
to home at Emory and was materially involved in any decisions
about golf that affected the family from now on. Bob knew that
if he was going to take off for a month overseas on a moment's
notice it wasn't going to happen without her blessing. She also
knew him well enough to say yes without putting up a fuss.
With two young kids at home she couldn't go with him, but it
would be the last trip of this kind on which she didn't. The
Colonel, Kiltie, and two other Atlanta friends jumped at the
chance to see Bob defend his championship; they caught a night
train to New York and sailed over on the *Transylvania*, landing
in Glasgow only five days before the Open.

Local qualifying had been restored after last year's regional
experiment; a round each on the Old and New Courses would
advance a hundred players to the championship. Entry fees for
professionals were £1; it cost amateurs twice as much, as they
were historically men of more means. The pros would contend
for a purse worth £275, with £100 of that going to the winner,
the largest payday in Open history. With a healthy surplus in
hand from last year, the R&A decided not to sell tickets. The
Old Course was so open and easy to access from every direction they couldn't keep anyone out who wanted to watch
anyway. But there would be no repeat of the mob scene at
Prestwick; the fans at St. Andrews were the most knowledgeable in the world and cared too much about their game to breach
its etiquette.

With no Walker Cup competitions that year, Bob was almost
the only American in the Open. After a poor practice round on
Saturday Team Jones moved to an American-style course at
nearby Gleneagles to get in more work before the tournament.
(An ancient ordinance in St. Andrews still prohibited playing
golf on the Sabbath; there was no such law in effect at Gleneagles,

a resort dependant on the American tourist dollar.) Bob regained his touch, setting a new course record of 67, but it left him again the following day during his first qualifying round on the Old Course. For one nervous night there was concern he might not make the cut. That worry vanished the next day when he tied the New Course record with a 71 and qualified easily.

The night before the tournament began Kiltie told Pop in an abnormal burst of enthusiasm that if Bobby kept hitting the ball the way he had been there wasn't a man alive who would beat him. As long as Pop had known him, Stewart Maiden had never predicted anything about golf before in his life.

Since his first visit to St. Andrews six years before, Bob had schooled himself in the traditions of the Auld Grey Toon, and embraced them as a student of the game. He had also grown to love and appreciate the nearby course that started it all. The Scots had been playing the game on this long, narrow fishhook of seaside ground a hundred years before Columbus discovered America. Two centuries before Shakespeare, before Queen Elizabeth I or Henry VIII. Golf is the oldest sport in the western world and St. Andrews is not just the physical and historical center of the game, it is its spiritual home. The genius of the Old Course lies not in its inherent difficulty, but in the overwhelming number of options it presents a golfer. Standing on the tee you are seldom if ever directed to follow any specific path to the green; what more often confronts you is a flat, featureless land-scape—alive with hidden dangers—through which you must care-fully plot your way. With its seven huge double greens—some of them over an acre in size—varied pin positions, and the infinitely changeable wind, you are almost never asked to play the same course twice. The Old Course requires great skill, but more than that it demands precise thinking and strategy; you first beat this golf course with your mind by creating a disciplined plan of attack, one shot setting up the next as if in a chess game, and then you had to go out and execute it.

By his own admission, Bob had disgraced himself here in 1921. His second trip in 1926 had brought forgiveness and redemption, and deeper understanding on his part of what riches the place represented. During this third tournament at St. Andrews, Bob earned the undying love and admiration of the British sporting world. Following the exacting approach he'd been formulating since his discussions with Tommy Armour, in the first round of the '27 Open Bob tied the Old Course scoring record with a 68. Par at this time was 73; it was the first time Bob had ever broken 70 in any Open competition. Along with his 66 at Sunningdale, it stands as one of the great single rounds of golf ever played. Calamity Jane II came into her own: at the fifth he canned a putt of 120 feet for an eagle. At the eighth he dropped a 30-footer for birdie. He saved par from 20 feet at thirteen. He did not miss a single putt of under 12 feet, needing only 29 in the round. Six came from more than 100 feet out on those oversized greens and he didn't three-putt once. In his room at the Grand Hotel afterwards, overlooking the eighteenth green, Bobby refused to give in to the rest of his brains trust's cautious optimism. Somebody would catch him.

Nobody did. Bob had grabbed a commanding lead he would never relinquish; the rest of the field seemed to part in stunned silence and let him pass. The next day in the second round he shot 72 while playing what felt to him like even better golf. Everyone fifteen or more strokes behind him at the halfway mark failed to make the cut: he had gone so low that the smallest number of players advanced since the Open introduced mid-tournament elimination. On the morning round of the final day Bob shot 73—even par—and although his score had gone up, he felt he played his best golf of the week. He began his fourth round that afternoon at six under par and held a four-stroke lead. That may not sound like much to fans of the modern game, so accustomed to the routine abuse of par, but at the time, and particularly in an Open at St. Andrews, this number was shocking. The weather had stayed fair, as it will sometimes do in July, and there hadn't been much wind all week, but Bob still had to make the shots.

He stumbled at the start of the final round, and Pop and the Colonel feared the strain was catching up with him. By the time he'd played eight holes he was four over par for the day and for the first time since the Open began his lead looked vulnerable. The Colonel couldn't take the tension, and headed back to the hotel; Pop stayed in the gallery. Bob was entering the part of the course known as the Loop, a stretch of four holes at the tip of the fishhook which criss-cross each other at the furthest outward point before beginning the return journey to the clubhouse. During his searing first round Bob had played this difficult passage at even par 4–4–3–4, and distanced himself from the field. Summoning up a ferocious burst of shot-making he went 3–3–3–3. He followed a 20-foot birdie at nine by driving the green at the 312-yard tenth. After narrowly missing a third straight birdie at eleven he ran his approach at twelve within 2 feet. He collected two more birdies on his way in to finish with a 72.

The year before, while winning at Lytham, Bob had tied the lowest winning score in the history of the Open with 291. He had just shattered his own record by six strokes, which turned out to be his winning margin over the nearest pursuer.

When Bob sank his final putt on the great open stage at eighteen Bernard Darwin was there in the crowd with Pop and Kiltie and the Colonel. Twelve thousand people swarmed the green, covering its broad expanse in an instant. "Not even when Francis Ouimet beat Vardon and Ray was there such a riot of joy," wrote Darwin. "Personally I thought Bobby was going to be killed in the very hour of victory. It was a real relief when, after what seemed whole minutes, Bobby reappeared, his putter held high over his head, borne aloft on admiring shoulders." As the mob closed in on him Pop shouted in alarm to anyone who would listen: "They're going to kill him!" Film and photos confirm that Darwin and Pop weren't exaggerating; it was a dangerous moment, resolved only when Bobby appeared hoisted above the crowd, still holding Calamity Jane. Six local policemen fought their way into the scrum, pulled him down and saw him safely to the doorway of the Grand Hotel, where the Colonel and Pop were waiting for him. At the sight of Bob hugging his father at the door, Pop discovered an urgent need to clean his glasses because all of a sudden he wasn't seeing clearly.

For a second straight year Bob had decided to play in the British Open at the last minute because of a disappointing performance in another event. In winning the way he did at St. Andrews he captured the undying affection of the true guardians of the game. The Scots had discovered in Bobby Jones the manifestation of their ideal golfer rendered in flesh, blood, and bone. It no longer mattered where he came from or what flag he played under. He was "their Bobby" now.

Neither did he do himself harm with his acceptance speech a short time afterwards. When they handed him the Claret Jug for the second year in a row he said: "Nothing would make me happier than to take home your trophy. It was played for here thirty years before I was born. I had rather win a championship at St. Andrews than anything else that could happen to me. You have done so many things for me that I am embarrassed to ask for one more, but I will. I want this wonderful old club to accept the custody of the cup for the coming year." If there were any die-hard nationalists left in that crowd who resented seeing the Claret Jug go to another American, those objections vanished on the soft westerly breeze.

"I have achieved the ambition of my life," he told them. "Because I have won at a place where golf was played nearly five centuries ago. This wonderful experience will live in my memory until my dying day. If I never win anything again, I am satisfied."

This was as fine a feeling as a competitor in his sport or any other could ever hope to have, and given the perfection of the moment, he could be forgiven the slight overstatement. He felt he had atoned for his poor performance at Oakmont.

But he was a long way from satisfied.

Although Bob had won his second straight Open overseas, his unprecedented streak of holding a USGA championship for four straight years was in jeopardy. He had confided in Pop two years earlier that his benchmark for walking away from the game might be reached if he could extend that streak to six. That ambition had already started to evolve into something even more audacious, but achieving the original objective meant a lot to him none the less. After returning home from Britain to another grand reception, Bob and company spent less than two weeks in Atlanta before leaving for Minneapolis and his last chance to keep the streak alive at the 1927 U.S. Amateur.

The tournament boasted the strongest field the Amateur had attracted since the Great War. After studying local weather patterns over a fifteen-year period, the USGA had decided the week beginning August 22 offered their best chance for perfect weather in Minneapolis, where the tournament was scheduled. Minikahda Country Club played host to the event, site of the 1916 U.S. Open, where Chick Evans won the first half of his historic double championship. Evans was back again; at thirty-eight he was no longer ranked among the game's élite and longed to restake his claim to the national limelight. Francis Ouimet was on hand, as was the reigning champion, George Von Elm, whose sleek feathers were ruffled once more when the USGA announced its seedings. Despite beating Bob in last year's Amateur, Von Elm still came in behind him at number two. Although he told reporters he wasn't bothered by the slight, complaints about the USGA's favoritism for Bob filled the air immediately.

Bob's arrival with Mary on August 18 generated front-page headlines in the Twin Cities. The contest to become Bob's caddie during the tournament also made the front page because every one of Minikahda's 175 caddies had requested Bob's bag. A lottery finally settled the issue and veteran Pat Doherty won the honor. "I'm mighty proud, and I guess I ought to be," Doherty told a local sportswriter. This was his first national event and he vowed to do everything he could "to help Bobby win the title."

The Twin Cities got their first look at Bob when he faced a press conference before playing his first practice rounds in a driving rainstorm. More than 150 journalists and correspondents from around the country and as far away as Great Britain were on hand to cover the event, and a 3,500-square-foot wooden shed had been put up to serve as their press center. When asked if anything was wrong with his game, Bob laughed and said: "Everything." Despite his win at the British Open, he claimed he'd been off form for months and had hardly played at all, but his radiant tan belied that statement; he'd put in many hours at East Lake to prepare for the Amateur.

As many as fifty thousand were expected to attend during the week; tickets sold for $1.10 per day, until the semi-finals when the price went up to $2.20. A pass for the entire week set you back $5.50. (As per the usual arrangement, Minikahda would split the proceeds 50:50 with the USGA.) As it did now wherever he played, Bob's presence attracted thousands who'd never seen a golf tournament in person. Believing that their well-bred Midwestern crowds would be better behaved than most, the club eliminated megaphones and whistles for the marshals, equipping them instead with a system of white, yellow, and red flags to handle the galleries; local papers published guides detailing what behavior the various flags were supposed to inspire. Pioneering local radio station KSTP announced plans to issue regular updates from the course throughout the week, with

Saturday's thirty-six-hole final match being broadcast live for the first time in its entirety.

Carrying the standard for Minnesota's golfers was thirty-one-year-old Harrison "Jimmy" Johnston, winner of seven straight State Amateur titles, a two-time Walker Cup teammate of Bob's who had turned in an impressive performance in the Open at Oakmont. In an interview before the Amateur Bob rated Johnston and Von Elm as the two men he was most worried about. George again took offense that Bob had expressed concern about anyone but him.

One hundred and fifty-nine other men attempted to qualify for thirty-two matchplay positions, beginning on Monday, August 22. Included in the field was the current amateur champion of Massachusetts, twenty-seven-year-old Eddie Lowery, Ouimet's friend and caddie from the 1913 Open.

Bob shot 75 in his qualifying round on Monday, tied for ninth, four strokes off the lead established by an unknown from New Jersey named Eugene Homans. The only man more upset than Bob at the end of the day was George Von Elm, who despite weeks of studying the course shot 79, which put him right on the cut line. Bob told Pop that night he wasn't going to risk flirting with the cut by playing a cautious round the next day. Although he believed the old superstition that the man who won the qualifying medal never went on to win the championship, Bob went out on Tuesday afternoon determined to shoot the works.

Bob's four-under 31 on the front nine shattered the record at Minikahda. He birdied the eighteenth and gave the crowd exactly what they'd come to see; he had won the qualifying medal and tied the Amateur record for lowest qualifying score (a Minikahda course record of 67), which earned him a headline on the Tribune's front page, just below Charles Lindbergh's homecoming parade.

Von Elm scratched and clawed his way to a 75 and narrowly

advanced to matchplay. So did George Voigt, local favorite Jimmy Johnston, Chick Evans, yesterday's leader Eugene Homans and Francis Ouimet. For his Wednesday-morning first-round match Bob drew a youngster from New York, Maurice McCarthy, who gave him a scare. McCarthy was one up through nine, and held that lead through fifteen, when the pressure hit him; he lost the last three holes, and the match, down two. Von Elm survived his first-round match, and in the afternoon played a veteran from Minikahda by the name of Harry Legg. Their battle went down to the wire, when Legg booted out the defending champ on the final green to the biggest cheers of the day. That afternoon Bob edged the other surviving youngster, Eugene Homans, 3 & 2, to advance to the final eight. Joining him were Evans, Ouimet, and Bob's next opponent, local boy Jimmy Johnston. The presence of Legg and Johnston in the quarter-finals generated excited speculation about an all-Minnesota/all-Minikahda final—as only East Lakers Bob and Gunn had done before in 1925—but Bob would have something to say about that. The eighteen-hole matches were behind him and he hadn't come close to playing his best golf.

Jimmy Johnston's dreams of glory died on Thursday morning. The Bob Jones they'd all come out to see showed up on the first tee. As he was able to do now whenever the stakes were highest, Bob came into his game and played untouchable golf. He was eight up by the end of the morning after winning seven holes in a row and nearly equaled his two-day-old course record with a 68. When they resumed play after lunch, Bob made quick work of it, and won the match 10 & 9. Johnston won two holes all day. Bob explained to a local reporter his merciless philosophy about matchplay as they set out that morning: "If you get an opponent one down, try to get him two down. If you have him two down, try to get him three down. And don't stop trying until he shakes your hand." Harry Legg also lost his quarter-final match, and the last local favorite was eliminated.

Four men were left standing, and three were former Amateur champions. On Friday Chick Evans faced current intercollegiate champion Roland McKenzie. Two old friends made up the other side of the bracket: Bob and Ouimet, meeting in an important match at the Amateur for the fourth time in the last seven years. Ten thousand people followed them that day, but of all the accounts written about their match, Ouimet left the most expressive: "Those of you who think Bobby is a bargain in a semifinal match should take him on sometime. Bobby was positively ruthless. I can only describe a match against Bobby in this manner: It is as though you got your hand caught in a buzz saw. If the young man were human he would make a mistake once in a while, but he never makes mistakes. He can drive straighter than any man living. He is perfectly machinelike in his iron play, and on the greens he is a demon . . . But he is more than a great golfer. He is a grand competitor."

Only Chick Evans now stood between Bob and his third Amateur title. The pairing offered an irresistible storyline: the veteran campaigner mounting a late-career comeback against the sport's reigning king. The men had never met in the finals of an Amateur; this would be their rubber match. The behind-the-scenes drama was pretty compelling too.

Although the rivals appeared friendly and sportsmanlike whenever they were face to face, Bob had heard about the backstage grumbling from Evans, Hagen and Von Elm for well over a year. As Von Elm confessed to journalist Lester Rice a few years later, by this point he "hated Bob's guts" and Bob sensed it. The reasons may have been more complex than simple envy: Von Elm was a teetotaler who took Prohibition seriously, and he disapproved of Bob's casual drinking, and also of Bob's smoking and casual locker-room cussing.

Evans was a different story. A prim, thirty-eight-year-old businessman still living with his mother, he never fitted in to the locker-room culture that was such a big part of the off-course atmosphere. Bob always respected what Evans meant to the game as a player but as two people they simply repelled each other. As they stood on the first tee being photographed that morning, Chick put on what Bob called a "typical Evans performance . . . he draped his arm around my shoulder, flashed that big grin and rattled on in a loud voice about how much fun it was going to be having a game with me, that neither of us cared who won. We would just go out and have a real good time, and all that sort of bosh." Bob knew exactly how much Evans wanted this win. More than any other opponent he ever faced, on this day Bob took satisfaction not just in beating Chick, but in crushing him.

The match began at 10:30 on Saturday morning. The Colonel, Clara, Mary, Pop, and Kiltie were all in the gallery. After they finished the morning round, the *Tribune* opened its front-page account the next day with the story of a determined Minneapolis matron who had stationed herself at the eighteenth green in order to secure a spot to watch the end of the championship. She was seven holes too late. Evans shot 75 in the morning, which would have kept him close to any other competitor, but Bob was already up three, and two under par, when they reached the ninth hole.

The ninth at Minikahda is 560 yards long, a par-five that plays steeply uphill to a small, fast green. Before the tournament began a Minikahda member offered a substantial bet that no one would make an eagle three at the hole during the championship. To do so required a long, perfectly placed drive and a phenomenal second to reach and hold the green. A few birdies had been recorded to date, but nothing close to an eagle. In fact, to that point in the club's history, no one had ever made three at number nine.

Bob hit a booming 300-yard drive that flirted with the out-of-bounds on the right, but cut 50 yards off the path to the green. From 230 yards out he powered a fairway wood that soared straight up that hill, bounced twice and came to rest a foot from the hole. Evans conceded the putt, but Bob sank the ball for eagle anyway; he putted out on every hole to stay sharp. The member lost his bet; Evans was down four. Pop quickly canvassed his fellow reporters, who agreed they had just seen the finest fairway wood shot a man ever played in a championship.

The stark difference in the two men's personalities was on display all afternoon. The extrovert Evans laughed and joked with the sympathetic Midwestern crowd, on a few occasions "dancing a little jig" when he sank a putt or pulled off a tough shot. Bob remained a study in composed concentration, going about his business while appearing substantially more relaxed than he actually felt inside. They spoke hardly a word to each other and some reported the tension between them as "thick." Evans looked annoyed at one point when Bob didn't concede him a breaking 3-foot putt for a half, and when Bob's back was turned he sarcastically tipped his hat. Whenever Evans conceded him a putt, Bob putted out anyway, prompting Chick at least once to look away and roll his eyes. Bob picked up one more hole during the back nine to stretch his lead to five; for the second time in less than a week he had shot a five-under-par 67.

Dark clouds rolled in and threatened as they began their afternoon round. Content to coast on his lead, Bob bogeyed two of the first six holes and Evans trimmed the deficit to four while playing his steadiest golf of the day. At the seventh, as the first rain started to fall, Bob turned it on and captured the next three holes in a row, capped by a birdie at nine, to stretch his lead to seven. After halving the tenth, both reached the par-three eleventh green with their tee shots when the day's most controversial incident occurred.

The rain that had been threatening all afternoon came down in buckets as they walked onto the green. Bob lagged his first putt close and tapped in for his par. Evans left his first putt a foot short. As he took his stance to tap in for par he seemed annoyed that Bob hadn't conceded it to him: it would have halved the hole, and left Bob seven up with seven holes to play. But if he missed it the match was over, and the rule of thumb in matchplay is you always make your opponent sink any putt he needs to extend a match. Evans knew that, and Bob knew that, and when Evans looked up at him he claimed Bob was glaring at him.

What happened next became the crux of the dispute: Evans's putter nudged the ball and rolled it slightly ahead as he addressed it, a clear one-stroke penalty if he had caused it to move. But according to Evans, his ball hadn't moved at all: Bob corrected him, politely but firmly. Bob's account was slightly different: he thought Evans had moved the ball *intentionally*—perhaps to get the match over with—then looked up and said: "I guess it moved." Bob answered that he agreed, and Evans stuck out his hand to congratulate Bob on winning the Amateur.

Both men smiled, seemed to put the awkward moment behind them, and walked back to the clubhouse as the skies opened and the crowd ran for cover. Neither mentioned it to reporters and paid proper, sportsmanlike respect to each other. No one covering the event made anything more out of it than an unintentional accident. But thirty years later this moment and his whole history with Evans still rankled Bob. When a television network was putting together the first comprehensive retrospective of Bob's career he asked that only one man be excluded from the list of people they planned to interview: Chick Evans.

Bob slipped on a thin black slicker and stood in the rain during the ceremony outside the clubhouse. Evans, who had changed into a dapper business suit, stood under an umbrella. USGA president Bill Fownes brought out the Havermeyer Trophy and said, "Here, Bob, you better hold the cup." Evans stepped forward and said, "Gee, I'd like to hold it for you." He got a big laugh from the crowd, then unintentionally summed up the last six years of his career: "But Bobby has me stymied." Bob later said that a photo taken of him a few minutes later, standing in the rain in his wet slicker, his hair all messed up, holding the Havermeyer Trophy for the third time, was his favorite shot taken of him during his playing years. There's a sly, mischievous twinkle in his eyes due in no small part to the fact that he had just decisively surpassed Chick Evans once and for all.

Bob's golfing "vacation" was over. It was time to begin his second year at Emory. Applying himself with the same single-mindedness he showed on the golf course, by the end of the fall semester—halfway through the three-year program—Bob decided to try and pass the Georgia State Bar exam. Living hand to mouth had worn him down, and living with his parents had created inevitable tensions at home between his wife and his mother. Mary wanted her own home, and she wanted Bob in it with her, not roaming around the golf courses of the world. Just after Christmas he learned that he had passed—no one could recall anyone passing the Bar after only three semesters of law school—so when 1928 began he left Emory and manned the desk that had been waiting for him all these years at his father's law firm.

Atlanta never tired of the parades, because Bob had done more to put their city on the international map than any other citizen in the twentieth century; in years to come he would often be referred to as Atlanta's ambassador to the world. But their gratitude was about to get him in hot water with the USGA. In November, at another dinner in his honor, they presented him with a check for $50,000 to help him and Mary build their own house. The money had been raised by friends as a charitable fund at the Atlanta Athletic Club, and thousands had contributed, their thanks for all Bob had done in promoting their city. News of the gift prompted a vigorous debate in the national press about the nature of amateurism in general, and Bob's unique status in particular. Two months later, after meeting with the USGA in New York during their annual convention, Bob returned the check to his friends.

The USGA did not order him to turn down the money— nothing in their by-laws covered this situation; there was no precedent for it—but they hadn't hesitated to point out the negative perceptions that could result. The example of his friend Francis Ouimet losing his amateur status over his ill-fated sporting-goods store in 1917 was fresh in Bob's mind. With a new career and a growing family to care for, Bob couldn't risk tarnishing the reputation he'd worked so hard to establish as an amateur sportsman. His decision was greeted with universal approval and cited as further proof of his exceptional character.

Soon afterwards he turned down another offer for help with their housing situation, from his own grandfather. When R.T. heard about Bob returning the Atlanta money, the old man quietly offered to lend him whatever he needed. Most assumed Bob accepted, but this part of the story wouldn't surface for decades: Bob and Mary talked it over, wrote to thank R.T. profusely, but declined, explaining they were determined to make it on their own. The young couple did buy their first home in Atlanta, at a substantially more modest price, in the spring of 1928. Bob also invested in a real-estate project with his father and some others from the Atlanta Athletic Club; they had their eye on a property in the mountains of North Carolina that they hoped to develop as a golf resort.

After trying, and winning, his first trial that spring, Bob turned his attention back to preparations for the summer golf season. He had already announced he wouldn't travel back to Great Britain to defend his Open title. This would prove to be the shortest competitive season of his career: only two events, with a month to practice in between; the U.S. Open and the Amateur.

The 1928 U.S. Open was played during the third week of June at Olympia Fields Country Club, twenty-five miles south of Chicago. Olympia Fields had already played host to a Western Open in 1920 and the 1925 PGA Championship, but this was its introduction to the Big Show. For the first time the USGA eliminated qualifying for the top thirty finishers from the previous year's Open. Bob arrived a few days early for practice rounds on a course he'd never played before.

Walter Hagen didn't show up until the day before the Open began, having just returned from England, where he'd won his third British Open at Royal St. George's. Hagen had made great strides since his first confrontations with the British class system. The current captain of St. George's, the Prince of Wales, presented Hagen with the Claret Jug and then invited him into the clubhouse for cocktails. The two hedonistic playboys had met that week and realized they were cut from the same cloth. One of the last citadels of the class system, Royal St. George's members sent their secretary in to remind their country's crown prince that professionals weren't welcome on the premises. The future King Edward VIII gave the secretary a blistering earful and sent him on his way.

Hagen arrived in Chicago a slight favorite over Jones: he had won the only two championships previously played at Olympia Fields, the reason he felt he could forgo any practice rounds. But he was now thirty-five years old, and, given the mileage he'd put on himself, he was an old thirty-five. Hagen started slowly on the first morning of the Open, with a 75, while Bob shot 75 that afternoon. The USGA reversed starting times on the second day and Bob returned an even par 71 to grab the halfway-point lead. Hagen played a lousy front nine, and then, as a torrential storm blew through, he shot 32 on the back nine to land in fifth place, a stroke behind George Von Elm. Behind Bob in second place was twenty-seven-year-old Johnny Farrell, a stylish short-hitting pro from Quaker Ridge Country Club in

New York, who'd had three top-ten finishes in the last five Opens.

The narrow Olympia Fields #4 Course was slaughtering the rest of the 150-man field, and Bob's presence had gotten into the heads of more than a few professionals. As Pop made his way around he could hear the cry of "How's Jones going?" flying back and forth between pros as they passed each other. For the uninitiated, the swarming crowds that followed Bob everywhere, not to mention the effect of the implacable par machine marching by you down the fairway, almost always translated into a two-shot deficit. (And yet not one of these men ever registered a complaint in public or private about Bob as a partner; he remained unfailingly courteous and supportive and they treated him like one of their own.) When Bob recorded what was, by his standards, a mediocre 73 in the third round, he still held a two-stroke lead. Hagen was three shots behind Bob, Farrell and Von Elm were five back. An unheralded twenty-one-year-old pro named Roland Hancock from Wilmington, North Carolina, stood six strokes back. Everyone else had already punched their ticket home.

Bob began his final round with a birdie, and picked up another at the fifth. He was cruising, and with the toughest stretch of the course behind him he had at least a five- or six-stroke lead to play with. Pop felt more certain this thing was in the bag than at any other event in Bob's career. But Bob had been scrambling for pars all week and on top of the customary tension he played with the effort had worn him down. He admitted to Pop that at this point he made "the fatal mistake of telling himself that he would just coast in." Bob wasn't built for coasting—he had to feel he was grinding to sustain his concentration—and the moment he took his foot off the gas disaster struck.

Bob hooked his drive on the sixth into the weeds. He punched out and salvaged a bogey. Leaking confidence, he began steering his shots, double-bogeyed the seventh, and followed with three more straight bogeys. Seven shots lost in five holes, he dropped from two under to five over par. Word of Bob's collapse whipped around the course, but only Johnny Farrell took advantage. Playing ahead, Farrell finished with 72; his total of 294 was now the number to chase. Hagen fell away, then Von Elm. Sarazen made a late rush but came up shy. After struggling through those awful five holes, Bob played eleven through seventeen in one over. He reached the eighteenth knowing he could still beat Farrell with a birdie, hooked his drive into deep rough, then punched out into a narrow, muddy ditch that ran across the fairway 100 yards short of the green. Forced to take an awkward stance with his right foot planted in the mud and the other hitched up onto the bank, he slammed a wedge as hard as he could down at the ball. It barely cleared the lip of the ditch. Ten thousand heads craned toward the green, where the ball sailed in, dropped and stopped 20 feet from the hole. A miraculous recovery. Making the putt would win him his third Open; a miss would drop him into his third play-off in the last six years. His ball had a clump of mud on it from the ditch, and the rules still didn't allow a player to lift, clean and replace it on the green; that wouldn't change until 1960.

Bob missed the putt.

Everyone was about to call it a day and prepare for the play-off when word came in that young Roland Hancock was taking the course by storm, making the turn in 33. He was about to reach seventeen; all Hancock needed to do was par the last two holes for a course-record 69, and the Open would be his by two strokes.

Farrell and Bob stayed out at eighteen to watch. As Hancock walked over a small bridge leading to the tee, unaware of where he stood, he heard people shout, "Make way for the new champion!" The cat was out of the bag. He was forced to wait twenty minutes while marshals tried to clear the fairway, and all the while the knowledge of what was at stake punched holes in his confidence. Hancock pushed his drive onto a patch of bare ground he thought might be part of a hazard. Instead of waiting for a ruling—it wasn't a hazard—he tried to advance the ball without grounding his club and topped it 15 feet into heavy rough. Two more shots to reach the green and then two putts and just like that he had double-bogeyed. Par at eighteen would still land him in the play-off with Jones and Farrell, but the patient died on the operating table; Hancock made back-to-back sixes and finished in third place, never to be heard from again.

After 1927's play-off win by Tommy Armour, the USGA had decided that in the event of a tie, eighteen holes didn't provide a definitive test for identifying the game's best player. This year's play-off would go thirty-six holes, played on the same day.

A light mist was falling as the two men stepped to the tee on Sunday, June 24. Johnny Farrell had a deserved reputation as a cool customer, but a play-off for the Open raised the ante on anxiety. He looked flustered on the first hole, where Bob collected an easy birdie. After halving the second, Bob double-bogeyed the third, a hole that had been giving him fits all week; Farrell collected his four for a one-stroke lead. By the time they made the turn it was clear Farrell had better command of his game; Bob made a series of unforced errors and had to scramble to stay even. Farrell finished the morning round with a brilliant kick, four birdies in a row for a one-under-par 70. He led Bob by three.

Pop thought Farrell appeared energized and Bob looked beyond exhaustion; he wondered if he'd even be able to finish. He should have known by now that Bob's pale, haunted look was the signal his friend was about to catch fire. He opened the second round with a birdie; Farrell slipped to double bogey. They were all square. Then it was Bob's turn to falter, with another double at the third, his jinx hole. Again, he climbed back into a tie that lasted until the ninth, where he lost two strokes to Farrell once again. A steady rain was falling by now but the gallery hardly seemed to notice. This was like watching a duel fought with rapiers.

With nine holes left, Farrell's nerves frayed; picking up a stroke on three straight holes, Bob took the lead for the first time since the first hole that morning. Farrell birdied the thirteenth to square them again with five to play. That held until the sixteenth, another par-three, when a rub of the green intervened: Bob's picture-perfect tee shot to the green ricocheted off the flagstick and bounced into deep rough. Two holes to play and Farrell had a one-stroke lead.

The par-four seventeenth. Bob outdrove Farrell, who pulled his into the rough. Playing his second over a low bush directly between him and the green, Johnny hit a beauty that rolled to 3 feet; a certain birdie. Bob reached the green in two as well, but left himself a 20-foot putt. He looked at the line from every angle then calmly sank the putt. The weight shifted to Farrell; he dropped his matching birdie and carried a one-stroke lead to eighteen.

The sky had turned black, the belly of the storm about to unleash a downpour. Four hundred and ninety yards, a reachable par-five, dogleg left to an elevated green. Farrell pushed his tee shot right, in light rough just short of a bunker. Bob split the fairway. Farrell played a wood, trying to reach in two, but the ball crossed the fairway and landed 60 yards short in the left-hand rough, halfway up the hill. Bob hit a rocket off the deck toward the left side of the green, but it nicked someone in the crowd near the green and kicked left. As the crowd scrambled out of the way, a policeman shepherding the gallery stepped on the ball, squirting it into the rough; an alert USGA official spotted the incident and allowed Bob to replace the ball in its original lie on the closely mown collection area.

Farrell played a dead-hands pitch out of the rough that arced right on line to the flag and stopped 8 feet short, lying three. The pressure shifted to Bob: he clipped his ball neatly off the turf and sent it running straight for the flag. For a fleeting moment an eagle three seemed in the offing. The gallery gasped . . . but the ball stopped 2 feet short. Bob holed out for his birdie and stepped away.

Farrell walked to his ball, studied the green, crouched down low to look at the line. As he took his stance a row of photographers opened fire, shutters shattering the graveyard silence. Farrell stepped away and quietly asked the referee to hold off the picture-taking until he completed his work. Then he walked right back to the ball, and without a moment's hesitation rolled it slowly into the heart of the cup.

Johnny Farrell had won the 1928 Open. Bob shot 73–71 in the play-off and came up a stroke short. Given the high level of play, with both men canning birdies on the last two holes, most considered it the finest play-off in USGA history. There was more rejoicing in the locker room afterwards; for the second year in a row a professional had prevailed in the Open against the relentless amateur from Atlanta. Pop thought Bob seemed more relieved than disappointed: he hadn't lost this title; Farrell had won it.

Slipping on a stylish beret, Johnny Farrell collected the Open trophy and his winner's check for $1,000. His performance that day changed Farrell's life to the better forever. He'd not only won the U.S. Open, he had joined the most exclusive outfit in the sport of golf, the "I Beat Bobby Jones" club.

After six weeks in his law office, Bob was back in Chicago to captain the United States Walker Cup team. During the ten practice rounds leading to the event, Bob worked out any lingering frustration about his loss to Farrell. He broke the scoring record at four different courses, shot eight of ten rounds under 70, averaging 68.5 for the stretch. In 1928 numbers, this was a level of play no one had ever approached. In the last tune-up, Bob won a one-day medal event at Flossmoor Country Club with a course-record 67. At one point in that round—Pop kept the card—Bob recorded seven straight threes. A scary thought circulated through the press and among his amateur teammates: twenty-six-year-old Bob Jones, the world's greatest golfer, had not yet reached his peak and was actually *getting better*. Looking at his career from a distance, from the Open through the upcoming Amateur, this was his greatest sustained period of play.

Ouimet decided to take advantage while he and Bob were rooming together in Chicago; he asked Bob for help with his putting. Bob's advice was to focus more on speed than on line: "Just hit it in the general direction of the hole and see what happens." Sure enough, during the Walker Cup Ouimet started dropping putts from all over the greens. If any further proof of Bob's mastery was needed, the U.S. team won the most lopsided victory in the five Walker Cups to date, 11–1. Bob won his singles match against Philip Perkins, the current British Amateur champion, by a score of 13 & 12.

Both teams hopped onto the *Twentieth Century* train afterwards and rode to Boston, where the 1928 National Amateur was held at Brae Burn. This was the last bachelor outing for Bob with his Atlanta contingent and Walker Cup buddies; Mary would accompany him on every subsequent expedition but the last. Rated the top seed, Bob qualified easily. Then came what for Bob now almost constituted a phobia: Wednesday's dual eighteen-hole matches. He survived the first, 4 & 3, then faced an old foe of Ouimet's from Boston, Ray Gorton. Gorton was a multiple Massachusetts Amateur champion and longtime member at Brae Burn who knew the course intimately and held its scoring record; the definition of a dangerous matchplay opponent. Both men played dreadful front nines. Then, wrote Pop, "came the fireworks." Bob birdied the tenth, a short par-five; Gorton topped him with an eagle to grab a one-hole lead. At the eleventh, Bob sliced his drive behind a stand of towering trees, 200 yards from the green in deep rough. The odds dictated punching back into the fairway and trying to get up and down for par, but Gorton had hit a perfect drive after his eagle and was heating up; Bob couldn't afford to hand him another hole.

Pop: "Bobby took a 4 iron, swung as hard as he could, tearing up a great strip of turf and long grass, and the fascinated gallery saw the ball soar over the trees and descend on the green, five yards from the hole."

A shot eerily reminiscent of the one they'd both seen Ted Ray pull off at East Lake fifteen years ago, Bob called it the best iron he ever played in competition. It didn't faze Gorton; he played his second to 20 feet and sank the putt for birdie. Bob dropped his putt as well to halve the hole, and for the moment blunted Gorton's momentum.

After trading holes, Bob squared the match at fifteen. They halved the sixteenth. At the 255-yard par-three seventeenth, Gorton missed the green short; Bob went long into a bunker. Gorton chipped close and assured himself of par. Bob blasted out to the edge of the green, leaving himself a ticklish, downhill 8-footer. He barely tapped the ball; it seemed to take a minute as it tracked toward the hole and then fell. When it did, Pop, watching from the hilltop behind the green, realized he was suddenly sitting on the grass. "I had dropped, too," he said.

At the eighteenth, Bob made a routine par. Gorton carded a stupendous four after popping up his drive to force sudden-death extra holes. The pressure finally hit Gorton. He sliced his behind a woodpile, while Bob played two safe shots to the green. Gorton reached the green in three, but his attempt to extend the match lipped out. Bob advanced to the field of sixteen, and the welcome refuge of thirty-six-hole matches.

Bob was never threatened again. He won Thursday's match with England's John Beck 14 & 13. In the semi-finals he pounded Phil Finlay 13 & 12. The finals brought him together with Philip Perkins, the British Amateur champion he had recently demolished at the Walker Cup. Perkins had made a lot of noise in the press after Chicago about how he wasn't going to let that sort of thing happen again. The beating he took at Brae Burn only differed by a matter of degrees; Bob won his fourth U.S. Amateur title 10 & 9.

Bob had tied Jerry Travers's record of four wins in the Amateur, and he'd done it in only five years. Add two wins each at the U.S. and British Opens and he now owned eight major titles. No man had ever won so many majors; the few who came close took decades to accumulate them. Bob had done it in only six years. He had also reached the goal he'd once set for himself of winning either a U.S. Open or Amateur for six years in a row. Pop didn't dare remind him; they were having too much fun, he didn't want it to end. But if fans and journalists felt there was a creeping sameness to Bob's domination of the game— the press had grown fond of calling him a "golfing machine"— no one experienced it more acutely than he did.

As he returned to Atlanta and settled down to work, content to spend time with Mary and the children, and weekends with Dad and the boys at East Lake, the public persona he'd created felt increasingly like an intrusion. The spotlight didn't keep him warm, and he was forced to spend more time trying to avoid ways in which he might be perceived as exploiting his status than he did enjoying it. He turned down big cash offers for movies, exhibition tours, personal appearances, even a Broadway musical set at a country club; saying no politely became a full-time job. The conflict arose out of the good news that he had started to define and discover who he truly was: family man, Atlanta lawyer, dignified member of his community, gentleman athlete. In that order. A low-key life of quiet satisfaction suited him best; he soon realized he didn't feel comfortable with trial work; shortly afterwards he settled on civil and contract work as his *métier*. The irony of his predicament was inescapable: by virtue of playing a sport he loved in pursuit of realizing a private, personal excellence he had become one of the century's most famous human beings, which in turn made a private life that much more difficult to manage.

Mary had begun to question his pursuit of this chimera. She was proud of everything Bob had done but also knew the price he paid during these ordeals more than anyone: the extreme weight loss, the physical pain and private anguish. She wanted what any loving spouse wants for their partner: happiness, contentment, wellbeing. If all he got from soldiering out there was suffering and a fame he didn't seem to enjoy, what exactly was the point of all this? She didn't disapprove, but she was curious: What did he want from this experience? What more could he hope to learn or gain? Most importantly, what would it take for him to feel satisfied enough to set championship golf aside and move on with the rest of his life?

Bob felt he had owed her an answer for a long time, and now he finally had one to give. Casting his eye ahead he had settled on 1930, the next time the Walker Cup team traveled to England. The British Amateur was scheduled to be played at St. Andrews, his favorite course in the world; the British Open followed at Hoylake, where he'd made his overseas debut in 1921. The U.S. Open would be held a few weeks later, in the Midwest on a course called Interlachen near Minneapolis. And at the end of that summer the U.S. Amateur was returning to Merion, where he'd arrived at fourteen and he'd come back to win his first Amateur title eight years later. What better stage on which to set the climax of the boldest assault on the record books anyone had ever imagined? Four majors. Four wins. That was his ticket out of the game and into private life.

If he lived to tell about it.

CHAPTER ELEVEN

PREPARATION

Pop Keeler estimated that Bob played ten rounds of golf between the 1928 Amateur and the 1929 Open. He was admitted to the Federal Bar in May and studying for that exam in addition to his regular workload kept him off the course more then ever before. During a brief business trip to New York City in late May, thieves broke into his car and stole both Bob and Forest Adair's golf clubs. Calamity Jane, Jeanie Deans and his thirteen other sticks had been kidnapped. The story made front-page news in New York and around the country: for curiosity value the theft of Bob Jones's golf clubs nearly rivaled the recent St. Valentine's Day Massacre in Chicago. Scheduled to leave town the next day and with the U.S. Open only a few weeks away, Bob urgently wired Old Tom Stewart in St. Andrews, asking him to build a duplicate set at once and ship them over-seas. (Stewart forged a number of extra sets, and later got into trouble for stamping them with the initials "RTJ" and selling them as "Bobby Jones's clubs.") By the end of the following day Bob's clubs and bag appeared, intact and untouched, in the office of a local garage owner; the thieves turned out to be two young kids who had robbed the car at random, with no idea what they'd taken. The clubs were put on the next train to Atlanta and followed Bob home.

In the middle of June Bob returned to New York, to spend ten days preparing for the Open at Winged Foot Country Club in suburban Westchester County. Home to two courses built in 1923, Winged Foot was the handiwork of another inspired amateur and one of the game's great eccentrics, Arthur W. Tillinghast, or Terrible Tilly as the people who often played his courses called him. Tilly moved 7,200 tons of rocks and cut down 7,800 trees to create the West Course, where the thirty-third Open would be played, and the end result was a tight, tortuous, 6,900-yard test of manhood. Of its twelve par-fours, ten measured more than 400 yards. Although he placed only sixty of them on the course, deep frightening bunkers protected most of his greens, leaving narrow openings for approach shots that had to be precise. Tillinghast himself said about these holes: "They were of a sturdy breed." Translation: Bring your best game.

Bob appeared to have done just that, turning in two 69s during practice rounds. Mortal men simply did not break par at Winged Foot, and Bob did it twice. He reckoned that if he could figure out the greased-lightning greens he had a good shot at the trophy; he decided to forgo his last practice round and spent the entire day on the putting green. The next day, Bob pinned another 69 on the West Course and led the first round of the Open by a stroke over Al Espinosa, a slow-footed thirty-four-year-old pro from the Monterey Peninsula in California. Hard as it is to believe, this was the first time Bob had ever broken 70 in a round at the U.S. Open. The next day a thunderstorm dampened his assault on Winged Foot; he fell back with a 75. Playing in the morning before the rain, Espinosa and Gene Sarazen ended up tied for the lead at 142, two strokes ahead of Bob.

Saturday's final day dawned bright and sunny. The USGA's raising ticket prices to $3 a head discouraged no one from showing up to watch when Bobby Jones was in the running. Yesterday's rain had slowed the greens, but done little to dampen the fast-draining fairways. Advantage Jones. Pop watched the morning round, noting that Bob "played with great confidence and boldness." Nothing troubled him, no one seemed to be in his way. He returned with 71, good for a three-stroke lead over Sarazen and four over Espinosa. Five strokes was then (and still is) considered the outside limit for comebacks in the final round of an Open. Although two men were inside that mark going against Bob, there wasn't a soul who would have bet against him. As he ate his traditional lunch of tea and toast, both Sarazen and Espinosa went out ahead of him; Sarazen shot six over on the front and waved goodbye to his chances. Espinosa played the front in a respectable 36, but a disastrous eight on the twelfth hole appeared to sound the death knell for him as well.

Bob sailed through his first seven holes showing magisterial command of his game and stepped to the eighth tee needing only to par the next two holes to match Espinosa's front side. Knowing Espinosa had tanked at twelve, Bob blasted his drive around the dogleg, leaving a four-iron to the green. With the wind blowing hard from the right he sent his approach toward that side of the green, but the wind didn't move the ball. It stayed dead on line, caught the edge of the green and bounced into a deep bunker.

The recovery didn't look difficult; he had a good lie and room to work with on the green. He even liked the shot as he hit it, but the green sloped away from him and a full day of sunlight had dried out the surface. The ball ran, past the flagstick, off the green, and didn't stop until it trickled into another bunker on the other side, settling just under the lip. Now he needed to get up and down for bogey.

Bob decided to blast the ball out to get past that lip. He did. All the way back across the green and back into the original bunker. The crowd reacted as if they'd been punched in the gut. After trudging across the green for the third time like a weekend duffer he lofted the ball softly out of the sand and it stayed on the short grass, but he needed two putts to get down for a triple bogey seven.

He appeared to shake it off with a birdie at the ninth. Bob had gone out in 38 and still held an insurmountable lead over Espinosa. But playing ahead, after his catastrophic twelfth, Espinosa figured he was out of it and had nothing left to lose. Nothing better illustrates Bob's oft-repeated maxim that golf is a game played entirely on the six inches of real estate between the ears. Thinking the pressure was off, Espinosa marched through the last six holes of his final round in one under par and finished with a 75.

Bob's escapades in the bunkers at eight had the opposite effect on his psyche. He called his back nine "an agony of anxiety." He finished the twelfth hole with a six-stroke lead over Espinosa, but instead of sprinting for the finish he started playing not to lose. Doubt crept into his mind, and spread to his arms and hands. He started steering the ball. He lost a stroke at thirteen, scrambled for par at fourteen, then sliced his drive on fifteen behind a stand of trees. After knocking a recovery back to the fairway he flew his next over the green into knee-deep rough, flubbed his pitch onto a little knoll between himself and the green, and ended up recording another triple bogey seven on the hole.

Most of his lead over Espinosa had been squandered. To hold

onto the single stroke that remained he needed to finish with three fours, and his next hole, the sixteenth, was a par-five. With the wind behind him Bob killed his drive, then played a splendid long iron onto the green only 20 feet from the flag. It was Calamity Jane's turn to go south. He left his first putt 5 feet short, missed his second and made five. Now Bob had to finish with two fours just to tie Espinosa, already in the clubhouse and more shocked than anyone at Winged Foot when he learned that he still had a chance at the title.

Bob collected his par at seventeen without incident. He hit a serviceable drive at the 440-yard eighteenth, leaving himself a long iron into a devilish, undulating green. He pulled the approach slightly and the shot came up less than a yard short of where it needed to land to hold the putting surface then slowly rolled back down, stopping just short of a bunker in deep rough. The crowd surrounding the green stood five deep as Bob reached his ball. Pop managed to see Bob play his delicate pitch up to the green; it rolled and stopped a dozen feet from the flag. Downhill, side-hill, on a surface that had turned to glass; if he missed it, Al Espinosa would win the Open.

Pop got swallowed up in the crowd, lost sight of the green and found himself standing next to a photographer perched on a step ladder. He quickly ran through all the calculations: Bob needed the putt not only to force a play-off but to keep his score under 80. He'd never scored below 70 or above 79 in an Open, and he'd already broken the record on the low side. If he failed on the high side Bob would be the first to say he didn't deserve to win. But what would that do to Bob's confidence? Six strokes lost on the last six holes? What would such a collapse do to his ambitious plans for 1930? "I knew in a sort of bewildering flash that if that putt stayed out," wrote Pop, "it would remain a spreading and fatal blot, never to be wiped from his record."

Pop couldn't even watch, afraid somehow that the ball wouldn't find the hole if he did. A gentle click from the green,

Calamity Jane meeting the ball. He heard another click, the shutter of the camera in the hands of the photographer above him, as the ball started its journey. A faint stirring from the crowd, no louder than the intake of ten thousand breaths . . . which grew steadily in volume, then started to change to a fatal gasp: the ball had tracked ever so slowly straight for the hole and then stopped on the rim—

It was over, it stayed out—

No, the gasp changed to a roar loud enough to wake the dead: the ball made one last turn and dropped.

Bob had salvaged a 79 and his tournament. Because of everything that followed, Pop later called that putt the most important shot of his friend's career. Al Watrous, who had dueled so memorably with Bob at the '26 British Open, later told Pop that Bob's last putt was so perfectly calibrated that if the hole had been a circle drawn on the green, the ball would have rolled to a dead stop right in the middle of it.

It would be Bob's fourth Open play-off in seven years. For Espinosa, his first; thirty-six holes, scheduled for nine o'clock Sunday morning. But Bob knew that Al Espinosa was a devout Catholic, from one of the founding Spanish families of California. Would the USGA mind delaying the start until ten so that Al could attend Mass? Bob meant it as a courtesy, but somewhere in the back of his mind another subliminal message must have gotten through to Espinosa; if any man hoped to beat Bobby over thirty-six holes he needed divine intervention. Both men attended the same service, as it turned out, and both took their wives. Al Espinosa was a combat veteran of the Great War, but he admitted he'd never faced anything like the pressures of an Open play-off before. When Bob stumbled coming out of the gate that morning—playing the first three holes in four over par—Espinosa's hopes rose for one brief shining hour. Then Bob remembered who he was playing—Old Man Par, not Al Espinosa—and restored the balance of nature.

Bob won the play-off by 23 strokes. It remains to this day the greatest margin of victory in a play-off of any important championship. Bob stamped his name on the big silver cup for the third time, and his national-championship-winning streak reached seven years.

If Pop's estimate is accurate, he had done it after playing only ten rounds of golf in the previous six months.

Once they were home in Atlanta Bob told Keeler that his quest for all four major titles in 1930 was officially on, but Pop was not to say a word to anyone. For the first time the city decided to hold off throwing a parade; maybe they sensed something bigger was on the horizon: Bob practically owned the deed and title to the Amateur and that tournament was only six weeks away. It was being played for the first time on the West Coast, at a nine-year-old course on the Monterey Peninsula in northern California that was part of the area's first big tourist destination, the Del Monte Hotel and Resort. They called the course that had been drawing such ecstatic reviews Pebble Beach. Bob's work schedule didn't allow the luxury of practicing full time, so he started going into the office early and squeezed in as many afternoon rounds as he could.

During one of those rounds at the end of July, Bob experienced his close encounter with the thunderbolt that took down the chimney at East Lake. Feeling lucky that he and his foursome escaped serious injury, if not death, he reported no ill effects from the blow he absorbed to the back of his neck. But there were already hints of persistent neck and shoulder problems that had lingered since the Amateur at Muirfield in 1926. If he felt any the worse for wear from the chunk of masonry that nearly took his head off after the lightning strike he told no one about it. The question of what this lighting bolt had done to him wouldn't be answered for twenty years.

A little over two weeks later, on August 17, Bob, his parents, Mary, Pop, and the rest of his Atlanta entourage—along with the Havermeyer Trophy—boarded a private rail car and headed west to Los Angeles.

The golf course at Pebble Beach opened in 1920, and like so many other classic American courses it was primarily the handiwork of a passionate amateur. Jack Neville was a real-estate salesman and former California State Amateur champion and Pebble Beach was the only golf course he ever produced. The stunning result has been stealing the breath away from visitors ever since.

Jones added his voice to the chorus of admirers. His first time around Pebble Beach on the afternoon he arrived, he tied the course record and spoke enthusiastically to reporters about the experience afterwards. Hundreds watched him that day and thousands more flocked from all over the Bay area to see the "Emperor Jones" practice his craft. By this time he had become much more than a sports hero; Bob had acquired the status of a cherished national landmark, and even if you had no interest whatsoever in his sport just saying you'd seen him swing a club had become the kind of thing you wanted to be able tell your grandchildren. A few days later some of them were treated to the sight of Bob breaking the record at Pebble with a 67—at one point collecting seven straight birdies—and shooting four under par on its picture-postcard back nine. Already established as the number-one seed, when Bob tied for the qualifying medal with Eugene Homans—one of his victims the previous year at Minikahda—predictions for a fifth Amateur title filled the columns of every golf writer in America. Pop thought Bob had never played better leading up to any championship but he found the air of invincibility that had been conferred on his friend by the world at large annoying. As great as Bob had become, not even he could ever master the world's hardest sport. "No man ever has had golf under his thumb," wrote Pop. "No man ever will have golf under his thumb. The game is greater than the man. Golf is like the game of life. No man ever will be its master."

Something was nagging at Pop, and had been ever since they first arrived at Pebble. Those early-round eighteen-hole matches were staring his man in the face; Bob might have four Amateur titles to his name, but he had also lost in every round of the tournament now but the first.

Enter Johnny Goodman. A blond, handsome twenty-year-old from Omaha, an orphan who had grown up poor and more or less stayed put. After working as a caddie through childhood, Goodman had developed into the best player ever produced by the state of Nebraska. The qualifying score that earned him his invite to the Amateur was the lowest of a thousand entrants' from around the country, and he had recently finished as low amateur—after Bob—in the Open at Winged Foot. Johnny Goodman was no fluke, no Andrew Jamieson; he was a tough, seasoned competitor who was desperately hungry to put his name on the map. He was also a devoted admirer of Mr. Bobby Jones, and had maintained his amateur status in order to emulate him, at considerable hardship.

Bob said afterwards the outcome had nothing to do with his taking Goodman lightly. After a brilliant week of play he started their match by missing every shot of the first three holes. When Goodman sank a 10-foot putt for birdie on third, Bob was down three to his unheralded opponent. He then rallied, birdying two of the next three to whittle Goodman's lead to one. Both men reached the green on the par-three seventh; when Bob tried to press for advantage and jam his putt home for a birdie it ran 6 feet past and missed the come-backer for par. Goodman went two up, and showed no sign of nerves. Bob fought back again and finally squared the match at twelve. On the thirteenth green, when Bob lofted a stymied putt over Goodman's ball and dropped it straight into the cup to halve the hole, the crowd went mad, certain Bob would capitalize on the momentum and sweep this persistent challenger from his path.

The match turned at the par-five fourteenth. When Goodman's drive landed in the rough, Bob decided to shoot for the green in two and instead found a deep greenside bunker. Goodman recovered brilliantly; short of the green in three he chipped up and saved par. Bob missed his putt to stay even and went one down again. They matched pars for the next three holes, Goodman standing tall against the mounting pressure of the Jones mystique. Needing a birdie at the long, seaside eighteenth to get back to square and force extra holes, Bob's last putt died two inches short. Goodman calmly two-putted for his par and eliminated Bob Jones from the 1929 Amateur.

Shockwaves reverberated from the stunned gallery to sports pages and radio reports across the country and around the world. Bob's devoted fans went into mourning. Initially irritated at himself for throwing the match away on those careless opening holes, by early that afternoon Bob had adjusted his reaction to one of relief. With the Open already in his pocket for the year and his string of championship years intact at seven, he'd lost nothing he couldn't afford. Most importantly, he'd exorcised that phobia about losing an early eighteen-hole match from his mind; when he added it all up the after-effects were nowhere near as dire as he'd imagined. In fact, his loss at Pebble had one positive effect: Bob was more determined than ever to capture the four championships up for grabs in 1930.

Bob gave Johnny Goodman all the credit he deserved for beating him and told Pop he was looking forward to relaxing and watching the rest of the action; he'd been so good for so long he'd never actually had a chance to watch much of the event in person. That same afternoon he saw Goodman lose his second-round match to a talented newcomer from Rhode Island, William Lawson Little.

The next day Bob and Ouimet decided to forgo the Amateur

and accept an invitation to play at a new course nearby they'd heard everyone at Pebble raving about. A few years earlier a former American Amateur champion and wealthy Eastern socialite named Marion Hollins had fallen in love with a heavenly slice of seaside land just north of Pebble Beach and hired the gifted Scots architect Dr. Alister Mackenzie to transform it into a golf course. Hollins named the result Cypress Point for the striking windswept trees that adorned the rocky coastline. Bob decided at first glance it was the most dramatic layout he'd seen anywhere in the world. So impressed was he with MacKenzie's routing and masterful eye for detail that when the moment came a few years later to select an architect for a dream course he planned to build, Alister Mackenzie was the man Bob tapped for the job.

The 1929 Amateur ended in disappointment for everyone but the eventual champion, St. Paul's Harrison "Jimmy" Johnston, who defeated a dentist from Oregon named O.F. Willing to win the title. With Jones, Von Elm, Ouimet and many other leading contenders eliminated so soon, attendance suffered drastically. More than any other sport, as it would years later with Arnold Palmer and Tiger Woods, by the end of the 1920s golf in America had become a one-man phenomenon.

Goodman had a bright future, and he joined George Von Elm, Cyril Walker, Willie MacFarlane, Johnny Farrell, and Andrew Jamieson in the game's most exclusive company: the "I Beat Bobby Jones" club.

Only one more name would ever join the list.

PART THREE

THE GRAND SLAM

"The price he pays for his success is too high."
                                                    —*Bernard Darwin*

"No one knows what will happen in golf until it happens. All you can do is work and suffer and wait for fate."
                                                    —*Bob Jones*

CHAPTER TWELVE

THE BRITISH AMATEUR, ST. ANDREWS

B ob and his entourage took the scenic route home from San
Francisco, traveling through Yellowstone National Park and
arriving in Atlanta near the end the September. Bob had noticed
during their California stay that the state's housing market
appeared to be in serious trouble; similar to what had happened
in Florida four years before, speculators had driven prices out
of the reach of buyers. The Golden State's land rush had turned
sour, supply exceeded demand, entire developments languished.
The same phenomenon now hit Wall Street. While the national
economy showed signs of weakening, the market's gyrations
grew increasingly volatile through 1929, experiencing sharper
downturns and steeper recoveries. By September, the wildly over-

valued Dow Jones industrial average had hit an all-time high of 381. Seasoned investors knew the market had reached its top and began quietly pulling out their money.

October 29, 1929, was soon nicknamed Black Tuesday. The single worst day that any publicly traded stock market had experienced in human history. The Jazz Age was over.

Bob Jones hadn't put together enough of a nest egg to risk losing any of it in the stock market. The Crash didn't affect his personal fortunes, nor did it catastrophically affect his father's law practice. Coca-Cola, the Colonel's biggest client, was and would remain for the next ten years the definition of a Depression-proof company.

Bob's sole focus now became the 1930 championship season. Throughout the 1920s he had averaged no more than three months in tournament competition, but this plan required a once-in-a-lifetime effort. He took the Colonel into his confidence and received his blessing to take time away from their practice to devote most of the coming season to the campaign.

The strain of winning nine championships during the last six years had left Bob progressively more fragile physically and emotionally. In addition to the increasing mental stress and severe weight loss, digestive problems were a regular part of any tournament now. He suffered from severe muscle spasms in his neck and right shoulder, the legacy of his injury at Muirfield, or perhaps the first symptoms of the injury caused by the lightning strike. He hid these traumas from everyone else in his life, but Mary could plainly see the toll they were taking on him. When Bob shared with her his goals for the coming year she insisted on going with him to Britain; she was staking her claim; she wanted Bobby back, for herself, for his own good and the good of their children. He welcomed the idea: his closest confidante would be there to either console him in defeat or share his greatest triumph.

Bob had come around to believing in the role of fate in human affairs, but Mary never needed convincing. Her religious convictions rested on the bedrock of destiny, and not long before they sailed for Europe she actually dreamed that Bob won all four tournaments.

For the first time in his life Bob began a rigorous training regime to condition himself for the coming ordeal. He made at least two trips to Highlands Country Club in North Carolina to get in some uncharacteristic early-winter rounds, where he also played tennis to stay in shape. Back in Atlanta he also spent an hour each day playing an aerobically intense indoor variation on tennis invented by his movie-star pal Douglas Fairbanks. In his honor they called the game "Doug": it was played with tennis rackets and a heavy badminton shuttlecock on an enlarged court, over a net hoisted somewhere between tennis and badminton standards. Bob set up a Doug court on the stage of an empty theater owned by a friend in downtown Atlanta near his law office, and stopped there on his way home every afternoon. Between Christmas and March, when his playing season officially began, Bob lost over twenty pounds and was in the best shape of his life. When the weather improved and he could comfortably play golf on a daily basis, during one of his first warm-up rounds at East Lake he matched his own course record of 63. Sufficiently encouraged, he entered his name in the Savannah Open, a mid-March tournament and an important event on the professionals' developing winter circuit.

Bob decided to room in Savannah with a twenty-one-year-old player from Missouri named Horton Smith, who had just taken the pro ranks by storm. His smooth, syrupy-tempo swing owed a lot to Bob, and the two men hit it off at once, talking theory and exchanging pointers, the beginning of a lifelong friendship. Bob picked up a pointer from Smith about cocking his wrists at the beginning of the downswing, which he felt allowed him to strike the ball more crisply with his short irons. Although they were never paired together once play began, the tournament at the Savannah Golf Club turned into a personal battle between them. Bob broke the course record during the first round with 67; it stood until Smith's second round the next day, when he lowered it to 66. Smith carried a five-stroke lead into the final day. In the third round, Bob dropped the record another notch with a 65. When Smith finished with 70 the two men were deadlocked going into the final round.

Playing half an hour ahead of Smith, Bob set the pace at par and Horton stayed with him, maintaining the tie through sixteen holes. The break came at seventeen. Trying to reach the long par-five in two, Bob hooked his approach out of bounds and carded a bogey. Despite recovering with a birdie at the last hole he'd left an opening that Smith exploited; he finished birdie-par to beat Bob by a single stroke, at ten under par, and miles ahead of the rest of the field. Horton Smith collected the winner's check for $1,000.

Two weeks later, just after Bob celebrated his twenty-eighth birthday, he and Smith renewed their rivalry at the Southeastern Open, played on two courses in Augusta, Georgia, a long-time winter retreat for residents of Atlanta and the South. The tournament sponsors had persuaded Smith to enter at the last minute, hoping to create another duel with Bob like the one they'd put on in Savannah. They paired the men for the first two rounds in anticipation of fireworks, but Bob had played these two courses since he was a teenager; Smith had never seen them before, and arrived by private plane too late to get in a practice round. They were tough, tight tracks, with frighteningly fast greens, cut so quick the sun glared off them like stainless steel. Benefiting from the hard work he'd put in over the winter, Bob came into full possession of his game at Augusta, months earlier than he'd ever done before. While he arrived fresh and rested, the pros were at the end of their winter schedule and showed signs of fatigue.

Bob had avenged his loss to Smith faster and more decisively than usual; this was the greatest margin of victory in his career. Superlatives rained down in the wake of his performance, with Keeler and Rice leading the chorus; sportswriters were running out of adjectives to describe him. After watching Bob dominate both courses at Augusta, the man Bob had beaten to win his first U.S. Open in 1923, little Bobby Cruickshank, took Pop aside and predicted that if he continued to play this way Bob would not only win the British Open and Amateur, he would return to the United States and win the Open and Amateur back home as well. Pop was so astonished anyone had hit on Bob's secret intentions, even inadvertently, that he didn't even mention the audacious prediction to Bob. This proved to be much more than idle-locker room chatter on Cruickshank's part, and he backed up his intuition by cabling $50 to his father-in-law in England, instructing him to place a bet with a London book-maker that Jones would win all four of the year's major championships. The gamble was so outrageous it wasn't even on the touts' boards; when they finally calculated probabilities, Cruickshank received odds of 210–1. Inspired by the gesture, a group of Bob's friends in Atlanta cobbled together a much larger wager—$2,500—that they placed on the same unlikely bet. The British touts who booked it asked Lloyd's of London to insure their long-shot gamble.

Before he left Augusta, Bob made a crucial discovery that would substantially affect the sport's future development. Right next door to Augusta Country Club stood an overgrown, decaying 365-acre property called Fruitlands Nurseries. An indigo plantation before the Civil War, the property was sold soon after the war ended to a visiting Belgian nobleman, Baron Louis Matheiu Edouard Berckmans. Under the direction of Berckmans and his son Prosper, for close to fifty years it had served as one of the principal supplies of exotic fruit trees and flowers in the country, but Fruitlands Nurseries' fortunes died with the younger Berckmans in 1910. After a decade of struggle the business shut its gates in 1920. Five years later a Miami developer bought the property out of bankruptcy with the hopes of turning it into a grand hotel and golf resort, but in the aftermath of the Florida real-estate crash his plans never came to fruition. Bob saw that the grounds had obviously gone to seed, but the lushly flowered landscape lingered in his mind long afterwards as the possible site for a project he had begun to envision after his retirement: building the perfect golf course.

The journey to Britain began with a grand send-off thrown by his friends at East Lake on April 21. The city presented him with a gilded four-leaf clover for luck, and Augusta Country Club contributed a grandfather clock in honor of his recent win there which sits in the lobby at East Lake to this day. The Colonel and Clara wouldn't be on this trip: they had been recruited to stay home and baby-sit the children. Bob, Mary, Pop and Eleanor Keeler and the rest of a small Atlanta entourage left a few days later and arrived in New York on April 28, where members of Bob's Walker Cup team had gathered. After a celebratory lunch hosted by the USGA at Engineer's Club on Long Island, two days later the Americans boarded the *Mauretania* and set sail for England. His teammates included Francis Ouimet, George Von Elm, current Amateur champion Jimmy Johnston, runner-up Dr. O.F. Willing, and two promising newcomers, nineteen-year-old Donald Moe from Oregon and George Voigt from New York. The stock-market crash had sufficiently disrupted the life of Wall Street broker Jess Sweetser that he'd been forced to drop off the team; he was replaced by first reserve Roland McKenzie.

In addition to the golfers a number of other luminaries were making the crossing, including Bob's friend Douglas Fairbanks, celebrated French entertainer Maurice Chevalier, and sixty-year-old Scottish music-hall comedian Harry Lauder.

After a convivial voyage, during which Bob kept himself in trim playing improvised games of Doug with the original Doug on the ship's topside tennis court, the *Mauretania* docked in Southampton on May 6. With ten days to prepare for the Walker Cup at Royal St. George's, the team took a motor coach into London and checked into the Savoy; Bob spent the rest of the day showing Mary the sights.

He led the team out for practice the next morning at a local London course, which also served as their initial meet-and-greet with reporters. The following day he and defending U.S. Amateur champ Jimmy Johnston were whisked out to Sunningdale to play a foursomes match with the Prince of Wales and Sir Phillip Sassoon, a prominent ruling-class social fixture. As a perquisite of royalty, the prince picked Bob for his playing partner; they won the last three holes on the strength of Bob's play to end the match in a diplomatic draw.

The next day the entire team traveled down to Sandwich, Kent, to begin practice rounds on the velvety turf at Royal St. George's. The R&A charged admission for the first time and drew huge crowds for the two-day event, but for the sixth straight outing the Americans made the Walker Cup no contest. After agonizing over his pairings for the first day of foursomes, Bob's selections won three of the four matches. Bob and his own partner, short-hitting "Doc" Willing, took their match 8 & 7. In his capacity as captain he also unselfishly named Jimmy Johnston as the team's number-one player for singles. The next day, with Doug Fairbanks and the Prince of Wales walking side by side in his gallery—prime specimens of New and Old World royalty—Bob won his singles match against British team captain Roger Wethered 9 & 8. Six of his teammates followed suit and the U.S. retained the Walker Cup by a score of 10 to 2. (Don Moe, America's youngest player and presumably weakest link, came back from four down to shoot 67, break the course record at St. George's, and equal the lowest score in Walker Cup history. In the locker room afterwards, as they were changing their shoes, Moe's British opponent Bill Stout ambled over to him and said sincerely, "Donald, that was not golf; that was a visitation from God.")

Three days later, on Saturday May 19, the Walker Cup team participated in a popular, relaxed annual amateur outing at Sunningdale sponsored by *Golf Illustrated* called the Gold Vase Tournament. Bob had agreed to appear for social reasons more than competitive ones—he partnered with Dale Bourne, an old friend and a former British Amateur champion—but after shooting 75 in the morning round, six strokes off the lead, his competitive fires kicked in.

He made a friendly lunchtime wager with Dale Bourne; Bob bet a single pound that he would break 70 that afternoon. Although reluctant to tax himself so close to the start of the British Amateur, only a week away, this was his last tune-up before the championship run began; just playing for that small a stake focused Bob's aggression like sun through a magnifying glass. He birdied three of the last four holes to shoot 68, break the tournament scoring record, and win the Gold Vase by a single stroke.

He would get in one last day of golf before the Amateur at Sir Phillip Sassoon's private estate, paired again with the Prince of Wales against their host and another future king, Edward's younger brother Albert, later George VI. Pop and Bob could only marvel about the experience afterwards: the little Dixie Whiz Kid had come a long way from short pants and playing golf holes fashioned out of wagon ruts on the dirt roads of suburban Atlanta.

The foundation of the Grand Slam was all riding on the British Amateur, the only major title in the sport Bob had never taken.

He later called it the most important tournament of his life. His loss to Johnny Goodman at Pebble Beach had softened his distaste for eighteen-hole elimination matches, but the British Amateur threw seven of them in his path over five days before the thirty-six-hole final, the toughest and most physically demanding test in the sport. He knew he would need more than incomparable shot-making and mental toughness, more even than good luck to climb that mountain. Fate would have to smile.

Play in the British Amateur began at St. Andrews on Monday, May 26. Bob arrived a few days earlier in time for a practice round on Saturday, and die-hard Jack McIntyre showed up to carry his bag every step of the way. The next day, just as he had three years earlier to get a round in on Sunday, Bob and company drove the 120-mile round trip to Gleneagles.

Monday morning dawned gray and benign; the sun would break through later, and the wind never stirred off the Eden all day. A dry, cold spring had left the Old Course in poor shape for the championship. What little grass there was had been mown to the nub; the fairways ran like parking lots and bare patches appeared on almost every green. The draw sheet listing every contestant's name was big enough to cover the side of a house. The enormous size of the field required some to play two matches on the first day, while others waited until the following afternoon to hit their initial drives. Bob began play as the top seed in the second bracket, a rating which earned him a bye in the first round. He walked out onto the first tee of the Old Course at 3:00 that afternoon to meet his opponent, Henry Sydney Roper, a former coalminer described by Bernard Darwin, the venerable correspondent for *The Times*, as "as player hitherto unknown to fame."

Syd Roper was the prototype of the player Bob dreaded facing in short matches. Most of his British friends had assured him Roper wasn't capable of anything better than bogey golf. Bob always believed he could accurately size up an opponent when meeting him on the first tee, not the quality of his game so much as the man's ability to withstand the scrutiny and pressure that a match with Bob guaranteed. "What I observed of Mr. Roper in this respect," Bob said, "was not at all reassuring."

About the same size as Bob, Roper had an efficient, athletic swing, and a calm look in his eyes. This young man was not just a golfer, Bob decided at once, but a competitor. When Roper pummeled his first drive, Bob signaled his own engine room to crank up the power to full speed ahead.

He rattled in a long downhill putt to birdie the first hole. Bernard Darwin, watching from the gallery, thought he detected signs of tension in Bob's putting stroke. That diagnosis appeared sound when he missed a much easier putt for birdie at the second. He gently dropped a short pitch shot at the third right next to the flag for another birdie that he could have putted with his eyes closed. After his 300-yard drive at the fourth dribbled into the infamous Cottage Bunker, Bob played one of the ten best shots of his life and holed a six-iron off the sand from 150 yards out for a double-eagle two—the rarest of all golf's avian deeds: an albatross. Pop heard a man in the gallery near him mutter, "They ought to burn him at the stake. He's a witch." Bob followed that thunderbolt by reaching the green of the par-five fifth in two and two putts later had another birdie. At the end of five holes Bob was five under par.

Any other man might have fled for his life after witnessing such an assault, but Roper, who played the first five holes in even fours, was one under par and only down three to Jones. What was worse, he looked utterly untroubled by the way Bob had just vaulted the first furlong at St. Andrews. In fact, he hardly seemed to notice.

Roper won the sixth hole when Bob three-putted. Bob restored his lead to three with another birdie at seven. After pushing his drive wide right at the eighth, Bob found himself stymied on the green; Roper had won his second hole of the last three and showed no signs of cracking.

They halved the ninth. Bob had played the outward nine in 33 strokes in a burst of supernatural golf. His lead over Roper was only two. Another half at the tenth. On the short eleventh, the scene of his unbecoming retreat nine years earlier, Bob nearly holed his tee shot for an ace; another birdie and the lead was back to three. At the twelfth Bob recorded his seventh sub-par score of the round and his lead for the first time grew to four.

Again Roper came back. They halved the thirteenth and Roper won the next with a superbly played approach. After halving the fifteenth, the match finally ended at sixteen, 3, & 2, when both men took fives. If they had continued, and Bob had finished with two fours, he would have equaled his own amateur record for the Old Course.

After predictions that Roper would play bogey golf, the man had made exactly one of them in the entire match, on their last hole. Bob told Keeler later that Roper would probably have beaten him on any other day of the tournament, but once again Bob had played his best when he needed it most. Thanks to the size of the field and the luck of the draw, on Tuesday he rested. He would have to play thirty-six holes, two matches a day, from this point forward through the finals; if he made it that far.

On Tuesday night the weather turned bitterly cold, the wind whipping from the west, the direction which made the Old Course play the hardest. Spectators went overnight from shirt-sleeves to coats and gloves. Bob arrived at the first tee at twelve minutes after eight, blowing on his fingers to restore feeling. His third-round opponent was Cowan Shankland, not the most promising name for a golfer, and for the better part of the morning he lived up to it. Playing slightly down to the level of his competition, after handily winning the first three holes Bob's concentration appeared to drift. A bogey at the ninth meant he had played the front nine in 40 and held only a one-hole lead.

Bob won the tenth with a par, then watched his opponent putt off the green and nearly into the Eden on eleven. Three more routine pars were all he needed to dispatch Cowan Shankland 5 & 3.

If Bob had been conserving his energy during his morning match, he had good reason. After lunch that day the fourth-round draw brought him up against current British Amateur champion Cyril Tolley.

Cyril James Hastings Tolley was thirty-five years old, a tall, burly, powerfully built natural athlete who had lettered (played varsity) in three sports at Oxford, after surviving thirteen months in a German prison camp during the Great War. Since winning the British Amateur in 1920 he had become a mainstay of their international teams. An aristocratic version of Ted Ray or John Daly, he possessed both intimidating power and exquisite touch around the greens. Having played with Bob numerous times in and out of formal competition in both countries, Tolley had become his closest friend in the game on this side of the Atlantic, and there was no one Bob feared or respected more in the entire field. This was the most anticipated match of the tournament. A local holiday in the nearby town of Dundee created an unwieldy crowd of over twelve thousand people who crammed around them on the first tee—the rest of the matches on the course that afternoon went almost entirely unwatched—and it would play a crucial, some would later say regrettable, part in the outcome.

The two friends were masters of studied indifference under fire, but tension showed on both men's faces as they shook hands at 1:35 and teed it up. Tolley topped his first drive forward less than 100 yards, and it cost him the hole when Bob collected a routine par. The gallery stampeded ahead to the next tee and down the second fairway, a pattern that would be repeated all afternoon, which led to aggravating delays, some as long as twenty minutes, before every shot they played. The wind had picked up, blowing ever harder, a three-club gale that swirled sand out of the bunkers and sent people scampering for cover between shots.

When Tolley won the second to square the match after Bob sliced his approach, it was clear neither man intended to yield an inch. This quickly settled into a primal battle that evoked allusions to every kind of combat from the assembled sportswriters; a saber duel to the finish, fought with the brutality of bare-knuckle boxers, summed up the prevailing point of view.

Tolley took his first lead at the fourth, when Bob again sliced an iron approach, this time into the crowd, and failed to get close with his recovery. Bob pushed his second shot into the gallery on the next hole as well, but after a lucky bounce back into the fairway saved his par, and the hole was halved. After the sixth was halved Bob squared the match at seven when Tolley three-putted. Bob seized his second lead with par at the eighth. The 306-yard par-four ninth was playing dead downwind and Bob tried to carry it with his drive but pulled it into the gorse; Tolley stepped up and slaughtered a ball that ran all the way onto the green. After his birdie the match was squared again.

The tension twisted tighter with every stroke. The immense crowd grew so still that as each man stood over his ball ready to strike all you could hear was the eerie whistling of the wind. After halving the tenth, both stumbled at eleven, but Bob stuck his third shot next to the hole and Tolley could only manage bogey. Bob had a one-hole lead for the third time, and for the third time gave it right back; both men hit magnificent drives on the 314-yard twelfth that bounced over and through the green, but Bob flubbed his second coming back while Tolley chipped dead to the hole for another birdie.

All square with six to play. The crowd churned around them like an immense school of fish; quiescent for long periods then startled into whirling, scrambling motion whenever a shot was played. The stewards toiled and strained to shepherd them but they were overwhelmed. The constant delays were hard enough for Bob and Tolley and downright impossible for anyone else. Every other match they encountered on the narrow links was forced to stand aside until the whole great throng had passed by. Some greens stood empty for half an hour, with players and caddies forced to stand guard over their ball against any mischief from the advancing masses.

As the end approached the two men starting banging at each other like two heavyweights going toe to toe. Bob sank a putt of nearly 40 feet for birdie at the thirteenth; he had his fourth lead of the match. Tolley answered at the 512-yard par-five fourteenth with his best shot of the day: after another booming drive he launched a soaring three-wood that landed on the fringe and rolled to within 3 feet of the flag: eagle. All square. At the long par-four fifteenth Bob stuck his approach inside of 5 feet; from 20 feet Tolley took a dead run at birdie, missed coming back for par and conceded Bob his putt. Bob had his fifth one-hole lead of the match.

Bob knew every bunker on the Old Course, open or concealed. One of the most dangerous of them all, a series of three actually, guards the right side of the sixteenth fairway and is known collectively as the Principal's Nose. Attempting to blast over the bunkers with the wind at his back and take a run at the green, Bob landed his ball in the Nose. Tolley scrambled for a par while Bob paid the price for his gamble with bogey. All square through sixteen.

Now every living soul on the course converged along the 467-yard par-four Road Hole; estimates run as high as fifteen thousand, a nightmarish collision of flesh and shouting stewards. The wait to restore order before the match could resume took more than twenty minutes. A photo of the two men waiting on the tee is a portrait of strain and battle fatigue: two boxers collapsed on the stools in their corners waiting for the final round to begin. Long celebrated in Britain as one of the game's greatest holes, what was about to happen would elevate the seventeenth at St. Andrews into enduring legend.

Both drives flew long with the wind behind them, Bob's to the left, Tolley's right center and slightly longer. The hole was cut close to the front, and right behind the deep and deadly Road Bunker. Bob had no direct line to the flag from his position, while Tolley's angle in appeared to be ideal.

Bob stared at the green and studied his options for nearly a minute, an eternity given his usual brisk pace. He then motioned the stewards to move the gallery away from the left side of the Road Bunker and all the way to the back of the green. A buzz ran through the crowd. No one ever played in at this flag from that side of the fairway; the traditional path from Bob's position was to shoot for the front of the green and hope to roll the ball in from the right, pin high.

Pop standing in the gallery with Alister Mackenzie, the golf architect whose work at Cypress Point he and Bob had so admired the year before, and who knew the Old Course as well as any man alive. He wasn't reassured to see Mackenzie shaking his head, a mixture of disbelief and admiration. "It's a very bold conception," he said.

Bob waited until the stewards had edged the crowd back as far as they showed any willingness to move. He stood to his work and drilled a four-iron exactly on the line he'd visualized, toward the swale just left of the Road Bunker where he hoped it would roll up onto the green and down the slope, but it took a huge hop off the rock-hard ground and looked as if it might bounce toward disaster, either onto the road behind the green or to the left toward the next tee. But the stewards had not moved the crowd as far as Bob had requested; the ball hit someone in the gallery on that first bounce and dropped straight down onto the fringe a few feet off the green, about hole high. Some complained afterwards that Bob had aimed for the crowd intentionally, but he had clearly just asked the stewards to move them out of the way; they were just so eager to watch Bob they weren't willing to move far enough. And as he wrote years later, "I should never have been so heedless of the possibility of inflicting injury upon a spectator."

The pressure shifted to Tolley and weighed on him; his short iron approach landed short, ran forward, curled a few inches just short of the top of the swale leading up to the green, and rolled back down to the front edge. The cavernous Road Bunker now sat directly between his ball and the flag. Bob was away. He chipped up to within 8 feet, leaving himself an uphill par putt from the left. Tolley had only one spot he could land his ball with any hope of ending near the hole: just over the edge of the bunker, dangerously close to the lip, at the top of the slope that ran from there down to the hole. Pop felt sure no man alive would be able to negotiate that shot under these conditions. "I could see nothing but a win for Jones."

Tolley hit his target as surely as if he'd floated over and dropped it by hand; the ball gently trickled down the slopes to within 2 feet of the flag. Bob years later wrote that it was the finest finesse shot he'd ever seen.

The pressure shifted again. Bob took one look at his "eminently missable" putt and dropped it for par. Tolley matched him. All square through seventeen. "Although it had been as tense a hole as I had ever played in my life," wrote Bob, "the result only served to increase the pressure."

With the wind behind them and no trouble in front of them, both men ripped their drives 340 yards to within 30 feet of the enormous eighteenth green. Another long wait ensued as the crowd poured in to surround the green, in some places standing ten or twelve deep. Bob was away and played a strong pitch that ran 25 feet past the hole. Tolley failed to press the slight advantage; his chip came up short through the Valley of Sin to about 15 feet. Bob putted first and left it on the edge of the cup, then went through "the most agonizing moments of that entire year" as he waited for Tolley to try his putt for the win. Bob fully expected him to make it.

Tolley's ball came close but stopped just short of the hole. Both men tapped in for pars. The match headed for extra holes and sudden death. The crowd turned and made a mad dash toward the first green while the players and caddies headed for the tee. By the time they reached it the crowd stretched all the way along either side of the fairway.

Both hit strong drives. Bob played his approach first to the left front of the green, a splendid piece of iron work, landing gently about 10 feet from the hole. Tolley pulled his second to the left of the green, then pitched up short, leaving himself 7 feet to the hole, inside and on the same line as Bob's ball.

Bob rolled his ball right on that line. It came to a stop a few inches short of the hole. With a gasp the crowd realized that Bob's ball had left Tolley's line to the hole almost completely stymied. He attempted to cut his ball around Bob's with an iron but it wasn't meant to be. Bob tapped in for his par: the match was over on the nineteenth hole. Policemen stepped in to escort both players back to the clubhouse as the crowd surged in on them. In one photo they appear to be holding Bob up on his feet.

"The release from the tension was almost unbearable," wrote Bob. "It was the kind of match in which each player plays himself so completely out that at the end the only feeling to which he is sensitive is one of utter exhaustion."

That night he told Pop he'd had a funny feeling out on the course against Tolley, not just once, but a few times. There had seemed to be something inevitable about the outcome, as if whatever he did had almost nothing to do with the final score. That uncanny certainty did nothing to reduce the strain, which had melted twelve pounds off him already; his belt tightened a notch, Bob looked gaunt, his eyes recessed in his head. His appetite had vanished altogether, but he seemed haunted by that strange sensation he'd had and couldn't stop talking about it.

Thursday morning, the fourth day of play. The western wind had vanished overnight, the skies cleared, the air warmed again; St. Andrews had drawn in its teeth. Bob's fifth-round opponent was an Englishman named G.O. Watt. After letting him hang around for a few holes, Bob threw down a string of four birdies in six holes and dispatched Watt, 7 & 6. He was grateful for a breather match, one that exerted no more than "ordinary pressure," requiring only twelve holes and forty-five shots, because another battle loomed after lunch that afternoon.

By the sixth round only three Americans were left in the field. Both Ouimet and Von Elm had fallen in the fifth; in addition to Bob both Johnston and Voigt had won through to the sixth round, both with comparative ease. For the first time the draw brought two Americans together when Bob faced Johnston, the reigning U.S. Amateur champion.

Johnston had begun his tournament by ousting fifty-year-old Bernard Darwin, who was covering the event for *The Times* of London, referring to himself in his account of their match only as "B. Darwin." Tough as ever, B. Darwin took Johnston to eighteen before bowing out. From there his path had grown progressively easier, until now. Darwin set out to follow their match with a bit of wishful thinking, stating he was eager to watch the two Americans "cut one another's throats before a big crowd." Jimmy started well, but Bob played slightly better; Johnston made only two slight mistakes through the first eight holes, and Jones made him pay for both, playing, as Darwin observed, "without fault and without mercy." Bob took a two-hole lead into the ninth, drove into a bunker and lost half his lead, then drove the tenth green and took it right back. When Johnston missed birdie by an inch at the eleventh, the match turned; after leaving his man stymied on twelve and Johnston's bunkered approach at the next, Bob's lead had grown to four with five holes to play. The gallery began to drift away to follow other players. Pop went off with them: this match was clearly over.

That's when the fun started.

Johnston played two superb wood shots to birdie the par-five fourteenth for a win, and then Bob made a gift of fifteen with a missed 4-footer for double bogey. After Bob collected par at sixteen, Johnston displayed his nerve by sinking a brilliant 12-foot putt to halve the hole and extend the match; Bob's lead was two, with two holes to play, but with Johnston suddenly on his game the result looked far from secure.

The Road Hole again. After a solid drive, Johnston found the green in two, while Bob's approach came up short of the Road Bunker, just as Tolley had done the day before. Bob couldn't match Tolley's miracle pitch and had to settle for bogey; Johnston two-putted for his par and the lead was down to one.

Both men hit solid drives at the Home Hole. Playing first, Johnston showed the strain on his second shot, pulling his pitch to the upper left corner of the green, a leave of nearly 90 feet from the cup. But the strain was working on them both; Bob followed with an only slightly less surprising pitch toward the same corner, 30 feet inside and to the right of Johnston's ball. Bob had the advantage; Johnston's putt would inevitably show him something of the line.

The colossal crowd that had earlier abandoned them came roaring in when they heard about Johnston's comeback. Ouimet, Von Elm, and the other members of the American Walker Cup team looked down on the eighteenth green from the balcony of the Grand Hotel. They watched Johnston putt first; the ball rolled and rolled and rolled, then curled right for the hole and stopped only a few inches short of a miraculous birdie.

Bob's touch failed him: Ouimet could see he was grinding, even from this distance. His putt stopped 9 feet short. Downhill, side-hill, with a foot of break from left to right. Nine feet to halve the hole, stave off Johnston and win the match. The moment of crisis.

"He'll make it," said Von Elm to Ouimet. "He's made hundreds like it. He'll pop it right in." Bob looked nowhere near as certain. He later told Pop it was the longest 9-foot putt he'd ever seen.

He hit it. The ball rolled right on line and dropped dead center. Match over.

Friday, May 30. Again no wind, but the day broke damp and cool. Bob's seventh-round opponent was a tall young Englishman from Stourbridge, Eric Fiddian. For the first time all week Bob lost the opening hole when he dunked his second shot in the Swilcan Burn. Fiddian's only lead of the match would last until the fourth; Bob went four up by the eighth. Bernard Darwin concluded, "the rest of the game was of purely academic interest. Fiddian postponed the evil day with a birdie at twelve, but there could be only one end and it came at fifteen." Bob eliminated Fiddian 4 & 3, and "it was all done without the faintest apparent effort." The gods had arranged another breather.

A curious episode followed. Bob had played his way into the semi-finals, and a longer than usual break followed as he awaited the results of the match that would produce his opponent. After a light lunch he and Mary walked upstairs to the living room of their suite at the Grand Hotel. Word arrived that Bob would be playing Voigt, the only other American left standing, in the semi-final round. Bob felt tired unto collapse, unaccountably agitated, his stomach roiling. A fugitive suggestion entered his mind that a short nip of something bracing might settle his nerves and revive his dulled senses. A decanter of sherry sat on the living-room sideboard, and Bob poured a glass for Mary and one for himself; for some reason he couldn't explain afterwards it seemed like a good idea at the time. He had never touched a drop of alcohol before playing a tournament round. "I could not have made a greater mistake," he wrote. "The wine flushed my face and caused me to be very keenly aware that my eyes were the slightest bit out of focus."

He couldn't shake the deleterious effects, even as he went down to prepare for the afternoon match with Voigt. He told no one at the time, reluctant as ever to use anything as an excuse, and kept the whole experience to himself for years afterwards, but as his starting time approached he came close to panic. The slight blurring of vision would persist until more than half the match had been played.

As he had admitted earlier to Pop, Bob had been feeling the influence of something like providence playing a hand at St. Andrews all week. The improbable eagle against Roper. The fortunate bounce off the crowd at the Road Hole with Tolley. The final putt on the Home Hole to beat Johnston. Bob had edged continually closer to the date he'd made for himself with destiny, and then, out of nowhere, came this casual, almost willful act of self-destruction. He'd had a few cocktails before playing at East Lake with the boys, but there was no precedent for this kind of behavior in any tournament he'd ever played. Even decades later he never arrived at an adequate answer. But the thought occurs that his intention might have been an unconscious testing of fate.

George Voigt was thirty-five, a mature, steady competitor who didn't shrink from the spotlight. He had dominated amateur golf in the Mid-Atlantic region for most of the 1920s as thoroughly as Bob had in the South. Many felt he had passed Von Elm to become the second best amateur in the game, and Grantland Rice thought he might be the best clutch putter in the world. A few compared not only his confidence and breezy manner to a slimmed-down Walter Hagen, but also the quality of his golf. His swing was compact, machine-like, repeatable, and he never faltered on the greens. He gave the impression of a man who had nothing to fear from his enemies, and he and Bob were friends. In fact it was no exaggeration to say that Bob was his hero.

The wind had picked up by the time they teed off, the temperature stuck in the low forties. Voigt arrived wearing a heavy sweater and fingerless gloves, to keep his hands warm. After both men reached the opening green in two, Voigt dropped his 15-foot putt for birdie. From about 10 feet out, Bob matched him, rattling the ball against the back of the cup.

Bob walked away from the first green aware that he'd been lucky again: his putt had been badly judged; only the wrong speed had kept it on line into the hole. The alcohol hadn't affected either his drive or approach, and wouldn't all day, but as he stood looking down at the green he'd realized he couldn't focus his eyes on the ball. He wouldn't make another putt of any consequence for over two hours.

Voigt gave away the second hole with a bunkered drive. Jones up one. They halved the third, and then the fourth when Bob missed his first short putt of the afternoon but Voigt failed to capitalize. Voigt squared the match with a birdie at the fifth, when Bob missed his own birdie putt of less than 4 feet. He missed another near-gimme of the same length two holes later, failing to take a hole that Voigt had all but handed to him. His play from tee to green remained flawless, but at the short eighth, Bob missed his third makeable birdie putt of the front nine. Another half.

At the par-three eleventh, just as his vision started to clear, Bob began paying the price for his mistakes. Voigt was on the green with his drive, while Bob overshot his into the Eden. Voigt had his first lead of the match.

After halving the twelfth, Voigt extended his lead to two at thirteen with a delicate pitch and run and a single putt. Bob flubbed his chip and missed his par putt. For the first time all week Bob trailed in a match by more than a single hole.

Voigt was two up with five holes to play. Even he started to believe he might win. Bob looked beaten and downcast; the way he had played, most of the gallery now expected him to lose. But there's a peculiar, age-old superstition at St. Andrews that says the golfer who is two up with five to play never wins his match. Francis Ouimet, who had been following the match all afternoon, heard at least a dozen local spectators spread the word with religious certainty that Voigt would now falter because he was two up with five to play. Bob heard the whispers too and found no comfort in them. George Voigt was not the kind of man who tossed away a lead.

As they stepped to the fourteenth tee the wind kicked up, blowing in off the water from the left across the long fairway. The gallery crowded in around them on the tee; maybe that was the reason Voigt couldn't feel the freshening wind. He elected to play his ball down the right side of the fairway and cut the corner, but the moment it climbed above the crowd the wind took hold and it drifted like a balloon just over the nearby stone wall, out of bounds into the gorse. Voigt couldn't believe his eyes; he'd been hitting the ball dead straight all day. Bob watched this unlooked-for gift arrive, then deliberately aimed way left, all the way onto the adjoining fifth fairway, where he safely landed his drive. Stroke and distance penalties applied to Voigt's mistake; he lost the hole and his lead was cut in half.

They halved fifteen when Bob missed another short putt that would have won it and evened the match. At sixteen, Bob played safely left again into the adjoining third fairway. Voigt aimed his drive down the left side as well, but again the wind grabbed his ball, blowing it all the way across into the dreaded Principal's Nose. He couldn't recover. The hole went to Bob; the match was all square with two to play, just as it had been against Cyril Tolley when they reached seventeen.

An enormous gallery again surrounded the Road Hole. Bob at last appeared to have full possession of his faculties; he followed a fine drive favoring the left through the rising wind with a solid approach that landed just short, kicked forward but then rolled back down into the swale when it failed to crest the small slope to the green. Desperate to seize the advantage and break Bob's momentum, Voigt went for broke, pulled a one-iron and hit a stalwart second that ran up the swale and onto the front of the green, only 10 feet past Bob, but with a clear line to putt. Bob played a bump-and-run chip toward the flag; it lacked conviction and stopped 12 feet short. Voigt ran his birdie attempt straight at the hole: it stopped less than a foot from the cup. He was assured of par; Bob was assuredly not. Voigt was certain Bob couldn't make that putt under these circumstances.

Ouimet watched Bob's behavior closely as he walked to his ball. "Ordinarily he takes a quick squint at the line, steps up and hits his ball. On this occasion he consumed quite a bit of time and looked his line over carefully from every angle."

An English lord with whom Pop had been walking as he watched the match chose this moment to announce: "The stars are with Bobby in this tournament. His luck is as fixed as the orbit of a planet." Pop, the student of destiny, wasn't half as sure.

Bob had an eerie feeling as he stepped up to the ball. "I could see the line as plainly as if it had been marked on the green. I knew before I swung the putter that I would surely hole the putt."

It dropped dead center. Darwin decided that with this putt Bob had just demonstrated "true greatness of soul."

The crowd broke ahead to line the eighteenth fairway. With the wind against them, Voigt left his drive 20 yards short of Bob. Smelling blood, an energized Bob ran up and leaped across the Swilcan Burn on the way to his ball. Now visibly shaken, Voigt had a tough decision to make. He carried no iron between an eight and a five and the distance put him dead between them. He elected to use the eight and punch the shot in low, but the coolness he'd shown all day had gone out of his touch after losing his lead. The ball missed reaching the plateau green by six inches, hit the bank and rolled back into the deadly hollow guarding the front edge that since time immemorial has been known as the Valley of Sin. Bob clipped a gorgeous high pitch that banked off the wind and gently fell within 8 feet of the hole. Voigt's chip up from the Valley was sound, but he was 6 feet shy of the flag and lying three.

Bob's 8-foot putt to win the match outright ran so straight and true he had stepped forward with his hand out to pluck the ball from the hole, when it hesitated on the last blade of grass and hung outside the lip. Voigt still had this 6-footer for par to extend the match into extra holes. He took his time, but his moment was gone. The putt lipped out. Bob had reached the finals of the British Amateur.

Two up with five to play; you would have heard that as the dominant theme running through conversations in all the pubs afterwards and long into the evening, where all were comforted by the warm reassurance of a fable confirmed. Why, the outcome was foretold!

Bob's diligent study of the Old Course had paid dividends on the one day his opponent had by all accounts outplayed him, but the strain had caught up with him; he told Pop as he walked off the course he felt more dead than alive. A drink, a hot bath, dinner with Mary and to bed, ordered Pop; tomorrow is another day.

This much was clear: whatever mysterious influence had been looking after Bob Jones all that week at St. Andrews watched over him still. If he had deliberately set out to test fate that afternoon, where temptation appeared in the unlikely guise of a glass of sherry, he'd just received as emphatic an answer as a man could ever hope to have.

Bob's opponent in Saturday's final would be thirty-one-year-old Englishman Roger Wethered. Universally liked and admired as the model of a sporting gentleman, he had appeared on the scene in 1921 while still an undergraduate at Oxford, losing the British Open in the play-off to Jock Hutchison. He had gone on to win the British Amateur in 1923, reach the semi-finals twice, and lose in the finals in 1928. He had also become a fixture on Britain's international teams, and his record in those matches showed he was equal to anyone. His only fault, if it can be called a fault, was that he was so nice a person he lacked a killer instinct. He couldn't even be considered the best player in his family; his younger sister Joyce, four time British Women's Champion, had claimed that title without argument. There's little question that up to this point in the game's history, she was the greatest female golfer who ever lived. Whereas the driver was the weakest club in Roger's bag, Joyce hit hers as straight as an iron rule. After playing in an exhibition against Joyce at East Lake the previous year, no less than Bob Jones had this to say about her: "I have not played golf with anyone, man or woman, amateur or professional, who made me feel so utterly outclassed."

Joyce Wethered might well have given Bob a harder time in this final; she could drive the ball as far as any man, equaled Bob's own formidable powers of concentration, and never backed down from a challenge. On the other hand, according to Bob, Roger was "a completely charming person without any semblance of aggressiveness on the golf course." Bob had been among a group of Roger's friends standing near the eighteenth green on the final day of the Open at St. Andrews in 1921 who'd had to persuade Roger that it was more important for him to stick around for the play-off with Hutchison than to return home for an amateur cricket match in which he'd agreed to play. They nearly failed to convince him.

Estimates of the crowd that gathered in St. Andrews from all over Scotland on the morning of Saturday, May 31 run as high as twenty thousand. With their favorite "bonnie Bobby" facing an upper-class Englishman, the native Scots handed Bob something he'd never experienced before in an overseas match: home-field advantage.

The sun was shining, a modest wind blowing from the east to keep things interesting. After introductions, as they waited for the gallery to settle, an official of the Royal & Ancient addressed the crowd at the tee with the following: "During the hundreds of years in which golf has been played at St. Andrews, every one of the greatest golfers in the world has as some time or other played the Old Course. Wonderful scores have been made, but no one has ever been able to play a round without having at least one five on his card." Francis Ouimet was standing close to Bob, and saw his mouth tighten at the comment, although he said nothing. But the challenge, whether or not that was the official's intention, waved in the air like a red flag before a bull. Just what Bobby needed to hear, thought Ouimet.

After splendid first drives, Bob foozled his second shot short of the Burn, then played a flawless pitch to within a foot and halved the hole for par. He recorded seven more fours on the front nine, and a three. Hitting a handful of erratic drives, Wethered had to work considerably harder to achieve the same result on the card, and after nine the match stood even, each man going out in 35. But this was where the longer length of the match served as a balm to Bob's nerves; time was on his side, he could hammer away at Old Man Par and let Wethered worry about his own problems. After they made the first turn, Roger began to crack.

On the tenth green, Bob holed a 6-foot putt for par. Wethered missed for par from five. Bob had the first lead of the match. As Wethered turned after picking up his ball, Bob read on the Englishman's face "his belief that he could not keep this up much longer."

They halved eleven, when Bob holed a side-winding 8-footer, and twelve, where Bob missed an easier putt for birdie. As they

turned into the home stretch Bob went to the whip: with three
pars sandwiching a birdie at fourteen, he won the next four
holes in a row. Wethered's driver had already faltered; now
through this crucial sequence his putter started to balk; Bob
seized on each mistake ruthlessly. They reached the seventeenth,
the eventful Road Hole, with Bob up five.

A quick glance at the scorecard at this point in their match
reveals that Bob had made two threes and fourteen fours. He
had yet to make a five.

Both men's drives at seventeen were perfect. Forced to gamble,
Wethered played a three-wood toward the Road Hole green.
The ball pitched into the ascending bank to the right of the
Road Bunker, took one hop and settled on the green 12 feet
from the hole. Bob pulled his three-wood and played his shot
along the exact same line, but it had a touch of draw on it, and
instead of hitting the bank it dove straight into the gaping, sheer-
faced Road Bunker.

Bob's ball was no more than 15 or 20 feet from the hole, but
the front edge of the bunker looked over his head as he took
his stance. This was still a year before Gene Sarazen invented
the modern sand wedge, with a flange below the leading edge
designed to slice down through the sand. Players as accomplished
as Walter Hagen still tried to pick the ball clean out of bunkers,
like a chip shot. Bob took one look and knew if he tried that
here the ball might very well scamper across the green and end
up on the road. But as he dug his feet in he also realized the
ball was lying on only a thin layer of sand. He split the difference. With perfect pitch he cut the legs out from under the ball,
and it rose up on a whisper of sand, barely cleared the top of
the bank, hit the down slope carrying so much backspin it nearly
came to a stop, then tricked down to pass the cup by 2 feet.
An old St. Andrews caddie standing next to Ouimet uttered a
then-unprintable oath, followed by "the finest shot I've ever
seen." Wethered left his putt for birdie hanging on the edge. All

Bob had to do to keep his streak of fours alive was can the 2-foot putt.

"Bob hurriedly took his stance and just as hurriedly hit his ball and—horrors!" wrote Ouimet. "He missed. Missed the two-foot putt. He whaled his drive a mile up the eighteenth fairway."

Bob finished the round with his four at the Home Hole, and maintained his five-hole lead at the halfway point of the match. He had shot a flawless, textbook 71, besting Wethered by five strokes.

Bob crossed the street to the Grand Hotel. Ouimet went after him and followed him up to his room. The minute the door was closed Bob paced, cursed and kicked a chair. "He was wild," wrote Ouimet. "He looked at me with disgust and I could not understand his attitude."

"What in the world's got into you, Bob? You're five up."

"Did you hear what that official said on the first tee?"

Ouimet thought for a moment, and then it came back to him.

"And I had to make a two-foot putt at seventeen to be the first man to play St. Andrews without taking a five." Bob had forgotten all about Roger Wethered or winning the British Amateur. Throughout that whole morning round—about which Bernard Darwin the next day wrote, "I do not think I ever saw golf so well played in all my life"—Bob had set his sights against a scoring record that had never been reached in five hundred years. One careless slip had cost him the achievement.

Bob was too disgusted with himself to eat lunch, but Pop pushed the tea and toast. Outside, spectators kept pouring off the trains. When they returned to the tee for the second round, the crowd had increased to twenty-five thousand, the largest ever gathered at the Old Course. Ouimet, Von Elm, and a couple of Bob's friends from Atlanta were recruited to serve as his personal escorts to keep him from being stampeded to death between holes. With anger still staining his mood, Bob took three putts for bogey at the first when Wethered stymied him and won the hole. That was Bob's second five of the day; there would be no assault on the "all-fours" record that afternoon, but then Bob had no intention of playing a full second round.

At the second Wethered hit a perfect drive. Bob hooked his into the crowd and the ball ended up on the road, just short of the out-of-bounds wall. After Wethered played up to the green, Bob hit a phenomenal recovery shot that cleared all the trouble and stopped on a bank behind the green. From there he chipped down and nearly holed his third shot, laying a perfect stymie between Wethered's ball and the hole. Roger three-putted. Bob's lead was back to five.

They matched scores until the sixth, where Roger's birdie trimmed the lead to four again. At seven Bob grabbed it right back with the help of another stymie. Two more halves and the lead remained five, with nine holes left to play. Wethered was running out of real estate.

Bob drove the front edge of the green at ten, took two putts for a birdie and his lead was six. After they both parred eleven the lead was six with only six to play. Par at twelve was all Bob needed to close out the match. He drove 300 yards to the green and after an easy par put an exclamation point at the end of his day—thirty holes played in two under par and the job was done.

Hats filled the air. The crowd swallowed him, a full mile from the clubhouse. A friend of Bob's was nearly trampled in a bunker. For a brief moment they lifted their hero up on their shoulders. Ouimet saw Bob's face turn white as the throng rushed at him, so he, Von Elm, and the two Atlanta friends dug him out of a great pile of well-wishers—Pop said they "apparently wanted to take the new champion apart to see what made him tick"—and formed a cordon around their friend until six burly Scots constables joined them. The cheering wouldn't stop. Bob turned to Ouimet when the police arrived and asked him to make sure that Wethered was all right. A brass band that had dutifully assembled to serenade the victor arrived too late; they broke apart on the human wave sweeping back toward the town and never played a note.

Pop knifed his way into the crowd to reach Bob about halfway back to the clubhouse, and they hugged and pounded each other on the back and shouted words that both could hardly hear. "I'm satisfied!" Bob shouted. "I'm satisfied! I don't care what happens now!" Pop shared his exhilaration, but remembered he had heard Bob voice those exact words once before, after his first win in the U.S. Open at Inwood.

When they reached the clubhouse doors Bob fell into Mary's waiting arms, and Pop saw to it that they were left alone for a while.

Only the third American to ever win the British Amateur after Travis and Sweetser, Bob had added the last and most elusive championship to his collection. All the jewels of golf now sparkled from his crown.

They soon called him out of the clubhouse for the trophy ceremony. He threw on a jacket and slicked back his hair and took the old silver cup, topped by the small stout figure of Old Tom Morris, into his hands for the first time. As exhausted and spent as he was, Bob couldn't stop smiling. He spoke of his love for St. Andrews, and how honored he was to be a member of the Royal & Ancient. "I was lucky to win," he told the crowd. "I never have been happier to get any cup, and I never worked so hard, nor suffered so much either."

Over three hundred matches had been played in five days. In every round Bob played, he turned in the best score in the field. Victory had required him to play a total of 143 holes, which he did in six under par.

"He has now caught up to Alexander the Great and has no more championships to win," wrote Bernard Darwin. He had no idea how wrong he was.

CHAPTER THIRTEEN

THE BRITISH OPEN, HOYLAKE

A special night train carried them away that evening from St. Andrews, the Americans all sharing a car and celebrating halfway to London, where they arrived at dawn. Bob and Mary left later the same day for a week in Paris; a change of scene to rest and restore his weary mind and body. He slept long hours and built his weight back up with five-star meals while they took in the sights of the city. France was a sound choice for seeking refuge; golf was a minor sport here so the only people who recognized him on the street were visiting Americans and Britons. He made room in his leisurely schedule for an exhibition match, pairing with Jimmy Johnston against a pro–am team of the current French champions—playing in a light rain, Bob and Jimmy beat them one up—and a few days later spent an afternoon taking in the French Amateur championship, which was won the next day by George Von Elm.

When they returned to England and made their way to Liverpool for the start of Open qualifying, Bob found to his dismay that the respite in Paris had recharged his spirits, but his swing had been left in the lurch. They checked into the Adelphi Hotel on Wednesday, June 11; Bob jumped in a taxi and went right out to the office for a practice round at Hoylake. He shot 71 but claimed he couldn't find a fairway or green; Calamity Jane did most of the work, saving half a dozen pars. Bob had played in his first international competition here in 1921, but hadn't laid eyes on it since. Hoylake is a long, flat and testing course that demands and rewards honest, straightforward drives and long irons. Bob spent over an hour on the driving range after his practice round—an eternity for him—trying to put things right with Jeanie Deans. Two days later he and George Von Elm lost a best-ball match to Horton Smith and Leo Diegel. His swing with the big clubs still felt awkward; Pop took one look at his game and saw it had gone "stale."

On Saturday the press announced that Pop had agreed to present daily radio summaries of the action at the Open back to America, the first live transatlantic sports broadcast. The BBC provided its local facilities in Liverpool; once they reached across the sea Pop's reports were to be beamed across the United States by David Sarnoff's National Broadcasting Company. (Eighteen years earlier, Sarnoff, a struggling, twenty-one-year-old Russian immigrant radio technician, was manning the control booth of New York City's most powerful radio station on April 14, 1912, when he picked up a faint distress signal from the *Titanic* and remained glued to his chair for the next seventy-two hours, relaying up-to-the-minute dispatches from the scene, the world's primary link to the unfolding tragedy.)

Fifteen other Americans attempted to qualify for the Open at Hoylake, a fraction of the record 296 entries. Others had traveled from as far away as Mexico, Greece, and South Africa; the Open was becoming an international event. Walter Hagen, on a lucrative exhibition tour of Australia, New Zealand, and the Far East with Joe Kirkwood, declined to defend the title he'd held for the last two years. He did, however, make certain that the Claret Jug arrived at Royal Liverpool in time for the tournament.

Two days of qualifying began on Monday, June 16, at Hoylake and a nearby course called Wallasey. The field was split between them, each side scheduled to change courses for their second round. When their names were called to the first tee at Hoylake, Gene Sarazen and Tommy Armour didn't report; no explanation was given. On the amateur side, Jimmy Johnston and George Voigt were last-minute scratches, serious losses to the American cause.

Bob played his Monday round at Hoylake, paired with a golfer from Havana, Cuba. A warm sun and only the slightest breeze greeted him—this uncanny weather had followed him throughout Great Britain for weeks—and Bob responded with an effortless 73. Pacing himself, thought Bernard Darwin; holding back his reserves. At 6,750 yards, the course was in spectacular shape, but like many of the classic British tracks offering narrow fairways and small greens, it depended on wind to enhance its defenses. Bob said after his that the only fault he could find with the greens was that they were running so true it gave a man no excuse for a missed putt. The galleries were large and some local fishermen had been recruited to help with crowd control, carrying ropes and clad in bright blue jerseys. The headlines were made that day by two others who tied the Hoylake course record of 70: Leo Diegel, the wiry, high-strung American terrier, and Archie Compston, the towering thirty-six-year-old Welsh giant, heir apparent to Ted Ray, Britain's best hope in the Open.

Archie Compston's strapping personality was scaled to his six-foot-five-inch frame. Admired as a dashing if not great golfer, Compston was also something of a national hero for standing up to the Inland Revenue, Britain's uncompromising tax bureaucracy. Rumored to have won considerable sums by betting on himself in matches played against a circle of aristocratic amateurs, the taxman had taken him to court for a share of those alleged winnings in 1929. When Compston emerged victorious, his Everyman image and popularity were considerably enhanced. Archie was a classic big hitter, wild and unpredictable, yet capable of mad streaks of red-hot play; two years before he had annihilated Hagen in a matchplay exhibition at Moorpark, handing Walter the worst defeat of his career: 18 & 17 in a thirty-six-hole match. Compston was equally capable of losing his temper over nothing and blowing up like a hand grenade. He had never been able to rein in his lumberjack's disposition long enough to close out a four round major, but his fans lived in hope this would be the week. Leo Diegel, on the other hand, had to be considered a legitimate contender in any event he entered. After long struggles to contain his jangly nerves, he had won the last two PGA Championships and finished second to Hagen at the British Open the previous year. The eccentric, elbows-akimbo putting style he'd developed to control his anxiety on the greens— Darwin described it as "a washerwoman at work over her tub"—only endeared him to knowledgeable fans, who always reserve a special place in their hearts for any poor soul who suffers the yips.

The second day of qualifying reduced the field to 112, eighteen of them amateurs. At Wallasey, a short, hilly course featuring a number of blind shots, Bob shot a limp 77. Most of his gallery from Hoylake had followed him over to Wallasey and many began to wonder if he had left too much of himself out on the Old Course during the Amateur. Darwin decided he was saving himself for the Open, "playing golf, rather than slaving at it," but some began to question the pre-tournament installation of Bob as the 2–1 favorite, an unprecedented vote of confidence. British fans took comfort in seeing that only eight Americans qualified to play on, with only two among the top twenty, the weakest qualifying performance for the invaders in five years. Leo Diegel finished third behind the medal winner Archie Compston and a stylish twenty-three-year-old named Henry Cotton, whose swing and relentless work ethic on the practice range put many in mind of a young Harry Vardon.

Henry Cotton was a ground-breaking figure in British golf: the first man from the upper classes to turn professional. He had spent the last two years playing in America, where Tommy Armour took him under his wing and taught him the secrets of the right-to-left draw. Although weak from a recent bout of flu, Cotton had been dubbed someone to watch by no less than Bernard Darwin. The second American in the ranks, George Von Elm, finished fifth, tied with Cyril Tolley for low amateur. Macdonald Smith, the old warhorse, shot the best round at Hoylake on the second day with 71, and came in eighth. Nine strokes behind the leaders and all the way back in twenty-ninth place was Bob Jones, and behind him by a stroke was the other American favorite, Horton Smith.

Bob headed out onto the first tee to begin his first round in the 1930 Open at Royal Liverpool early on Wednesday, June 18. The tradition of amateur champions in the British Open had started and ended at Hoylake; aside from Jones, the only two who had ever won it were both born and bred there: John Ball and Harold Hilton. Now seventy and sixty years old respectively, both Ball and Hilton were on hand to watch Bob hit his opening drive. So were Harry Vardon, J.H. Taylor, James Braid, Ted Ray, George Duncan, Sandy Herd, and seventy-six-year-old Allan McFie—another Hoylake native; winner of the first British

Amateur in 1885—virtually every citizen of the British Empire who'd won a major championship in the last fifty years. Watching them assemble near the clubhouse, Darwin remarked that it was as if all the gods of Olympus had descended to earth. With their presence, and in light of the Americans' poor showing during qualifying, expectations for a British revival in the Open ran high.

Bob could not have felt less prepared to face their scrutiny. He wasn't much of a nationalist by nature; he'd grown too fond of all the British greats, and had no interest in showing up the English because they played under a different flag. On this day he was only worried about embarrassing himself. Before moving to the tee he told Pop that on the practice range he had no idea where the ball was going with the driver. He looked as close to being undone mentally at the start of a tournament as Pop had ever seen him. Thunderclouds rolled in from the west, reinforcing Bob's gloom.

The first hole at Hoylake is called Course, a 458-yard par-four that demands one of the most delicate and difficult opening drives in golf. All along the left side of the narrow fairway sits the clubhouse, out of bounds. Two hundred and fifty yards from the tee the fairway dogs to the right, along a low mud wall called a "cop" that borders the practice ground, also out of bounds. The cop runs all the way in to hug the right side of the green. A hook off the tee, a slice on the first or second shot is deadly. Hit it straight, or else.

As Bob took his club back to swing, "some imbecile clicked a camera at him, and he had to begin again," reported Bernard Darwin. He then pushed his drive to the right, flirting with the out of bounds, and rolled into the shallow ditch in front of the cop. Digging it out from there to the fairway, Bob steered his third onto the front edge of the green. As he was about to chip up "a lady spectator made explosive noises behind him and he had to break off, walk around like a caged lion and begin again."

Bob chipped close and sank his putt for bogey. After another bogey at the third—the hole called Long that would plague him all week—Bob found his stroke for the first time since the Amateur.

"One hole in par followed another in monotonous perfection," wrote Darwin. "Not a single exciting thing happened for a long time." He finished by tying the course record with 70. "Not too good to be terrifying to others, and yet good enough to inspire confidence in himself," pronounced Darwin.

When he returned to the hotel late that afternoon Bob saw a headline that read EIGHT INCHES OFF A WORLD'S RECORD; his final putt had failed by that distance to break the Hoylake scoring record. He couldn't for the life of him imagine that they were describing his round; as a subjective experience his golf had felt miserable. He told Pop his game felt hopeless; even when shots ended up where he wanted them to go it felt like an accident.

Two other men matched Bob's opening 70: steady old Macdonald Smith, still chasing his first major title at forty; and the young Englishman Henry Cotton, shaking off his influenza and the thunderstorm that passed through in the middle of his round. (The same storm system moved on to drown out Derby Day at nearby Ascot Racecourse, a major event of the English racing season, reducing the lords and ladies in their smart frocks to bundles of dripping rags.) A few local favorites played decently but there was no avoiding the fact that, of the eight Americans who'd qualified, six had placed in the top ten; Horton Smith stood two off Bob's pace.

The weather cleared and warmed on Thursday; the British hoped for a wind that never blew. On the scorecard Bob's second round looked like a portrait of consistency: even par 72. But this was misleading; fine recoveries out of deep rough near the greens concealed the fact that Jeanie Deans had again lost her way. Time and again he scrambled to the green where Calamity

Jane saved par. Without her he might not have broken 80. In conversation with Keeler that night—which Pop declined to share with his radio audience—Bob said he hadn't been "sure for six collected minutes what my game would do. I simply don't know where the damn ball is going to go when I hit it. The fairways are so tight I keep trying to steer the ball off the tee, and it's the most hopeless job I've ever tackled." His win at the British Amateur had played like a forced march with intermittent pitched battles; the Open at Hoylake was going to be a war of attrition.

A veteran English pro named Fred Robson slipped into second place, a stroke behind Bob and two ahead of Horton Smith. By midday the air had grown unseasonably warm, and without a cooling breeze it sapped the strength of Macdonald Smith and a visibly ailing Cotton; with 77 and 79 they tumbled down the leader board. Archie Compston improved his position with 73, five strokes off Bob's pace, tied with Macdonald Smith and Diegel. Pop predicted for his radio audience that evening that this Open would come down to the two Southerners who'd dueled earlier that season in Savannah, Bob Jones and Horton Smith.

The halfway cut reduced the field to sixty-one men who would contend on the final day; fifty-two professionals and nine amateurs. The focus of every surviving player remained firmly fixed on just one man, the pole star everyone was chasing. Not only national pride was at stake for the British, but also professional; like Hagen, the British pros were tired of Bob having his way with them. Americans had won the last six Opens in a row, eight of the last nine; someone had to stand up for the Union Jack and stop this man in his tracks. Whoever found it in himself had two rounds on Friday to try.

One Briton resolved to do something about it publicly. In the breakfast room of his hotel on Friday morning, Archie Compston told anyone who would listen he was going to march and out and beat Bob Jones. He was quoted as saying he felt "good enough to go around Hoylake in nothing."

The final day began. Horton Smith teed off at 8:00, the first contender out on the course in the third round. Bernard Darwin watched Smith three-putt the first green from the window of his hotel bathroom. Smith's fortunes unraveled and after a 78 the young American was out of the running in his first major. Englishman Fred Robson soon followed Smith onto the course, and into the also-ran category: another 78.

Grey scudding clouds threatened rain as Bob reached the tee a little before nine. After another wayward drive that just missed the ditch, he recovered for his first par of the tournament at one. At two he pushed his drive into the hay, hit his second in a bunker, and was lucky to make bogey. At the par-five third he hooked his drive out of bounds, then pushed his third shot into the cabbage; he ended up, by drilling a long putt, with six. Then the evil spell that had affected his starts all week lifted again and he played out the front nine like an avenging angel: 37, distancing himself from Smith and Robson.

The cheers started behind Bob at five and quickly rippled forward to him: Archie Compston was going crazy. After par at the first, the Welshman ran off three straight birdies; playing the first four holes in thirteen strokes, he had chewed up all of Bob's five-stroke lead. The crowd, waiting for any British-born human being to play like this in an Open for nearly a decade, went nuts right along with him. Compston fed off their energy, striding down the fairways like an enraged Highland chieftain who couldn't wait to clobber his ball another fatal smash. He made the turn in 34.

Bob stepped to the fourteenth tee, the first of five monstrous finishing holes that cover over a third of the course's total yardage. During the first two rounds he had saved his best play for last; par was 22 for this brutal stretch and he'd taken 20 and 21 strokes respectively. During the third round, with cheers for Compston ringing in his ears—after missed drives, timid irons, and a three-putt green—he played it in 24.

Compston wasn't through. He carried his mad streak into the back nine: three more birdies in the first four holes. "And at every fresh exploit a wild yell of defiance or exultation rent the air," wrote Darwin. The Welshman looked invincible; wild rumors of impossible scores reached the old champions in the clubhouse. Some were seen jogging out onto the course to join the thousands watching Compston come in. He faltered only once, a bogey at sixteen after a missed short putt, then finished strong with two fours and was nearly carried off the course.

Compston had played Royal Liverpool in 68 strokes, smashing the course scoring record by two, and in four hours had revived the spirits of a sporting nation that had stood by helplessly for years as America hijacked their native game. After playing one of the greatest rounds in the history of the Open, Compston pulled ahead of Bob by a stroke and led Leo Diegel, the next closest competitor, by three.

The morning's gray sky shaded toward black and a light mist started to fall. Bob knew he didn't have anything close to his best game. Tension and uneasiness had been gnawing at him without relief since his arrival in Liverpool. As popular a figure as he was throughout Great Britain, after Compston's charge no one here was wishing him well. He felt he had less energy and sharpness of mind at such a crucial moment than at any other tournament he'd ever played, but it wasn't in his nature to back off from a fight. After winning the Amateur he had told Pop it didn't matter what happened at Hoylake, but now that the moment was here it mattered like life and death. Darwin had observed that Bob never seemed greedy for victory, but once he was in the arena he could not help fighting to the death; that's what separated him from every other golfer alive, that force of will. He put the whip to his resolve by telling himself that no matter what the outcome, he was about to play his final round in a British Open.

Bob parred the first hole for the second time that day. At the second he smashed a high towering drive that drifted right toward the gallery. From the tee it appeared to be tracking toward a steward (identifiable by their red skullcaps) standing with his back to the play. The ball bounced right off the man's head and shot dead left for 50 yards, rolling into a bunker on the adjoining fourteenth fairway. The steward was uninjured; Bob said later, "I have often wondered what that fellow's head had been made of."

His ball was sitting cleanly in the sand, a huge break compared to the knee-deep rough surrounding the bunker. The longer Bob examined his next shot the more he liked it. The distance, lie, and angle to the green were nearly identical to the eagle he'd holed at St. Andrews in his first-round match. Fixing the memory of that shot in mind, he played one nearly as good, landing the ball 20 feet below the hole. He knocked in the putt for birdie; the bounce off that steward's head turned out to be the only luck he'd had all week. After a par at the third he had traversed the minefield where he'd blown up in every round at a stroke under par. That steadied him through the seventh; if he could par eight and nine he was on track to match his best nine of the tournament.

Archie Compston returned from his lunch hour still fired up and brimming with confidence. Crowds swarmed around him and he welcomed the attention. Instead of regrouping before setting out on his final round, against the advice of his caddie he decided to warm up again. Compston strode to the practice ground, pulled balls out of his bag, and belted them with his driver and long irons for fifteen minutes. When he reached the first tee, still laughing like a buccaneer, he learned about Jones's strong start; Bob had pulled back in front of him by two strokes. For the first time that afternoon Compston's broad grin disappeared.

Ahead at the eighth, a 480-yard par-five hole called Far, Bob
followed a strong drive with a three-wood that rolled off the
left edge of the green and down a small slope. His ball came to
rest in a shaved hallow, 20 yards from the cup and 15 yards
from the edge of the green, that perched on a small knoll; from
there the fast surface ran straight down toward the flag. He
badly wanted birdie here, feeling he could ride the momentum
all the way in and build a lead that left Compston in the dust.

Bob tried to finesse a chip just over the front edge of the green
and trickle it down to the hole. He misjudged it by a fraction
and came up inches short of the crest. Worried about the speed
of the green, he decelerated his second chip and left the ball 10
feet short of the hole. His putt for bogey slipped a foot past the
hole. Unsettled, he tapped carelessly at the ball and missed the
putt coming back. Five strokes to get down from 20 yards.
Double bogey seven. He felt as if someone had just hit him with
a mallet.

> As I walked to the ninth tee, I was in a daze. I realized that
> in one brief span of only a moment or two, all the effort of
> the past three days had been just about washed out. I
> wasn't looking at any Grand Slam, only one championship.
>   I was badly shaken and knew it. I was even confused
> mentally. At this point I was completely incapable of making
> any calculation either of what score I might ultimately
> achieve or of what it would be necessary to do to stave off
> the challenge of others. I simply resolved to keep hitting the
> ball as best I could, to finish the round in an orderly
> fashion, if possible, and let the result be what it would.

Unaware of Bob's gaffe at eight, Compston hit a good drive off
the first tee, came up short with his approach, and left a long
putt from the fringe less than 2 feet shy of the hole. A gimme.
He took a quick stroke, reached down to pull his ball from the

hole . . . and saw it still hanging on the lip. He stepped back and stared at it in disbelief, and in that moment the magic that he had conjured up and carried with him all day vanished. The missed putt stunned him worse than a physical blow. At the second, after another decent drive, he shanked a short iron dead right and ended up taking double bogey six.

"And so began the rot," wrote Darwin. "One hooked shot followed another and there was a long and gloomy string of fives. The story is too sad to tell at length, even if it were worth it. The thunder clouds overhead were no darker than his expression."

From the high peak he'd reached during his heroic charge in the third round, Compston fell like a stone down a well. There would be no suspense, no struggle or last-minute reversal, only a quick and violent tumble from the summit. The crowd that had set out to follow him with such high hopes slumped away from his gallery in droves. Archie Compston shot 82 in his final round, a fourteen-shot swing from his record 68. He would finish in fifth place, but the hangover lingered long after this Open; Compston never seriously contended in another major during his lifetime. Within a few years, on a recommendation from Walter Hagen, he took a job as private instructor to the Prince of Wales. He and the Prince of Wales were spotted cruising the Mediterranean on board the Royal Yacht, knocking golf-balls off the top deck into the sea.

Unaware of Compston's disintegration, Bob climbed to the ninth tee looking like a beaten man, shoulders sagging, inex-pressibly weary. A brisk wind had arrived with the advancing stormclouds, toughening the obstacle course in front of him. There would be no more thoughts of attacking holes or defending a lead, scoring above or below par. All he could focus on now was playing one shot at a time until this ordeal was over. Unable to remember playing the hole afterwards, he somehow managed a birdie at the ninth and finished his front nine in 38, the highest he'd scored there all week.

He began the final nine with four straight plodding fours, barely strong enough to put one foot in front of the other. Pop and the others who'd been with him since the quest began looked so lost and forlorn it helped bring Bob out of his melancholy; he felt so bad for Pop that he started joking with him as he walked between shots. The effort did as much for his own spirits as Keeler's.

It wasn't until he reached the fourteenth tee and Hoylake's strenuous finishing stretch that word reached them about Compston's breakdown. Bob inhaled the news like pure oxygen. He played two outstanding shots just short of the green and got up and down for a birdie. He handed that stroke right back over with a bogey at fifteen.

The sixteenth, par-five, 532 yards. Dogleg to the right around the corner of a dike, leaving 270 yards to a wide, flat green. Bob's last realistic chance for birdie in the round. A well-placed drive hugged the right side, then he went all out for the green with his brassie. The shot bounced into a bunker guarding the left side of the green. The ball had rolled out of its pitch mark, sitting up, 25 yards from the hole, but close enough to the steep far wall of the bunker to seriously limit his swing. He would have to stand with his right foot on the bank outside the bunker, then chop down at the ball with a sharply descending blow. It would come out low and hot; it remained to be seen if he had enough green to work with.

Bob pulled a large, concave-faced wedge from his bag that Horton Smith had given him at Augusta. An early forerunner of the sand wedge, it weighed twice as much as an ordinary club. He'd used it only twice in England, but it was built for exactly this kind of situation. If he dropped it just behind the ball, making contact above the center of the clubface, the loft would be just about right to play a running shot across the green. He placed his right foot on the bank, dug in with his left and practiced the move down at the ball a few times. Then he played it for real.

The ball popped out of the sand, barely cleared the face of the bunker, hopped onto the green. Backspin grabbed the grass, acting as a brake; the ball slowly rolled and rolled, tracking straight for the hole. It just missed falling in the side door and came to a stop two inches past the cup. He had the birdie he needed.

Bob dropped a testing 6-foot putt to save par at seventeen. Hitting both fairway and green, he closed out the final round with one last par for a score of 75. Newsreel footage of his finish shows a shockingly small group of people around the eighteenth green. When his last putt fell there was no celebration or rejoicing from either Bob, Jack McIntyre or his gallery; there was no reaction whatsoever. He shook his partner's hand and walked off, signed his card in the scorer's tent, then ducked into the clubhouse and, as he had done so often over the years, fortified himself behind closed doors in the secretary's room upstairs, and sat down to wait and see if anyone would catch him.

When Pop found him there, Bob looked as white as a sheet. His hands were ice cold, his eyes darted around like a caged animal's. He asked Pop to pour him a stiff whiskey, but his right hand trembled so severely he couldn't hold the glass. He had to steady it with both hands, downed it in a couple of gulps, then asked for another and slumped into a chair looking like a man twice his age. He was utterly spent, past speech. Pop watched with something closer to pity than pride. Bob had survived the round, but at what cost? Pop sat beside him for a while before saying anything.

"When are you going to quit this foolishness, Bob?" he finally asked.

"Pretty soon, I think," he said. "No game is worth these last three days."

Two Americans still had chances to catch him and were closing fast. Leo Diegel, playing an hour behind him, and then Macdonald Smith, alone and unwatched near the end of the field. Diegel had been two strokes behind Bob starting his final round; Smith was six back—a lot of ground to make up, but Bob had left the door wide open.

A cold rain finally fell from those sullen clouds shortly after Bob finished his round. Leo Diegel played stoutly all afternoon, picked up two strokes on Bob by the turn, and stood in a flat-footed tie with him when he reached the sixteenth. Knowing he needed to match Bob's birdie, Leo put every ounce of his 140 pounds into a second shot that found the same bunker Bob had been in earlier, but he failed to get up and down and ended with a bogey six. Now he needed two birdies to catch Bob, and the best he could manage were pars. One down, one to go.

Macdonald Smith mounted a valiant run, shooting even par on the front and, one under on the back for 71, the lowest round of the day, but he'd started too far behind. Smith reached the eighteenth hole needing an eagle to tie Bob for the lead.

From the clubhouse window Bob watched Smith's caddie walk ahead to the green to pull the flag. When he saw Smith's approach fail to find the hole he knew this Open was his. He put down his drink. Pop saw no joy, no happiness, only relief. Bob's hands finally stopped shaking and the color slowly returned to his face.

Eleven major championships in seven years. He had equaled John Ball's forty-year-old record—winning the Open and the Amateur in the same year—and the grand old man was the first of the long line of British champions to congratulate him. It was the highest score Bob had shot in any British championship. Pop wrote afterwards: "If experience and patience and philosophy and grim determination were enough to produce that score from his game at Hoylake, I will say he never played a greater tournament, perhaps never one so great."

For the first time reporters began to contemplate the scale of what Bob was halfway to finishing. He was already the only man who had ever won all four of the sport's major titles, and as defending U.S. Open Champion he held three of them simultaneously. Speculation about what he might do in next month's U.S. Open filled columns around the world. Some dared to wonder if he had it in him to win all four in the same year. Although Bob had not taken Darwin into his confidence, the game's most perceptive and sensitive commentator predicted that Bob would indeed win all four of the year's major tournaments.

When they called him down to receive the Claret Jug, Bob felt so disorientated at first he hardly knew why he was there. The club secretary saw him crumpled in a chair just before the ceremony, his face pinched and ghastly. Bob rallied long enough to offer a small speech, nearly identical to the one he'd given at St. Andrews, and smiled as he posed for the traditional photographs holding the trophy. Weariness looked etched into his features. Mary hovered protectively; Pop realized she'd never seen Bob look like this before.

A few hours later, slightly revived, Bob leaned out the window of his train as it left for London to tell his friend Al Laney he could now write about the idea of his winning all four majors. There was no point in keeping it a secret anymore. As the train pulled away, Bob called back to him: "But don't forget to keep your fingers crossed!"

Eager as he was to start the voyage home, Bob had one last commitment in England he was determined to honor. During qualifying rounds at Royal Liverpool, Ted Ray had asked if he'd be willing to play a charity match at Ray's home club before he left the country. Bob said he would be glad to participate, but only if Ray played with him and invited Vardon, Taylor, or Braid to complete the foursome. What better way to complete his final visit to England than a best-ball round with Ted Ray and two-thirds of the Great Triumvirate?

On Saturday, June 22, Bob paired with James Braid against the grand old partnership of Vardon and Ray in a best-ball match at Ray's home course of Oxhey. Playing his first carefree round in nearly six weeks, Bob shot 66 and broke the course record. He and Braid edged Vardon and Ray at the last hole. After watching Bob drop his drive on a par three within a foot of the pin, as old Harry stepped forward to tee up his ball Bob heard him say in his soft quiet voice: "Ah, Master Bobby's 'ot today."

This turned out to be the last round Bob ever played with Vardon, Ray, or Braid. A game played among friends, who just happened to be four of the ten greatest golfers who'd ever lived, away from the crowds and the pressure of competition, with no trophy or national pride at stake. Ray presented him with a gold cigarette case after the match, inscribed: "To a great golfer and a great sportsman." There could be no more fitting conclusion to Bob Jones's British career.

But there was no more telling sign of Bob's mental and physical exhaustion than this: when he and Mary departed London for the cruise ship home he left his golf clubs behind at the hotel. An enterprising bellboy at the Savoy found them in the lobby, jumped in a cab, and tried to catch him at Waterloo Station. He arrived just as Bob's train was rolling down the tracks, so the bag followed him to Southampton on the next train, but Bob and the *Europa* sailed for New York ten minutes before it arrived. After an urgent exchange of ship-to-shore cables, officials sent the clubs steaming after him the next day on the *Aquatania*.

CHAPTER FOURTEEN

THE U.S. OPEN, INTERLACHEN

During the last day at Hoylake, news about Bob's final round reached his friends in Atlanta via radio and hole-by-hole telegraph updates. Newspapers reported that the city came to a standstill as the bulletins arrived, with crowds gathering in the early-morning hours around newspaper and Western Union offices. A former Georgia Amateur champion and playing partner of Bob's named Chick Ridley camped out at the *Journal* all night and kept Big Bob up to date with constant phone calls. At home, the Colonel paced the floor from well before sunrise until the results were conclusive. When the news finally came across the wire that Diegel and Smith had failed to catch Bob in the final round, there were "wild scenes on downtown streets,

in office buildings and out at East Lake." Reporters were immediately dispatched to the Colonel's house and noticed that little
four-year-old Bob the Third and five-year-old Clara were
"romping with glee," resonating with the unbridled delight being
expressed by their grandfather. Plans were made by Atlanta's
mayor, John Cohen, to greet Bob and Mary with a hometown
reception when the *Europa* docked in New York on July 2. A
special train—the "Bobby Jones Special"—carrying well-wishers
north from Atlanta was arranged.

When he was informed that his most famous pupil had just
completed a sweep of the British majors, Kiltie broke down in
tears. When he collected himself he summed up his feelings with
his usual economy: "There are no words for me to use to tell
how pleased I am."

After a crossing Bob described as restful and tedious—he made
so few appearances during the crossing that as they neared
America members of his party felt compelled to issue a public
statement denying rumors that he had experienced an unspeci-
fied physical breakdown—the greeting New York gave him this
time around dwarfed the reception he had received after his
British Open win in 1926. As the *Europa* sailed into harbor,
twin fireboats sprayed geysers and hundreds of Atlanteans sailed
out on the *Mandalay* as a brass band played "Valencia." After
he had bypassed customs and granted a mass interview to the
assembled press, a police escort hurried Bob and his party to
City Hall, where Mayor Walker greeted them again on the front
steps, and then introduced him to a nationwide radio audience
as the crowd cheered wildly. Nothing he'd ever experienced, no
acclaim or excitement from his fans, prepared Bob for the adora-
tion they showered upon him this day. Newsreel footage shows
him looking stunned by the depth and scale of their tribute. The
Mayor called New York the "Atlanta of the North" to express
how deeply his city had embraced their mutual hero. When
Walker turned over the radio microphones to him, Bob's voice

sounded husky with emotion, and he could only offer a few gracious sentences in response:

"I have not experienced anything like this before. All I can say is that I am overwhelmed by the welcome I have received from the people of New York and the people of Atlanta. I have never been so impressed."

To this day, Bob Jones is the only individual to ever receive two ticker-tape parades down the canyons of Broadway. This was a typically hot and humid midsummer afternoon and in surviving film of the spectacle it appears as if the entire city has shut down to greet him; on Wall Street, Wednesday, July 2 turned out to be the slowest trading day in two years, and not only because of the deepening Depression. Bob's accomplishments and personality had touched a chord in the American soul, and their gratitude for the thrills he'd given them would now pour out of every village, town, or gathering he moved through. Although he played his part without complaint and endured the rituals of championship with grace and courtesy, this outpouring of unconditional devotion ran deeply contrary to Bob's modest instincts. One reporter described him as "gasping for breath and looking about almost wildly as if for some avenue of escape." A grand dinner for four hundred followed in his honor that night at the Vanderbilt Hotel, where despite his efforts to look engaged he seemed equally uncomfortable.

Grantland Rice, who acted as the dinner's master of ceremonies, caught up with Bob after the festivities that night. In his column he said the greeting he thought this day of celebration had been even harder on Bob than his final rounds at St. Andrews or Hoylake.

Bob let his guard down with his old friend Rice and talked about his toughest moments in the Amateur and Open. He said tournament play is often "a matter of who gets the breaks and there are times when the final result seems to be beyond your control. Things can happen before you know they're happening. They break your soul before you know what has taken place."

He sidestepped the question of retirement, but did say he would not return to Britain the following year—"I have to get back to work and make a living"—then added that he was looking forward to the Open at Interlachen, against the toughest field in the world, but refused to predict another victory: "No one knows what will happen in golf until it happens. All you can do is work and suffer and wait for fate."

Bob left by train for Minneapolis at two o'clock the following afternoon. His parents, grandfather, Pop, Rice, and a large percentage of the "Bobby Jones Special" crowd traveled on with him, while Mary returned home to Atlanta to take care of the children. His golf clubs, fresh off the *Aquatania*, were rushed through customs and conveyed by police escort to Penn Station, where they showed up minutes before the *Broadway Limited* was scheduled to depart. Bob carried his own bag onto the train and kept it in his compartment the whole way.

Cyril Tolley told a reporter, "Bobby did not play well in Britain—that is, for Jones—but I am confident he will be Bobby, himself, again in the west. And if he is, this championship is over before it starts."

The clubhouse and eighteen original holes of Interlachen— German for "between the lakes"—opened in July of 1911 and gave Minneapolis its first real country club. After playing host to a Western Open in 1914, and a Trans Mississippi championship in 1916—won by the area's first local hero in the sport, Harry Legg—the members decided their golf course needed an upgrade. They did what so many other upscale clubs in the postwar era decided to do: hired architect Donald Ross to redesign and shape a new layout. The peripatetic Scotsman reversed the nines and reworked half a dozen holes; his resulting parkland masterpiece opened in 1919 to universal acclaim.

After a day's layover in Chicago, where he caught up with Cyril Tolley and Horton Smith and got in a round of holiday golf, Bob arrived in Minneapolis early on Saturday, July 5. Weary but buoyant, Bob claimed to be sufficiently rested for the Open but denied that he had his heart set on winning all of the year's championships; he pointed out that no one had ever won three of the majors in the same year, let alone four.

After checking into his downtown hotel Bob drove out with Tolley and Jimmy Johnston for a practice round at a local country club called Woodhill, where he matched the course record with an effortless 69. As they would all week, reporters and photographers dogged Bob's movements, both on and off course, every step of the way.

Every golfer in the country of any consequence poured into the Twin Cities that weekend: Walter Hagen motored in from Detroit in the latest of his extravagant touring cars with Tommy Armour, Al Watrous, and twelve-year-old Walter Jr., along to watch his father compete in an Open for the first time. Jock Hutchison, Don Moe, Chick Evans, Willie Hunter, Leo Diegel, George Von Elm, Long Jim Barnes, George Voigt, Bobby Cruickshank, Johnny Farrell, Gene Sarazen, Johnny Goodman, Willie MacFarlane, Al Espinosa, Lighthorse Harry Cooper, Joe Turnesa, Ralph Guldahl, Wild Bill Melhorn, and Macdonald Smith were all in the 150-man field; a roll-call of the game's past and future champions, all of whom had at one time or another memorably locked horns with Bob Jones in a major. With Bob halfway to the Slam, everyone sensed something special was in the air. Figuring in the endorsement income of the last few years, an Open championship could mean as much as $100,000 dollars in extra income to a victorious professional. One slogan united all the pros: "Beat Jones."

Bob's quest attracted an equally star-studded cast of American sportswriters to join Pop Keeler in the press corps: Rice, Paul

Gallico, Bill Richardson of the *New York Times*, Westbrook Pegler of the *New York News*. Two hundred and twenty-six reporters covered the event from papers all across the country. One hundred and fifty typewriters, dozens of telephones and scores of telegraph transmitters were installed in a large wooden shack built beside the course that would serve as a temporary press headquarters. An extra twenty-five long-distance operators were added to the local phone system to handle the increased traffic. The Minneapolis *Tribune* reprinted a primer written by Granny Rice on gallery etiquette for the uninitiated ("Don't walk across the course if any player is on the tee. You may be hit"). On the same day the paper reported the approach of an ominous heatwave that broke long-standing records in Oklahoma and Kansas and appeared to be headed toward Minnesota.

On Sunday Bob picked up his local caddie, a teenager named Dale Donovan whose name had been pulled from a hat, and played his first two practice rounds at Interlachen, matching even par 72 each time. Only club members and their families were allowed on the course that day to watch, but Bob still drew a gallery numbering in the hundreds.

On Monday Bob and Diegel played together and both equaled the course record with 70; Johnny Goodman finished right behind them with 71 on his first circuit around the course. Hagen broke the front nine's record that morning with 32, pronounced his swing ready for action, called it a day, and drove off to go fishing with his son.

Two long days spent in the rising heatwave gave Bob a painful case of sunburn, and he played Tuesday's practice round with a wet table napkin wrapped around his neck like a bandanna. In an exclusive interview he revealed to Granny Rice that he had still not regained control of the driver and long irons that troubled him at Hoylake.

By Wednesday morning the heatwave had arrived and parked on top of the upper Mississippi River valley; temperatures edged over one hundred degrees. Accustomed to spending the final day before a tournament resting and reading quietly in his room, the hotel's lack of air-conditioning drove Bob to seek relief outside. He spent the morning fishing with Jimmy Johnston on nearby Lake Minnetonka—where even the fish were too over-heated to bite—then played a late-afternoon nine with Johnston, Tolley, and Moe. Over a thousand people followed them around in the stifling heat, which seemed to bother everyone but Bob; he told Pop after he came off the course that for the first time since Augusta in the spring his game felt as if it had all come together.

"This battle will be the hardest championship that any man ever won," Hagen told Rice that night. "Here are 150 of the best golfers in the world, the survivors of 1200 entries, and yet it is the field against one man—Bobby Jones. Nothing like this has ever happened in golf, from the days of Vardon and Taylor and Braid to the present moment."

Everyone of note on the grounds was asked to pick their favorites by reporters that night. A surprising number failed to name Bob as their first choice; many felt he would buckle under the strain of his battles in Britain. Hagen was mentioned by most; although eleven years had passed since his last U.S. Open win, he had arrived in the best physical condition he'd displayed in years. While most of the field rested or played abbreviated rounds on Wednesday, Hagen played thirty-six in the scorching heat and walked away none the worse for wear. Even Pop talked up the old pirate as a man to look out for, noting that he had recently converted to steel shafts and revitalized his iron play—Bob was now one of the last in the field still using hickory. Many pointed to the meteoric rise of Horton Smith; as the last man to beat Bob at Savannah and the heir-apparent to Hagen in the professional ranks, he posed the greatest threat to Bob's quest. Others liked the chances of the two men who chased Bob down to the wire at Hoylake, Leo Diegel and Macdonald Smith.

Plans to accommodate ten thousand fans a day were in place; how many would show up beyond that was anyone's guess. The chairman of the Gallery Committee spent the final evening going over last-minute instructions on how to shift the crowds around with his 150 marshals, studying a map of the course like a field general looking over a battlefield. Workmen spent the long northern twilight stringing rope through the posts hammered into every fairway. In anticipation that ropes alone would not prove sufficient, volunteers assigned to Bob's gallery were equipped with 16-foot-long bamboo fishing poles that they would extend like toll gates to hold back the hordes. Two dozen Interlachen caddies who had not caught on with players in the field were armed with red flags and assigned to spot drives that missed the fairways and landed in the ankle-deep rough; on the course's sharp dogleg holes they were told to stand in the fairway and serve as human targets for players teeing off. Last-minute checks verified each station of the radio recording system installed to relay scores from every green to a large central score-board near the clubhouse. So many festive tents dotted the land-scape it looked as if the circus had come to town. The Big Show was about to begin.

Professional Jack Burke from Houston, Texas, led off the 1930 Open at 8:30 in the morning on July 10, teeing off in front of a few dozen spectators. By the time Bob was called to the starting line with Jock Hutchison at a few minutes after ten, the crowd around the first tee had grown to over five thousand and the temperature had reached ninety-three degrees. By noon it was 103 in the shade, on its way to a high of 108. Humidity hovered between 80 and 90 percent all day, with no afternoon thunderstorms to alleviate the pressure; the smothering peak of the heatwave had arrived. This was the hottest day on which a round of the U.S. Open had ever been played, setting a record that would stand for thirty-four years. One writer described the galleries as "lying in casual water from start to finish, and it all came from open pores." The Red Cross tent treated at least twenty people for heat prostration, and a small number of golfers withdrew, too dizzy to finish their rounds.

Bob's teenage caddie, Donovan Dale, had signed on with a national newspaper syndicate to provide a ghost-written first-person account of each day's round. In his first column Dale professed amazement at Bob's patience with his gallery. The vast crowd pressed in around them from every angle and shut out any breath of fresh air, adding to the oppressive atmosphere. After his introduction at the first tee, Bob hit a perfect drive, then had to gesture for the sustained applause and cheers to stop as Hutchison walked out to play his first shot. Hutchison plucked Bob's tee from the ground, dropped it in his pocket, and then made a show of looking around for more, drawing a big laugh. When an official asked again for quiet, he said to the crowd: "That's all right, this doesn't bother me a bit." Then he laced his drive down the middle just short of Bob's.

As they set off, two friends from East Lake flanked Bob, acting as his escorts, bodyguards and water boys: Chick Ridley and Charlie Cox, Adjutant General of the State of Georgia, the commanding officer of the Georgia National Guard. Each tee at Interlachen was being patrolled by members of the Minnesota State Militia and General Cox struck up conversations with most of them while they waited for the gallery to settle. Bob later heard one of the local guardsmen say to another: "I don't know what sort of golfer this Jones fellow is, but he's got the goldangest highest-ranking water boy I ever saw."

Bob had it going from the jump. Using fifteen of the seventeen clubs in his bag—he never called on his one-iron or over-sized concave wedge—he carved a 34 out of Interlachen's front nine by collecting seven pars and two birdies at the par-fives. Jeanie Deans was back at the top of her form; he missed only three fairways all round, and two of those by only a foot. His only bogey of the day came at the par-four tenth, his last missed fairway, when a middling recovery from the rough found a green-side bunker. Young Mr. Dale was amazed by his speedy, no-nonsense pace. He realized that Bob seldom spoke during a round because he was sizing up his next shot as he walked to the ball. By the time he reached it he'd already decided what he was going to do, asked for his club, made the shot, and moved on. Dale could find no fault with his master's game, but thought Bob could have bettered his first-round 71 by at least three strokes; wary of playing the fast greens too aggressively, three short birdie putts had hung on the front lip and failed to drop. The blast-furnace heat, as far as he could tell, failed to trouble Mr. Jones for a moment. In spite of his lifelong exposure to extreme Southern summers, Bob later said this was the hottest day he could ever remember, with the air so humid it must have been "only a very little shy of liquidity."

When Bob and Hutchison came off the course, their soaked clothes hung off them as if they'd jumped into one of the state's ten thousand lakes. People in the clubhouse thought Bob had wounded himself; his red foulard tie had bled the front of his white shirt crimson, and the paint from the Reddy Tees he carried in the pocket of his light gray plus-fours had sent a red streak all the way down his leg. When he met Pop in the locker room, he was so worn out and cramped from dehydration that his fingers couldn't undo the soaked, shrunken knot of his tie; Pop had to clip it off him with a pocket knife. Bob had lost ten pounds by the time he came in that afternoon, and for once couldn't attribute it all to nerves. Only after twenty minutes under a cold shower and a few glasses of iced water did he begin to feel human again. Some wondered out loud after his clockwork performance in that blazing inferno if he was human at all: Bob had established the early first-round lead.

Almost the entire rest of the field yielded to the heat. Englishman Cyril Tolley went out in the noonday sun, was repeatedly besieged by swarming mosquitoes, lost nine pounds and shot 80; by the time he dragged himself in, his crisp white flannels looked as limp as dishrags. Long Jim Barnes carried around a huge umbrella to keep the sun off his face. Chick Evans nearly had to quit after nine because of light-headedness and shot an 81. But the game's other old lion announced he wasn't ready to put out to pasture yet: attracting the day's second largest gallery, Walter Hagen finished with an even par 72. The Haig played without a hat as usual, since he was still under contract with Brylcreme, but endorsement be damned, announced he wouldn't be venturing out into that inferno again tomorrow without a big straw boater covering his head. Harry Cooper and Horton Smith joined Hagen at 72 a short time later; Smith said afterwards he intended to have words with a local friend who had issued a warning about Minneapolis's unpredictable weather and urged him to "bring an overcoat." Johnny Farrell began his round with an 8 and a 6, then excelled himself to finish the front nine at even par and ended with a 74. A salty old pro from Dyker Beach (a public course in Brooklyn) with the irresistible golf name of Whiffy Cox matched Bob's 71; a former sailor with a gravelly Popeye voice, Cox seemed immune to the blistering heat. Minneapolis golfers fared poorly, and Tom Vardon withdrew from the tournament, exhausted after an 81, while local favorite Jimmy Johnston struggled to an 80, his worst competitive round in years. Willie Kidd, Interlachen's resident pro, scraped together a 77, then, alone among the men who'd finished their struggles that day, went back out into the flaming heat to watch the rest of the action. The rest of the field remained huddled inside Interlachen's "Sobbing Room," a chamber set aside for members to tell sad stories about their rounds, which on this day had been converted into a cooling oasis with lounge chairs, pitchers of iced water and electric fans. Tolley summed up the prevailing mood when he shuffled in and asked no one in particular: "So, what did the Great Man do today?" Everyone knew exactly who he was talking about.

Beginning his round after noon under the full hammering zenith of the sun, Tommy Armour sent a messenger scurrying back to the clubhouse after four holes to ask for a big bag of ice. Before every subsequent shot he rubbed down his face, neck, and forehead with chunks of ice wrapped in a handkerchief; it seemed to do the trick. The Black Scot blistered the back nine in 33 to match the course-record 70, and edged ahead of Bob by a stroke. Later in the day another native Scotsman made news: Macdonald Smith came to the eighteenth tee needing only a par-four to shoot 69, break the course record, and take sole possession of the lead. His approach to the elevated final green fell a foot short and rolled back down the hill into a thick clump of clover. Smith's bogey five netted him 70, and tied him with Armour for the first-round lead in the Open.

Sixteen people in the Twin Cities succumbed to the intense heat on Thursday. Scores of others died all across the Midwest and the Deep South, where the high pressure had started to intrude. Some small measure of relief arrived in Minneapolis when a drier wind blew in from the east on Friday morning and moderated the humidity; temperatures ran about seven degrees cooler and attendance at Interlachen increased by 30 percent, with over twelve thousand tickets sold. Many of those ticket holders started out to follow first-round leaders Macdonald Smith and Tommy Armour, but by the end of the morning nearly the entire crowd had circled around two men playing in consecutive pairing: Horton Smith and Bobby Jones.

Granny Rice bounced back and forth between their twosomes all day long and had this to say about Smith: "It was as fine a round of golf as anyone has ever seen in an open championship when you consider the way he went about it. Horton adopted a unique idea and put it into effect. This idea consisted in hitting his drive smack down the middle and then rapping an iron shot six or eight feet from the pin. It is a system that seldom fails, even if you are putting with a broom."

After their battles at Savannah and Augusta, no other professional in the field seemed more eager or unafraid to take on the Emperor Jones. The lanky young Missourian sent an early message to the famous amateur playing just behind him with every shout that issued from his gallery. Riding a birdie at the second and a steady string of pars, Smith had picked up a shot and pulled into a tie with Bob by the time he reached the 485-yard par-five ninth. After another rifle-shot drive he gambled on his second and spanked a two-iron that cleared the lake then ran up onto the green, coming to rest only 20 feet from the hole. While Smith advanced to his ball, Bob played an equally strong drive behind him and was waiting to play his second in the fairway when a huge cry went up from thousands packed around the distant green; Smith had dropped his putt for an eagle and jumped ahead of Jones.

Bob stared at the distant green but betrayed no reaction. His caddie watched him closely as he pulled his three-wood and stood to the ball; Bob had reached this green in two in every round he'd played, and birdied it the day before, but today the wind was directly in his face; the shot demanded both power and precision, a carry of 200 yards over the lake then up a thin throat to a green protected by a deep bunker on the left. The gallery narrowed around him, forming a human tunnel down the line of flight. Bob stepped away from the ball, urging the crowd to move back and give him more room, then took his stance again. As Bob reached the top of his backswing, two little girls in the gallery just behind him broke from the crowd to run across the fairway; their motion disrupted his peripheral vision, and he came down to impact a fraction of an inch off plane. He struck the ball thin and it shot off, low and hot, toward the water.

The crowd gasped. They watched the ball hit the surface of

the lake at tremendous speed 60 feet short of the far bank, but instead of sinking it skipped forward, hit the water a second time, then bounced out onto the grass on the opposite side and rolled to a stop only 30 yards short of the green. "The crowd's groan," wrote Rice, "before it reached full utterance, took a queer turn into a frenzied shout."

They cheered him all the way as Bob walked around the lake— given what they'd just witnessed, some might have expected him to walk across it—and a legend immediately arose from some eyewitnesses who insisted they'd seen the ball bounce forward off a lily pad. Although it came to be known forever after as the "Lily Pad Shot," Bob always maintained that no vegetation was involved, simply the elementary laws of surface tension and aerodynamics. Whether the beneficiary of luck, fate, a lily pad, or a hard-headed bullfrog, Bob regrouped during his stroll to the ball, pitched up to within 2 feet of the cup and sank his putt for a four. What could easily have ended up a bogey score or worse had, in a moment's act of grace, turned into a birdie. The ovation that arose from around the ninth green did not go unnoticed by Horton Smith standing on the tenth tee; when he saw Bob's ball bounce across the water, this exact thought entered his mind: It is not destined for me to win this championship. After a good drive, Smith jacked his approach over the tenth green and wrote a bogey five on his scorecard. The two men were back in a tie. After a 40 on the front nine, explaining that he didn't want to slow Bob down, his playing partner Jock Hutchison called it a tournament and withdrew; Bob would play the back nine alone, which further underscored his head-to-head battle with the man in front of him.

With a sizeable percentage of the gallery shuttling between them on every hole, Smith steadied down and played the last eight holes in perfect par. Bob's game was less solid; he ground out pars, bogeyed the thirteenth, then stumbled badly at fifteen, missing a 4-foot putt and taking double bogey. By the end of the round Smith had bested him 70 to 73, and seized a two-stroke lead at the halfway mark of the tournament.

The duel between Mr. Smith and Mr. Jones dominated the day's headlines: GALLERY QUITS FIRST ROUND LEADERS FOR NEW GODS sums up the tone. Their golf had provided such compelling theater, everyone else seemed to shrink back and grant them center stage. Tommy Armour and Macdonald Smith shot 76 and 75 respectively, still in the running, but unattended by galleries by the time they finished their rounds. Lighthorse Harry Cooper clung to par for the second straight day and stayed two shots back. An obscure twenty-three-year-old expatriate Englishman named Charles Lacey, resident professional at Pine Valley, stepped into the role of this year's dark horse; he matched Smith's best round of the day and jumped into a second-place tie with Jones and Cooper. Hagen had struggled manfully to a second-round 75 and stood five shots back. The second-round leader board ended like this:

Horton Smith	72–70 –	142
Bob Jones	71–73 –	144
Harry Cooper	72–72 –	144
Charles Lacey	74–70 –	144
Macdonald Smith	70–75 –	145
Johnny Farrell	74–72 –	146
Whiffy Cox	71–75 –	146
Tommy Armour	70–76 –	146
Walter Hagen	72–75 –	147

Sixty-nine men survived the halfway cut, ten amateurs among them. Chick Evans withdrew even before the cut, halfway through his second round; he had a contract to cover the event for a Chicago newspaper and spent the rest of the tournament working as a journalist.

That evening during his radio broadcast (to New York from

local radio station KSTP) Pop Keeler did his best to dispel the growing legend of the lily pad, but did remark that the fortunate bounce boded well for Bob's chances: "That's the way it goes in championships. If your name is up, the ball will walk on water for you." He stopped well short of saying Bob's path to the title was clear, and fretted that the pros were really gunning for him this time; he had a premonition that somebody was about to play like a superhuman and close this thing out before it was over. Horton Smith, who had shown an unprecedented willingness to stand up to Bob's game, worried him the most.

If Bob shared his friend's concern that night he didn't show it; he and his father joined Jimmy Johnston for an excursion on a private yacht around Lake Minnetonka during the warm, lingering twilight. Smith turned in early to rest for Saturday's final two rounds. Four former U.S. Open winners, and two others who had lost them in play-offs, sat within five shots of his lead; he didn't sleep very soundly.

Bob woke early on Saturday morning, July 12, knowing with absolute certainty he was about to play his last two rounds in a U.S. Open. He was scheduled to tee off early in the third round, at 9:15, and saw it as a chance to make a statement, to set the tone before any other contenders were on the course. He had always liked playing just off the lead, preferred it; he could go flat out without feeling he had something to protect. He would be partnered for both rounds that day with Joe Turnesa, the man he'd battled to the wire in the U.S. Open at Scioto in 1926, another advantage; Turnesa was a friend, a pro's pro, steady, respectful, and solid. For the next few hours, hardly a soul at Interlachen even noticed Joe was playing.

The mercury fell a few more notches that morning, but the humidity returned; the air was thick, a mix of clouds and sun with a constant threat of thunderstorms. Ten thousand people had already assembled, a sea of white shirtsleeves and hats, to watch Bob tee off. Chick Ridley and Charlie Cox were on hand, armed with full canteens to act as his seconds; the Colonel lurked somewhere near the tree line toward the back of the crowd, still leery after all these years of letting Bob see him watching; Pop was there for him, as he had been from the beginning, front and center.

The golf swing is as pure a reflection of personality as any athletic action a person can perform, as unique as a snowflake, more telling than a signature. Bob's swing never said more about him than it did that morning at Interlachen: languid and unhurried, equal parts poetry and power, a portrait of efficiency with no wasted motion or energy. He sank a 10-foot putt for par at the first, collected effortless pars at two and three, not pressing for anything, like an orchestra tuning up, and then came the music; his second shot to the par-five fourth found a bunker. He clipped the ball off the sand to within 6 feet, then holed the putt for birdie.

After a scrambling par at the fifth, he left his drive at the sixth in deep rough 100 yards short of the green. After a short iron pitch to 5 feet of the hole he canned his second birdie of the round. On the seventh he improved his odds; his approach landed only 3 feet from the cup. Another birdie. Two routine pars followed at eight and nine. Bob had played the front nine in 33.

The announcer at his post beside the ninth green shouted out the result for all to hear as Bob moved in. The crowd at the clubhouse erupted in a sustained cheer. Horton Smith was on the practice green near the first tee, preparing to begin his round, when the mob swept around him at a gallop. As Smith moved upstream to his starting line, Bob walked ahead to the back nine.

By this point in the round Bob was hitting with full power, his tempo on the downswing increasing with nearly every stroke. Gone was any thought of safe or conservative play; he couldn't afford to let up for a second, not when his swing felt like this. His features looked set and determined, unstoppable; he hardly spoke a word. After another easy par at ten, he crossed the street to the par-five eleventh—a reachable dogleg right, with a pond in the crook of its elbow protecting the shortest route to the right side. Bob placed a mammoth drive in the perfect spot to the left of the water, and then played just short of the green with his second; he chipped up to within 3 feet and collected another easy birdie. Smith could hear that roar on the second tee half a mile away:

The twelfth hole mirrors the eleventh, another par-five, 535 yards long, a narrow, tree-lined dogleg left that ends in a steep climb to an elevated green. Bob blasted his drive 290 yards, then stood over the ball and debated whether to wallop a wood to the green or lay up short with an iron. He chose the latter: a ripple of disappointment ran through the crowd. He played his wedge shot to level ground and a perfect lie at the foot of the hill. Looking up at the green, he could barely see the top of the flag and waited for his caddie to climb up to show him the line; he played another short wedge and watched it arc up and disappear from sight. The gallery packed in around the green up top let out another roar; the ball grazed the flag on the fly and came to rest 8 feet from the hole. Bob climbed the hill and when he saw the result he cracked his first smile of the day. A minute later he rolled in that putt for a birdie four.

Five under par.

After a wayward drive he saved par at thirteen with another brilliant chip. At fourteen a 20-foot putt for birdie missed by an inch. Routine par at fifteen. At sixteen, a challenging short par-four, he planted his approach within inches of the pin. He could have fanned it in for birdie with a feather.

Six under par. Two more pars coming home would bring Bob in at 66 and shatter the U.S. Open single-round scoring record.

The crowd danced around him, delirious with excitement; as

word spread about his round he'd drawn nearly every person on the course to his gallery and was being followed by the largest audience ever to attend one man in American golf. They stood ten or twelve deep, shoulder to shoulder; most could barely catch a glimpse of him, but no one wanted to miss the opportunity to say they'd been there on the day that Bobby Jones made history. He still had to fight his way through a human wall to reach every tee and green, and without ropes to restrain them on the tees they thundered after them down every fairway. Kids darted around between shots, but after yesterday's lily-pad incident the gallery had become more self-policing; whenever Bob stood over his ball marshals stared at the crowd like bird dogs, no one moved, and the air grew as still as church.

The hole has since been shortened, but in 1930 the seventeenth was a terrifying par-three, downhill, at 262 yards the longest of its breed in the USGA directory and perhaps the world. Surrounded by bunkers, the green is further defended by a small lake on the right and a stream to the rear. From the tee the available target area appears about the size of a dinner plate. Bob's tee shot with a two-wood came up 20 yards short and landed in heavy rough beside the slope of a bunker. He negotiated another delicate pitch to 12 foot, and then watched the putt slide just by the hole for his first bogey of the day. The way the field played this hole, anything less than four felt like a birdie.

The finishing hole at Interlachen is a big, brawny test of character; the fairway favors a fade, leaving a steep uphill second to a severely contoured green tucked against the side of the clubhouse. Bob applied a touch more fade than he wanted to his drive and watched it bounce off the fairway into a cluster of trees. For the first time all day, Pop saw a hint of fatigue in Bob's face, the toll he would pay for this burst of perfection. His stance was problematic, leaving barely enough room to swing a club, but with an abbreviated action he slugged the ball back out onto the fairway near the base of the hill. His third shot, a short pitch to the green, took a hard bounce and kicked into a bunker dead behind the flag. He settled into the sand, lofted the ball gently onto the edge of the green, then watched it trickle slowly toward the hole and stop one roll short of dropping in for par. Bogey five.

No person in any form of competition had ever broken 70 at Interlachen. The average score on this day was 77.96. Bob had just shot 68 in the pivotal third round of a U.S. Open, his personal best in the event, the one and only time he felt he had reached and sustained his highest level of excellence in a national championship. He had hit three approach shots during the round with seven-irons; each landed less than a foot from the hole. He had eleven one-putt greens. Driver, irons, putter; everything clicked. Now his only anxiety was whether anyone would catch him from behind.

Horton Smith stood up to this hurricane for a while. He played the front nine in even par 36, remarkable under the circumstances, but after he made the turn, as more and more of his gallery deserted him and the booming shouts and cheers for Bob's heroics continued to rise in volume and frequency and echo across the course, he began to falter. Not obviously, but with a slow leaking of confidence. A double bogey at seventeen ended Smith's slide. He played the back nine in 40, for a grim 76. He'd gone from a two-stroke lead to a six-stroke deficit in less than four hours.

While Bob went into the clubhouse to rest and repair for the final round, news of his thunderbolt spread through the tournament; players collapsed internally at the news, decided to call it a day and wait till next year. Walter Hagen, for so long the pro game's standard bearer against the great amateur, could only match Horton Smith's 76; thirteen strokes down, he was out of the running. Halfway through Hagen's third round even his own son deserted him for Bob's gallery. Toward the end of the back nine, playing to an empty house, Hagen was so bored and dejected he started putting left-handed; he would shoot 80 that afternoon and finish tied for thirteenth place. The twin curiosities of Charles Lacey and Whiffy Cox vanished into history. Johnny Farrell and Macdonald Smith both faded; they were seven strokes back. Tommy Armour stumbled to 75: nine back, over and done. Chick Evans reported that the locker room was deathly silent; that was the sound of men packing it in.

Only two men remained within striking distance of the lead: Horton Smith was six strokes behind, and given the way Bob had just passed him no one gave a nickel for his chances that afternoon. His closest competitor was Harry Cooper; with a steady third-round 73, the Texan sat five strokes in back of Jones.

That was it. Bob Jones had blown everyone else in the field off the golf course.

The Midwestern heatwave had spread to Atlanta: 103 degrees that Saturday afternoon. The *Journal* reported that every human being over the age of ten spent the entire day glued to a radio set. Mary huddled in Bob's parents' big house with their kids, receiving or passing on regular updates from friends on the phone, the radio turned up full blast so she could listen as she chased the toddler from room to room. With all the windows open for the heat and every radio within a hundred miles turned on, you could have walked down any street in the city and never missed a word of the coverage.

Bob walked out of the clubhouse to the first tee at 1:15. The crowd had grown as large as sixteen thousand; some estimates put it closer to twenty thousand. No one could read it on his face but Bob was spent, dead tired; the relentless pressure, the incessant attention and lack of privacy, fighting the crowds and himself and this cruel, intractable game. He had spent a restless hour inside, nibbling at some chicken salad and a glass of iced tea, trying to prepare mentally. He knew he couldn't hope to repeat what he'd done in the third round; the bill for his morning's burst of brilliance was about to fall due.

His first drive betrayed no unsteadiness; nearly 300 yards long, just right of center. His long iron approach found the back of the green; two putts for a routine par. The crowd roared its approval. Two good shots landed him on the second green, but he three-putted for bogey, the first symptom of trouble. At the short par-three third he pulled his drive 20 yards left into a bunker. He recovered onto the green, but three-putted for the second straight hole. Double bogey. Three strokes lost to par after three holes. A shudder rippled through the crowd.

At the par-five fourth Bob cracked another soaring drive, 300 yards dead down the middle. A strong three-wood left him just short of the green; he later called this his most important shot of the tournament because it staunched the bleeding. Bob pitched up close and sank the easy putt for a birdie. Steadied, he played the next four holes in even par, but still gave the gallery cause for concern; during that stretch he missed two makeable putts for birdie. As Bob teed up his ball on nine, the immense mob trampled over the right of way of Walter Hagen, playing his second hole of the afternoon, alone and unnoticed; the Haig had to wait until Bob played on before he could proceed, which told him all he needed to know about his current status.

Bob collected par at the ninth without aid or comfort from a lily pad. Out in 38, two over for the first half of the ride. Far from disastrous, but five strokes worse than his morning effort. And he was about to hear footsteps coming up behind him.

Macdonald Smith teed off half an hour behind Bob at 9:45. Now forty-two, after falling two strokes short of Bob at Hoylake, Smith knew this might well be his last chance to win the major that had eluded him for over twenty years. Both his older brothers had a U.S. Open title to their name, but Mac had come up short so often people tended to disregard him.

Starting seven strokes in back of Bob, with only a small gallery watching, Smith began his final round with two pars, then birdied the par-three third—the hole Bob double-bogeyed—with a driver that nearly went in the hole. Almost no one on the course knew it, but Bob's lead was already down to three.

Even before he had any inkling about Smith, Bob's face was a mask of worry as he made the turn. His energy and concentration were flagging, and when he called on them, his reserves hadn't answered. The crowd jostled him, claustrophobic; Ridley and Cox had to muscle through a human wall to forge a path for him. Starting the final nine he found a rhythm with his driver and played the opening third of the side conservatively for three straight pars. He felt better, but the two par-fives he'd birdied that morning, the last obvious chances on the back, were behind him. His strategy was obvious: Take no chances. Make pars. Force the men behind him to go for broke.

As Bob walked onto the thirteenth tee, word reached his gallery for the first time that Mac Smith had birdied the ninth and finished his front nine in 34. Only three strokes separated them; the crowd thrummed with news of this dawning threat.

A difficult, downhill par-three, the 192-yard thirteenth hadn't presented Bob with any problems all week, but now he pulled his drive to the left and watched it bounce down a steep bank toward Mirror Lake behind the green. He tried to shave his recovery from the rough too closely; it hit the crest of the hill and rolled back down a few feet shy of the green. His next chip found the green, 12 feet short of the hole, but the putt wouldn't fall. He had to tap in his second get-down for a double bogey five.

Bob's lead over Smith in the final round of the Open was down to a single stroke. Messengers began sprinting back and forth between the two players, forming a network of nerves.

Rice and Keeler looked at each other in the gallery at four-teen as the crowd bustled around. They both watched Bob closely as he passed, eyes to the ground, deep in concentration. The dangerous moment had arrived. Fate and will were about to collide. If Bob faltered one more time from here on in both of the men who'd watched him play his entire career knew that the game, the Open, the quest for the Slam, would all be over.

The fourteenth hole is an intimidating uphill 444-yard par-four. Bob's drive soared up the right side of the fairway but got no forward kick off the hill. He had 210 yards left to the green. He roped a three-wood that bounced up and rolled to a stop within 15 feet of the cup. When he sank the putt for birdie the biggest shout of the day went up. Smith heard the eruption from a few hundred yards away, where he was lining up his putt on the twelfth green. Ten seconds later, he responded by sinking the 8-footer for birdie, and the cheer echoed back toward Bob.

Bob's lead was back to one stroke, and he knew it before he teed off again. He smashed a fine drive and iron to the green at fifteen. His bid for birdie, from only 8 feet, lipped out. Par four, but given the lost opportunity it was hard to feel good about it. The crowd tried to rally him, shouting encouragement, slapping him on the back as he walked to the next tee. Then word arrived that Smith had bogeyed thirteen; the lead was back up to two. The news lifted his spirits; Bob decided to press the advantage at the short par-four sixteenth. He pounded his drive over the trees protecting the dogleg, going for the green as he had that morning, but as so often happened when he swung too hard he pulled it left. The ball settled in the rough, short of a string of bunkers, 30 yards shy of the putting surface.

He walked up to the green to examine the surface around the flag, headed back to his ball and took out his lofted, heavy wedge, the only time he used it in the entire Open. A short, crisp swing; the ball lifted cleanly out of the tangled grass . . . and dropped and stopped dead less than 3 feet from the hole.

His birdie putt would have gone in from there on the desire of the gallery alone, but Calamity Jane did the job for them.

Three-stroke lead, two holes to play.

Hope came out of hiding. At last Bob had closed the door, all his fans assured themselves. Two birdies in three holes would stop Smith in his tracks. Bob was now even par through the back nine; surely that would be enough to see him to the finish.

Bob climbed up to the elevated tee at seventeen, a narrow chute perched on a plateau dug out of the hill, the launchpad to the mammoth 262-yard par-three. He studied the green below and the lake to the right. He glanced up at the treetops; a brisk wind blowing from the left toward the water. He pulled his two-wood and lined up to start the ball at the right edge of the green, then draw it back into the wind toward the flag.

He hit it on the heel of the club; the ball didn't hook. The gallery watched in horror as it arced out, found the wind, and faded toward the lake. It appeared to encounter a tree as it neared the swampy waterline, then disappeared. Of fifteen thousand eyewitnesses looking on, not one could say for certain what had happened to the ball. The crowd followed Bob down toward the water. Even the forecaddie who'd been stationed there to watch drives couldn't locate it. They dug and poked around for minutes. Someone finally came across a ball embedded in the mud on the shore of the marshy water, and the rejoicing began; they knew he'd get a free drop from such a lie, and suffer no penalty at all. Bob had a better suggestion: "I think we'd better make sure that's my ball." After prying it out of the muck with an iron Bob determined that it wasn't his.

A clutch of local and national officials descended to consult about how to proceed as Bob and the crowd waited breathlessly. A lost-ball ruling would send him back to the tee, playing his third shot. A triple bogey six seemed almost guaranteed; his entire lead over Smith could vanish with this one mistake.

The senior official, former USGA president Prescott Bush,

emerged from the huddle to announce that the lake had been designated a parallel water hazard by the committee and cards had been given to all players stating the rule when the Open began, therefore Bob was entitled to a drop within two club lengths of the hazard, at a penalty of one stroke. No loss of distance. No return to the tee.

Knowledgeable observers questioned the ruling. Didn't the ball have to be found first to receive the lesser penalty? This was clearly a lost ball. Didn't that call for loss of stroke *and* distance?

Bob didn't question the ruling; that wasn't his job now. He dropped a ball on the fairway and pitched to the green, lying three. He needed two strokes to get down for his double bogey five. His third of the round on a par-three.

The lead was back to one. Mac Smith was still alive. Bob heard grumbles all the way to the eighteenth tee: doubts that he could rise from the canvas for a third time in the same round. Questions about whether he'd been given another favorite's advantage by the ruling at seventeen. If that uncalled penalty turned out to be his margin of victory, he knew that controversy threatened to taint his win and the entire campaign for the Slam. It made him mad. Mad was good.

His drive at eighteen carried 300 yards, ideally placed down the right side, leaving the angle he needed to the hole, perched on the green's upper tier, back and left. Bob asked for an iron: Donovan Dale handed it to him, a look of reverence on his face. A wild roar rose from the crowd as he made his swing; after overshooting this green that morning, his approach faltered in the opposite direction; the ball hit the apron of the putting surface and reached the green, but failed to kick up onto the back tier.

The crowd stampeded to the green, forming a dense wall up and around the hill. The empty green looked like a stage waiting for the lead to appear; a break formed in the crowd like a curtain parting, and as Bob came through the opening he was greeted with thunderous applause. His ball sat on the front of the green, 40 feet from the hole, breaking hard right to left up the slope. He looked it over. A four for par from this spot was a long way from guaranteed; this was three-putt territory. Three putts for bogey here and Smith could easily close the gap to force a play-off, or even win the Open outright.

Newsreel cameras cranked away from the clubhouse and the back of the green as Bob walked all the way up to the hole and back, examining the contours and the line. Pop, Rice, his parents, his friends, and countless thousands of strangers looked on; people surrounded that green and spread out in every direction almost as far as the eye could see. Bob took his stance, looking cool and collected. "I was quivering in every muscle," he admitted to Pop later.

The last shot Bob Jones ever hit in a U.S. Open rolled up that hill, took the break of the slope as if it was riding a rail, turned right 6 feet from the hole, gently clicked against the center of the back of the cup, and stayed down for a birdie three.

It took five minutes to clear all the hats that were tossed into the air off the green so his partner Joe Turnesa could putt out. Bob and Joe shook hands. Ridley and Cox wrestled a path for Bob through the crowd to the scorer's tent where he turned in his card: 37 on the back, for a final-round 75 and a total score for the Open of 287. He had finished only one shot off the all-time Open record set by Chick Evans at nearby Minikahda in 1916. Alone in that enormous crowd, Evans heaved a small sigh of relief.

Bob had scouted out a small room upstairs in the clubhouse between rounds as the private sanctuary where he would sweat out the results from the rest of the field. Pop arrived moments later with a whiskey and soda, and the news that Smith had parred seventeen. Bob's lead was two. The rest of the news was good: Horton Smith and Harry Cooper had been unable to mount a charge on the final nine. Only Smith was left with a chance to catch him, and he had one hole to do it.

Bob's hands weren't shaking this time as he held his highball. Pop thought he looked completely worn out, but peaceful in a way he hadn't seen for some time. Maybe years.

"So, what do you think, Pop?"

"I think it's almost over, Bob."

Outside the clubhouse, in Bob's absence Donovan Dale was mobbed by reporters. "Besides being the world's best golfer, Bobby is a real gentleman to caddy for," he told them. "And that, if you know the things a caddie runs up against, is saying plenty." In his pocket was the $85 Bob had tipped him (the average wage for a caddie was less than a dollar a round).

Just as he had at Hoylake only two weeks earlier, Macdonald Smith came to the final hole needing an eagle two to tie Jones for the lead in an Open championship. His drive found the fairway and left him 150 yards to the green; the same gallery that had followed Jones now surrounded Smith. He waited for his partner to play up to the green, took his time, stared down the flag, then made his swing.

The shot looked good all the way. It bounced on the front of the green and started rolling up the slope on line to the hole . . . and hit his partner's ball, knocking them both sideways. That was the end. Two putts later, just as it had at Royal Liverpool, Macdonald Smith's four at eighteen secured him first-place money, second place on the scoreboard and a footnote in history. Horton Smith, just as he had at Hoylake, finished third.

Pop came back to the room—known today as the "Bobby Jones Room"—with the news. They grinned at each other and Pop asked him how he felt.

"Well," said Bob. "I'm pretty happy." Back to back U.S. Opens. His fourth American Open, tying Willie Anderson's record. Counting both British and American events, his seventh Open win overall, equaling Harry Vardon's record. His third major championship in the last seven weeks, the twelfth of his career in eight years; alone and in the clear now, ahead of anyone in history who had ever played the game.

"So tell me," asked Pop, "are you going to quit this damned game now?"

"I'm going to play in the Amateur in September at Merion, anyway," he said, and smiled. "Don't print it yet, but that's going to be the end."

Almost no one left the grounds before the awards ceremony. Bob had time to shower, change his shirt and put on a coat and tie. Players and officials from Interlachen and the USGA walked out in formal procession onto the broad green lawns below the clubhouse, the happy throng arrayed above them all in white. Smiths Horton and Macdonald both paid tribute to Bob, but vowed to keep on fighting as they collected their checks. When they handed him the silver cup Bob gave his thanks on live radio: he returned the compliments given him by the company of Smith and Smith, but couldn't quite explain how he managed to better them. "I was just a little lucky, that's all."

"Make that plucky," Horton Smith interjected, and got a big laugh.

When the ceremony ended, Walter Hagen said on radio that after Bob's display of greatness at Interlachen and throughout that summer, it would no longer be appropriate to criticize any golfer who got himself into trouble by saying that he "played like an amateur." Another reporter elicited a rare word from Bob's grandfather. During the last couple of years even old R.T. had come around to appreciate the wonder of what Bob was doing, even if the credit should go elsewhere: "The arms of the Lord are around the neck of my boy this day," he said. "God be praised."

Bob Jones played in eleven straight U.S. Opens. He won four of them, finished second in four others, tied for fifth, eighth and eleventh. For eight of the last nine years that he competed in the national championship, he finished either first or second.

A few hours later that evening, not long after dark, a reporter ran into Bob standing by the tracks of the Great Northern railway station. A private railcar had been requisitioned to convey Bob and his friends to Chicago and from there home to Atlanta, and he was waiting patiently for it to be coupled onto the train. Many other players from the Open had boarded that same train. There was no explanation as to where the other members of Bob's party had gotten to, but for the moment he was alone and almost unnoticed.

The reporter wrote that there was little to catch the eye in a very tanned young man, in modest gray coat, white knickerbockers and gray turn-down hat, quietly checking over his traveling bags and a black leather golf bag. From the way he carried himself—bone weary, self-contained, lost in thought—he could have been any of a hundred thousand men traveling by train that night across America, for business or a convention somewhere. A salesman, perhaps. Or a lawyer. Homesick. Tired of travel.

Bob graciously answered this last reporter's questions—he was "sorry to leave" so soon; he had enjoyed Minneapolis and the tournament, but he was "anxious to get home."

A porter arrived to help with the bags; the special car had at last been coupled onto the train and they were ready to depart. Would Bob mind posing for a final photograph? Not at all, said Bob.

There was one last burst of flashlight powder, and a pair of gray-stockinged legs beat a hasty retreat to the sanctuary of a railroad car.

CHAPTER FIFTEEN

THE U.S. AMATEUR, MERION

He had pushed himself to the limit of endurance. He lost seventeen pounds in three days during the Open at Interlachen. His neck and shoulders ached; he was constantly beset by muscle spasms. The stomach problems that had troubled him since his trip to Paris, the weak link in his system since childhood, had now become chronic and continued to plague him throughout the rest of the summer: by the time he reached the Amateur championship he was treating it with tincture of opium. He had not slept in his own bed, sat at his desk, or held his children since the last week in April, nearly three months before. He never gave voice to any complaint, and refused to let his closest confidant write one word about these trials. He had enjoyed far too much good fortune to ever ask for public sympathy, he told Pop. It wouldn't seem fair: "Other fellows have their troubles, too." But, having already done more to redraw the map defining the vast gulf between the very good and the truly great, as the end of his journey came into view, tired, buffeted, and bruised, did he have the strength and reserves to reach for greatness one last time?

After years of discussion with Pop about the role of fate in his game and in life, the incredible events of that summer convinced Bob he had been delivered into the influence of forces larger than himself, a destiny over which he could no longer pretend to exercise any control. What does one do in those circumstances, pulled by the currents of such powerful forces: how do you make decisions? If he had any lingering doubts about its governing presence in his life, as his train sped from Minneapolis toward Chicago that night, they were about to be removed altogether.

A pioneering aviator named "Mail" Freeburg had been flying the airmail route between the two cities for over three years, a round trip each day, morning and night. He was headed south to Chicago on that same Saturday night, using the major rail lines to navigate as pilots liked to do. As he neared the Wisconsin border a little after midnight, he noticed an unusual reddish glow on the horizon and banked down toward it to investigate.

The wooden railway trestle spanning the river was on fire and near collapse, engulfed in flames. Freeburg remembered that he'd flown over a train about ten minutes before, the regular night train to Chicago, and it was headed directly for that bridge.

Freeburg turned around and sped back along the tracks, flying low. When the train's headlight came into view he swooped down repeatedly toward the locomotive, dipped his wings, trying to attract the attention of the engineers. The train was closing toward the bridge, but it was around a distant bend; they couldn't see the fire. Freeburg flashed his lights, but the train didn't respond. He made one last run, leaned out the window and dropped a series of lit flares on the tracks ahead of the train. The engineers responded at last and slammed on the brakes. The train came to a halt just as it rounded the curve toward the river, and came to a stop less than a quarter of a mile from the burning bridge.

The members of the party that was in progress aboard the special car stepped out to have a look when the train stopped. Bob and his father and Pop and Tolley watched the fire for a while until the engineer received his orders to reroute the train and cross the river farther to the south.

Mail Freeburg landed in Chicago a few hours before the train arrived on Sunday morning. No one made that big a fuss about Freeburg's actions at the bridge: it didn't even appear in the papers for a couple of days, and then only as a small item in the back pages. Freeburg was hard to grab for an interview because he was already back in the air, flying the mail.

Bob never got a chance to thank the man who had saved their lives.

As they headed south on Sunday, airplanes kept regular track of the train's progress, reporting back to his hometown. A holiday had been declared on Monday in Atlanta, and plans created for the biggest parade of all to welcome Bob home. Those plans were telegraphed ahead to his train as they traveled through the night. The train stopped a few miles short of the downtown station early Monday morning so Bob and his party could climb into waiting cars and be escorted to the start of the parade route. Mary and the kids greeted him as he climbed down, and Bob the Third delighted his dad with a demonstration of his new-found ability to whistle.

GREATEST DEMONSTRATION IN CITY'S HISTORY MARKS GOLF

KING'S RETURN TO NATIVE HEATH was the headline on the front page of the Atlanta *Constitution* on Tuesday morning. Half the population of the city turned out to see him; with businesses closed that morning, over 125,000 people crowded the parade route on Peachtree Street. The heatwave lingered, muggy and oppressive, but there were rainclouds on the horizon.

The parade began at the stroke of noon. The guest of honor was preceded by a procession of three hundred caddies from courses all over the city, marching bands, motorcycle police, veterans of the Great War, politicians, friends, and family. On every block thunderous ovations greeted Bob, perched on the back seat in the first open car, adorned by the American flag and the Union Jack. Mary, wreathed in smiles, sat below him. The Colonel, Clara, and the children rode in the next car. Just in front of Bob's car rode the three trophies he'd brought home, grouped for the first time, arrayed on the back of a flatbed truck with a sign that read BOB IS HOME—HERE'S THE BACON! Confetti and ticker tape billowed from overhead office windows—"Pity the poor street cleaners," wrote Pop—as Atlanta tried to outdo the welcome their favorite son had received in New York two weeks before. At City Hall Bob and the principals climbed onto a dais draped in bunting. The Mayor presented Bob with a key to the city. Pop said a few words—the event was carried on radio—and introduced the phrase he'd come up with to describe the championship sweep that his friend was one win away from completing: the Grand Slam. Bob's brief, modest speech thrilled the crowd, who cheered every sentence. He spoke, as was his custom, from the heart, no prepared or written words, with the same plain sincerity and economy he showed with a club in his hand:

"Your welcome makes it impossible for me to say much. It has fairly taken my breath away. I had no idea any such affair was planned. I appreciate all the things you have done for me, and I just want to say you don't think any more of me than I do of you."

Bob didn't touch a club until the following Saturday, when he played his regular game with the Colonel and his buddies at East Lake. He went back to work at the office, trying to rest and settle into his normal routine, but there would be nothing close to normal for him now, not this summer. A barrage of requests for interviews from around the world poured in; he accommodated as many as his schedule allowed, answering them all in prose as crisp and efficient as his golf swing. Bags of fan mail collected at his door. He never used a press agent, never hid behind a mouthpiece, despite having become one of the world's most famous people. He remained startlingly accessible; if you wanted to correspond or talk with Bob Jones, and you weren't an obvious crank or crook, he would most certainly write or speak back to you. Yet all he craved was peace, diligent work, a quiet life with his family and friends. The unending assault he experienced on his privacy that season may have been possible to bear only because he knew it was so close to being over.

He took Mary and the kids for a quiet vacation at Highlands Country Club in North Carolina, and played recreational golf with his dad and some friends, but for the month of July he mostly left the sticks alone. As the weeks passed he began to feel restored, the reservoirs of energy he'd depleted during the quest slowly seeping back to level. Then, out of nowhere, came another stark reminder that fate wasn't through with him yet.

On a warm Friday near the end of July, he had a lunch engagement at the downtown Atlanta Athletic Club, and set out to walk the eight blocks from his office. Preoccupied, his mind elsewhere, he registered that the sidewalk was empty ahead of him and was halfway down the block to the door of the club when he heard a voice from somewhere behind shout: "Look out, mister!" He turned, startled: a speeding car had just jumped the curb and was bearing directly down on him. He stopped and leaped backwards—pure athletic reflex, his powerful legs carried him close to 10 feet—as the car rushed right over the spot on the sidewalk where he'd been passing and crashed into the side of the building. No one was behind the wheel of the smoking wreck. When Bob looked around, he was unable to spot the person who'd shouted out the warning to him. The street was empty.

After the police arrived it was determined that the car had been parked at the top of the hill a block away without the handbrake being set. At some point, for some unknown reason, the car began to roll, and missed maiming or killing Bob Jones by no more than eighteen inches.

The lightning bolt. The train. Now this. His third close call in less than a year. At which point he had to ask: was fate putting him in harm's way, or delivering him from it?

Last stop: Merion.

Speculation built through the summer about the possibility of Bob leaving the game, while emotional investment in his completion of the Grand Slam built to a fever pitch. As the Depression's chill settled into the bones of everyday life, shaking faith in the American dream, the prospect of this young man from Atlanta completing his impossible mission offered a ray of hope. Thousands hitched their fading dreams to his, in a way all too familiar to us now but unheard of at the time. This wasn't some cynical marketing campaign co-opting a championship athlete's image to sell tennis shoes or soft drinks; people possessed the common sense to realize that the reasons driving him toward this goal came from a place both authentic and good-hearted. That he sought no obvious profit from it made his effort all the more meaningful and real; this was a man worth emulating, strong and unhurried in the face of adversity, patient, resilient, and unassuming. There was more to life than money. He had quietly gone about his business and, without ever setting out to do so, when his country had never needed one more, Bob Jones now showed the world how to stand up to troubled times. The man had crossed over into myth.

Bob remained mute on the subject of withdrawing from the game, but as he began practicing again in earnest for the Amateur the pressure grew almost unbearable. They had recently learned Mary was pregnant with their third child; she would not be going with him to Philadelphia. He would feel her absence acutely: she had replaced Pop, naturally and appropriately, as the emotional rock in his life. As the date drew near Bob's stomach pains resumed, he found it increasingly difficult to concentrate on work, and suffered through many sleepless nights. He became fixated on the idea that another accident might strike and end the quest a few steps from the summit: every time he shaved he remembered a friend who'd been forced to withdraw from a tournament because he'd grabbed instinctively at a razor blade he'd dropped and severely cut his hand. Always mildly superstitious—he wore a gold shamrock on his watch chain, and liked to wear the same outfit every day when he was playing well—for Bob the simple act of shaving, along with a dozen other mundane daily rituals, became infused with unseen danger. Thoughts of completing the Slam consumed his waking and sleeping hours.

Pop estimated that he and Bob had logged over 120,000 miles together during his playing years, but in terms of life experience they had traveled a much greater distance. With the dramatic wholeness characteristic of his entire career their last trip would take them back to where it all began. By the time they were ready to leave for Merion, Bob's stomach problems had grown so severe that he was under constant medical care. He had agreed to play in a charity exhibition for war veterans at East Lake on Sunday, September 14, the day before departure. The night before, he was stricken with such severe pain he couldn't stand and was rushed to the hospital; the first diagnosis was acute appendicitis—for two tense hours the Slam appeared in jeopardy—but another round of tests revealed that this was the result of a nervous disorder. Bob was given new medication and cleared to travel to Philadelphia, but only if a doctor accompanied him. Refusing to cancel his commitment to the exhibition, Bob left the hospital for East Lake, played the event, and helped raise over $5,000 for the charity.

On the way, he stopped for a day in Washington to play in another charity event at Columbia Country Club with Horton Smith, and before the game Pop visited the White House for the first time, where President Hoover offered his congratulations and best wishes for continued success. (Hoover was not and never had been a golfer: far too time-consuming.) Bob played the round at Columbia in a steady rain, then boarded a night train. By the time he arrived in Philadelphia early the next morning, slightly hungover, the muscle spasms in his neck and shoulder had flared up again. A crowd of journalists and photographers were waiting for him; every paper in town had assigned at least one reporter to follow his every step. The Philadelphia *Evening Bulletin* assigned sixteen writers and photographers to Bob and the Open.

Among them was a young cub reporter named Joseph Dey, Jr., who nailed an exclusive when Bob arrived; as they wheeled Bob's bags into the lobby of the downtown Barclay Hotel, a bellman dropped one of the packages and the unmistakable odor of bootleg liquor filled the room. Pop spread a little cash around to keep the incident quiet, and recruited the guilt-ridden bellman to find a local source for their hootch. (Joe Dey, who hadn't covered golf before, became so intrigued by Bob and his performance at Merion that he pursued golf-writing full time; a few years later, when the USGA was looking for its first executive director, Dey applied for the job, and stayed at his post for the next thirty-five years, thereafter serving as commissioner of the PGA Tour.) Security was heightened at the Barclay, with extra men stationed at the stairwells leading to their famous guest's room. Bob's two-bedroom suite offered the only privacy he would experience for the next ten days.

He had five days before qualifying. When he arrived at Merion on Wednesday for his first practice round he discovered that over four thousand people had paid a dollar apiece for the privilege of watching him that day. Although a few marshals had been assigned to his twosome in anticipation of a crowd, the massive gallery that showed up made the kind of concentrated work Bob needed impractical. Every time they surrounded him he was left with a 10-foot-wide corridor through which to make his next shot, and he lived in constant fear of injuring someone if it went off line. Marshals carried ropes and were supposed to stay ahead of the crowds, directing their movement. When they stampeded forward after every shot the marshals failed to stay in front of them; Bob could never try the same shot twice, a primary objective in practice rounds. He shot 73, three over par, and felt completely out of sorts afterwards. A new sprinkler system had been installed and the rough had grown to six inches in some spots, more severe than Bob had ever seen at Merion. The greens were cut to $3/16$ of an inch, a championship standard for putting surfaces that would endure into the 1960s.

The next day the crowd around him was even larger and more unruly. A nineteen-year-old caddie named Howard Rexford had won the Jones lottery at Merion and would carry his bag throughout the tournament. During his practice round on Thursday, a hot and humid day, the crowd's rowdy behavior and his own loose play prompted Bob to toss a few clubs back to Rexford after some poor shots, the closest he'd come to his old temperamental ways in almost a decade. He shot 78 that day, and despaired about his game; as well as he knew this course, he couldn't get a handle on it, and the greens baffled him. He tried one putt ten times before it dropped. His close friend Jess Sweetser, eighth seed in the amateur field, joined Bob's gallery for the final two holes. He could see that the crowd made it impossible for him to practice; he called Bob that night and invited him to the private sanctuary of nearby Pine Valley.

Bob, the Colonel, and Pop traveled to Pine Valley with Sweetser on Friday morning. With no one watching them but the ducks, Bob soon began to settle down. By the turn Sweetser thought he was starting to look more like himself; Bob shot a two-under-par 33 on the back nine. After they returned to the hotel that night, Bob grew ill again, vomiting repeatedly. Rumors had begun to spread that he was seriously sick. Despite feeling weak, he knew the only way to quell those reports was by showing up at Merion. He played a four-ball match on Saturday morning with Sweetser, Jimmy Johnston, and Max Marston, shooting 71, and his fine round put a stop to the chatter about his health.

Sweetser's hospitality didn't stop at Pine Valley; after the round he took Bob, the Colonel and Pop out to a local ballpark to watch the Phillies lose to the first-place Cardinals. Both Bob and his dad were lifelong baseball fans—Bob had recently been named the ceremonial vice-president of a minor-league team in Atlanta called the Crackers—and the game relaxed him even more. By the time they got back to the hotel, his stomach pains had subsided for the first time since Atlanta, and his neck and shoulders felt pain-free.

For the second consecutive tournament Bob decided to forgo his habit of relaxing in his hotel on the day before play began; he felt on the verge of coming onto his game, but needed confirmation more than rest, so when the USGA asked him if he wouldn't mind playing one more practice round so they could pad their box-office take during these troubled times, Bob agreed to appear. But when he hit the opening shot of his final practice round at Merion, another emergency presented itself, on the first tee. The ball made a peculiar sound coming off his driver and upon examination Bob realized the duckhorn plate on the face of Jeanie Deans had cracked. A small crack had also started to appear at the back of the club's persimmon head. The Colonel took charge and rushed her into the pro shop, where George Sayers diagnosed the problem: Bob's unerring ability to hit the ball on the center of the club every time had worn a small hole where the edge of the tee met the inset. The fracture had turned into a fissure, but Sayers assured them he could handle the repair. Knowing that Jeanie Deans might be as close to retirement as he was, Bob played with his second-string driver in the bag and shot 69 on Sunday. He had made another small bet with his English friend Dale Bourne that he could shoot even par that day.

"With a little luck, I may qualify," he told a reporter afterwards, with a twinkle in his eye. On the eve of the tournament Bob had found his game.

Realizing he was going to be facing galleries at Merion larger than any he'd ever seen before, Bob's Interlachen bodyguard Charlie Cox had placed a call to colleagues in Washington and Philadelphia. By the time the qualifying for the Amateur began on Monday morning, a contingent of fifty U.S. Marines in full dress uniform had arrived from the Philadelphia Navy Yard to supplement the USGA's marshals and serve as Bob's last line of defense. Cox and Ridley would once again be at his side, walking stride for stride, carrying his water. Forty policemen would also be roaming the grounds.

That night at the Barclay, Bob received a telegram from Johnny Boutsies, owner of a Greek restaurant that the Jones family frequented in Atlanta. Johnny knew that with Bob's grounding in the classics he would be able to decipher the cryptic message, which read: "E TON E EPITAS." Bob shared it with Pop; he had translated it, but wasn't sure of the reference. "With it or on it." Pop reminded him that it was the traditional farewell that wives and mothers in ancient Sparta gave to their warrior husbands and sons when they buckled on their shields and sent them off to battle.

One hundred and sixty-eight contestants would attempt to qualify for thirty-two matchplay slots. The second floor above the clubhouse, originally the old farm's barn, was converted into the press room for over 150 reporters who descended on Merion. Fourteen years earlier, when Bobby made his debut, twenty-nine sportswriters had covered the entire tournament. Three radio networks arranged for live hook-ups, and three motion-picture outfits had sent crews to cover the event, including Grantland Rice Newsreel, a company Rice owned and operated. A telephone system had been installed on the golf course, with a station every three holes, so scores could be constantly relayed back to the press and the big scoreboard.

Bob began his first qualifying round at 9:18 on Monday morning. Not one of the seven thousand people who bought tickets and followed Bob around that day had come to see his playing partner, Emory Stratton from Brae Burn. Jeanie Deans had been returned to Bob's bag by Merion's pro George Sayers as promised, and appeared as good as new, but Bob pushed his first drive down the right-hand side and found a bunker. A long recovery shot landed within 10 feet of the flag, and the par he collected appeared to steady him. With a phalanx of Marines providing security, Bob settled into the brand of cold-blooded concentration that had always separated him from the pack. He assayed a superlative round: nine pars through the front, two birdies and a bogey on the back for the day's best score of 69. Only sixty other men in the entire field broke 80 that Monday. Avoiding a crush of reporters, he left for the Barclay, and spent a quiet evening with Pop and the Colonel.

The next day Bob wasn't scheduled to tee off until nearly one in the afternoon. With final positions on the line, many of the players ahead of him on Tuesday slowed their pace to a crawl. His second round became an exercise in patience, waiting on nearly every tee for the fairway to clear. His gallery grew so enormous it spilled over into adjoining fairways, disrupting other twosomes; one exasperated player pleaded with the crowd to step aside so he could play his next shot: "After I fail to qualify, you can come out and watch Bobby all week."

Bob stayed within himself, and shot even par on the front. At the fifteenth a man in his gallery broke into applause as he stood over his putt; Bob looked up and glared at the man—the only time he ever showed anger at a spectator—then missed the putt for bogey. He came to seventeen needing only to par in for 71. He also knew that score, added to his 69 in the first round, would lower his existing record for an Amateur qualifier. These smaller accomplishments within the context of his larger pursuit helped keep Bob in the moment, and he was determined to break this record. The wait at the seventeenth tee, a long dangerous par-three played down and over Merion's old quarry, dragged on for half an hour, testing his patience to the breaking point. Bob got his par at seventeen, but had to wait again at eighteen. Five groups were bottlenecked between tee and green. The home hole at Merion asks for a knee-knocking drive that must carry 200 yards to the fairway back across the quarry. When Bob finally stepped to the tee, he took out all his frustrations on the ball.

The tee shot rocketed across the quarry, kicked forward down the descending slope of the fairway on the far side and carried close to 350 yards, leaving him a blind, uphill shot into the green. This was an unfamiliar distance to a target he couldn't see; no one could ever remember a drive landing here before. Bob misjudged the shot and the ball bounced into the rough behind the flag. He left his chip coming back short and then missed the 8-foot putt for par that would have broken the record. He had tied his own record for lowest qualifying score in the

Amateur, and won the gold medal for a record sixth time, but as he walked off the green he was furious at himself for failing to capture the record outright.

The final field of 32 included ex-Amateur champions Francis Ouimet, George Von Elm, and Jess Sweetser. Also reaching the matchplay rounds were Watts Gunn, Johnny Goodman, and George Voigt. Five former Amateur winners failed to make the cut, including defending champ Jimmy Johnston, Jess Guilford, and Chick Evans, who lost out in the play-off, as did Cyril Tolley.

Bob couldn't sleep again that night. Wednesday would bring the two eighteen-hole elimination matches of the tournament and reduce the field to eight, the last obstacle he feared on the path to the title. He called Pop after midnight, who came in and sat with him for a while. "There's something on my mind I can't shake off. I go to sleep all right from fatigue, but then around midnight I wake up and have to get up. I've always been able to sleep. Something's bearing down on me in this tournament that was never there before."

Pop thought he knew what it was: the specter of the fourth championship and all it implied, bearing down on him like a horseman he could not see. He called it the Fourth Horseman of the Apocalypse of Championship.

Bob wasn't sure. After all he'd been through, it may have been own his mortality. Death had brushed him with its wings three times in less than a year. What price was he ultimately going to pay for this perfection?

Ross "Sandy" Sommerville was considered the best golfer to ever come out of Canada. A triple-threat athlete—varsity half-back in football at the University of Toronto, first-string center on the hockey team with offers to turn pro—he had already won three Canadian Amateur titles on his way to a total of six, and he would go on to become the first Canadian to ever win the American title. Only twenty-seven, a physically impressive specimen, Sommerville had a deserved reputation as a pressure player. The gallery of ten thousand strangers who greeted them on the first tee at ten o'clock that Wednesday morning didn't seem to bother him at all.

The weather was ideal for scoring—no wind, warm and oppressively calm. Bob and Sommerville played the first two holes even; Sandy bogeyed the third to send Bob one up. The next three holes were halved in par; at one under for his round, Bob was still only one up. Bob had an instinct that the match would turn at the seventh, a short par-four, after both hit good drives and solid approaches to the right of the hole; Bob was 8 feet out, Sandy 7, on a slightly different line.

Bob walked all the way around the green, viewing the line from every angle, grateful he had to putt first; if he could hole this birdie Sandy's putt would get a lot tougher. If he missed Sandy would almost certainly make his and pull even; then all bets were off. "I never worked any harder on any putt than I did on this one," Bob wrote later.

The green was scary fast, slightly downhill, with an un-detectable right and left break that Bob knew was there only from experience. He tapped the ball gently and watched it crawl down to the hole, hesitate, then curl and drop in through the side door. Sommerville saw the line from Bob's effort but didn't embrace it with the same conviction; his ball grazed the top of the cup and stayed out by an inch.

Bob was two up. The swing in momentum elevated his game. He birdied the par-four eighth, then rammed in a 25-footer right past a partial stymie at nine for his third birdie in a row. Sommerville kept making pars but it wasn't enough; as they made the turn Bob was four up. The Canadian never challenged again. The match ended on the fourteenth green, 5 & 4. Playing flawlessly, Bob had taken care of Sandy Sommerville in only two hours and ten minutes to advance to the field of sixteen.

Bob drew the tournament's remaining Canadian in the afternoon's second round, Fred Hoblitzel, a far less accomplished player than Sommerville. But Bob's nervous stomach was acting up; he ate only toast and iced tea during a brief intermission.

From the moment they walked out to play that afternoon the immense gallery terrified Fred Hoblitzel. After a scrambling par at the first, he picked up at the second, conceding the hole. He bogeyed the fourth, then double-bogeyed both the sixth and the eighth. He scratched out only three pars on the entire front nine. The larger surprise at this point was that Bob was only three holes up. As brilliantly as he'd dispatched Sommerville that morning, his game went slack that afternoon; playing down to the level of the competition, he shot 41 on the front—including a drive he shanked out of bounds at the sixth—eight strokes more than he'd taken earlier, but Hoblitzel was so hapless that Bob held an identical lead. No one, including both contestants, appeared to have any doubt about the outcome from their opening drives. Bob finished Hoblitzel off by the same score— 5 & 4—and at the same hole—the fourteenth—where he'd earlier ended his match with Sommerville. He had advanced to the quarter-finals, and the last of the eighteen-hole elimination matches was behind him. Despite his aversion to them, in the last four years his record in those short sprints was 17–2.

Sensing that Hoblitzel wasn't capable of putting up a fight, by the time they reached the back nine a large percentage of Bob's gallery had deserted the match in search of bigger thrills. They found them in a second-round battle between George Von Elm and New Yorker Maurice McCarthy. They slugged out nine extra holes shot for shot, putt for putt, the longest extra-hole battle in the history of the Amateur. As darkness fell, on the twenty-eighth hole—his forty-seventh of the day, another record—McCarthy knocked out Von Elm with a birdie.

By Wednesday night they were calling the action on the course that day the greatest collection of upsets during any Amateur in memory. Ouimet and Johnny Goodman both bowed out in the first round—Ouimet to an eighteen-year-old from Detroit; he owned socks older than that—and now Von Elm was gone. George Voigt lost a second-round match to an unknown kid from California named Charlie Seaver. Of all the former champions and top-ten-seeded players who had started the tournament, only Jones and Sweetser were left standing in the field of eight.

Immediately after his dust-up with McCarthy, George Von Elm announced his retirement from the amateur ranks. He would elaborate a few days later when the tournament ended in a printed statement remarkable for its thinly veiled bitterness.

> I have retired from amateur golf because competing in the American and British amateur and Walker Cup international match isn't worth the $10,000 a year it costs me. For ten years I've had the "Mr." stuck in front of my name, and that insignia of amateurism has required more than $50,000 of hard-earned money . . .
>
> It isn't nice to treat the subject of my amateur status in cold terms of dollars. The USGA's Amateur Championship is a highly organized commercial project, while the thirty-two performers play their hearts out for honor and glory. Not a penny of the money the USGA makes is contributed to the expenses of the players. Tournament golf today is show business in a big way. The finger of suspicion points to many players of amateur golf today, but the show must go on, and the USGA is busy a good part of the time straining at gnats and swallowing camels.

A heavy rain soaked the greens and fairways late Wednesday night; Bob woke up during the storm and was unable to get back to sleep until after 3:00 A.M. This time he declined to call Pop, sitting out the long hours before dawn alone. The morning papers predicted an open run for Bob to the title, which was exactly why he didn't read them. He might have been particularly upset by a small article which claimed that a Hollywood movie studio was about to sign him to a contract worth $200,000 for some unspecified film work. When he was questioned about it by reporters that day Bob denied any such offer had been made; in fact the idea had been floated, but he cut off the man making the offer and refused to discuss it until after the tournament was over.

First he had to get by a golfer from Culver City named Fay Coleman, the current southern California champion. For years golf writers had leaned on the idea of describing Bob as a "mechanical man," but as he progressed deeper into the Amateur that image began to break down. He bogeyed four of the first nine holes but still led the match one up. Anyone walking out to face Bob in this tournament was up against a host of obstacles in addition to the man himself, but Coleman hung tough; when Bob hooked his drive out of bounds and double-bogeyed the fifteenth, Coleman evened the match. The young man played capable golf, but at no point did he persuade the thousands watching that he could seize control of the match. Bob settled down to par the final three holes; Coleman recorded back-to-back bogeys to end the morning round two down.

Bob was pacing himself, thought Pop, like a long-distance runner, saving his kick for the decisive moment when he can sprint ahead and finish the job; classic matchplay strategy. When they went back out after lunch, overcast skies threatened rain all afternoon but Bob bent to his task. They halved the first with pars. Coleman won the second hole with a stymie to draw within one—Bob tried to chip over his ball into the cup and failed—but he had reached his high-water mark. Starting at the long par-five fourth hole, Coleman began to crack: three straight bogeys to Bob's perfect line of pars. Smelling blood, Bob called on the kick; with a birdie-par finish to close out his front side,

Bob seized a commanding six-hole lead with nine to play. When it grew to seven after the tenth the match was all but over; Bob coasted for two holes which Coleman won, then closed him out on the thirteenth, right next to the clubhouse, 5 & 4. As they shook hands and walked off the green the heavens opened in a heavy downpour and sent thousands scattering for cover.

When he reached the shelter of the locker room, Bob learned he would be playing his old friend Jess Sweetser in the semi-finals. The other bracket was a surprise: nineteen-year-old tournament rookie Charlie Seaver against the former Princeton champion, Eugene Homans.

With two young and relatively inexperienced golfers in the other semi-final, experts agreed that Sweetser remained the last serious threat to Bob's completion of the Grand Slam. They also sought comfort in the startling fact that Bob had never lost a match to the same man twice, and in every rematch he avenged his earlier defeat. Sweetser knew the only way to beat Bob—as he had done at Brookline, when he handed Bob the worst matchplay beating of his life, 8 & 7—was to get him down early and keep the pressure on. He also knew that the ten thousand in atten-dance—with the exception of his own wife and parents—and millions around the world listening by radio or reading coverage in print were unanimously hoping he would fail. Even the waiters at Merion were pulling for Bob; one famously threatened to remove a reporter's soup because the man was slurping while Bob prepared to putt on a distant green.

Homans and Seaver teed off at 8:30 on Friday morning. Bob and Jess began their match a half-hour later, and thousands who set out with the two younger men came rushing back to the first tee after they'd played only a single hole. On every hole during their match, including the long par-fives, the gallery would reach all the way from each tee to the green.

Hoping for a fast start, Sweetser stumbled out of the gate; he found two bunkers on his way to the green and lost the hole with a double bogey six. Bob calmly sank a 15-footer for birdie. At the par-three third, Jess half-topped his drive into another bunker and couldn't recover; another par for Bob and he was two up. Sweetser hit his approach short at four for bogey; a second birdie for Bob. Three up. At the fifth, Sweetser hooked his drive into a brook and had to accept a penalty stroke; double bogey six. Another par for Bob, and he was up four. Well, thought Sweetser, so much for a fast start.

But after they halved the sixth, the "mechanical man" sputtered, slicing his drive over a fence out of bounds; when he missed his approach to the green he conceded the hole. They halved the eighth with pars, then Bob put his tee shot in a bunker on the par-three ninth, chipped out short and two-putted for bogey. Sweetser took advantage and made par; he was two down as they made the turn. After Bob made his second straight bogey at ten, which cut his lead to one, Pop heard the crowd murmur its disapproval. Heads wagged, eyebrows were raised. Most of these people were watching Bob play for the first time—many were watching *golf* for the first time—and didn't understand: Bobby Jones wasn't supposed to make mistakes, was he? It got worse: two more bogeys followed at eleven and twelve. What the heck was going on here? Sweetser double-bogeyed because of a well-laid stymie to lose the eleventh, then scratched back to one down again with a par at twelve.

The least concerned man on the grounds appeared to be Bob; as he'd been able to do all that week, he let the bad shots go and flushed the mediocrity from his system. The next two holes were halved with pars, both men hitting fairways and greens, with Sweetser laying his approach inside of Bob's on both occasions. The crowd warmed up with the Indian-summer sun; they were starting to feel they might be about to witness something special.

At the fifteenth, both men found the green in two, but Bob

ran in a 15-footer for his third birdie of the round to go two up. They halved the sixteenth, but the tone of the action was changing. Bob had mastered himself and withstood Sweetser's run; in the gallery Pop could physically feel the pressure shifting back onto Jess. Their tee shots at the long par-three seventeenth would be crucial: Bob, playing first, found the green, while Sweetser came up just short. Facing an uncomplicated chip, Sweetser stumbled again; he came up short and missed a 4-foot putt for par. Bob made par. Up three.

Bob kept the pressure on with a spectacular drive across the quarry at eighteen. Sweetser's effort ended up 20 yards behind him, increasing the pressure on his long approach to the green. He watched it flare to the right and land in a bunker: another bogey, while Bob cashed in for his par. At the intermission, Bob had regained all of his early four-hole lead. In the other match, young Californian Charlie Seaver had taken a commanding lead over Eugene Homans, up five.

Bob followed his lunchtime rituals: a few bites of chicken salad on toast, iced tea. He looked calm, collected, didn't talk much. Pop didn't even try to speak to him. Not today.

On their opening drives of the afternoon, both men found bunkers, both reached the green. Bob missed an easy 6-footer for birdie and they halved the hole with fours. At the long, intimidating par-five second, Bob striped another bullet down the center; Sweetser popped his drive up high to the right and watched it soar onto adjoining Ardmore Avenue, out of bounds. Just like that, Bob was five up, but he handed that gift right back by overshooting the green at the third. Sweetser saved his par; Bob's scrambling putt failed to find the hole. Four up.

They halved their twenty-second hole of the day. When they reached the next tee, the par-four fifth, Pop saw something come into Bob's expression; eyes set like stone, his movements a fraction slower and more deliberate. Here comes the kick, he thought.

Sweetser hit a serviceable drive down the middle. Bob's ball passed him on the fly and kept running another 15 yards. After Sweetser played to the front, Bob stuck his approach 20 feet from the hole on the challenging, right-to-left-sloping green. Sweetser missed his long try for a three and took par. The putt Bob faced was downhill, side-hill and fast, with a break of at least 2 feet; he rammed it dead into the center of the cup for birdie. The lead was back to five.

Another half at six. At the seventh, Bob drilled an 8-foot putt for birdie. Jones up six. Sweetser looked dazed. At the short eighth, Bob stuck his iron second on the green. Sweetser's approach flew over the flag and bounced into a pot bunker; he failed to get out, and conceded the hole. Jones up seven. At the par-three ninth, both men reached the green. Bob took a quick look at his line, feeling it now, and his 24-foot birdie putt tracked straight for the hole and dropped. Jones up eight, with nine to play.

Both men hit good drives at the par-four tenth, with Bob the longer again. Sweetser hit a high-pitch second to the right side of the green, 20 feet from the hole, pin high. Bob took his wedge in hand and played an elegant pitch and run that landed on the front edge, rolled and rolled toward the flag and came to rest four inches from the cup and an eagle two. Over fifteen thousand people had jammed into their gallery by this time and most of them went berserk; the Marines snapped to their task, holding back the throng. Walking to the green, Bob looked over at Sweetser and grinned sheepishly. When Sweetser missed his last birdie attempt he stuck out his hand, conceding Bob's tap-in. The match was over, 9 & 8.

As they walked to the clubhouse Bob put an arm around his old friend and said, "I feel sort of mean about that last shot. It was like a stab in the back, or a shot in the dark."

"Bob, it wasn't any shot in the dark. It was a great shot." Sweetser patted him on the back, and mopped his own brow. "I'd about had enough anyway."

In reaching the finals Bob had also avenged the most lopsided defeat of his career; for the two matches they'd played together, over fifty-seven holes, Sweetser now stood one down to Bob Jones, a fact Jess was proud to tell you for the rest of his life.

The gallery rushed ahead of them to catch up with the Seaver–Homans match, which had turned into a corker. Five down at the halfway mark, Homans chipped away at Seaver's lead during the afternoon; he stood three down at the turn. Homans won the eleventh with a par. They halved the next two holes, at which point Seaver stood two up with five to play; the dreaded St. Andrews matchplay lead. Only nineteen and playing in his first Amateur, great things were predicted for Charlie Seaver, but alas they weren't to be. Only Eugene Homans now stood between Bob Jones and the Grand Slam.

Bob soaked in a hot tub back at the Barclay, and drank his first highball. He had a second afterwards, sitting with Pop and his dad. Despite the relative ease with which he appeared to be winning his matches, he told them this was the toughest, most grueling campaign of the four he'd been through that summer. It wasn't the golf—getting to the course was almost a relief— he felt like a creature in a zoo, on constant display wherever he went. His natural inclination to polite, sincere interaction was under constant assault by strangers pushing and pulling at him for favors or autographs. He would have been happy to go on playing, but much more than the satisfaction that playing well and winning gave to him, he wanted his life back. He spoke with Mary on the phone before retiring to bed, said goodnight to his kids. Downstairs at the front desk a snowdrift of telegrams wishing him luck accumulated through the evening. Reporters huddled in Merion's press room, churning out copy late into the night. Families gathered around their radios all over the country, eager for any news about Bob. Atlanta papers prepared hourly editions in order to update Bobby's progress. Extra operators were called on duty to handle the anticipated crush of telephone traffic the following day. Granny Rice said it was no exaggeration that you could almost hear the entire country holding its breath. Bob was one step from the summit.

Bob slept better that last night than he had all week, uninterrupted, then woke half an hour before sunrise. Another rainstorm had passed through during the early morning and sweetened the air; you could taste the first hint of fall, cool and bracing. He ate breakfast alone in his room, then drove out to Merion, arriving at 7:30. The match was scheduled to begin at 9:00. He changed shoes at his locker, then followed all his small daily rituals, as if this was just another round of golf. Outside the USGA braced itself for a record crowd. They underestimated. Homans's nickname on the course was "Gabby" because he never opened his mouth during a match unless spoken to. He was only twenty-two, bespectacled, scholarly, and painfully slender; some thought he looked anemic. On the contrary, he was under normal circumstances a capable and tough-minded opponent. But when he walked out to the first tee on Saturday morning, the eighteen thousand people who were already packed around the first fairway felt little else for Homans than pity. He looked frail next to Bob, a commoner beside a beloved and handsome crown prince. In fact, another wave of nausea had fluttered into Bob's system just prior to the match that was so strong he couldn't button his collar. Bob may have been more adept at concealing it, but the nerves of both men were frayed to the seams as they teed up their first shots. No Amateur championship in the game's history had ever attracted a crowd like this.

They were off. Homans hit driver in the fairway; Bob outdrove him with a three-wood. Homans pulled his approach into a bunker; Bob pitched to within 20 feet. Homans's recovery left him 35 feet from the hole and he missed the putt for par. Bob lagged his close and took his par. Jones up one.

They halved the second with bogeys, both men showing the

strain; Homans found two bunkers along the way. Bob three-putted from the front of the green, and failed to capitalize. At the par-three third, Bob steered his drive onto the green. Homans, needing a three-wood on the 195-yard hole, found yet another bunker. He failed to get up and down. Bob calmly two-putted for par. Jones up two.

At the par-five fifth, Bob drove into a bunker, but hit a brilliant three-wood far down the fairway. Homans found the fairway, but pushed his second into the rough. Both reached the green in three. Homans three-putted, Bob needed only two. Jones up three.

The overcast weather had brought in a stiff wind; blowing across, it pushed both tee shots at the fifth into bunkers. Bob's recovery was stronger, but he missed a 4-footer for par. Both men bogeyed the hole. Five holes into the match, Homans had failed to record a par. Pop took a nip from a flask; Bob looked more relaxed than he did. Homans got his first par at the sixth for another half. After both men reached the seventh green in two, Bob left his first putt 3 feet short. Homans putted to within a foot and stymied Bob's ball; Bob couldn't get around or over him. Homans tapped in for par and won his first hole. Jones up two.

They played the eighth even in par. At the downhill par-three ninth, Homans's drive found the creek short of the green. Bob gently dropped an iron off the tee within 20 feet. After taking a drop, pitching up and missing his putt, Homans conceded Bob's second putt for par. Bob had played the front nine in three over par and was up three. Homans had 43 on the front, and showed no signs that he could turn himself around.

Bob kept the heat on with a perfect drive at the par-four tenth. Homans hooked his drive into the rough, then pitched over the green into a bunker, where it rolled into a heelprint left by the retreating gallery. Bob pitched safely to the middle of the green. Homans misplayed his shot out of the bunker, and needed two putts for bogey. Another two-putt for Bob for par. His lead increased to four.

The 378-yard par-four eleventh hole asks for a downhill tee shot to a blind landing, bearing slightly to the left. The green sits in the elbow of a stream called the Baffling Brook; trees protect its right side and a bunker the left, asking for one of the most demanding second shots on the course. The premium is on accuracy over distance off the tee, and Bob used his three-wood to find the fairway; Homans outdrove him slightly using a driver. Bob's approach stopped 25 feet past the hole. Homans pitched to within 8 feet. Bob looked the line over from both sides, unusual for him, then drained the putt for his first birdie of the day. The crowd erupted. Homans missed his birdie try. Jones up five.

They halved twelve and thirteen. At the 412-yard par-four fourteenth, Bob was on in two, 15 feet from the hole. From the same distance Homans hooked a three-wood into the rough. He left his chip 7 feet shy of the flag. Bob lagged close: Homans missed his putt; Bob tapped his in. Jones up six. Whatever fight was left in Homans appeared to leak away; Bob brought the hammer down. At fifteen, he stuck his approach 6 feet from the flag. Homans's found a bunker; he failed to get up and down and conceded Bob's putt. Bob knocked it in one-handed for birdie. Jones up seven. At sixteen, both hit good drives, then spanned the quarry to reach the green with their second. Homans three-putted from 60 feet. Bob two-putted from 25. Jones up eight.

A brief respite: Homans collected his first birdie of the day at seventeen to trim the lead to seven, and it stayed that way when both men parred the eighteenth. Bob had shot 72 and Homans 80, but after Bob's birdie at eleven and his hard, implacable play coming in, the crowd knew the match wasn't even as close as the score. Bob was tough enough to beat anyone who'd ever lived; on this day, on the brink of this triumph, there wasn't another man alive who could have beaten him.

Once the crowd realized the outcome they craved was not going to be in doubt, a party atmosphere took hold. Celebration replaced anxiety. They cheered wildly after Bob's every shot. Marshals, Marines, police, and state troopers did everything they could to contain them, but hundreds broke ranks on every hole, rushing ahead to line up on the next one.

They halved the first two holes of the afternoon in par. Bob used his oversized wedge to carve out a sensational bunker shot at the third that stopped within a foot of the hole. Homans putted past the hole and left himself stymied behind Bob's ball; he missed for par, Bob sank his. The lead was eight. At the fourth, their twenty-second hole of the day, Bob played every shot safely to a smooth five, while Homans struggled for bogey. Jones up nine.

Bob took a breath, content to match shots with Homans for a beat. They halved the next four holes without incident.

Homans bagged his second birdie at the twenty-seventh hole, holding off the end for a brief moment. By now the crowd's excitement was impossible to contain. Slack with emotion and the weight of what was coming, both played the tenth/twenty-eighth as a comedy of errors. They found bunkers with their second shots; Bob failed to get out on his first try, while Homans skulled his across the green into another bunker. Both took double bogey sixes; Bob later wrote "Ha-ha" next to his score for ten on the card.

He was eight up with eight to play.

They walked to the eleventh tee. Homans still held the honor from his birdie at nine and drove deep down the right side. Bob crushed his final drive long and down the left, leaving the best angle to the green. The gallery packed into the tightest corner of the course surrounding the eleventh green. A solid mass of people who didn't make it there in time backed up the hill halfway back to the tee box.

Silence. Homans played first, a neatly judged wedge shot that rolled to a stop 25 feet past the hole. Bob's drive had nearly reached the stream, traveling close to 300 yards. He asked for a wedge from his caddie, took his stance and fired a precise pitch that landed on the front and bounded forward to within 13 feet of the flag. An enormous roar crashed around them as he traversed the small bridge to the green. Pop thought Bob looked haggard and drawn, but he was white as a ghost himself, the enormity of the moment crushing.

The crowd settled. Eighteen thousand people. The Colonel was in that crowd, and Pop Keeler, Grantland Rice, Francis Ouimet, Cyril Tolley, and four-time Amateur Champion Jerry Travers, the man whose record Bob was about to break. All the people who'd watched him grow into the man he was gathered in solemn silence around this sylvan green, the quiet broken only by the gentle splash of water flowing in the stream.

His caddie handed him Calamity Jane, the world's most famous golf club, then pulled the stick. Bob lined up the putt, and cocked his head, that familiar quizzical last glance at the line and the hole, then the slight economic hinge of the wrists and Bobby Jones's last putt rolled forward to within six inches of the cup.

Gene Homans knew the moment wasn't his; it wasn't his turn. Bob Jones's name had been written in this Book, perhaps as long as fourteen years ago. He took hardly a moment to line up his putt, just this side of careless, and then let it go and even before it creased the side of the hole and rolled past Homans started walking toward Bob with a big smile, extending his hand, the first to reach him.

And then shouts and cries and tumult filled the air. They all came at him in a wild rush, hundreds and thousands. Only the quick reaction of Ridley and Cox and the fifty Marines who leaped to his side protected him from certain harm. In the middle of the chaos Howard Rexford had the foresight to replace the stick and pick up Bob's ball. The cheering would not dissipate for five full minutes. Runners dashed back toward the clubhouse; a call was placed from the phone at the twelfth tee to the press room, but the crowd was so loud the man on the other end of the line couldn't hear a word—he didn't have to. The cheer had traveled the half-mile back to the clubhouse; operators were already toggling their telegraph keys, spreading the news around the world.

Jones had won the Grand Slam.

Chick Ridley and Charlie Cox had rehearsed this drill earlier with their fifty Marines; they formed a corridor and Bob edged his way back through it inside their protective cordon. The trip to the clubhouse felt as if it took forever, but Bob didn't seem to mind. He smiled and waved to the crowd and their cheers attended him all the way back in.

"All at once I felt the wonderful feeling of release from tension and relaxation that I had wanted so badly for so long a time. I wasn't quite certain what had happened or what I had done. I only knew that I had completed a period of most strenuous effort and that at this point, nothing more remained to be done."

Before he went inside, Bob slipped $150 into Howard Rexford's hand, a small fortune for a caddie. Rexford hung on to Bob Jones's last ball for thirty years until for some reason he put it in play during a match and lost it in the woods. Pop Keeler fought his way through to Bob as they entered the clubhouse and there was some whooping and hollering to do, and songs to sing as his friends crowded him one last time. Any thoughts of Prohibition went out the window as they broke out the champagne and the hootch and the forty-dollar Scotch. No one lucky enough to be on those grounds or in that building ever forgot the moment.

The Colonel couldn't locate him in the crowd and finally made it into the building shouting, "Where's my boy? Where's my boy?" They found each other just inside the locker-room door;

the Colonel threw his arms around his only son and wept, tears in both their eyes—and Keeler wept when he saw them crying—just as there had been twenty years before when Bobby had shown him the scorecard for his first 80 at East Lake.

Pop hustled everyone away. For a few moments, everyone left Bob alone with his dad.

CHAPTER SIXTEEN

RETIREMENT

All three national radio networks carried the live presentation of the Havermeyer Trophy at Merion. After he'd said all his thank-yous, Bob was asked about retirement, but this was neither the time nor place to make an announcement of that magnitude; the joyous mood of the crowd and the moment would have been shattered. Bob answered diplomatically: "I expect to continue to play golf, but just when and where I cannot say now. I have no definite plans, either to retire or as to when and where I may continue in competition. I might play next year and lay off in 1932. I might stay out of the battle next season and feel like another tournament the following year. That's all I can say about it now." He was letting them down easy, and with that he quietly stepped away.

Jubilation broke out in Atlanta, but he let them know that this time he'd prefer to return home quietly, without a parade. He'd had enough of crowds and noise and cheering that summer to last a lifetime. The inevitable dinner at East Lake was all he would allow, when the four trophies of his conquest were for the first and only time in their colorful histories united, with the Walker Cup as a chaser.

National interest in Bob crested with his final victory; the win at Merion made the front page of every newspaper in the country. No single sports figure in history had ever received the attention or affection that he attracted now. The USGA reported record receipts for the tournament of over $55,000, a windfall that would help sustain it through the difficult years ahead. Reporters announced that Bobby Cruickshank had cashed his winning long-shot bet on the Grand Slam—Pop's phrase quickly became omnipresent; others later took and were given credit for it, but it started with Pop—and collected $10,500. According to some estimates, the group of Atlantans who had pooled their resources on a similar wager split a small fortune worth $125,000.

As he looked back on the experience, his final season took on an air of unreality. He attributed his success during the Slam to perseverance more than skill—he felt he had played his best golf of the year at Augusta, before the quest officially began. Aside from a few stretches at the British Amateur and his stunning third round at Interlachen, he had never sustained his highest level of excellence. Even when he was being outplayed, which by his reckoning had happened in three of the four tournaments, the decisive element had been his ability to think his way through the patches when his swing deserted him. He never gave up, and that in the end had made all the difference; his mentality and will carried him almost to the top. Then, during the toughest part of the climb, when each step was burdened with the weight of the world's expectations, he never trailed during his five matches at Merion for a single hole.

Bob had won his first British Amateur, his third British Open, his fourth U.S. Open—a new record—and his fifth U.S. Amateur, another record. He had won thirteen matches in a row, and three medal competitions, including the Amateur qualifier at Merion. He had tied both countries' records in winning the Double; he had won the Double twice over no matter which way you counted them. He knew he could never duplicate such a feat and he had no intention of trying. Bob had now captured thirteen major wins, more than any other player in history. Darwin's words after the British Amateur at St. Andrews that he had no worlds left to conquer had come to pass.

He rested. He took stock. He went back to practicing his profession and enjoying quiet time with his family. He played casual weekend golf at East Lake with his dad and their friends and found a natural rhythm to his life again. He fielded questions about his future on a daily basis, and politely deflected them. Eventually they slowed.

He still played the game with the old hickory shafts he grew up with, at a time when almost every other man had changed to steel. During the 1920s he played an average of only four tournaments a year against full time professionals, generally practiced for only a few weeks to prepare himself and was still, without argument, the greatest player who ever wore cleats. Since 1923, Bob had played in twenty-one major championships and won thirteen of them, a winning percentage of 62. At the time of writing in early 2004, golf's all-time leading money winner Tiger Woods is the same age Bob was in the second half of 1930. Counting his three U.S. Amateur titles as majors, Woods has played in thirty-six championships and won eleven of them, a winning percentage of just under 31. When he was Bob's age, Jack Nicklaus had nine majors under his belt. Arnold Palmer had won one Amateur. Ben Hogan hadn't won a single major.

No one in their right mind could imagine Nicklaus or Woods or Hogan retiring at that point in their lives and it's important to remember that no great athlete in any sport up to that time had ever quit the field at the top of his game. Bob Jones was about to blaze another trail. He called in Pop Keeler one day to confirm the news with him. Pop had been expecting the moment, dreading it, longing for it himself.

"I'll never give up golf," Bob told him. "I love it too well, and it has meant too much in my life. But I think I'd like to play the sidelines for a while. It'll be an easier and more gracious trail from now on."

Pop found that he couldn't speak for a moment. He just held out his hand.

"It was grand, Bob. Wasn't it grand?"

"Yes it was, Pop."

"I was happy, in a way," he wrote afterwards. "And I was— well you don't come to the end of 15 years with the grandest sporting competitor, and the greatest boy who ever lived, without something that hurts."

Keeler had been at his side from the first step, through the darkest days and the greatest glory. His devotion to Bob Jones had carried him from an obscure corner desk of a small-town news department to a deserved reputation as one of the most respected sportswriters in the world. He had devoted himself to making this young man realize his extraordinary potential, the net effect of which made him one of the world's most famous men. The way had been long and uncertain for years, but Pop's faith had never wavered and the riches he'd derived from the journey were more precious to him than gold. He was forty-eight now and would work and live on a much beloved figure, for another two decades; his friendship with Bob would never falter, and their time together still had one of its brightest chapters to come, but their paths would inevitably start to diverge.

Bob's goodbye to golf was, in effect, his own as well. Shortly after Merion, foreshadowing what was to come, Pop announced his retirement from writing about championship golf.

"I could still say what I had said to people all over the world," wrote Pop.

> They could see for themselves if he was a golfer, but I could tell them that he was a much finer young man than he was a golfer. Wholly lacking in affectation, modest to the degree of shyness, generous and thoughtful of his opponents, it is not likely that his equal will come again. It would be immeasurably more pleasant to write of Bobby Jones himself than of his exploits, but you cannot pick out the details of a winsome personality, or properly hold up for inspection the graces of modesty and the strong heart. Besides, good-natured as he is, he would be furious if any chronicler who knew him should attempt a thing like that.

Bob found himself as an athlete before he even knew who he was. He had only recently found himself as a man, but what he'd found was solid and sure and grounded. Having lived a fantasy life, reality demanded his attention; he had a family to support and another child on the way. Times were tough and about to get a lot tougher. Fame was fleeting. An Atlanta friend who owned a string of movie houses interested him in exploring the idea of a series of instructional films about the game. He could teach what he knew to the masses in a way that had never been done before; Bob warmed to the idea at once. When he entered into active negotiations with Warner Brothers, Bob knew the time had come to issue a public statement.

Bob signed his Warner Brothers contract on November 13, 1930. The deal called for him to create and star in a series of twelve short films, ten minutes in length, a staple in the motion-picture business at the time, the appetizer course to an evening at the movies, which usually included a newsreel and a cartoon as well before the main feature. The contract included an option for six additional films. Bob was scheduled to receive $10,000 a film, and 50 percent of the net receipts from distribution over the next five years, potentially worth a great deal more. With his father's help he made arrangements to put most of the money into a trust for his children.

Teaching golf was a job reserved for the professional golfer. About to tread in a very gray area, Bob decided he couldn't in good conscience announce the movie deal without first renouncing his amateur status. He did both in the statement he released on November 17, 1930, read to the press in New York by a USGA official less than two months after his win at Merion. It ended:

> I am not certain that the step I am taking is in a strict
> sense a violation of the amateur rule. I think a lot might be
> said on either side. But I am so far convinced that it is
> contrary to the spirit of amateurism that I am prepared to
> accept and even endorse a ruling that it is an infringement.
>
> I have chosen to play as an amateur not because I have
> regarded an honest professionalism as discreditable, but
> because I have had other ambitions in life. So long as I
> played as an amateur, there could be no question of
> subterfuge or concealment. The rules of the game, whatever
> they were, I have respected, sometimes even beyond the
> letter. I certainly shall never become a professional golfer.
> But, since I am no longer a competitor, I feel able to act
> entirely outside the amateur rule, as my judgment and
> conscience may decide.

With that, Bob Jones let the game of competitive golf slip from his hands.

His statement inspired stories and editorials from around the country and Britain, praising his decision. In spite of their disappointment, no one could deny that he left in the same style and spirit with which he had thrilled his fans for so long.

He had made his entrance on the world stage fourteen years earlier as a callow, cocky boy. He took his leave from it as golf's greatest player and a gentleman, in the best and truest sense of the words.

Bob and Mary's third child, a daughter named Mary Ellen, was born on January 29, 1931, and their family was complete. Just after finalizing the deal with Warner Brothers Bob agreed to appear on a weekly radio series for David Sarnoff's NBC Network, and he called on Pop Keeler to co-host the show with him; it ran for twenty-six weeks, with episodes recreating his greatest triumphs.

A personally satisfying business arrangement came soon afterwards with the Spalding Sports Goods company, now the largest manufacturer of golf clubs in the country. Working with their resident designer J. Victor East and his own Tom Stewart set of clubs as a model, Bob drew up plans to create a mass-produced set of irons. Applying his considerable skills and knowledge as an engineer to the process, the result was the first high-quality matched set of irons ever produced on American soil. He took great pride in them, put his name on them, and appeared in advertisements to endorse them. Bob joined Spalding's board of directors; his relationship with the company would last for over thirty years.

In late February of 1931, Bob and Pop ventured out to Hollywood to begin work on his film series. (Pop's luggage included eleven typewriter boxes: ten of them contained jugs of corn liquor.) They began shooting in early March, turning out the first twelve films at a rate of four a month. With typical modesty Bob wanted to call the series *How I Play Golf*—not "*how*" to—starting with the putter and working his way up through the bag to the driver. In a unique amalgam of entertainment and instruction, each film folded a fluffy incidental comic scenario around a more nourishing nugget of Bob's advice on the subject under discussion. Warners initially recruited their own contract players to round out the casts that surrounded him, but interest in working with Bob was so great that for the first time every studio in town signed releases for their own stars so they could appear in the series. Almost all appeared without benefit of salary, but the golfers in the group received a much more valuable in-kind remuneration: hands-on personal instruction from the Great Jones about their games. A group of actors and directors who became friendly with Bob during filming soon began inviting him into their weekly fun-filled scrambles.

James Cagney, Edward G. Robinson, Loretta Young, Walter Huston, Douglas Fairbanks, Jr., W.C. Fields, and Joe E. Brown were only a few of the luminaries who pop up in the films; they usually played fictional characters, and on occasion themselves, but in every instance Bob played himself without any introduction, on the reasonable assumption that everyone in the world already knew who he was. Each story contrived to bring its principals, suffering from some urgent and quickly defined golf deficiency, into contact with the famous golfer while out on the course. Watched in succession the series suggests that Bob is an almost mystical being who materializes from out of the woods to offer soothing words of advice and a laying-on of hands to his anguished supplicants.

The curious effect of these films today is that all these Hollywood big shots, busily hamming it up or acting their hearts out, come across as utterly synthetic when juxtaposed to Bob's self-possessed authority. He's good-natured, game for whatever the films demand, and never condescends to any of the goofy proceedings around him, but his own relaxed personal magnetism and natural gravity exude more genuine "star quality" than everyone else on screen combined.

When each film gets past the clunky plot and requisite

clowning to the meat of Bob's instruction, his advice is first-rate: clean, precise, and practical. Taken as a whole—and visually reinforced by one startling demonstration of his masterful skills after another, often with the experimental use of slow-motion photography—the approach Bob presents to the game remains as fresh and useful today as when it was first filmed over seventy years ago. The films are the best surviving record of his understated charisma—despite all the movie stars, there isn't a better-looking or more interesting person on screen in the series—and his powerful physical vitality (Pop wrote that at the height of his powers Bob could tear an entire deck of playing cards in half with his hands). When you see his swing repeatedly from every angle and in slow motion as often as you do in these films, you begin to comprehend how he was able to accomplish so many of the unbelievable things he did with a golf club in his hand.

The first twelve films in the series rolled out in April, 1931, and continued through the summer at a rate of one a week. Screened in over six thousand theaters, they were an immediate smash, well reviewed and financially successful; it was later estimated that with his back-end profit participation, Bob doubled his up-front salary. Warners picked up his option for the additional six films, which due to scheduling conflicts didn't go into production until early 1933. Warners titled the second series *How to Break 90*, still one of the staples of every golf magazine. One of the Hollywood trade papers reported that by mid-decade the eighteen films Bob shot for Warners had been seen by over forty million people and for most audiences this was their first real introduction to the sport. Bob always looked back on his two brief seasons in Hollywood as one of his happiest professional experiences. More films would undoubtedly have followed, but the deepening Depression put an end to the movie-short business. Like so many other perishable products of the early studio system, the films disappeared from circulation and nearly died from neglect; over forty years later a distant cousin of Bob's by the name of Ely Callaway found what were believed to be the last surviving celluloid prints slowly decomposing in a storage room. They were restored and transferred to video just in time, and are still readily available to anyone curious about seeing the real Bob Jones.

They say a great athlete dies twice, the first time when he leaves his sport, but Bob never regretted his decision to retire or indulged in nostalgia for days of glory past, something that plagued a born showman like Hagen. Bob was happy in his own skin and had also learned to live in the moment, one of the master skills in life; playing a game for so long which demanded that ability in order to succeed helped give it to him. He would still have enjoyed the personal satisfactions that came from winning championships, but was no longer willing to pay the price: the travel and time away from his family and home, the profound loss of privacy and the physical and mental stresses that nearly brought him to the brink of collapse. Twice during the Grand Slam year alone only the timely intervention of friends, police, and the U.S. Marines had saved him from serious injury at the hands of a jubilant mob.

After reaching and losing in the semi-finals of the National Amateur five times during the 1920s, Francis Ouimet was the first to benefit from Bob's absence. Even Watts Gunn, a loyal friend to both men, came to Ouimet before the next Amateur began and said, "Francis, I feel like a new man altogether with Bobby and George [Von Elm] out of the way." Ouimet won the 1931 National Amateur at Beverly Country Club, near Chicago, at the grand old age of thirty-eight. After beating four golfers nearly half his age to reach the finals, seventeen years to the day and almost to the minute after capturing his first Amateur title, Ouimet bookended his career by defeating Jack Westland to win his third major championship. Bob walked in his gallery that day, reporting on the action for *American Golfer*, and shared in his old friend's triumph. Bob took in a few of the major tournaments during the early part of the decade, as a spectator. Reluctant to steal any player's thunder by calling attention to himself, he could occasionally be spotted watching from a hill or distant vantage point away from the galleries. A short time after his own last great victory, Ouimet announced his retirement and joined Bob on the sidelines. For the rest of his life, a beloved member of the Boston community until he died in 1967, whenever he was asked why he hadn't won more championships, he always reminded people that they had no idea how good Bob Jones really was.

Despite thrilling finishes and popular victories in both championships that year, with Bob out of the picture attendance at USGA tournaments fell by more than 50 percent. A trend began; without the electrifying presence of a star like Bob or Hagen, general interest in the sport gradually sank to its lowest levels since the Great War. As the Depression hit bottom during the middle of the decade the golf industry suffered considerable hardship; country-club incomes dropped by 65 percent. The repeal of Prohibition in 1933 helped slow the losses, when liquor sales could once again legally supplement club income, but along with the rest of the country, the sport would not fully find its footing again until after World War II. Deprived of the most compelling player in its history, golf in America would not come close to enjoying the same level of popularity it had experienced during Bob's heyday until the arrivals of Ben Hogan and Arnold Palmer.

If he didn't miss the pressure and strain of championship golf, Bob's love for the game never diminished. After returning home from Hollywood in June of 1931, he found the ideal outlet for his affection in the design and creation of Augusta National Country Club. He remembered that languishing old nursery next door to Augusta Country Club and, with the partnership and guidance of a New York investment counselor named Clifford Roberts, purchased the property for $15,000 cash and a $60,000 mortgage. Bob hired Dr. Alister Mackenzie, whose designs for Cypress Point he had so admired, to help him transfer the course he had in his mind onto paper and then sculpt it from the grounds they now owned. Roberts took control of the club's business and they began soliciting members from around the country; charter memberships cost $350, with annual dues of $60. Grantland Rice was one of the first to be invited and accept; his own fame and enormous popularity proved indispensable as a recruiter of additional members. Those new members were slow in coming: Jones and Roberts could not have picked a less promising moment to open their doors. For the first few years of its existence Augusta National's survival was far from assured; with the Depression at its worst, the club nearly went under more than once.

Routings and features from dozens of immortal courses echo throughout Augusta National, but the total exceeds even the sum of its extraordinary parts; the passage of time has confirmed that with Mackenzie's help Bob had created something unique and transcendent, an American original that can be copied but never duplicated. Volumes have been written about the course and its genesis, but a neglected point in understanding its finest quality is the many ways in which the course suggests nothing so much as the man who conceived it: graceful, guarded, fair, tough-minded, and touched by a mysterious divinity.

When the USGA declined to move the date of its championship forward into April and hold the 1934 Open at Augusta—where it was conceded that greens and fairways would not hold up under midsummer Southern heat—Bob and Roberts decided to organize a tournament of their own. Bob called on all his friendships within the sport to attract a field of the game's greatest players. From the beginning Roberts wanted to call this event the Masters; Bob's modesty prevented him from approving, but Rice and other sportswriters started using the name and it gradually caught on. Six years later, Bob relented and it became official.

Sixty-nine amateurs and professionals played in the first Annual Invitation Tournament at Augusta National in late March, 1934. For the first time at any tournament in memory, the traditional "Mr." prefix in front of amateurs' names did not appear in any of the printed material. Since his own status fell somewhere between the two definitions, Bob felt there was no longer any need to make that distinction. Whatever the reason, the message it sent was clear: golfers capable of playing at this elevated level were seen, at last, as equals; friends, competitors, and social peers. The news that Bob intended to play in the event generated enormous heat and attracted reporters and spectators from all over the country, as did news that he had set an early course record at Augusta with a 65 during a practice round. Bob felt compelled to clarify that this was the only tournament in which he intended to compete and did not signal his formal return to the game.

Although he was only thirty-two years old, after four years away from competitive golf Bob quickly discovered that he possessed neither the keen mental focus nor the overriding desire that would allow him to perform to the standards he'd set during his championship run. His inimitable flowing swing looked as rhythmic and powerful as ever, but his extraordinary putting touch under pressure had vanished. "I grew nervous when I played in the Masters," he said, "and it hurt my game. It's perfectly obvious why. I wasn't keyed for the tension any more." Bob finished in a tie for thirteenth, eight strokes behind eventual winner Horton Smith, and made it clear he would thereafter be playing in his own tournament in a purely ceremonial capacity.

Through the 1930s Walter Hagen contended in occasional tournaments but never bagged another major; his life trailed slowly away in an endless succession of attempts to recapture past glories. In 1934, while in St. Paul, Minnesota, for a tournament, he accidentally killed a young boy who ran out in front of his car. He was cleared of any wrongdoing in the official inquiry that followed, but some who knew him said the Haig was never quite the same afterwards. He did make a concerted effort to get closer to his own neglected son as a result, and a decade later with his only grandson. His last twenty-five years were spent in affluent retirement and slowly deteriorating health, the bill coming due for his hedonistic lifestyle. An almost forgotten figure by the end, he died of cancer on October 6, 1969.

In 1936, Bob and Mary traveled to Europe with Robert Woodruff, the president of Coca-Cola, Mrs. Woodruff, and Granny and Kit Rice to attend the Olympics in Berlin. On their way they made a stop in Scotland, at the Gleneagles resort, to relax and play some golf. Finding himself less than sixty miles from St. Andrews with a free day on his hands, Bob could not resist the idea of heading over to play the Old Course again; his hotel sent a driver over to put in a request for a tee time under the name "R.T. Jones, Jr." When Bob and his partners arrived the following day he noticed a substantial crowd gathered on the Old Course, and feared he'd come to play on a day when an important local tournament was scheduled. It wasn't until they reached the clubhouse that Bob realized that this crowd had come for him; word had spread about his impending visit, businesses had shut their doors and the entire town had turned out, over six thousand people by the time he teed off. Rice reported seeing grown men cry simply at the sight of Bob. Inspired by the town's affection and the lighthearted holiday mood, Bob turned back the hands of time and shot a 32 on the front nine. He never played another shot on the Old Course again.

After he capped off his afternoon with a birdie at eighteen, for a 71, the gallery cheered and crowded around as if he'd won the Open all over again. Bob retreated to the clubhouse for a drink with his partners, then stood on the portico and signed autographs for an hour as people lined up around the building.

He continued to make his yearly appearance at the Masters, and on a few occasions played in exhibitions to support various charities, but he turned down most invitations for public speaking and showed no interest in pursuing life as a public figure. Now a pillar of the Atlanta business community—he was named president of the Chamber of Commerce in 1938—his role at the family law firm became as ceremonial as his playing career. He spent the majority of time attending to various business ventures, which now included seats on a number of corporate boards, an active role as vice-president of Spalding, and controlling interest in three Coca-Cola bottling plants. As they grew older he also spent more time with his three children, with whom he was by all accounts a strict but affectionate father.

Bob remained accessible to presidents and paupers alike, serving as an advisor to Franklin Roosevelt on the Works Progress Administration, and answering every letter written to him with the help of a full-time secretary. By 1939, his rising income afforded a move into a luxurious Italianate four-bedroom house in one of Atlanta's best neighborhoods, on Tuxedo Road. They owned a second home in the resort at Highlands, North Carolina, and spent part of every winter in nearby Augusta. As their city grew with them, Bob and Mary moved in social circles unimaginable to their fathers' generation; the South truly had risen again, with Atlanta leading the way, in no small measure because of the achievements of its most famous native son. After leaving competitive golf behind less than a decade earlier, Bob Jones had become the man he once and always hoped to be.

In the aftermath of the attack on Pearl Harbor and the outbreak of World War II, at the age of forty-one Bob lobbied

for and received a commission as a captain in the United States
Air Force, then found himself stuck for months on an air base
in Florida. Resisting entreaties from higher-ups that he stay home
and play exhibition golf to raise money while keeping an ocean
away from the line of fire, Bob kept pushing for an overseas
role and eventually entered training as an intelligence officer,
specializing in prisoner interrogation. In 1943 he was promoted
to major and received a posting to an air base in northwestern
England with the Ninth Air Force, where he served under a man
who would become one of his greatest friends, General Dwight
D. Eisenhower. Bob landed with his division at Normandy Beach
on June 7, the day after D-Day, and spent the next two months
working near the front lines under constant threat of artillery
fire. By the time he was discharged and sent home near the end
of 1944, after two years of active service, Bob had earned the
rank of lieutenant-colonel.

Along with the rest of the sport's major championships on
both sides of the Atlantic, the Masters was canceled during the
war years and once again Augusta National nearly went under;
the course was literally put out to pasture, with a herd of cows
grazing on its fairways. After six months of intensive work to
put the course back in shape, much of it done by German pris-
oners of war from nearby Camp Gordon, the Masters tournament resumed in 1946. Just coming into his own as a player
after a decade of hard knocks, thirty-four-year-old Ben Hogan
finished in second place by a stroke to Herman Keiser, just as
he had to winner Byron Nelson four years earlier in the last
Masters.

In the immediate aftermath of the war, Bob became involved
in the creation of another golf club even closer to home,
Peachtree, in Atlanta. Like everything else he touched in his
career, it became a great success. He could still turn in extraordinary stretches of golf; as late as 1946, he played the front nine
at East Lake in 29 strokes, six under par.

His businesses were thriving, he was all but set for life financially, he had been happily married for nearly a quarter of a century, he had three healthy children and was looking forward to grandchildren who would not be long in coming. He hunted and fished and played tennis and golf as he pleased with a select and favored few whose company he adored. He had friends in the highest places around the world, many more who were nearer and dear to him, and the universal regard of anyone who'd ever seen him play or followed his career as the greatest sportsman of his generation, if not the century. After nearly twenty years of struggle, Augusta National and the Masters were on the cusp of achieving the recognition and reverence that they enjoy today as a cornerstone of American sport.

Bob turned forty-six on St. Patrick's Day in 1948. His lucky streak had held; he had made the turn onto the back nine and should have been looking forward to the best years of his life. Fate had different plans.

CHAPTER SEVENTEEN

DECLINE

In the summer of 1950, the USGA held its fiftieth annual U.S. Women's Amateur Championship at East Lake. As part of the festivities the club announced a plan to host a dinner honoring the anniversary and the amateur tradition. The winner of three of those first fifty titles, Atlanta native Alexa Stirling Fraser, accepted an invitation to attend. She was now fifty-three years old, a happily married mother of three, living in Toronto with her distinguished physician husband. Long retired from the game and the spotlight, Alexa had not returned to Atlanta in over twenty years, and decided to go primarily out of desire to see her old childhood friend Bobby Jones. Perry Adair, the third member of their Dixie Whiz Kid trio, would be there as well; Alexa felt it was time for a reunion. When Bob learned she was coming he insisted on meeting her at the station with a sportswriter friend, who found Alexa as she came off the train and escorted her to where her old friend was waiting at the top of a flight of stairs.

She had been expecting the handsome, vibrant champion she'd enjoyed watching on newsreels and in newspapers all through his great sporting years. Alexa refused to believe her eyes. This man standing at the top of the stairs was a physical ruin, his face a pale and deathly gray, swollen by the use of cortical steroids. He carried a cane in each hand, and wore a cumbersome metal brace on his right leg. Bob took in the shock on her face without alarm, kissed her warmly, and told her not to worry. When they started for the car Alexa realized with another jolt that Bob could no longer walk. "He dragged his feet along without being able to lift them, his face set against the pain each movement cost him."

Over the next few days, Bob shared details of his still undiagnosed illness with his old friend that he had never confided in anyone. He could no longer drive or climb stairs; he needed to be carried to his fourth-floor office in a wheelchair. He had lost all feeling in his hands, and could only write his name by using a pen attached to a tennis ball that he gripped in his palm. "One morning a few weeks ago, I woke up without remembering my condition," he told her, "and I stepped out of bed to walk to the bathroom. I fell flat on my face, of course. I lay on that floor and beat it with my fists and cursed at the top of my lungs. For ten minutes nobody dared come near me. I would have bitten them."

Over the course of her visit, Alexa's profound sadness at Bob's condition slowly changed to admiration. He had been stripped of his magnificent physicality in the cruelest imaginable way, but somehow his spirit, fine mentality, and sharp sense of humor remained untouched. How had he done it, she wanted to know.

"There were times I didn't want to go on living," he told her. "But I did go on living, so I had to face the problem of how I was going to live. I decided I'd just do the very best I could."

"And he'd be damned if he was going to have any soupy sympathy," wrote Alexa afterwards. "About this point he was profanely specific."

Two years earlier, during the first rounds of the Masters in 1948, the pain in Bob's neck and shoulders had flared up again. Far from an uncommon complaint, he paid it little mind. But this time the soreness didn't go away. He experienced a six-week spell of double vision for distant objects, like greens or flags. He became aware of an alarming tendency to stumble, particularly with a right foot that seemed reluctant to follow orders. A creeping numbness in his right hand followed; one day while fishing a friend noticed a fishhook deeply embedded in his thumb: Bob hadn't felt a thing. He began searing his fingers with cigarettes that burned down too close to the nub without his noticing; he began using a cigarette holder to avoid injury, joking that he had to "tee them up." The numbness and tingling spread to his arms and legs.

His doctors sent him to specialists, who were baffled and sent him to surgeons. He was X-rayed, poked, and prodded. A precise diagnosis remained elusive, but there was agreement that what appeared to be clusters of bone spurs were massing in and between his cervical vertebrae. None of the physicians he consulted had a definitive idea of how to treat the condition; it seemed to depend on how much pain Bob felt he could tolerate.

Within months he could not longer take a full swipe at a golfball without severe burning pain in his back. His long graceful swing shortened and soon lost its music. Not long after-wards, on the final hole of his regular weekly game, Bob hooked his drive into the trees and neglected to even go in after it. He confided in Tommy Barnes, a young protégé of his, after the round was over that he wouldn't be playing golf again for awhile. He had decided to have an operation.

The head of surgery at Emory University hospital performed the work on October 30, 1948, and in a seven-hour procedure removed a number of bony growths from between his fourth, fifth, and sixth cervical vertebrae. Bob's doctors were quoted in the local papers as saying that the operation had been a complete success; they believed the growths they'd found had been pressing on his nerves, creating constant pain and inhibiting movement. Bob began an aggressive rehabilitation program soon afterwards, but in truth it was two weeks before he could even attempt to walk again. Another cruel blow came while he was recuperating in hospital; Bob was shocked to learn about the sudden death of Kiltie Maiden, victim of a heart attack.

Within a few months it became clear that the operation had not alleviated his symptoms; on the contrary, the numbness and atrophy in his right leg and arm only grew worse. By early the next year, the loss of motor control began spreading to his left side. He continued a rigorous program of physical therapy but soon he could no longer walk without the use of a cane. Before long, he needed two of them; a friend ordered some made of hickory from the same firm that used to make the shafts for his golf clubs. After consulting with the best surgeons and specialists around the country, he underwent a second operation at a clinic in Boston in early 1950; doctors there seemed to feel his troubles derived from a damaged cervical disc and put him under the knife for five hours. For the second time, extensive surgery did nothing to alleviate his condition; shortly afterwards, his right side became almost completely paralyzed.

Bob had another encounter with an old friend not long after seeing Alexa Stirling while visiting New York City for the USGA's annual meeting. He was sitting on a low chair at the end of the dais when Al Laney—who had not seen him since before his illness—stopped by to pay his respects. "He took my hand in both of his and pulled me down toward him in a semblance of an embrace, and as he did I saw steel braces showing below the cuffs of his trousers. As soon as I could I moved away from him for fear he would see the shock of it on my face."

A few months later at the Masters, Laney was walking the course when Bob pulled up alongside in a small motorized cart that he now used in order to get around. They exchanged small talk, then "in his gently understanding way he placed his not yet gnarled hand on my knee and said quietly, 'You ran away from me at the meeting.'"

Laney tried to explain, awkwardly saying that he hadn't wanted to impose.

"Never mind that," said Bob. "I want my old friends to impose on me. I love my old friends and I want to be bothered by them."

Encouraged, Laney asked about his condition and Bob quietly explained all that he'd been through, and then spoke of his prognosis. "I've known you now longer than anyone in golf, Al," he said. "I can tell you there is no help. I know I can only get worse. But you are not to keep thinking of it. You know, in golf we play the ball as it lies. Now, we will not speak of this again, ever."

A precise diagnosis would not come until 1956. After examining his voluminous case history, Dr. H. Houston Merit of the Columbia Medical Center Neurological Institute in New York informed Bob that he was suffering from an extremely rare illness called syringomyelia. Striking fewer than one out of a million people each year, the disease causes the spinal cord to expand and the spine itself to contract. The result is a slow strangulation of the nervous system, as the nerves are compressed into dysfunction, with atrophy and complete paralysis the inevitable result. The pain this causes is widespread, severe, escalating, and unrelenting; it is, in short, a living hell.

Subsequent medical advances now make earlier diagnosis and treatment considerably more effective, but at the time the average lifespan of a person diagnosed with syringomyelia was five to seven years from onset. By the time they figured out what he was suffering from, Bob had already been living with the disease for eight.

The most common form of syringomyelia is congenital, a defect inherent from birth that reveals itself in childhood. Far less common, but more often the case in instances involving adult onset, it can be induced by severe trauma to the neck or spine. Because of the late diagnosis in Bob's case the precise cause of his disease could never be pinpointed, but Bob's mind went back to the injury he had suffered in the British Amateur at Muirfield. And three years after that, to the cluster of bricks and mortar that had struck him on the back of the neck when a lightning bolt blew up the chimney at East Lake. The disease was a one-in-a-million shot; he had been struck by lightning again.

Pop Keeler finally retired from the *Atlanta Journal* in April, 1949, at the age of sixty-seven, and received a magnificent send-off from his friends in Georgia and around the country: a sit-down dinner for three hundred, with speeches, medals, and a gift of a brand-new Buick. Bob spoke last and presented Pop with the keys, remarking on "all the suffering I caused poor old Keeler and how he held my hand through the critical moments of my career. I thought he might need someone to hold his hand tonight, and I am glad to be here to do it."

Pop had lost weight; he looked tired, his face drawn. He announced he'd given up drinking recently—"because of the wife and the kidneys"—but there were suspicions that he wasn't well. After fighting back tears, when he finally got up to speak, for one of the only times in his life O.B. Keeler found himself at a loss for words: "Life has been good to me, but this is the finest moment of all. I can't thank you folks for this night. I can only say God bless you."

A little over a year into his retirement, Pop was diagnosed with liver cancer. After all his close brushes in the past with what he referred to as "the Old Man with the Hourglass," Pop didn't have much left to fear from death. He faced it with the same humor and grace he'd shown to every setback or triumph that came his way.

Bob visited him in the hospital on a Saturday afternoon near the end. Pop came out of a coma, lucid and calm.

"I'm glad you're here," he said. "I'm well down the eighteenth fairway." He closed his eyes. "Hold my hand a minute. I'm sick, I'm so sick I'm almost crazy."

A short time later Bob let go of his friend's hand, and the next day the Old Man with the Hourglass arrived. Oscar Bane Keeler died at 2:40 Sunday morning, October 15, 1950.

Bob received word late the next day at the Greenbrier Hotel in White Sulphur Springs, West Virginia, where he'd just arrived with a group of friends. The news stopped him cold.

"He was my dearest friend," said Bob, then excused himself from the reporter who'd told him about it, too emotional to say another word. Bob returned to Atlanta at once and, along with Grantland Rice, served as an honorary pallbearer at Pop's funeral.

Determined to continue living his life, Bob remained as active as his deteriorating condition would allow. He suffered a mild heart attack in 1952 that further defined his limits. He hunted until he couldn't feel the trigger with his finger and accidentally discharged a round that could have killed somebody. He fished until his crippled hands could no longer hold a rod and reel. Denied those former pleasures, he poured his competitive instincts into bridge. Stripped of all vanity, he held his head up and never hesitated to appear to public. His annual role as the host of the Masters became increasingly important to him. He held court in his cabin near the tenth tee, a warm, august presence to old friends and a patient mentor to new players. His regular appearances during the green-jacket ceremony on television introduced him to a whole new generation of Americans who had never known him as a golfer.

A registered Democrat his whole life, for the first and only time Bob became active in politics, supporting his friend Dwight Eisenhower's successful 1952 campaign for president. Four years earlier Bob had been instrumental in bringing General Eisenhower into the fold at Augusta National and their deep friendship now became one of the enduring joys of his life. Knowing better than few others alive the trying demands of public life on a private man, Bob arranged for a special cabin to be built at Augusta for the President, which became his favorite retreat.

After the death of Pop Keeler, Grantland Rice assembled *The Bobby Jones Story* from the vast stockpile of columns and stories he'd written through the years, a project Pop had left unfinished at the time of his passing. The book was published in 1953, the same year that Perry Adair died, only fifty-three. Granny Rice himself passed in the summer of 1954 after suffering a stroke. Bob attended the funeral in New York, which took place not long after the USGA announced that they were creating an annual award for sportsmanship which would bear Bob's name. The first recipient, fittingly, was his old friend Francis Ouimet, who agreed to accept the honor only because it came to him in Bob's name.

Two years later, in July of 1956, Bob's father died at the age of seventy-six. With the Colonel gone, he had lost his dearest friend.

In 1958, Bob accepted an invitation to serve as the non-playing captain of the American team in the first World Team Championship, a biannual event played by four-man amateur squads from twenty-nine different countries. He accepted in part because the competition would be held at St. Andrews and after a twenty-two-year absence he longed to see the place again, realizing it might be his last opportunity. Shortly afterwards he received a telegram from the town's clerk asking if while he was there Bob wouldn't mind accepting an award naming him a freeman of St. Andrews. Assuming this was something along the lines of the many ceremonial awards extended to him during this period of his life, he accepted.

When Bob, Mary, and two of their children arrived in St. Andrews on October 3, he soon realized that being offered the title of Freeman of the Royal Burgh meant a great deal more than another key to the city from another chamber of commerce. The town was in effect granting him genuine citizenship, the first and only time they had extended that honor to an American since 1759. The only previous recipient: Dr. Benjamin Franklin.

Among the ancient rights of citizenship granted by the ceremony were free license to catch rabbits, to dry his washing on the Old Course, and to take divots whenever he pleased. The Provost (major) concluded by saying that Bob "is free to feel at home in St. Andrews as truly as in his own home of Atlanta. One of our own number, officially now, as he has been so long unofficially."

No one expected what happened next. Bob rose from his seat, without canes, refusing assistance of any kind, and shuffled the 8 feet to the lectern, the first steps he'd taken unaided in years. He realized during those few moments that he had "no need for the notes in my pocket. I knew that I would have no difficulty finding things to say to the people of St. Andrews."

He spoke at length of his first visit to St. Andrews, and the youthful errors in judgment and temperament that led to his disqualifying himself from the third round of the 1921 Open competition at the eleventh hole. He talked of how his bewilderment at the Old Course had led to curiosity and finally wisdom as he discovered her secrets. "The more I studied the Old Course, the more I loved it, and the more I loved it, the more I studied it—so that I came to feel that it was for me the most favorable meeting ground for an important contest."

He spoke of his astonishment at the warmth and approval he had received from the people of the town when he returned six years later and won the Open, and three years after that when his victory at the Amateur started him on the road to the Grand Slam. He recalled the exquisite miniature replica of the British Amateur Championship Trophy that his fellow members of the R&A had mailed to him to Atlanta, bearing an inscription "which at this point I could not trust myself to repeat . . . It has remained my prized possession." He described his first return visit to St. Andrews in 1936, how the presence of the huge crowd which spontaneously turned out to see him inspired him "to play the best golf I had played for four years, and certainly never since."

"And now I have this. I could take out of my life everything but my experiences at St. Andrews and I'd still have a rich full life."

He spoke of friendship, and expressed with a full heart and his precise lawyer's language exactly how much that overused expression meant to him. The spiritual clarity of his emotions rose to meet the eloquence of his words, and in his steady gaze and warm, measured baritone Bob reflected back to his audience the love he felt from them.

"When I say that I am your friend, I have pledged to you the ultimate in loyalty and devotion. In some respects friendship may even transcend love, for in true friendship there is no place for jealousy. When I say that you are my friends, it is possible that I may be imposing upon you a greater burden than you are willing to assume. But when you have made me aware on many occasions that you have a kindly feeling toward me, and when you have honored me by every means at your command, then when I call you my friend, I am at once affirming my high regard and affection for you and declaring my complete faith in you and trust in the sincerity of your expressions. And so my fellow citizens of St. Andrews, it is with this appreciation of the full sense of the word that I salute you as my friends.

> Friendship should be the great note of this world golf meeting, because not only people, but nations need friends. Let us hope that this meeting will sow seeds which will germinate and grow into important friendships among nations later on.
>
> I just want to say to you this is the finest thing that has ever happened to me. Whereas that little cup was first in my heart, now this occasion at St. Andrews will take first place always. I like to think about it this way that, now I officially have the right to feel at home in St. Andrews as much as I, in fact, have always done.

Thunderous applause, then the room fell silent, the air hushed with gravity. Everyone stood to sing "God Save the Queen." Bob was escorted down the stairs to the center aisle, where an electric golf cart sat waiting for him. He climbed on board, and as the cart drove slowly up the aisle toward the exit, someone with a bright tenor voice broke spontaneously into a lilting old Scottish folk song called "Will Ye No' Come Back Again." Within moments, almost every other voice in that hall had joined in. They reached out to touch Bob and his family as he passed. This was the kind of tribute seldom given or received while the person being honored still lives, made possible only if that person has moved past longing and pride and illusions of the self into the rarest wisdom.

The great American golf writer Herbert Warren Wind was in the audience that afternoon. He reported that after he and his friends left the hall, ten full minutes passed before any of them were even able to speak.

Bob later called it the most emotional experience of his entire life.

Bob Jones had long ago exhibited a genius for the game of golf. The road of life is littered with broken dreams and squandered talent, but he had mastered his own brash, unruly nature and honored the brilliant gift he had been given with uncommon discipline and faith. Anyone can fall short, and most stumble, but the truth is that the consequences of success are often harder to live with. "Hero" has become the most overworked word in the world of sports, and people are justifiably cynical about the breed of "heroes" these days. It's all too easy to mistake remarkable physical ability for uncommon personal character, a greater achievement that most young athletes, steeped in self-interest and short on experience, aren't remotely prepared to meet.

Bob Jones is and always will be the greatest exception to that rule. His record in his sport cannot and never will be equaled, but it was the way in which he went about realizing his abilities that matters even more. Because he stood for something rare and true, without trying to or saying so in speeches and empty gestures; he never talked about the meaning of what he had accomplished, he simply did it as he lived it, and in so doing left others with a far more meaningful path to follow. That's why his dedicated pursuit of the excellence that was born in him still holds the power to inspire. Some may discount his legacy by saying he only played a game, but what he achieved remains in its own right as powerful and permanent an expression of the human longing for perfection as any poem or song or painting. Greatness is rare and a solemn responsibility and because he offered himself in service to his talent with a strong mind, a committed heart, and every ounce of strength in his being, he deserves a lasting place in our memory.

Away from the golf course his virtues were quiet ones that

he felt no compulsion to exaggerate or advertise: loving son, devoted husband and father, diligent and disciplined worker, loyal and generous friend. You have only to read the countless statements left by gifted writers like Pop Keeler, Grantland Rice, Al Laney, and Paul Gallico, who loved him like a brother, or the hundreds of other people whose lives he touched, who without exception felt honored to have known him, basked in his affection, benefited from his wise counsel, and shared his warm, embracing humor. It was his presence alone, they all said, that gave you such a wonderful feeling. Alistair Cooke, who knew him only as an older, infirm man, tried to explain it by saying that Bob radiated simple goodness without a smidgen of piety. His modesty wasn't an act and there was nothing false about it; it was a genuine expression of his character so out of the ordinary in the famous of our contemporary world that it seems unimaginable. When athletes finally came along who surpassed some of his records, and to whom he was constantly compared, instead of retreating to the fortress of his past he extended a hand to them, and helped them any way he could; and like so many of the men he played against in his own time, Arnold Palmer and Jack Nicklaus became his close and devoted friends.

This was who he was. A man who did such wondrous things he had the world at his feet, but kept his feet on the ground. A man who always behaved decently, treating both the proud and the poor with unfailing courtesy and abiding respect. A man who gave hope to a country at its darkest hour, and asked for nothing in return. A man who stayed true to his principles, and kept his dignity when he could have auctioned it off for any price he named. He was no plaster saint, but he was a man's man; he smoked and drank, sometimes to excess, and was very much at home in the rowdy enclave of the locker room, but he stayed faithful to the one woman he loved throughout his life. Bouquets of hotel-room keys were tossed his way during the bright shining years of his youth; there's no shred of evidence that he listened to any of those sirens' songs. He was a socially conservative gentleman from the Deep South, born in the Victorian age, who lived to see men walk on the moon, an era of bewildering upheaval and change, but he remained resolutely fair in his treatment of individuals, black or white; no one who knew him ever recalled a single racist epithet passing his lips. As early as the late 1920s, over the protest of many, Bob helped promote Woodrow Bryant, an African-American caddie and club maker, to the position of assistant professional at East Lake, where Bryant remained employed for the next fifty years. It's easy to judge any man's actions retroactively when viewed through a contemporary lens, but it's as futile an exercise for reaching a fair conclusion as is arguing how athletes from a different era would stand up against those playing today.

When in the second half of his life the countless blessings he'd received turned into a spiraling nightmare of pain, suffering and diminishment, he found the strength not only to endure, but to triumph; nothing said more about the way he lived his life than the way in which he took his leave from it. Bob Jones lived for twenty-three years with that dreadful disease. He fought, he railed against, he suffered and despaired at the relentless cruelty of it, but he never asked for pity. He soldiered on, and by the end it had stripped him of everything but the diamond sharpness of his mind. He spent his last few years bedridden, helpless, and paralyzed; in many ways this was a fate worse than death. Near the end he weighed less than ninety pounds, his once-powerful hands reduced to useless claws. Betrayed by his failing body, Bob found a form of grace as he made his peace with these hideous indignities because he knew that the hardest lesson learned during his playing days applied equally to matters of life and death: this was his fate, it had all been written in the Book, and he accepted it. For everything he had

given to his game, the game gave him back this lasting gift—
the strength to bear his trials—and called it even.

Bob converted to his wife's Catholic faith during his final
days. Some thought he had done it to please Mary; others said
he came to it of his own accord. Whatever the reason, by all
accounts it seemed to give him comfort. Bob died at home,
peacefully, in his sleep, on December 18, 1971. His funeral was
brief and private, for family members only, as he had requested.
There would be no parades now, no "great fuss". He'd had
more than his share while he was alive. Modest to the end, he
was laid to rest in Atlanta's Oakland Cemetery beneath a simple
headstone bearing only his name and the dates of his birth and
death. His beloved Mary would join him there only four years
later.

The flags at East Lake, Augusta, and St. Andrews, and a thousand other places, were lowered to half-mast.

For decades Clifford Roberts had tried to build a statue of Bob
at Augusta National, but Bob always rejected the idea. His
instinct was correct: his essence can't readily be captured in an
image of marble or bronze, because it was his life as he lived
it among the people whom he loved that made him who he
was, not numbers on a scorecard or trophies on a shelf. If you
want to catch a glimpse of his spirit, sit down by the water at
East Lake on a cool April morning and remember a small fragile
boy testing himself against the world's toughest game on this
old hard ground and never yielding. Walk the fairways some
afternoon at Augusta during Masters week, far away from the
crowds and the tumult, when the setting sun filters pure golden
light through starbursts of azalea, and feel the divine blueprint
of a masterful mind creating beauty and order out of chaos.
Stroll out to the Eden at St. Andrews on a gray, windswept eve
during a long summer's twilight, near the hole they now call
"Bobby Jones," and look back at that ancient arena where men

first practiced to pit their hearts and souls against nature in this supreme and impossible game. Stand on a first tee, or confront a bad patch in life, anywhere in the world, and then ask yourself: Do I in this moment have what it's going to take to face the troubles this earth has set in front of me?

You'll find him there.

I remember a farmer who knew nothing about golf, but who happened to watch Bobby playing one morning on a suburban course near London. He did not know who Bobby Jones was, but was so fascinated by the rhythm of his swing that he suddenly turned to a journalist I knew and said: "This man is the greatest golfer in the world."

—*Bernard Darwin*

ACKNOWLEDGMENTS

I am indebted to Sidney L. Matthew, without whose guidance and unfailing generosity this book could not have been written. If he were the only man alive who had been touched by Bob Jones there would be no cause for concern that his memory will ever be forgotten.

At the start of this journey Dr. Katherine Lewis at the Atlanta History Center and her husband John Companiotte provided me with a map and perfect directions, and for their assistance I am most grateful. Tom Williams, formerly of the USGA, helped enormously with the research, and Rand Jerris, a friend and valued counselor still very much with the USGA, led me to him. Many thanks to Doug Stark, Patty Moran, and Shannon Doody at the USGA Library for their great patience and assistance.

A special thanks to Bill Stitt, Bob Bowers, and John Capers at Merion, Joe Ford at Augusta National, Dr. Lloyd Pearson at Interlachen, and two extraordinary gentlemen in Atlanta who represent a great living link to Bob, Charlie Yates and Tommy Barnes.

I wish to thank all the professionals in the golf world who extended a hand to this effort: Rick Burton and Chad Parker at East Lake Golf Club; Jock Olson and William Kidd, Jr., at Interlachen; Mike Schultz at Hazeltine; Scott Nye at Merion; Matt Massei at Pinehurst; Brian Morrison at Olympia Fields; Rick Anderson and Kevin Clark at the Atlanta Athletic Club; Bob Linn, Doug Hoffort, Marianne Huning, Chris Powel, Patrick Boyd, and Jeff Brockman at MountainGate. A very special thanks to a man I'm privileged to call my friend, Eddie Merrins of Bel-Air.

In the publishing world, love and gratitude to my friend and literary agent Ed Victor, first, last, and always. At Hyperion, many thanks for their continued faith and partnership to Bob Miller, Will Schwalbe, Jane Comins, Christine Ragasa, and my wonderful editor Gretchen Young. I am most grateful for the help of George Peper and Kevin Cook, and the continued friendship and support of Gaetan Burrus, Ian Chapman, Francis Esminard, Bob Oberneir, Jack Romanos, Bill Shinker, Will Sieghart, Ron Weir, and Peter Workman.

I am especially grateful for my long friendship with David Steinberg. Thanks also to John Walsh at ESPN; Dick Cook, Nina Jacobson, and Jason Reed at Disney; Leslie Moonves, Mary Murphy, Jason Sacca, and Jim Axelrod at CBS; Sandy Mendelson; and Judy Hilsinger. Thanks for a hundred different reasons to Steven Altman, Mark Andrew, Scott Baker, Larry Brezner, Jeff Freilich, Peter and Connie Goetz, Adam Krentzman, Steven Kulczycki, Martin Leren, Pat Miles, John O'Hurley, Susie

Putnam, Doug Richardson, Martin Spencer, Jerry Stein, Stuart Stevens, Scott Turow, Sonny and June Van Dusen, Bruce Vinokour, Alan Wertheimer, Harley Williams, and Michael Zinberg.

One of the great joys of writing *The Grand Slam* has been the number of new friends it has brought into my life; chief among them many thanks to Ric Kayne, Bill Paxton, Brad Faxon, Todd Field, Billy Andrade, Charley Norris, Selwyn Hirson, Mack Clapp, Mike Kaiser, Frank Bredice, and Tom Yellin. Continued and undying gratitude to J. Louis Newell, Bob Donovan, and all my friends at the Francis Ouimet Scholarship Fund; Denny Goodrich, Dick Connelly, Bill Foley, Anne Marie Tobin, and Denny Kelly among them.

My son Travis was born as I began writing this book. To him, my wife Lynn, my parents, brother, sister, nephews, and brother-in-law, thank you for your love during this journey, and for teaching me the meaning of family.

PICTURE CAPTIONS